THE GREATEST MYSTERY EVER REVEALED:

THE MYSTERY OF THE WILL OF GOD

THE OBEDIENCE OF FAITH.

BOOK 3

MICHAEL LEE KING

authorHOUSE®

AuthorHouse™
1663 Liberty Drive
Bloomington, IN 47403
www.authorhouse.com
Phone: 1 (800) 839-8640

Published by AuthorHouse 11/21/2016

ISBN: 978-1-5246-4631-8 (sc)
ISBN: 978-1-5246-4630-1 (e)

Print information available on the last page.

This book is printed on acid-free paper.

CONTENTS

PREFACE

And A Note On How To Use This Work

(For the Complete Four Volume Set)

Greetings in the name of our Lord and savior Jesus Christ! I trust that upon reading this page you are ready to be reminded of, or to learn and be taught the strong meat of the word of righteousness. For, he that attempts to study this work must be of an humble mind and teachable spirit. This work possesses many statements and scriptures sure to cause great controversy for babes in Christ and the carnal Christian alike. This work began through a prophecy from the Lord, to the writer, through another preacher, prophet. It has been through the obedience of the writer and his being taught directly by revelation of the Holy Ghost, that this work has proceeded this far. The writer declares to know nothing except what the Spirit of Christ has taught him and led him to place upon paper. This work is intended to help, remind, reprove, instruct, correct and provide a roadmap for those who dare to approach the way called Holiness.

A note here is necessary to warn that most of this work was taught to and learned by the writer as he wrote, and therefore, from time to time his own human frailties may have been inserted within the text, unknowingly. Please forgive. For this reason, you are admonished to read every scripture text and citation given, for every statement made. Be not afraid to question the conclusions, but do so not with a mind to condemn but to get a better understanding. Always pray before you open these pages, asking the Lord to lead, guide and teach you more perfectly what the writer has attempted to do.

The writer suggests the following method of studying this work: **(1)** Do not use it as a crutch. Get an understanding; **(2)** Study one, small section at a time, for this is the manner in which the Spirit of Christ taught the writer. The work does not attempt to read as a novel, but as a complete, resource text for the subjects covered; **(3)** After studying a section, try teaching it to a friend or incorporating it into your preaching sermon. This will help your understanding even more. **(4)** Tape record your teaching and preaching sessions. Then, when you are alone, only with the Lord, listen to it. If you are sincere the Lord will teach you, remind you and open up your understanding even farther. **(5)** Use a King James Version of the Holy Scriptures, the Hebrew, Chaldees and Greek Dictionaries of the Strong's Exhaustive Concordance of the King James Version, and a Webster's dictionary. For these are the earth-bound tools used by the writer. **(6)** Abbreviations and symbols and their meanings used throughout this work are as follows:

(a) When a book, chapter and verse citation is given such as '(Ge 2:7a)', this means that the writer is using only the first half or portion of the verse cited. For example, *"And the Lord God formed man of the dust of the ground...."* (Ge 2:7a) Here, although this is not the complete verse, the writer wants to discuss at this point only the first portion of the verse.

(b) When a book, chapter and verse citation is given such as '(Ge 2:7b)', this means that the writer's intent is to use only the second half or portion of the verse cited. For example, *"...breathed into his nostrils the breath of life; and man became a living soul."* (Ge 2:7b) Here, although this is not the complete verse, the writer wants to discuss at this point only the last portion of the verse.

(c) The cite 'e.g.' means 'for example'.

(d) The cite 'i.e.' means 'that is', or 'in other words it means this...'

(e) The Bible, Book Abbreviations used throughout this work are:

Ge—Genesis	Ex—Exodus	Le—Leviticus
Nu—Numbers	De—Deuteronomy	Jos—Joshua
Jg—Judges	Ru—Ruth	1Sa—1 Samuel
2Sa—2 Samuel	1Ki—1 Kings	2Ki—2 Kings
1Ch—1 Chronicles	2Ch—Chronicles	Ezr—Ezra
Ne—Nehemiah	Es—Esther	Job—Job
Ps—Psalms	Pr—Proverbs	Ec—Ecclesiastes
Ca—Canticles (Song of Solomon)	Isa—Isaiah	Jer—Jeremiah
La—Lamentations	Eze—Ezekiel	Da—Daniel
Ho—Hosea	Joe—Joel	Am—Amos
Ob—Obadiah	Jon—Jonah	Mic—Micah
Na—Nahum	Hab—Habakkuk	Zep—Zephaniah
Hag—Haggai	Zec—Zechariah	Mal—Malachi
Mt—Matthew	Mk—Mark	Lu—Luke
Joh—John	Ac—Acts	Ro—Romans
1Co—1Corinthians	2Co—2Corinthians	Ga—Galatians
Eph—Ephesians	Php—Philippians	Col—Colossians
1Th—1Thessalonians	2Th—2Thessalonians	1Ti—1Timothy
2Ti—2Timothy	Tit—Titus	Phm—Philemon
Heb—Hebrews	Jas—James	1Pe—1Peter
2Pe—2Peter	1Jo—1John	2Jo—2John
3Jo—3John	Jude—Jude	Re—Revelation

(f) 'Read' means stop! Do not go any further until you have read the scriptural citation.

(g) '[]', anything in brackets is either added by the writer to make the point clearer or, it means that the section being quoted is not the beginning of the verse. Something may have been left out or changed such as a small letter being made a Capital letter or vice versa.

(h) '...' means that some of the verse has been left out.

The writer has attempted to assist the reader with the correct pronunciation of difficult and foreign words. This is done by placing the phonetic spelling of the boldface English, Greek, Hebrew or Chaldees words being discussed, in italics, within parenthesis. For example, the word **boule** is pronounced ***(boo-lay').*** This work has been broken down into small sections and chapters for ease of study.

To assist the disciple of Christ even further, this work includes a Table of Contents, an Index and a Table of Scriptural Citations. The Table of Contents allows one to get an overview of the major topics and themes covered in the complete work. The Index allows one to find specific words and phrases within each separate Book. By using the Index the researcher is able to easily locate the places in the work where the word or topic is discussed. The Table of Scriptural Citations will assist the seeker in locating a specific scriptural verse on the pages that the verse is mentioned or discussed. Each Book has its own separate Index and Table of Scriptural Citations.

This work is a work in progress as you read. For, the writer has learned that line must be placed upon line, precept upon precept, here a little and there a little. *(Isa 28:10, 13)* This work was written as one book with each chapter picking up where the last or preceding chapter left off. However, for purposes of making it affordable for the less fortunate the one book is published in four separate volumes or books, called Book 1, Book 2, Book 3 and Book 4. To get a complete understanding the reader will need to study all four books, because some topics are discussed a little in all four books, depending upon how the Spirit of Christ revealed and opened up the scriptures to the writer. *"For I neither received it of man, neither was I taught it, but by the revelation of Jesus Christ..." (Ga 1:12)* has this work come to be. Please pray for the writer that the Lord may continue to reveal Himself to him and that the writer may be able to teach others.

Your comments are welcome. If you have additional scripture that you believe agrees with, disagrees with or clarifies what you find here, please send your thoughts and your scriptures to the writer that they may be considered and the text amended as required. The writer's goal here is to be completely and totally correct in all that lies within these pages as much as this is possible with the Holy Ghost leading and inspiring human flesh. Thank you. A battle warrior in Christ Jesus.

MICHAEL LEE KING

MAIN

INTRODUCTION

(For The Complete Four Volume Set)

There have been many stories rehearsed, fables told and secrets revealed from generation to generation, since the fall of man, referred to herein, as the Genesis Affair. Many of the fables, stories and secrets attempt to teach some moral lesson or ethical grace. However, the greatest mystery ever revealed was first hidden by God, Himself, in Himself, *(Eph 3:9-10; 1Co 2:7-8)* long before the first man, Adam, was formed from the dust of the earth. This mystery, having been kept secret since the world began *(Ro 16:25-26)*, from ages and from generations *(Col 1:26)* was revealed only after the last Adam, Jesus Christ, *(1Co 15:45-47)* had died *(Joh 19:30)*, rose the third day *(Lu 24:46)*, ascended into the Holiest of Holies *(Heb 9:11-14)* and returned to the earth as the Comforter on the Day of Pentecost. *(Joh 14:18, 26; Ac 2:1-4)*

Several years after the mystery began to unfold the mystery itself was revealed and its preeminence impressed upon, one, Saul of Tarsus. *(Eph 3:1-6; Eph 1:9-10; Ac 22:13-21)* The mystery referred to here, is that mystery embodied in the first chapter of Ephesians, verses 9 through 11, namely, *The Mystery Of The Will Of God*. For, the writer wrote,

> **9 Having made known unto us the** *mystery of his will*, **according to his good pleasure which he hath purposed in himself:**
>
> **10** *That in the dispensation of the fullness of times he might gather together in one all things in Christ, both which are in heaven, and which are on earth; even in him:*

11 In whom also we have obtained an inheritance, being predestinated according to the purpose of him who worketh all things after the counsel of his own will:
Eph 1:9-11 *(emphasis added).*

Within the Kingdom of God, the church and beyond, we hear people discussing in earnest what they deem to be God's Will. By the term God's Will, we mean here, the ultimate goal of God. For centuries the Will of God remained a mystery. *(Mt 13:10-11, 16-17)* Not everyone who says they know God, knows him. Many know of God only through a third source. But, yet they lay claim to having been imparted with the responsibility to do His Will. The problem here is one that escapes them. For to know God is to know Christ. For, God is the Father. And Christ and the Father are one. *(Joh 10:30; 1Jo 2:1)*

Therefore, Christ is God, manifested in the flesh. *(1Ti 3:16; Joh 1:1-3, 14)* God, being a spirit, can be worshiped only in spirit and in truth. *(Joh 4:23-24)* It is only the Spirit of God, the Holy Ghost that knows the Will of God. *(1Co 2:7-13)* And it is He, the Holy Ghost that reveals what His Will is. *(1Co 2:10; Eph 3:5)* Therefore, without God through Christ indwelling, one cannot know God's perfect Will with understanding or perform God's perfect Will. *(1Co 2:11, 14; Mt 13:10-11, 15)*

Many would have you believe that God's ultimate goal and main purpose for stepping into the likeness of sinful flesh and suffering the burden of Calvary was only to save individual souls. However, this cannot be the case in light of revealed scripture, such as *Ephesians 3:2-6, 7-11.* Scripture reveal that personal salvation through Jesus Christ is the means or manner by which God shall accomplish and fulfill the end, which is reconciling all things back to Himself. *(Eph 1:9, 10)*

Thus, there is a larger purpose and aim behind the saving of individual souls. Therefore, a person can be called and given gifts by God and still miss out on eternal life—by being in violation of the ultimate Will of God. This thought is vividly portrayed by Jesus' parable of the ten virgins as recorded in Matthew 25:1-12 *(Read Mt 25:1-12)*, and by His statement that,

> **21 Not every one that saith unto me, Lord, Lord, shall enter into the kingdom of heaven; but he that doeth the 'WILL' of my Father which is in heaven.**
>
> **22 Many will say to me in that day, Lord, Lord, have we not prophesied in thy name? and in thy name have cast out devils? and in thy name done many wonderful works?**
>
> **23 And then will I profess unto them, I never knew you: depart from me, ye that work iniquity.**

Mt 7:21-23 *(emphasis added).*

From Jesus' statement, here, one can plainly see that the Will of God is more than prophesying and preaching in Jesus' name, casting out devils in Jesus' name, and doing wonderful works in Jesus' name. *(Mt 7:22-23)* Moreover, Jesus declared that those who prophesy, cast out devils and do wonderful works in his name, but fail to do the Will of the Father, are workers of iniquity. And, that he, Jesus, never knew them. *(Mt 7:22-23)* The word **iniquity** *(in-ik'-we-ti)* is translated from the Greek word ***anomia*** *(an-om-ee'-ah),* which means wickedness, a violation or transgression of the law, unrighteousness.

Thus, we see that the goal and main objective of the Mystery of the Will of God is God's intent to gather together in one all things in Christ Jesus, *(Eph 1:9, 10)* thereby reconciling all of mankind back to himself. *(Eph 2:13-17)* And that, preaching, works of deliverance and other wonderful works done in Jesus' name are mere incidents and reconciliation by-products of the Will being fulfilled.

Reconciliation *(rek'-ən-sil'-ē-ā'-shən)* is a term used in the law, meaning to re-establish friendship between; to settle or resolve a dispute; to reunite. If there is a need to reconcile, to re-establish friendship and to reunite man with God, his maker, then there had to have been a falling away from God first. With the fall of man came sin. This sin brought divisions amongst the people based upon sex, race and wealth or lack thereof. By fulfilling the Will of God in our individual, personal lives we assist in the fulfillment of the Mystery of the Will of God.

The Original Will and Plan of the Lord God for Man

The Lord God announced his original Will and plan for the creation and existence of mankind here on this earth in the book of Genesis. We find the Lord God declaring,

> **...Let us make man in our image, after our likeness: and let them have dominion over the fish of the sea, and over the fowl of the air, and over the cattle, and over all the earth, and over every creeping thing that creepeth upon the earth.**

Ge 1:26.

Before Genesis 1:26, the word of God does not mention man. But, when man is brought into the creation picture we hear immediately what the Lord God has in store for his glory—the man. Verse 26 plainly states that God's Will and plan for man, even in the beginning, is that man should live and exist in God's image and in his likeness. God, being a spirit, must be worshipped in Spirit and in truth. *(Joh 4:24*) And so, if the man was going to exist in God's image and likeness it must be accomplished in the spiritual realm, rather than the natural. Because, as the Apostle Paul stated,

> **…the natural man receiveth not the things of the Spirit of God: for they are foolishness unto him: neither can he know them, because they are spiritually discerned.**

1Co 2:14.

Therefore, except that man existed in the image of God spiritually, there was no way for him to resemble God, who is a spirit. We find that man did in fact resemble God, because God breathed himself, the **neshamah** *(nesh-aw-maw'),* breath of life into man, and man then became a living soul. *(Ge 2:7)* A soul is a spirit. Therefore man became a living spirit as God is the living God *(Jer 10:10),* who is a spirit. *(Joh 4:24)* With the neshamah of life indwelling him, Adam was able to exist upright and holy *(Ec 7:29)* as God is upright *(Ps 18:25; Ps 25:8; Ps 92:15; Isa 26:7)* and holy. *(Le 11:44-45; Le 19:2; Le 20:26; Ps 22:3; Ps 99:9; Isa 6:3; Isa 43:3)*

Thus, Adam resembled God and existed in his image and in God's likeness. He was able to worship God in truth and in spirit by loving the Lord God with all his heart, with all his soul, with all his mind, and with all his strength. *(Read Mk 12:29-30)* The words, love, heart, soul, mind and strength, all point to and deal with that part of man that is invisible and cannot be seen with the natural eye. This is the same physical trait associated with a spirit—invisible to the natural eye. Thus, during the creation event, Adam was made and formed according to God's plan. This plan is known as the Will of God, because when God planned to create man, he willed it—purposed it—to be so.

Within the original Will of God, there was one Spirit indwelling one man, Adam. Adam represented not only God, but the whole of humanity. There was one race of people, speaking one language, living for the one true God, with the one true God indwelling the whole human race. There was no division amongst man or between God and man. Everything existed and worked together for the good of the man, Adam, who loved God, so that the Lord would receive his glory. Even after God made a physical division of the man by making the woman, there was still one people, one race, one language, one flesh and one Spirit indwelling the two pieces of the one flesh. Because she was bone of his bone and flesh of his flesh *(Ge 2:23,)* the woman and the man carried the same DNA genetic code. They acted and desired alike, and it was that same Spirit that gave them the same mind so that they could think spiritually, holy and in an upright manner like the Lord God.

A reconciling became necessary because man's disobedience and sin resulted in a separation and divorcement between God and mankind during the Genesis Affair. *(Ge 3:1-7, 24)* By the term the Genesis Affair we mean that part of the Book of Genesis that deals with God's commandment given to man—not to eat of the tree of the knowledge of good and evil *(Ge 2:16-17);* God's declaration that man's situation of being alone was not good *(Ge 2:18)*; God's separating the flesh of man and forming the woman *(Ge 2:21-22)*; the separated piece called the woman being reconciled back to the man through and by the institution of marriage *(Ge 2:21-24)*; the woman's transgression of the one flesh *(Ge 3:1-6)*; the woman's transgression of the commandment not to eat from the tree of the knowledge of good and evil *(Ge 3:1-6)*; the woman being used as an instrument of unrighteousness by Lucifer and thereby tempting and enticing her husband Adam to transgress the commandment not to eat from the tree of the knowledge of good and evil *(Ge 3:1-6; Ro 6:13, 16)*; man's transgression of God's commandment *(Ge 3:6)* and thereby, his fall from grace with God; God's sentence of punishment upon man for the violation *(Ge 3:14-19)*; and, man being put out of his home, the Garden of Eden. *(Ge 3:23-24)*

Due to man's fall from grace with God during the Genesis Affair, all of mankind received a sinful nature, *(Eph 2:3; Ro 5:12),* and by this same man, Adam, came death. *(1Co 15:21)* Within man's nature is his sinful desire to fellowship with others based upon his having respect of persons. By having respect of persons man discriminates against man causing divisions amongst the people. Divisions amongst the people hinders God's Will to reconcile mankind back to God, back to himself. This respect of persons is an attempt to place undue importance upon one person rather than another person, based solely upon a worldly, and carnal standard. Put simply, to have respect of persons is to hate. For, love has no respect of persons. God is love *(1Jo 4:8, 16)*, and he respects the person of no man, but loves all the same. *(Joh 3:16; 1Jo 4:10; Ro 12:9)* And there is no middle ground between love and hate. We either love or we hate. We either serve God in love through obedience or serve Satan in hate by rebellion and sin. *(Mt 6:24; Ro 6:16)* We either have a strong fondness, or a strong dislike. For, a double minded man is unstable in all his ways. *(Jas 1:8)* Although the hatred may be subconscious, it still is hatred.

To divide a thing is to break it into more than one part, therefore bringing about the need for reconciliation. The Mystery of the Will of God then, is, through Jesus Christ, the divisions, the desire to hate, and the need to have respect of persons, amongst the people are eliminated. Thus, together in one all things exist in Christ, *(Eph 1:10; Eph 2:16, 17)* in love. We exist, not as Jews or Gentiles, male or female, bond or free, but as the Church, the one body of Christ, all in the name of Jesus. *(Eph 1:20-23; Eph 2:6; Eph 4:4; Ga 3:28)* So, as we exist together in one, as one in Christ, we are hereby reconciled back to God in the state and spiritual condition—that mankind dwelled in before they sinned in the Garden of Eden.

Within the law of commandments contained in ordinances the reader will find the enemy of the Mystery of the Will of God, hatred. *(Eph 2:15)* For within the law is found the middle wall of partition, which were the rules of physical separation and non-involvement of God's people, the Israelites, with the Gentiles. The Gentiles are the non-Israelites, who did not know God. *(Eph 2:15, 16)* The rules of physical separation and non-involvement were necessary to maintain God's standard of holiness and reverence for Him. However, through Christ and the workings of the Mystery of God's Will, the need for the middle wall of partition is eliminated. *(Eph 2:14, 15)* For, Christ,

> **15 Having abolished in his flesh the enmity, even the law of commandments contained in ordinances; for to make in himself of twain one new man, so making peace;**
> **16 And that he might reconcile both unto God in one body by the cross, having slain the enmity thereby:**

Eph 2:15-16.

Therefore, in Christ, in things spiritual, we are all one. *(Ga 3:28; Col 3:11; Ro 10:12) For as many as are led by the Spirit of God, they are the sons of God, (Ro 8:14);* regardless of their gender, race or societal status. *(Ga 3:28)*

The Truth Of The Gospel

The gospel of Jesus Christ and its salvational plan is the means by which God has determined to fulfill the Mystery of his Will: to make in himself of twain (two) one new man. *(See Eph 2:15-16)* For,

> **...it pleased God by the foolishness of preaching to save them that believe.**

1Co 1:21b.

When the preacher honors hatred and has respect of persons he frustrates the grace of God and violates the truth of the gospel. One can have respect of persons based upon race, gender or societal status, called bond or free. The Lord Jesus said,

> **16 For God so loved the world, that he gave his only begotten Son, that whosoever believeth in him should not perish, but have everlasting life.**
>
> **17 For God sent not his Son into the world to condemn the world; but that the world through him might be saved.**

Joh 3:16-17.

God loved not only the Jews, but every person in the world that he gave Christ to die for the sins of the world. The one body of Christ must continue in its strivings to eliminate the ranks, influence, power, and workings of the enmity—having respect of persons—within the Kingdom of God. The Apostle Paul began the work of eliminating this evil from the body of Christ at Antioch. For, the record reflects that,

11 But when Peter was come to Antioch, I withstood him to the face, because he was to be blamed.

12 For before that certain came from James, he did eat with the Gentiles: but when they were come, he withdrew himself, fearing them which were of the circumcision.

13 And *the other Jews dissembled* likewise with him; insomuch that *Barnabas also was carried away with their dissimulation.*

14 *But when I saw that they walked not uprightly according to the truth of the gospel*, I said unto Peter before them all, If thou, being a Jew, livest after the manner of Gentiles, and not as do the Jews, why compellest thou the Gentiles to live as do the Jews?

Ga 2:11-14 *(emphasis added).*

In the above passages we learn that Peter had respect of persons when certain people were present, and therefore was not walking uprightly according to the truth of the gospel. When we are not walking upright we are walking in sin. Furthermore, Paul called them hypocrites. For, the word **dissimulation** is translated from the Greek word **hupokrisis** *(hoop-ok'-ree-sis).* **Hupokrisis** means deceit, condemnation, hypocrisy, acting under a feigned part, dissimulation. Peter's hypocrisy required immediate, open rebuke due to his status in the Church. For, by his actions he caused the other Jewish brethren to be carried away and to follow in his sin. *(See Ga 2:12-13)* Had Peter not been aware or understood what the '*truth of the gospel*' was at the time, then his sin would not have been hypocrisy, but it would have been a mistake borne out of ignorance.

However, Peter knew and understood. For, the Lord had shown him in a trance, that while heaven opened, a great sheet descended to the earth,

12 Wherein were all manner of fourfooted beasts of the earth, and wild beasts, and creeping things, and fowls of the air.

13 And there came a voice to him, Rise, Peter; kill, and eat.

14 But Peter said, Not so, Lord; for I have never eaten any thing that is common or unclean.

15 And the voice spake unto him again the second time, What God hath cleansed, that call not thou common.

Ac 10:12-15.

Peter's reference about not eating animals that were common or unclean involved the commandments found in the law of Moses. This is what Paul called *"the enmity, even the law of commandments contained in ordinances..." (Eph 2:15)* A good example is Leviticus 11:4, where it says

Nevertheless these shall ye not eat of them that chew the cud, or of them that divide the hoof: as the camel, because he cheweth the cud, but divideth not the hoof; he is unclean unto you.

By revelation and the leading of the Spirit of Christ, Peter entered the house of the Gentile named Cornelius. *(Read Ac 10:17-33)* After, entering the house and hearing the testimony of Cornelius, Peter was given the revelation of what the truth of the gospel is.

34 Then Peter opened his mouth, and said, Of a truth I perceive that God is no respector of persons:

35 But in every nation he that feareth him, and worketh righteousness, is accepted with him.

Ac 10:34-35.

Thus, the truth of the gospel is that God is no respecter of persons, because he so loved the world that he gave his only begotten son to die for the sins of the world. *(Read Joh 3:16-17)* God did not so love only the Jews, but he so loved the whole of the human race. Therefore, Peter knew and understood that his having respect of persons was a violation of the truth of the gospel. And, his failure to walk upright according to the truth of the gospel, frustrated and hindered the very gospel that he, as a preacher, was commissioned to proclaim. *(Read Ga 2:20-21)*

The law was the Israelite's schoolmaster to bring them into an inward holiness unto Christ, that they might be justified. *(Ga 3:24)* The Keeper is He that gives us the power within, to live a holy life in the midst of evil. The Keeper, who is Christ the Holy Ghost, had not indwelled all of mankind, since the fall of man during the Genesis Affair. For the law was before the dispensation of the fullness of times, wherein Christ came to indwell. *(Eph 1:10)*

Therefore, after the fall of man, **(1)** which was a direct result of the violation of the one flesh, **(2)** which in-turn provided the temptation and opportunity to violate God's commandment causing the first divorce, **(3)** the common man was not able to live holy without the rules of physical separation. Now, man had lost his state of innocence and had become like God, to know good and evil. *(Ge 3:22)* So, the need arose for **(1)** the rules of physical separation and non-involvement to bring about reconciliation of man back to God; **(2)** the rule wherein men became rulers over their wives *(Ge 3:16)* to insure a reconciliation of man back to the woman, and to prevent the wife from leading the husband based upon her desires; and **(3)** the rule that the Lord would put enmity between the serpent, Lucifer and the woman *(Ge 3:15; See also Re 12:13),* to destroy the friendship, trust and admiration between them which led to Eve's stealing God's glory, the man, for Lucifer's use. *(See Isa 42:8; 48:11)*

These rules, left in the hands of un-regenerated men, eventually led to **(1)** absolute male dominance and a selfish sense of ownership of the institution of marriage, **(2)** gender discrimination, **(3)** racial discrimination in the sense of racial superiority, and **(4)** wealth based classifications.

These results came about due to man's sin and his continued desire and nature to sin. For, the Gentiles, who are the non-Israelites were

> **...aliens from the commonwealth of Israel, and strangers from the covenants of promise, having no hope, and without God in the world:**

Eph 2:12.

And, the woman's sorrow was greatly multiplied when the Lord said,

> **[T]hy desire shall be to thy husband, and he shall rule over thee.**

Ge 3:16.

What the law attempted, but could not accomplish by the letter alone, Christ, born of a woman and made under the law, *(Ga 4:4-6; Ge 49:10)* accomplishes and fulfills through and by His Spirit. *(Mt 5:17)* For, with the coming of Christ through faith, *"...we are no longer under a schoolmaster." (Ga 3:25)*

For centuries, discrimination and therefore a division of the people in the world, at large and in the Kingdom of God, the visible church has consistently occurred in three basic forms, namely: gender, race and wealth. These three basic forms of discrimination are hatred, the enemy, and are actively engaged in a direct, spiritual conflict with the revealed Mystery of the Will of God.

The intent here, then, is to trace the development and expose the existence and workings of the enemy of the Mystery of the Will of God. Next, it shall be prudent to consider the means and manner by which God has chosen to defeat the enemy in all its forms, through and by the plan of salvation in Christ Jesus, and the power of His Word. Finally, it is hoped that you, the reader, will be enabled to see why Galatians 3:28,

> **There is neither Jew nor Greek** [ELIMINATION OF RACIAL DISCRIMINATION], **there is neither bond nor free** [ELIMINATION OF WEALTH BASED DISCRIMINATION]**, there is neither male nor female** [ELIMINATION OF GENDER BASED DISCRIMINATION]: **for ye are all one in Christ Jesus..,**

a declaration by the Apostle Paul, serves as a word picture showing the ultimate fulfillment of the Mystery of the Will of God. This ultimate fulfillment is achieved when Christ indwells the male and female, the jailed and the free, and the Jew and Gentile alike. The indwelling Spirit of Christ, because he is one Spirit, causes all who possess him to become one and equal in importance. For, they all become members of the one body of Christ. *(1Co 12:12-13)*

> **5 And the angel which I saw stand upon the sea and upon the earth lifted up his hand to heaven,**
>
> **6 And sware by him that liveth for ever and ever, who created heaven, and the things that therein are, and the earth, and the things that therein are, and the sea, and the things which are therein, *that there should be time no longer*:**
>
> **7 But in the days of the voice of the seventh angel, when he shall begin to sound, *the mystery of God should be finished*, as he hath declared to his servants the prophets.**

Re 10:5-7 *(emphasis added).*

Amen.

The Obedience Of Faith

Book 3

Introduction

In **Book One**, '*The Image of God*', of this four volume set, we learned and discussed the truth that God's Will for man was that man should be created and then he should be made to exist in the image and likeness of God. *(Read Ge 1:26-27; Ge 2:7)* This Original Will of God for man, was accomplished, by God himself, as the writer recorded,

> **And the LORD God formed man of the dust of the ground, and breathed into his nostrils the breath of life; and man became a living soul.**

Ge 2:7.

Later, in Book One we discussed the events that led to the fall of man and his losing the image of God. After man lost the image of God, God being the faithful creating father, shifted into the salvation mode and announced a plan for the saving of his creation called man in Genesis 3:15. For, there the LORD God prophesied and proclaimed the coming of the Christ, stating,

> **14 ...unto the serpent...:**
> **15 ...I will put enmity between thee and the woman, and between thy seed and her seed; it shall bruise thy head, and thou shalt bruise his heel.**

Ge 3:14-15.

This prophecy of the LORD God was fulfilled after the son of perdition *(2Th 2:3)* Satan, entered his seed *(Lu 22:1-6),* Judas Iscariot who became the son of perdition *(Joh 17:12)* and brought about the betrayal of Christ with a kiss. *(Lu 22:47-48; Mt 26:47-49; Mk 14:41-46; Ps 41:9; Ps 109:4-8; Ac 1:16-20; Ps 69:21-25)* Christ was the seed of the woman *(Mt 1:16; Mt 11:11; Lu 7:28; Lu 1:35; Php 2:7-8),* whose heels were bruised when he was crucified *(Mt 27:34-35; Mk 15:25; Mk 16:6; Ps 22:16-18)* and therefore rendered unable to walk upon the earth for three days. *(Mt 12:40; Mt 16:21; Mt 17:22-23; Mt 20:18-19; Mt 26:61; Mt 27:40, 63; Mk 8:31; Mk 10:33-34; Lu 9:22; Lu 13:32-33; Heb 5:7-9; Lu 24:6-7; Lu 17-21; Lu 24:46; Ac 10:38-41; 1Co 15:3-4)* While unable to walk upon the earth, the seed of the woman, Jesus the Christ, went into the heart of the earth *(Mt 12:40)* and bruised the head of the serpent when he took from Satan the keys and the power of death. *(Heb 2:14; 2Ti 1:10; Re 1:18; Ps 68:20-21; Col 2:15)* As the prophet Habakkuk declared,

> **Thou wentest forth for the salvation of thy people, even for salvation with thine anointed; thou woundedst the head out of the house of the wicked, by discovering the foundation unto the neck...**

Hab 3:13.

By wounding and bruising the serpent's head, Jesus started the process that began the destruction of Satan, his kingdom and his works. *(Heb 2:14)*

Book One proceeds to discuss how today, man is enabled to re-acquire the image of God, thereby making peace with God and being reconciled back to God. In the end, Book One concludes that

"...in the beginning, Adam and Eve possessed the indwelling Spirit of God, the neshamah of life, the Holy Ghost."

Book Two, *'Growing In Grace'*, continued our search for the full and deeper understanding of the Mystery of the Will of God, through the scriptural Mystery of Godliness. *(See 1Ti 3:16)* Beginning with Chapter 6 the work briefly discusses the problem and root of gender discrimination—also known as having respect of persons based upon one's gender. Chapter 7 then points us to a greater and deeper walk in Christ by teaching us how to walk in the Spirit and what it means to

> **Be ye therefore perfect, even as your Father which is in heaven is perfect.**

Mt 5:48.

For, it is through obedience to the Word of God that we reach perfection, which means to be of full age in those things that we know and understand about the Kingdom of God and his ways.

Later on in Chapter 8, after having re-acquired the image of God, and having begun our walk in the Spirit towards perfection, the work then discusses God's plan and means to help us in our 'Growing in Grace'. For it is through and by the operation of the gifts of the Spirit that the saints are perfected, the work of the ministry is performed and the body of Christ is edified,

> **13 Till we all come in the unity of the faith, and of the knowledge of the Son of God, unto a perfect man, unto the measure of the stature of the fulness of Christ:**
>
> **14 That we henceforth be no more children, tossed to and fro, and carried about with every wind of doctrine, by the sleight of men, and cunning craftiness, whereby they lie in wait to deceive;**

15 But speaking the truth in love, may grow up into him in all things, which is the head, even Christ:

16 From whom the whole body fitly joined together and compacted by that which every joint supplieth, according to the effectual working in the measure of every part, maketh increase of the body unto the edifying of itself in love.

Eph 4:13-16.

And finally, Chapter 9 lets us know that although we have received his image, but because we are yet in the flesh, we are subject to backslide into carnality and become the dreaded Carnal Christian. It is hoped that by discussing the problem and the attributes of the Carnal Christian that more of us will refuse to remain in a carnal state, because

6 ...to be carnally minded is death; but to be spiritually minded is life and peace.

7 Because the carnal mind is enmity against God: for it is not subject to the law of God, neither indeed can be.

Ro 8:6-7.

In this book, **Book Three**, *'The Obedience of Faith'*, which begins as Chapter 10, of The Mystery of Godliness, we discover the ten original commandments of the Lord God to man. While discussing the commandments we learn about the potter's house—the place where God, the creator, forms, shapes and fashions us. Book Three is subtitled, *'The Obedience Of Faith'*, because it strives to teach and show the children of the Kingdom of God that to have faith is to obey the commandments of God; and that,

> **...without faith it is impossible to please him: for he that cometh to God must believe that he is, and that he is a rewarder of them that diligently seek him.**

Heb 11:6.

For, it is through faith that the children of the Kingdom are enabled and empowered to overcome the world in the same manner as did the saints of old,

> **33 Who through faith subdued kingdoms, wrought righteousness, obtained promises, stopped the mouths of lions.**
>
> **34 Quenched the violence of fire, escaped the edge of the sword, out of weakness were made strong, waxed valiant in fight, turned to flight the armies of the aliens.**
>
> **35 Women received their dead raised to life again...**

Heb 11:33-35.

Finally, in the end, it is hoped that as the children of the Kingdom of God,

> **That ye be not slothful, but followers of them who through faith and patience inherit the promises.**

Heb 6:12.

Amen.

The

Mystery Of Godliness

(Continued From Book 2)

Chapter 10

Faith And The Commandments Of God

Faith in God and his word sustains and strengthens our obedience. Since man must search the scriptures *(Joh 5:39, 46)*, seek the kingdom of God and his righteousness *(Mt 6:33)* and study the word of God *(2Ti 2:15)* before he can know, understand and obey the commandments of God, he is therefore, first, justified by faith *(Ro 3:28)*, through his belief in God.

The question is asked, "*What is Faith?*"

Now Faith is the substance of things hoped for, the evidence of things not seen.
Heb 11:1.

And, without faith it is impossible to please God *(Heb 11:6)*, because *"...whatsoever is not of faith is sin." (Ro 14:23)*

But, what is sin?

The word **sin** *(sin)* in Romans 14:23 is translated from the Greek **hamartia** *(ham-ar-tee'-ah).* **Hamartia** means an offence, sin, sinful. And **sin** means the breaking or violating a religious or moral law, especially through a willful act; any offense. Therefore, we learn what sin is by acquiring knowledge of the existence of a specific command-ment or law of God. For,

...by the law is the knowledge of sin.
Ro 3:20b.

That is, we know and are made aware of how to offend and sin against God when we acquire knowledge of specific commandments and laws of God. Because, when one sins, he offends God by violating or breaking a specific law of God. Therefore, when a member of the body of Christ lives a life based upon what he can see, do and accomplish outside of placing his faith in God—he offends God. And this offense is sin against God. Because, as God, ***God desires:*** *to be petitioned (Ps 20:5; Ps 20:1-9), to be asked (Mt 6:8; Mt*

7:11; Mt 21:22; Lu 11:9-13; Joh 14:13-14; Joh 15:7), to be called upon *(Ps 4:3; Ps 31:17),* to be desired *(Ps 55:22; Isa 31:1),* to be prayed to *(Ps 6:9; Ps 32:5-6; Mt 6:6, 9; Mt 21:22),* to be sought after *(Ps 34:4; Mt 7:7-8; Lu 11:11-13),* to be wanted *(Ps 55:22; Isa 31:1),* to be hoped for *(Ps 146:5; Ps 147:11; Jer 3:23),* to be worshipped *(1Sa 7:3; Ps 29:2; Joh 4:23; Jer 7:2),* to be cried to *(Ps 3:4; Ps 6:8; Ps 9:12; Ps 18:6; Ps 22:24; Ps 28:2, 6; Ps 30:2, 8; Ps 31:22; Ps 34:6, 17),* and to be praised *(Ps 9:1; Ps 33:1-3; Ps 50:23; Ps 106:1; Ps 117:1-2; Ps 135:1; Ps 149:1; Ps 150:1),* **for: his defense** *(Ps 5:11; Ps 7:10; Ps 20:1; Ps 31:2-3);* **his pastoral care** *(Ps 23:1-5; Ps 34:10);* **his name** *(Ps 8:1, 9; Ps 9:10; Ps 29:2; Ps 33:21; Ps 34:3);* **his forgiveness** *(Ps 25:18);* **his secret** *(Ps 25:14; Ps 31:20);* **his healing** *(Ps 30:2);* **his pardons** *(Ps 25:11);* **his favour** *(Ps 5:12; Ps 30:5, 7);* **his safety** *(Ps 4:8; Ps 12:5);* **his shield** *(Ps 5:12; Ps 18:35; Ps 28:7; Ps 33:20; Ps 115:9);* **his refuge** *(Ps 9:9; Ps 14:6);* **his judgments** *(Ps 9:4, 7-8, 16-20; Ps 10:17-18; Ps 19:9; Ps 25:9; Ps 33:5);* **his mighty acts** *(Ps 145:4; Ps 150:2a);* **his light** *(Ps 27:1);* **his holiness** *(Ps 30:4);* **his marvelous works** *(Ps 9:1; Ps 139:14);* **his wondrous works** *(Ps 8:3-8; Ps 26:7);* **his works** *(Ps 33:4);* **his mercy** *(Ps 5:7; Ps 6:1-2, 4; Ps 13:5; Ps 18:25, 50; Ps 21:7; Ps 23:6; Ps 25:6-7; Ps 31:7, 16; Ps 32:10; Ps 33:18-19, 22; Ps 100:5; Ps 118:1, 4; Ps 145:8; Ro 11:30-32);* **his faithfulness** *(Ps 9:10; Ps 36:5; Ps 37:28);* **his goodness** *(Ps 16:2-3; Ps 21:3; Ps 23:6; Ps 25:7; Ps 27:13; Ps 31:19; Ps 33:5; Ps 34:8; Ps 100:5);* **his lovingkindness** *(Ps 17:7; Ps 25:6; Ps 26:3; Ps 36:7, 10);* **his marvelous kindness** *(Ps 31:21);* **his merciful kindness** *(Ps 117:2);* **his instruction** *(Ps 32:8; Mt 28:19-20);* **his counsel** *(Ps 16:7; Ps 33:11);* **his gifts** *(Ps 37:4; Ro 6:23);* **his gentleness** *(Ps 18:35);* **his righteousness** *(Ps 11:7; Ps 24:5; Ps 31:1; Ps 33:5; Ps 36:6);* **his hiding place** *(Ps 32:7);* **his eye** *(Ps 33:18-19; Ps 34:15);* **his salvation** *(Ps 3:8; Ps 6:4; Ps 7:10; Ps 9:14; Ps 13:5; Ps 17:7; Ps 18:27; Ps 20:5-6, 9; Ps 21:1; Ps 24:5; Ps 25:5; Ps 27:1; Ps 34:6, 18);* **his blessings** *(Ps 3:8; Ps 5:12; Ps 21:2; Ps 37:5, 9, 18-19, 29);* **his preservation** *(Ps 25:21; Ps 31:23; Ps 32:7; Ps*

37:28); ***his upholding power*** *(Ps 11:7; Ps 17:5; Ps 37:23-24);* ***his pavilion*** *(Ps 27:5; Ps 31:20);* ***his vengeance*** *(Ps 18:47);* ***his redemption*** *(Ps 31:5; Ps 34:22);* ***his voice*** *(Ps 29:3-5, 7-9);* ***his peace*** *(Ps 29:11);* ***his law*** *(Ps 19:7);* ***his word*** *(Ps 33:4, 6, 9);* ***his testimony*** *(Ps 19:7);* ***his statutes*** *(Ps 19:8);* ***his commandments*** *(Ps 19:8);* ***his truth*** *(Ps 100:5; Ps 117:2);* ***his fear*** *(Ps 19:9; Ps 34:11; Ps 112:1);* ***his help*** *(Ps 10:14; Ps 27:9; Ps 30:10; Ps 33:20; Ps 115:9);* ***his deliverance*** *(Ps 18:2, 17, 19, 43, 48, 50; Ps 22:4-5; Ps 25:20; Ps 31:1-2; Ps 33:18-19; Ps 34:7, 17, 19; Ps 35:10; Ps 37:32-33, 40);* ***his power*** *(Ps 21:8, 13);* ***his strength*** *(Ps 18:32, 39; Ps 19:14; Ps 21:1, 13; Ps 27:1; Ps 28:7-8; Ps 29:11; Ps 31:4, 24; Ps 37:39);* ***his promotions*** *(Ps 37:34);* ***his pleadings*** *(Ps 35:1; Ps 45:1; Ps 119:154; Pr 22:22-23; Pr 23:10-11);* ***and all the benefits*** that he has bestowed upon man. *(Ps 103:2)*

Furthermore, God is the Father of all creation. And, as a true father ***God desires: to provide for his own*** *(Ps 34:9-10; Ps 37:25);* ***to be honored*** *(Pr 3:9);* ***to be needed*** *(Ps 55:22; Isa 31:1);* ***to be believed*** *(Joh 3:16; Ro 10:9, 14, 16);* ***to be imitated*** *(Jer 4:2; Ro 6:22; Mt 5:48; Eph 5:1; Lu 6:36; 1Pe 1:16);* ***to be appreciated*** *(Pr 3:9);* ***to be loved*** *(Ps 31:23; Mt 22:37);* ***to be thanked*** *(Ps 18:49; Ps 30:4; Ps 35:18; Ps 100:4; Ps 106:1; Ps 107:1; Ps 118:1; Ro 14:6);* ***to be praised*** *(Ps 33:1-3; Ps 106:1; Ps 117:1-2; Ps 135:1; Ps 149:1; Ps 150:1);* ***to be sung to*** *(Ps 33:1-3; Ps 47:6; Ps 100:1-2; Ps 105:2; Ps 108:1; Ps 135:3; Ps 138:5; Ps 144:9; Ps 147:7; Ps 149:1, 3, 5-6,);* ***to be looked up to*** *(Ps 5:3; Isa 17:7; Isa 31:1; Isa 45:22; Isa 51:1);* ***and to receive glory from his offspring*** *(Ps 50:23).* But when man lives outside of faith in God, he fails to recognize God as his father, and thereby offends God. Because, his attempt to live in a manner that does not recognize God as his provider, protector and sustainer of the breath and wind of life—is an attempt to take away God's glory and praise. And this is surely an offense and sin against God, because the Lord said,

I am the Lord: that is my name: and my glory will I not give to another, neither my praise to graven images.

Isa 42:8 *(Read also Isa 48:11).*

And since it is sin that separates man from God, thereby we understand that God is not pleased with sin—whether it is due to a lack of faith in Him or otherwise. Therefore, he that is upright and just must live by faith in order to obey and thereby please God. *(Heb 10:38)* The word **faith** *(fāth)* in the Hebrews 11:1 passage above is translated from the Greek word **pistis** *(pis'-tis).*

Pistis means persuasion, credence, moral conviction of religious truth or the truthfulness of God; constancy and continuity in one's belief, reliance upon or persuasion of the truthfulness of God; assurance, believe, belief, faith, fidelity. Furthermore, the Greek word **pistis** is derived from the Greek word **peitho** *(pi'-tho)* which means to convince by argument, to rely by inward certainty. **Peitho** also means to agree, be content, believe, make friend, obey, trust, yield, persuade and to assent to evidence or authority.

The trying of your faith brings about and worketh patience. *(Jas 1:3)* The trying of your faith is actually accomplished through personal temptations, which leads to perfection through the process of overcoming. For, the writer said,

But let patience have her perfect work, that ye may be perfect and entire, wanting nothing.

Jas 1:4.

Now, let us return to Adam and his quest to maintain his created state of uprightness. When we review the scripture we learn that God commanded Adam to be perfect, in the same manner that Jesus commanded us in Matthew 5:48 where he commanded us to

Be ye therefore perfect, even as your Father which is in heaven is perfect.

Mt 5:48.

The commandment of God to Adam and Eve to be perfect came in the eighth and ninth commandments given to man, although the specific word perfect was not used. The writer of Genesis wrote,

> **And God blessed them, and God said unto them,... replenish the earth and subdue it:...**

Ge 1:28.

The word **replenish** *(ri-`ple-nish)* is translated from the Hebrew word **male** *(maw-lay').* **Male** means to fill, be full of, accomplish, confirm, to consecrate, satisfy, furnish, to replenish. In the book of Hebrews Chapter 5, verses 8 and 9 the writer declared,

> **8 Though he were a Son, yet learned he obedience by the things which he suffered;**
> **9 And being made perfect, he became the author of eternal salvation unto all them that obey him;**

In the above passage of scripture the word **perfect** *(`per-fikt)* is very close in meaning to the word **replenish**, discussed above in Genesis 1:28. The Greek **teleioo** *(tel-i-ŏ'-o),* from which the word perfect is translated, means complete, consummate, to accomplish, consecrate, finish, fulfill, make perfect. When God commanded mankind to replenish and subdue the earth, the commandment was first to them. So, the question is then asked,

Replenish what earth, subdue what earth?

The answer is simple—*The earth that is in you*—mankind's flesh. For, mankind was created from the dust of the earth. *(Ge 2:7)* And, although man was created with an upright soul that was from God *(Ecc 7:29),* his flesh was of this world and therefore, naturally, possessed no desire for heavenly things or heavenly beings, such as God. *(Ga 5:17; Ro 7:18)* This being the case, it was necessary for mankind to train and consecrate the earth made flesh. This consecration of the flesh would be accomplished by and through obedience to the commandments of God.

In order for Adam to accomplish and fulfill the process of consecrating himself, also known as perfection, he first would have to subdue the earth, subdue the will of the living dirt that was in him. The word **subdue** *(səb-dū')* in the Genesis 1:28 passage is translated from the Hebrew word **kabash** *(kaw-bash').* **Kabash** means to tread down, to keep under and bring into subjection. While discussing the perfection and obedience of Christ Jesus, the Apostle Paul declared,

> **And being found in fashion as a man, he humbled himself, and became obedient unto death, even the death of the cross.**

Php 2:8.

In this Philippians 2:8 passage, wherein Jesus humbled himself and became obedient, the word **humbled** *(hum'b'ld)* is taken from the Greek **tapeinoo** *(tap-i-nŏ'-o).* **Tapeinoo** means to depress, humiliate, abase, bring low, humble self. When we bring low our mind and therefore our thoughts and our will into subjection to the law and will of God, then we have subdued and humbled the earth that is in us. And, after we have humbled our mind, we are then capable and empowered to become obedient to the law and will of God.

Mankind was first created with an upright soul, an upright mind. By and through his initial, intentional and knowing sin the soul of man died and lost its uprightness. *(Ec 7:29)* God, who is the Holy Ghost, has set into motion again the 'creation process', by redoing, renewing the dead, corrupt soul of man. For, it is the Holy Ghost that renews our mind *(Tit 3:5)*, that is, it creates in us an upright mind, a mind to live for God. After our mind is renewed and our mind becomes upright, or we possess within us an upright spirit, then it is our job, our service to perfect our way in holiness. *(Ro 12:1)* We perfect our way by and through our obedience to the commandments of God, thereby substituting his way for our way. The ways of God are perfect because he is obedient in all that he knows. And, he knows all things.

Furthermore, obedience to the commandments of God is actually a 'putting off' of the old man by abandoning our own ways and deceitful lusts *(Eph 4:22; Col 2:11; Ro 6:6)*, and putting on the new man by taking on the ways of God. We take on the ways of God by taking on the mind of Christ *(Php 2:5-8)* and thereby possessing, walking, talking, and living within the thoughts of God. *(Ga 2:20)* For, the thoughts of God are not our thoughts. *(Isa 55:8-9)* And, a thought is the 'product' of a thinking mind. The old man is the sum total of the thoughts, will and desires of mankind's fallen, sinful, fleshly-minded soul.

The Law and Freewill Praise

After God created mankind he gave them his word in the form of Ten Commandments. That is, God gave them a set of rules to live by so that they would be able to live long and happy lives, and enjoy each other, while in the service of God. For, the conclusion of the whole matter is,

> **[F]ear God, and keep his commandments: for this is the whole duty of man.**

Ec 12:13.

These commandments or statutes made up the law of God as given by God to Adam and Eve. The commandments were necessary to insure that mankind possessed a freewill of his own and was afforded the opportunity to exercise that freewill as he so desired. As the Psalmist declared,

> **Accept, I beseech thee, the freewill offerings of my mouth, O LORD, and teach me thy judgments.**

Ps 119:108.

A **nedabah** *(ned-aw-baw')*, Hebrew for **freewill** *(`frē-wil)*, is that which is spontaneous, voluntarily, willingly and freely. Where there is no choice, and thus no decision to make, there is no opportunity and thus no freedom to exercise one's own freewill.

Man's freewill is the result of God having created him subject to vanity *(Ro 8:20)*, and not subject to the law of God. *(Ro 8:7)* Therefore, since man's vain nature makes him naturally not subject to God's law, he must make a conscious, voluntary choice to become subject to God's law. This conscious choice is contrary to man's nature, his make up, because there is none that seeketh after God. *(Ro 3:11)* For, God is good, but by nature no good thing dwelleth in the flesh. *(Ro 7:18)* And, there is none that doeth good of his own accord. *(Ro 3:12)* Therefore, when man chooses to obey God, as God has commanded, this obedient, righteous choice is in honor, and praise of God. And such praise glorifieth God. For, the Lord himself declared,

> **Whoso offereth praise glorifieth me: and to him that ordereth his conversation aright will I shew the salvation of God.**

Ps 50:23.

When man is obedient to God, others who are witnesses of the obedient acts give praise to God in recognition of the man that was obedient. Therefore, when man goes against his nature of vanity and chooses God's law instead, he exercises his capacity and freewill to choose.

Man's subjection to vanity was not in agreement with man's own will, but was done for God's personal reasons.

> **For the creature was made subject to vanity, not willingly, but by reason of him who hath subjected the same in hope.**

Ro 8:20.

For, God desires to be worshipped *(Joh 4:23)* and to be praised. Praises to God from mankind are sacrifices, because they are the exercise of man's freewill. *(Heb 13:15; Ps 54:6; Ps 50:14)* The word **vanity** *(`va-ne-tē)* is translated from the Greek word **mataiotes** *(mat-ah-yot'-ace)* meaning moral depravity, transientness, inutility. **Mataiotes** is derived from **mataios** *(mat'-ah-yos)*, which means that which is empty, profitless, vain, and vanity. Thus, we see why the scripture declared that the carnal mind is opposed to God. *(Ro 8:7)* It desires, naturally, those things that are morally depraved, empty, and is of no gain nor profit to the spirit man, his soul. And except the thing desired benefits and profits the soul of man, it cannot be in favor of nor a benefit to God, because man can only serve and worship God in spirit and in truth. *(Joh 4:24)* For God is a spirit. *(Joh 4:24)*

Man was created with an upright soul residing in carnal flesh. **Carnal** *(`kärn-el)*, from the Greek word **sarx** *(sarx)*, means pertaining to the flesh, not spiritual and relating to fleshly desires and appetites. That which is vanity relates to the flesh, because it is useless to the upright soul. In this life, because man resides in a fleshly body, he will inevitably engage in the acquisition and use of things vain in nature and pertaining only to this world. However, the fact that man must exist now within carnal flesh, that is, with a mind born of the flesh, he does not have to live carnally minded.

> **For to be carnally minded is death; but to be spiritually minded is life and peace.**

Ro 8:6.

To be carnally minded is to be always mindful and desirous of the acquisition and fulfillment of the desires and appetites of the flesh. Those who are carnal minded walk after, that is, are overly concerned with seeking after the needs and wants of the flesh *(Ro 8:1, 5)*, rather than being more concerned with seeking after the needs and wants of the soul as they relate to the Will of God. When we are carnally minded we become slaves to our fleshly desires and needs and therefore remain in total subjection to vanity. To be in **subjection** *(sŭb-jĕk'shen)* means in the Greek to be **hupotage** *(hoop-ot-ag-ay')*, or in subordination; a slave to it.

Likewise, where there is no law, there can be no sin. *(Ro 4:15)* Because, by the law comes the knowledge of sin. *(Ro 3:20)* That is to say, when the law says to not do a thing, then, the hearer immediately understands that to do the thing, once forbidden, is wrong and therefore sin. And, also, when the law commands a person to do a thing, then, the person immediately understands that to not do the thing, once commanded, is wrong and therefore sin.

Furthermore, *"[s]in is not imputed when there is no law (Ro 5:13), because [s]in is the transgression of the law." (1Jo 3:4)* Therefore, it was the law of God, which was necessary to give man a choice between serving vanity and serving God's law, that brought about the knowledge of sin, right and wrong, righteousness and unrighteousness. Man could choose to obey God and live *(Pr 7:2)* or not obey God and die. *(Ge 2:17)* When man chooses to serve and obey God, without being forced to do so, this is a sacrifice of man's will, and, is in praise of God. God is a god who desires the sacrifice of praise from mankind. *(Heb 13:15; Ps 50:14, 23; Ps 54:6)* It is God's desire that mankind would obey his voice, whereby we keep his charge, his commandments, his statutes and his laws. *(Ge 26:5)*

Moreover, God is love. *(1Jo 4:8, 16)* And, because he is love, it was this love that required that God allow man the opportunity and liberty to choose to serve God, rather than forcing man to serve him, without a choice.

The Commandments of God

Let us now seek out the commandments given by God to Adam and Eve. For, to understand how man fell from God, we must first determine what commandments were given and what commandments were violated.

The commandments given by God can be divided into four different categorical types. *First*, there are the commandments of commission, which requires that certain acts be taken or certain events take place. In the commandments of commission, sin arises only when the person commanded to perform the act required, fails to perform the act as commanded. *Secondly*, there are the commandments of omission, which commands that certain acts not be performed or events not take place. In the commandments of omission, sin arises only when the person commanded not to perform a certain act, disobeys and performs the act once forbidden.

Thirdly, there are the commandments to the creator, which are commandments given by God, to himself, because no one else can ever qualify to perform the commandment. And *fourth*, there are the commandments to the creation, which are commandments given by God, to the thing or person created, that are meant to be performed only by the creation. All commandments, given by God, will fall within two of these categorical types, namely: the commandments of commission, the commandments of omission, the commandments to the creator and the commandments to the creation.

Within the first several chapters of the book of Genesis the writer, of the book, uses several words, phrases and methods to inform the reader that God had commanded or given a commandment about a certain thing or topic.

The first phrase used was *"And God said..." (Ge 1:3, 6, 9, 11, 14, 20, 24, 26)* The word **said** *(sĕd)* is translated from the Hebrew word **'amar** *(aw-mar')*. **'Amar** means to charge, require, to command, to give a commandment and to declare. In each of the above referenced verses God declared and gave a commandment that something should happen or that an event should take place. Immediately after the commandment or declaration was given, it is written that something did happen. Each time, the event occurred through and by the power of God, because God obeyed and performed his own commandment. This was so, because there was no one else who could obey and perform the commandment given.

For there is but one God and he knows of no other. *(Ge 44:8)* And, with no other being capable of performing God's command, God himself had to perform it, because his commandments are true. *(Ps 111:7, 8; Ps 119:142, 151, 152, 160; Isa 40:8; Mt 5:18; Joh 17:17)* To not make it so, that is, to not make his commandments a reality would make God out to be a liar. And it is an impossible thing for God to do, to lie. *(Heb 6:18; Tit 1:2)* Also, if God were a liar, then, Satan would be the creator and not the creation, because then he would be the father of God. God forbid! For, Satan is the father of the lie. *(Joh 8:44)*

In these first sets of commandments we see only God acting in obedience to his own commandments. For example, Genesis 1:3 reads, *"And God said, Let there be light: and there was light."* The Apostle Paul wrote that God commanded the light to shine out of darkness. *(2Co 4:6)* Immediately after God spoke the command, verse three records, *"[A]nd there was light."*

Again, we see God commanding in Genesis 1:6, *"And God said, Let there be a firmament in the midst of the waters, and let it divide the waters from the waters."* Then, in Genesis 1:7 we see God obeying his own commandment: *"And God made the firmament, and divided the waters which were under the firmament from the waters which were above the firmament: and it was so."* We call these first sets of commandments, wherein we see only God acting in obedience to his own Word, commandments of commission to the creator.

The second phrase used by God to give a commandment was, *"And God blessed them, saying, Be fruitful, and multiply..." (Ge 1:22)*, which was given to all the animals in the sea and that flew in the air. *(Ge 1:21)* This is a commandment wherein God's blessing upon them placed within the animals' nature, an automatic 'instinct' to obey the command, without the free-will ability or need to have a choice in obeying God's commandment. For, animals have no free-will and no capacity to reason. They were made subject to the law of God, that is, animals were not given a choice of serving vanity, their flesh, or God's law; obedience or disobedience. Nor were they created in God's image or his likeness.

When animals and the forces of nature work or act in the manner that God has commanded or intended, this action taken by the animal or force of nature is in praise and honor of God. For, the Psalmist commanded all things that were created to praise the LORD, including: the heavens, angels, sun, moon, stars, fire, hail, snow, vapors, wind, mountains, trees, animals, birds, insects, and all people. *(Ps 148)* And, when the thing created fails to praise the LORD, by performing the particular act commanded, the Lord punishes the creation, even when the creation does not possess the ability to reason. This was vividly portrayed when Jesus hungered and expected to receive fruit from a fig tree in Bethany, but found none, because the tree had bore no fruit. *(Mt 21:17-19; Mk 11:12-13)* Jesus punished the tree by declaring, *"...Let no fruit grow on thee henceforward for ever." (Mt 21:19)* And because the tree had been created to bear fruit, to feed man, but now was forever stopped from doing so, the tree became useless to God. *(Mk 11:14)* The tree's uselessness was due to the fact that, now it could not serve its purpose in praising God, by feeding man with its fruit. *(Ps 148:1, 5, 9; Mk 11:14)* Therefore, with its ability to fulfill its purpose lost, the tree was cursed by Jesus *(Mk 11:21)* and lost its life, *"...And presently the fig tree withered away." (Mt 21:19-20; Mk 11:20-21)*

Again, we see the forces of nature in honor and praise of God, when Jesus rebuked the stormy wind, *"...and said unto the sea, Peace, be still. And the wind ceased, and there was a great calm." (Mk 4:37-39; Mt 8:24-26; Ps 65:7)* Then, the Lord received honor and praise from others, the disciples, who actually witnessed the wind and the sea obey the spoken commandment of Jesus Christ. *(Mk 4:37-41; Mt 8:23:27)* In honor and praise, the disciples *"...said one to another, What manner of man is this, that even the wind and the sea obey him?" (Mk 4:41; Mt 8:27)*

Mankind is blessed when plant and animal life obey the commandments of God and praise his name by fulfilling their created purposes. For, if all plant and animal life did not praise God through obedience, mankind would die from a world-wide famine and starvation, unless and except God would send manna from heaven, as he did in times past. *(For example see Ex 16:2-4, 15; Ps 78:23-29)* These type commandments are commandments of commission to the creation.

Again we see the phrase, *"And God blessed them, and God said unto them, Be fruitful, and multiply..." (Ge 1:28)* Here, God blessed the man and the woman. But unlike the animals, mankind was given a free will and was able to choose not to obey God's commandment. Man's capacity and ability to think and reason provides him with the opportunity to obey or not to obey, depending upon where his desire is. This is a commandment of commission to the creation, Adam and Eve.

The Ten Commandments Given To Man in the Beginning

God gave mankind ten commandments in the beginning. ***First,*** God put the man in the garden and told him to work by dressing the garden. *(Ge 2:15)* This is a commandment of commission to the creation. ***Second,*** God put the man in the garden to keep the garden. *(Ge 2:15)* This is a commandment of commission to the creation. ***Thirdly,*** God commanded the man, saying, *"Of every tree of the garden thou mayest freely eat..." (Ge 2:16-17)* This is a commandment of commission to the creation. ***Fourth,*** God commanded the man saying, *"But of the tree of the knowledge of good and evil, thou shalt not eat of it: for in the day that thou eatest thereof thou shalt surely die." (Ge 2:17)* This is a commandment of omission to the creation. ***Fifth,*** God told Adam to cleave unto his wife and once again live as one flesh. *(Ge 2:24)* This is a commandment of commission to the creation. ***Six,*** God commanded ***them,*** the man and his wife, to be fruitful. *(Ge 1:28)* This is a commandment of commission to the creation. ***Seventh,*** God commanded the man and his wife to multiply. *(Ge 1:28)* This is a commandment of commission to the creation. ***Eighth,*** God commanded ***them*** to replenish the earth. *(Ge 1:28)* This is a commandment of commission to the creation.

Ninth, God commanded ***them*** to subdue the earth. *(Ge 1:28)* This is a commandment of commission to the creation. And, ***tenth,*** God commanded ***them*** to exercise dominion, control over the sea life, the birds of the sky and over every living thing that moves upon the earth. *(Ge 1:28)* This is a commandment of commission to the creation.

Let us now consider each commandment given to mankind and determine what was actually required by God.

Chapter 11

No. 1: The Commandment to Work by Worshiping God

> ***And the LORD God took the man, and put him into the garden of Eden to dress it...***
>
> ***Ge 2:15.***

Adam, first being the only human being in existence, was given the first commandment which was to dress the Garden of Eden. *(Ge 2:15)* In essence, Adam was first a gardener set over the work of God's hands. During his work we learn that

> **19 ...out of the ground the LORD God formed every beast of the field, and every fowl of the air; and brought them unto Adam to see what he would call them: and whatsoever Adam called every living creature, that was the name thereof.**
>
> **20 And Adam gave names to all cattle, and to the fowl of the air, and to every beast of the field; ...**
>
> **Ge 2:19-20.**

The word **dress** *(dress)* in the Genesis 2:15 passage is translated from **`abad** *(aw-bad').* **`Abad** means to work, to serve, till, bondman, husbandman, keep, labour, set a work, worshipper. And so, the Lord God put the man in the garden of Eden to perform the work of the ministry as a labourer and a tiller, a worshipper, a servant, a bondman and a husbandman unto the Lord God. For, even today we are admonished to work as if we are working unto God *(Eph 6:5-8),* even while performing our job duties for a human employer. Also today, the Lord is yet calling and causing men and women to go forth into the world to perform in the work of the ministry. And to be sure that they possessed the ability and power to perform the work commanded, the Lord

> **11 ...gave some, apostles; and some prophets; and some, pastors and teachers;**
> **12 For the perfecting of the saints, for the work of the ministry, for the edifying of the body of Christ:**
> **13 Till we all come in the unity of the faith, and of the knowledge of the Son of God, unto a perfect man, unto the measure of the stature of the fullness of Christ:**
> **14 That we henceforth be no more children, tossed to and fro, and carried about with every wind of doctrine, by the sleight of men, and cunning craftiness, whereby they lie in wait to deceive.**

Eph 4:11-14.

And the Lord God has admonished us to,

> **19 Go ye therefore, and teach all nations, baptizing them ...**
> **20 Teaching them to observe all things whatsoever I have commanded you...**

Mt 28:19a, 20a.

Upon studying Genesis 2:19-20 we learn that before man sinned there was no enmity or fear between man and the beast of the field and/or the fowl of the air. For, we learn by scripture that it was God who caused the animals to come to Adam willingly by bringing them to Adam. *(Ge 2:19)* Therefore, Adam did not have to chase them or to trap them, as man has done since sin entered the world through the life of mankind. For, we know that the whole of creation did not begin to groan until after man sinned. As the Apostle Paul stated,

> **22 For we know that the whole creation groaneth and travaileth in pain together until now.**
> **23 And not only they, but ourselves also...**

Ro 8:22-23a.

When we consider the phrase "*...and brought them unto Adam...*" in the Genesis 2:19 passage above we learn that God led the animals to Adam by his spirit. For, God is a spirit *(Joh 4:24),* and for Him to have brought the animals to Adam God had to do it by His spirit, because at that time, '*In the beginning*', the Son of God, the physical body of God, called Jesus, had not been manifested in the flesh. *(Joh 1:1, 14; 1Ti 3:16)* So, God did not use a pair of physical legs to bring the animals to Adam. Therefore, God gave the animals a spirit *(Ec 3:21)* that could be led by His Spirit, by Him, just like He caused the fish to swallow Jonah *(Jon 1:17; Jon 2:10)*, the chicken to crow three times *(Joh 18:27; Joh 13:38)*, the donkey to speak like a man *(2Pet 2:16)*, and the raven birds to feed Elijah while he was in the wilderness. *(1Ki 17:1-6)* Also, the fowls of the air are flying animals. These animals were also brought to Adam by God. A spirit, being invisible, is not bound by the laws of gravity, like the wind is not bound by gravity. For,

> **The wind bloweth where it listeth, and thou hearest the sound thereof, but canst not tell whence it cometh, and whither it goeth...**

Joh 3:8a.

Likewise, the Spirit of the Lord easily flew with the fowls of the air to assist in bringing the birds, bats and other flying fowl to Adam.

So, God placed in the spirit of the animals a willingness and desire to come to the man without fear, in contrast to the spirits possessed by animals after Adam and Eve sinned. For then, after they had sinned, the Lord God said,

> **2 And the fear of you and the dread of you shall be upon every beast of the earth, and upon every fowl of the air, upon all that moveth upon the earth, and upon all the fishes of the sea; into your hand are they delivered.**
>
> **3 Every moving thing that liveth shall be meat for you; even as the green herb have I given you all things.**

Ge 9:2-3.

But, before Adam sinned, God did not place the animals on a natural leash to guide them to Adam. And because the animals have a spirit also *(Ec 3:21)* the Spirit of God was able to lead their spirit to Adam, because he 'brought them' to Adam. That is, the Spirit of God brought, led, the spirit of the animal to Adam. If God brought the animals to Adam, then God was with the animals when they were presented to Adam. God did not 'send the animals'. Nor did he cause the animals to go to Adam. But more importantly when God brought the animals he accompanied them. He was with them. This point of God being with the animals that he 'brought' to Adam teaches us that God was concerned about and cared for the welfare of the animals. *(Ps 36:6; Ps 147:9; Pr 12:10; De 25:4; Ge 7:1-4)* And then, after the animals were brought to Adam, Adam considered them and gave them names in obedience to God's request for him to name the animals. *(Ge 2:19-20)* This naming of the animals was a type of working for the Lord God by worshipping, because Adam was obedient to what God required. A part of the work of dressing the garden of Eden was determining first what the things in it would be called, thereby establishing order within the garden and within the world.

So, to answer the question, *"How do we worship God?"*, we must review scripture. For, there it says,

God is a Spirit: and they that worship him must worship him in spirit and in truth.

Joh 4:24.

But, then John 4:24 raises more questions such as, **(1)** How do we worship in spirit?; and **(2)** How do we worship in truth?

Worshipping In Spirit

First, to worship God in spirit does not mean that one must be in an excited, emotional state to worship him. Nor does it mean that we must wave our hands and sing some particular song, praise or hymn. To worship God in spirit means to apply the Word of God to your life, obey it and allow the truth of that Word to become your way of life, your manner of living; your manner of speech, your manner of doing business, your hope and your aspirations. Because Jesus said,

…[T]he words that I speak unto you, they are spirit and they are life.

Joh 6:63b.

So, when the application of the Word of God becomes your way, manner and means of life, then you possess this life in Christ—because, Christ is the Word of God *(Joh 1:1-2, 14)* and the Word of God has become your life style and standard for living. And, in another place,

53 Then Jesus said unto them, Verily, verily, I say unto you, Except ye eat the flesh of the Son of man, and drink his blood, ye have no life in you.

54 Whoso eateth my flesh, and drinketh my blood, hath eternal life; and I will raise him up at the last day.

55 For my flesh is meat indeed, and my blood is drink indeed.

56 He that eateth my flesh, and drinketh my blood, dwelleth in me, and I in him.

57 As the living Father hath sent me, and I live by the Father: so he that eateth me, even he shall live by me.

58 This is that bread which came down from heaven: not as your fathers did eat manna, and are dead: he that eateth of this bread shall live for ever.

Joh 6:53-58.

The John 6:57 passage above is the basis for why Jesus rejected the devil and his temptation when the devil said unto Him,

...If thou be the Son of God, command this stone that it be made bread.

Lu 4:3b.

And straightway,

...Jesus answered him, saying, It is written, That man shall not live by bread alone, but by every word of God.

Lu 4:4.

Jesus said *"I live by the Father"* in John 6:57. And in Luke 4:4 he said that man shall live *"...by every word of God."* Therefore, if Jesus was living by the Father he was living by the Word of God. So, if he had obeyed Satan and commanded the stone to be made bread, then he would have begun living by the bread that was made by the word of Satan and not by the Word of God. Thus, by the act of turning the stone into bread, for food, Jesus would have begun applying Satan's word to his life by obeying it. And, by eating Satan's word, through the consumption of obedience to Satan's word, Jesus would have been worshipping (obeying) Satan rather than God. And so, his worshipping would not have been in Spirit and in truth, because there is no truth in Satan. *(Joh 8:44)* For, in agreement, the Lord Jesus said later, in a different place,

> **Ye are of your father the devil, and the lusts of your father ye will do. He was a murderer from the beginning, and abode not in the truth, because there is no truth in him. When he speaketh a lie, he speaketh of his own: for he is a liar, and the father of it.**

Joh 8:44.

Therefore, to worship God in Spirit one must apply the Word of God to one's life and obey it.

Chapter 12

No. 2: The Commandment to Work By Keeping the Garden: The Watchman

And the Lord God took the man, and put him into the garden of Eden ... to keep it. Ge 2:15.

The word **keep** *(kēp)* in this Genesis 2:15 passage is taken from **shâmar** *(shaw-mar'),* meaning to hedge about; to guard, protect, attend to, beware, be circumspect, take heed to self, keeper, keep self, mark, look narrowly, observe, preserve, regard, reserve, save, save self, sure, watch, watchman. So, while Adam was working and worshipping the Lord by dressing the garden he was also required: **(1)** to be the Lord's watchman; **(2)** to guard and protect the garden of Eden for the glory and praise of the Lord God; and **(3)** to keep the way of the tree of life *(Compare Ge 3:24)* and thereby to keep himself by obeying the commandments of God. For it is by man's obedience to the commandments of God that his soul and spirit are preserved and kept in the image and likeness of God. *(Ge 1:26-27)* Because, when God made man he made him upright. *(Ec 7:29)* And as King David stated later,

Let integrity and uprightness preserve me…

Ps 25:21a.

Here, the word **preserve** *(pri-`zərv)* is translated from the Hebrew **natsar** *(naw-tsar')* which means to protect, preserve, maintain, obey, to guard in a good sense, to keep, keeper, observe, watcher, watchman, preserver, hidden thing. Therefore, when we compare the word **keep** in Genesis 2:15 with the word **preserve** in Psalms 25:21a we learn that they mean the same thing with regards to—protecting, guarding, keeping, preserving, watching and being a watchman.

It was necessary for the man to possess a mind and will to obey the commandments of God, because, in the midst of the garden stood two different and opposite trees. The **first** was the tree of the knowledge of good and evil. And, the **second** tree was the tree of life. *(Ge 2:9)* These two trees were exact opposites in their effect upon man when eaten by man.

The Tree of the Knowledge of Good and Evil

For, the tree of the knowledge of good and evil, when eaten by man, was a pathway of death leading to the loss of life. For, the Lord God said,

But of the tree of the knowledge of good and evil, thou shalt not eat of it: for in the day that thou eatest thereof thou shalt surely die.

Ge 2:17.

Thus, because eating of it would result in sure death, the tree of the knowledge of good and evil represented man's carnal state before God,

…breathed into his nostrils the breath of life; and man became a living soul.

Ge 2:7b.

For, when you study the creation of man, before he received the neshamah (breath) of life from God, we learn that man was in existence, but only as dust formed into human flesh. *(Ge 2:7)* That is, when God first formed the man he existed as did the animals, as a brute beast, created, but without the soul, mind and spirit of the Lord God. For, it was the Spirit of life that caused the man to **'become'** a living soul. *(Ge 2:7b)* Therefore, before he **'became'** a living soul—he existed as spiritually dead, carnal dirt and not yet a living spirit. For, even though God had formed him from the dust of the ground *(Ge 2:7a),* he did not begin living in the spirit, as a living soul, until after God breathed into his nostrils the neshamah (breath) of life. *(Ge 2:7b)*

It is important to remember that the life of the flesh is in the blood of the animal and man *(Read Le 17:11, 14; De 12:23),* and that this life is called the **ruwach** *(roo'-akh)* of life. The word **breath** *('breth)* of the phrase **breath of life** as found in the Genesis 7:15 passage is translated from the Hebrew **ruwach**. For, in Genesis 7:15, the writer wrote,

> **And they went in unto Noah into the ark, two and two of all flesh, wherein is the breath of life.**
> **Ge 7:15.**

Ruwach means wind, breath, life, anger, blast, courage, mind. All living animals, beast and man possess the ruwach of life. However, only man was given the **neshamah** *(nesh-aw-maw')* of life which is translated from the word **breath** in the Genesis 2:7 'breath of life' phrase above. **Neshamah** means a puff, a vital breath, divine inspiration, intellect, soul, spirit. So, when God *"...breathed into his nostrils the breath of life...",* God actually blew into man his soul, his spirit, his intellect. *(Ge 2:7)* And it was only after this breathing into man that *"...man became a living soul." (Ge 2:7; Job 33:4)* That is, man had already been created, but he had not become a living soul. The neshamah *(breath)* of life is the Spirit of life and it is in Christ

Jesus. *(Ro 8:2)* Therefore, the neshamah *(breath)* of life is life in the spiritual, inward man.

Dirt is carnal and has no life, although God did command the dry land—which is earthly dirt *(Ge 1:10)*—to bring forth living things. *(Ge 1:11-12, 24-25)* However, those living things came into existence by the operation of the power of God through Jesus Christ. *(Joh 1:3; Col 1:16)* Because

> **All things were made by him; and without him was not anything made that was made.**

Joh 1:3.

And in agreement, the Apostle Paul wrote, that

> **16 For by him were all things created, that are in heaven, and that are in earth, visible and invisible, whether they be thrones, or dominions, or principalities, or powers: all things were created by him, and for him:**
>
> **17 And he is before all things, and by him all things consist.**

Col 1:16-17.

For, Christ is the power of God. *(1Co 1:24)* Furthermore, God has life in himself *(Joh 5:26)* and He has ordained that life should be also in Christ Jesus, and not in the dirt. *(Joh 1:4; 1Jo 5:11-12)* And so, even though the flesh of man was formed and created from the dirt *(Ge 2:7),* and the dirt was created by God *(Ge 1:1),* it was never a part of God and did not come from God. For, God is a spirit. *(Joh 4:24)* He is not carnal, of a carnal nature, or carnal minded. For to be carnal minded is to be dead in the spirit, to be the enemy of life and the exact opposite of life.

> **For they that are after the flesh do mind the things of the flesh; but they that are after the Spirit the things of the Spirit.**

Ro 8:5.

Therefore, when man was first formed, if he had a mind at all, he was mindful only of the things of the flesh, because he had no spiritual life in him. At the point that he was formed, God had not breathed the neshamah (breath) of life into the dirt that had been formed into the flesh of man. And as such, the carnal man that existed without the Spirit of life, the neshamah (breath) of life, was not yet God's son. He was God's possession, because God created him. *(Ge 2:7)* But, he was not yet God's son, because God had not created him in his image through the preservation process. For, until God breathed the neshamah (breath) of life into man, he did not exist in the image of God. As the writer declared,

> **...Now if any man have not the Spirit of Christ, he is none of his.**

Ro 8:9b.

And, in another place he said,

> **But we all...are changed into, the same image from glory to glory, even as by the Spirit of the Lord.**

2Co 3:18.

Thus, before God breathed the neshamah (breath) of life into the nostrils of man, man did not exist in God's image and was not subject to the law of God

> **Because the carnal mind is enmity against God: for it is not subject to the law of God, neither indeed can be.**

Ro 8:7.

And, for this reason, when one studies the creation of man he learns that God did not give the man a commandment until after the man had become a living soul. *(Read again Ge 2:7-15)* Because, to have given man a commandment before he had been given the power and therefore the ability to obey the commandment would have been a futile, unjust and idle use of words, resulting in no praise or glory to God. But we know that God does not speak idle words. *(Read Mt 4:4)* For man would have possessed only a carnal mind—mindful only of those things pertaining to the flesh and to the world. His mind would have been the enmity of God and not subject to the commandment or to the law of God. *(Ro 8:7)* And as such, although man would have been alive in the flesh by the ruwach (breath) of life *(See Ge 7:14-15),* which is in the blood *(Le 17:11, 14; De 12:23),* he would have existed in spiritual death having possessed only a carnal mind unable and incapable of pleasing God. *(Ro 8:8).*

> **6 For to be carnally minded is death; but to be spiritually minded is life and peace.**
>
> **...**
>
> **8 So then they that are in the flesh cannot please God.**

Ro 8:6, 8.

And, if a man cannot please God, then, he cannot be God's son, nor his image or his likeness, because, only they that are

> **...led by the Spirit of God, they are the sons of God.**

Ro 8:14.

Therefore, by existing only in the flesh, before God breathed the neshamah (breath) of life *(Ge 2:7)* into him, if man possessed a mind at all, it was only carnal and mindful of fleshly things. And so, he was not yet God's son.

However, he was not a sinner either, because there was no law or commandment yet given to man. Because, where the law has been given, there is the knowledge of sin.

...for by the law is the knowledge of sin.
Ro 3:20b.

Likewise, where no law has been given there is no knowledge of sin. **Sin** *('sin),* here, is translated from the Greek **hamartia** *(ham-ar-tee'-ah).* **Hamartia** means sin, an offence, sinful. Also, when we consider the first mention of the word sin within the Holy Scriptures, we find the word being used in Genesis 4:7, in a conversation between Cain and the Lord God. There, the Lord had rejected Cain and his sacrifice, but He had accepted Abel and Abel's sacrifice. While admonishing Cain about why Cain and his sacrifice was not accepted, the Lord God said unto Adam's first *(Ge 4:1)* son,

If thou doest well, shalt thou not be accepted? and if thou doest not well, sin lieth at the door.
Ge 4:7a.

In this Genesis 4:7a passage the word **sin** is translated from the Hebrew **chatta'th** *(khat-tawth'),* which means an offence (sometimes habitual sinfulness), an offender, punishment of sin. Thus, we learn from comparing the word **sin** in Genesis 4:7a with the word **sin** in Romans 3:20 that both words mean an offence. That is, when a person commits a sin he commits an offence. And the offence is a specific action against or contrary to the law or commandment of God. So, a person cannot knowingly, or by the exercise of his free will offend God through sin if no law has been given. Because without knowledge of the law's existence there can be no choice, no decision and thus no exercise of a person's free will. And when there is no exercise of a man's freewill, for good or evil, God gets no glory and no praise. And there is no concept, awareness or knowledge of things good or things evil. This is the same state that animals exist in, although they possess a spirit by the ruwach (breath) of life. *(See Ge 7:14-15; Ec 3:18-21)* The animals and the beast of the field do what they do without regard to right or wrong, good or evil, righteousness or unrighteousness. They have no free will to choose what they will be in life or what they will do in life, or whether what they do is good, evil, right or wrong. And so, when they die the spirit of the animal goes down and not up to God. *(Read Ec 3:18-21)*

Thus, if man possessed a mind only by the ruwach (breath) of life *(Ge 7:14-15)* it was a carnal mind and he was not yet God's son. *(Read Ro 8:9)* And so, without the Spirit of Life indwelling him, man was only a mere possession of the creator God who had created all things by Christ Jesus *(Joh 1:3; Col 1:16-17),* who is the Word *(Joh 1:1-3, 14),* the wisdom *(1Co 1:24)* and the power of God. *(1Co 1:24)* For, in Genesis 2:7a where it says *"God formed man from the dust of the ground...",* the man was in the flesh and not in the Spirit, because the Spirit of God had not begun to indwell him *(Ro 8:9a)* until after God breathed the neshamah (breath) of life into him. *(Ge 2:7)* And so he was not yet God's son, which is the same state that he would end up in, later in the life of the flesh, after he had received the neshamah (breath) of life, and then sinned by eating from the tree of the knowledge of good and evil. *(Ge 2:17; Ge 3:7)* For,

> **...if any man have not the Spirit of Christ, he is none of his.**

Ro 8:9b.

The Tree of Life

The **second** named tree that was in the midst of the garden of Eden *(Ge 2:9)* was the tree of life. The tree of life represented man's spiritual state and condition after God

> **...breathed into his nostrils the breath of life; and man became a living soul.**

Ge 2:7b.

For, it was only after man received the neshamah (breath) of life did he possess life within his spiritual, inward *(Ro 7:22)* man. For, life is in Christ Jesus. *(Joh 1:4; 1Jo 5:11-12)* And, in keeping the garden of Eden, man was required to guard and preserve the garden of Eden and to protect it by keeping himself within life, within the image of God. Because on the day that he would lose life and step into death, is the day that he would no longer be capable or empowered to properly guard or preserve the Garden of Eden. This is partially so, because he would be put out of the garden of Eden and therefore rendered unable to perform the duties and the work of a keeper, watchman. *(Read Ge 3:22-24)* If man is not present, on his watchman's tower *(Isa 21:5-6)* and on his keeper's post, then he cannot perform the work for the Lord God in the Garden of Eden or within the Kingdom of God. Even the Lord Jesus stated in another place that,

> **...No man, having put his hand to the plough, and looking back, is fit for the kingdom of God.**

Lu 9:62.

For, it was through man's being in God's image that he was able to be the glory of God, the praise of God and God's watchman over God's creations. The presence of the tree of the knowledge of good and evil in the midst of the garden, with the tree of life was the spiritual environment that allowed man to have a free will. This freewill allowed him to choose between keeping the garden and thereby keeping himself or disobeying the law of God by going carnal by eating from the tree that represented his existence before God breathed into his nostrils the neshamah (breath) of life. Adam's stepping out of life into death through disobedience would actually be a 'looking back' to a time in his creation existence *(Read Ge 2:7)* when he did not possess life, through and by the neshamah (breath) of life. This time in his existence is between the time when the Lord God *'formed man of the dust of the ground'* and, when God sometime later, after man was formed and was in existence, *'breathed into his nostrils the breath of life and man became a living soul.' (Ge 2:7)* The Apostle Paul declared,

> **21 (Touch not; taste not; handle not;**
> **22 Which all are to perish with the using;) after the commandments and doctrines of men?**

Col 2:21-22.

When man tastes, touches and handles the doctrines of men and of angels, he perishes. *(Col 2:21-22)* And during Adam's day this would occur only if and when Adam chose to disobey the commandment and eat from the tree of the knowledge of good and evil. But, so long as he refrained from eating from the tree of the knowledge of good and evil and only ate from the tree of life—he would maintain life and tend to it through righteousness. *(Pr 11:19; Pr 10:16; Pr 12:28; Pr 19:23)*

When we consider why Eve was deceived and that Adam was not deceived we need only look to the truth that Eve had never existed in a carnal state and that the rib from which she was made-up from—was holy to the bone *(Ge 2:18, 21-22),* because when the Lord God took the rib from Adam, Adam was living in the image and likeness of God. *(Ge 2:7, 19-20)* And this was possible only because he was filled with the Spirit of life which is Christ Jesus. So, when God took a part of the upright and holy son of God called Adam and formed the woman from that holy part, all that resulted from it—from Adam's wound was also holy. Therefore, not ever having experienced the state of being carnal, without the indwelling Spirit of God—Eve did not understand what was meant by 'surely die', which meant to die first spiritually and then later, naturally. But, Adam had experienced what it was like to be in the flesh and without life in the Spirit—which is spiritual death. For the Apostle Paul said,

46 Howbeit that was not first which is spiritual, but that which is natural; and afterward that which is spiritual.

47 The first man is of the earth, earthy: the second man is the Lord from heaven.

48 As is the earthy, such are they also that are earthy: and as is the heavenly, such are they also that are heavenly.

1Co 15:46-48.

For, man was created with a natural, outer man first, which is earthy and is mindful only of those things pertaining to the flesh—which makes it carnal. For the scriptures declare that

...the Lord God formed man of the dust of the ground...

Ge 2:7a.

And then, after the natural man was created, the man was made to possess the inward, spiritual man in the image of God. Because, then the Lord God

...breathed into his nostrils the breath of life; and man became a living soul.

Ge 2:7b.

So Adam was aware and understood what the phrase 'surely die' meant—he would revert back to the carnal state to which he began, but in a worst state, because his carnality would have resulted from the violation of a given and known commandment and law. Thus, his carnality would have been of a spiritual nature—now carnal in the inward, spiritual man and carnal in the outward, natural man. For, when a man is carnal within his inward, spiritual man, the carnality will show up and manifest itself on the outside, in the outward, natural man. In agreement, the Lord Jesus declared,

16 ...Are ye also yet without understanding?

17 Do not ye yet understand, that whatsoever entereth in at the mouth goeth into the belly, and is cast out into the draught?

18 But those things which proceed out of the mouth come forth from the heart; and they defile the man.

19 For out of the heart proceed evil thoughts, murders, adulteries, fornications, thefts, false witness, blasphemies:

20 These are the things which defile a man: but to eat with unwashen hands defileth not a man.

Mt 15:16-20.

So, spiritual carnality affects the whole of man, whereas natural carnality is passed through the body—when there is no understanding of the law concerning the matter. When a man is carnal spiritually, he is mindful only of those things that please the flesh, and therefore he walks after the flesh *(Ro 8:4-5),* serving the law of sin with the flesh. *(Ro 7:25b)* Because, when man is upright, and walking in the image of God, he will

...delight in the law of God after the inward man:

Ro 7:22.

And with the inward man that dwells in his mind, the upright man serves the law of God. *(Ro 7:25)*

The Watchman

The keeper's job also involves the work of a watchman. But to be a watchman for the Lord God, he that watches must be of God. That is, to worship God through the gift or work of the watchman, the watchman must do so in spirit and in truth. *(Joh 4:24)* In agreement years later, the writer declared,

But ye are not in the flesh, but in the Spirit, if so be that the Spirit of God dwell in you. Now if any man have not the Spirit of Christ, he is none of his.
Ro 8:9.

Just as Adam was a watchman over the work of the Lord's hands, in the garden of Eden, so were all the other prophets who followed after him, from Enoch to Noah to Moses through Malachi to John the Baptist. And just as the first keeper and watchman over the work of the Lord possessed the indwelling Spirit (neshamah) of life *(Ge 2:7)* so did all the other prophets of the Lord who were sent by God.

Enoch

14 And Enoch also, the seventh from Adam, prophesied of these, saying, Behold, the Lord cometh with ten thousands of his saints,
15 To execute judgment upon all, and to convince all that are ungodly among them of all their ungodly deeds which they have ungodly committed, and of all their hard speeches which ungodly sinners have spoken against him.
Jude 14-15.

As a prophet and watchman for the Lord God, it was said of Enoch, that he

...walked with God: and he was not; for God took him.
Ge 5:24.

And,

By faith Enoch was translated that he should not see death; and was not found, because God had translated him: for before his translation he had this testimony, that he pleased God.
Heb 11:5.

And we know by the scriptures that if he pleased God, he walked not after the flesh, but after the Spirit, because

> **...they that are in the flesh cannot please God.**

Ro 8:8.

We also know by the scriptures that the Spirit of God, the neshamah (breath) of life indwelled him because

> **... ye are not in the flesh, but in the Spirit, if so be that the Spirit of God dwell in you...**

Ro 8:9a.

Therefore, for Enoch to have walked with God and pleased God he had to do so within the Spirit and not in the flesh. And if he was in the Spirit he possessed the Spirit of God.

Noah

Likewise, the scriptures spoke of Noah, saying,

> **8 ...Noah found grace in the eyes of the LORD.**
> **9 ... Noah was a just man and perfect in his generations, and Noah walked with God.**

Ge 6:8-9b.

> **And the LORD said unto Noah, Come thou and all thy house into the ark; for thee have I seen righteous before me in this generation.**

Ge 7:1.

Noah could not have been a just and perfect man without the indwelling Spirit of God, because the scriptures have declared that all men are under sin *(Ro 3:9),* because of Adam's original sin in the garden of Eden.

Wherefore, as by one man sin entered into the world, and death by sin; and so death passed upon all men, for that all have sinned:

Ro 5:12.

The writer wrote further saying,

10 ...There is none righteous, no, not one:

11 There is none that understandeth, there is none that seeketh after God.

12 They are all gone out of the way, they are together become unprofitable; there is none that doeth good, no, not one.

Ro 3:10-12.

Moreover, Noah could not have walked with God and been a righteous man without the neshamah (breath) of life indwelling him, because,

God is a Spirit: and they that worship him must worship him in Spirit and in truth.

Joh 4:24.

Moses

Also for Moses, the law giver and leader of God's people, it was necessary for him to possess the Spirit of God in order for him to righteously lead God's people and to preside over the law and commandments of God. For, the scriptures declare,

11 Then he remembered the days of old, Moses, and his people, saying, Where is he that brought them up out of the sea with the shepherd of his flock? where is he that put his holy Spirit within him?

12 That led them by the right hand of Moses with his glorious arm, dividing the water before them, to make himself an everlasting name?

Isa 63:11-12.

Joshua

And the same goes for Moses' minister, Joshua, when it was time for Moses to be replaced as the leader of God's people. *(Nu 27:12-23)* For,

15 …Moses spake unto the LORD, saying,

16 Let the Lord, the God of the spirits of all flesh, set a man over the congregation,

17 Which may go out before them, and which may go in before them, and which may lead them out, and which may bring them in; that the congregation of the Lord be not as sheep which have no shepherd.

18 And the Lord said unto Moses, Take thee Joshua the son of Nun, a man in whom is the spirit, and lay thine hand upon him;

Nu 27:15-18.

Old Testament Prophets

Furthermore, all of the Old Testament prophets of old, who were sent by the Lord God, possessed the neshamah (breath) of life, which is in Christ Jesus. For, the Apostle Peter declared,

10 Of which salvation the prophets have enquired and searched diligently, who prophesied of the grace that should come unto you;

11 Searching what or what manner of time the Spirit of Christ which was in them did signify, when it

testified beforehand the sufferings of Christ, and the glory that should follow.

12 Unto whom it was revealed, that not unto themselves, but unto us they did minister the things, which are now reported unto you by them that have preached the gospel unto you with the Holy Ghost sent down from heaven; which things the angels desire to look into.

1Pe 1:10-12.

John the Baptist

Even the forerunner of Christ *(Read Lu 1:57-77),* John the Baptist, was born possessing the Holy Ghost, the neshamah (breath) of life, from his mother's womb. For, it is written,

13 … the angel said unto him, Fear not, Zacharias: for thy prayer is heard; and thy wife Elisabeth shall bear thee a son, and thou shall call his name John.

…

15 For he shall be great in the sight of the Lord, and shall drink neither wine nor strong drink; and he shall be filled with the Holy Ghost, even from his mother's womb.

16 And many of the children of Israel shall he turn to the Lord their God.

17 And he shall go before him in the spirit and power of Elias, to turn the hearts of the fathers to the children, and the disobedient to the wisdom of the just; to make ready a people prepared for the Lord.

…

76 And thou, child, shalt be called the prophet of the Highest: for thou shalt go before the face of the Lord to prepare his ways.

Lu 1:13, 15-17, 76.

Thus, we learn from the recorded lives of the prophets that man's sin in the garden of Eden did not change God's requirement that to be a watchman for the Lord and to lead God's people one must be of an upright spirit. Furthermore, even King Solomon wrote,

Lo, this only have I found, that God hath made man upright; but they have sought out many inventions.
Ec 7:29.

God, being the most upright *(Isa 26:7),* requires his people who are called by his name to be upright and therefore perfect. As the Lord Jesus has admonished all that will obey him to,

Be ye therefore perfect, even as your Father which is in heaven is perfect.
Mt 5:48.

The Watchman's Diet

Therefore, in order for Adam, as a watchman, to maintain the proper watch for the Lord God he had to maintain his strength in his outward (fleshly) man and in his inward (spiritual) man. And we know that God was concerned about man's diet and what type of foods Adam would eat, because

16 …the Lord God commanded the man, saying, Of every tree of the garden thou mayest freely eat:
17 But of the tree of the knowledge of good and evil, thou shalt not eat of it: for in the day that thou eatest thereof thou shalt surely die.
Ge 2:16-17.

In this above passage of scripture we learn that the Lord God placed a restriction upon Adam's diet. Adam was allowed to eat from all of the trees in the garden of Eden except one, *the tree of the knowledge of good and evil.* The tree of the knowledge of good and evil would give Adam knowledge of what was good and of what was evil. But eating of it and therefore worshipping and obeying it would also cause Adam to enter into death which is carnality of the spirit man, and step out of life. For, at the time that Adam received the diet, restricting commandment he existed and lived in the image and likeness of God. *(Read Ge 1:26-27; Ge 2:7)* He had been given the commandment and duty to work, worship, keep and watch for the Lord God. But, Adam was required to obey and fulfill the commandments of working, worshipping, keeping and watching within the image and likeness of the Lord God. And, in order to maintain the watch within the Lord's image and likeness Adam was required to maintain his natural life and his spiritual life within life. Adam could maintain life only by eating from the tree of life. The Word of God is the way of the tree of life. *(Joh 1:1-2, 14; Joh 14:6)* Life is in Christ Jesus. *(Joh 1:4; 1Jo 5:11-12)* And in the beginning before, during and after Adam was created, Jesus existed as the wisdom of God, the power of God *(1Co 1:24)* and the Word of God. Because, the writer wrote,

> **1 In the beginning was the Word, and the Word was with God, and the Word was God.**
>
> **2 The same was in the beginning with God.**
>
> **3 All things were made by him; and without him was not any thing made that was made.**
>
> **4 In him was life; and the life was the light of men.**
>
> **…**
>
> **14 And the Word was made flesh, and dwelt among us, (and we beheld his glory, the glory as of the only begotten of the Father,) full of grace and truth.**

Joh 1:1-4, 14.

In this John 1:1-4, 14 passage above we are enabled to follow the progression of Jesus Christ first existing in the beginning as *"the Word" (Joh 1:1),* then as the *"Word...with God" (Joh 1:1),* next the

"Word was God" (Joh 1:2) and finally the same *"Word was made flesh". (Joh 1:14)*

The Word of God is written in a book. This book is a volume and collection of pages concerning specific things, namely the Lord God and His Will. And, collectively we call this volume the Holy Scriptures. As Jesus came in the volume of the Book to do the Will of God the Father *(Heb 10:5-7; Ps 40:7-8),* the Word of God that is found on the pages within this Book, has the power to heal, to deliver, to encourage, to build up, to cut, to rescue and to save. As the writer declared,

> **For the word of God is quick, and powerful, and sharper than any twoedged sword, piercing even to the dividing asunder of soul and spirit, and of the joints and marrow, and is a discerner of the thoughts and intents of the heart.**

Heb 4:12.

The pages of a book are also called the leaves of the book. *(e.g. Read Jer 36:1-32)* And the pages and leaves of the book make up the fullness of the book, just as the leaves of a tree make up the fullness of the tree. And when the leaves are present the tree and the book produce fruit that is good for food, for the nourishment and healing of the body. In like manner, in Christ Jesus,

> **...in him dwelleth all the fullness of the Godhead bodily.**

Col 2:9 *(Read Col 2:8-10).*

Jesus Christ was righteous and therefore a green tree. And he referred to himself as a green tree on his way to be crucified. *(Lu 23:26-31)* For the scripture records,

26 And as they led him away, they laid hold upon one Simon, a Cyrenian, coming out of the country, and on him they laid the cross, that he might bear it after Jesus.

27 And there followed him a great company of people, and of women, which also bewailed and lamented him.

28 But Jesus turning unto them said, Daughters of Jerusalem, weep not for me, but weep for yourselves, and for your children.

...

31 For if they do these things in a green tree, what shall be done in the dry?

Lu 23:26-28, 31.

And during his life on earth, as the Son of God, as a green (righteous) tree he healed the sick *(Mt 8:14-16; Mt 9:20-22; Mt 9:35; Mt 11:2-5; Joh 4:46-53; Lu 5:17-25);* gave sight to the blind *(Mt 9:27-30; Mt 12:22; Mt 21:14; Mt 15:30-31; Mt 20:30-34; Joh 9:1-11*); restored hands that had withered up *(Mk 3:1-5);* made the lame to walk *(Mt 21:14; Mt 15:30-31);* made the dumb (the deaf mute) to talk *(Mt 9:32-33; Mt 12:22; Mt 15:30-31);* set free those who had been captives of demonic spirits *(Mk 5:1-6; Mk 9:14-27; Mt 17:14-18; Lu 9:37-42; Lu 8:1-3; Mt 8:16; Mt 9:32-33; Mt 15:22-28);* healed every manner of disease *(Mt 8:1-3; Mt 9:1-7*); rebuked fevers *(Lu 4:38-39);* and gave life to the physical dead. *(Joh 11:38-44; Lu 7:11-15)* In like manner, the Word of God describes the tree of life, saying

In the midst of the street of it, and on either side of the river, was there the tree of life, which bare twelve manner of fruits, and yielded her fruit every month: and the leaves of the tree were for the healing of the nations.

Re 22:2.

From this passage above we learn that just like the Word of God is written on the leaves of a book that heals, the leaves of the tree of life heals also. For, they are one and the same. The cherubim angels were placed at the east of the garden of Eden,

> **...to keep the way of the tree of life.**

Ge 3:24b.

And, in another place Christ Jesus said,

> **...I am the way, the truth, and the life: no man cometh unto the Father, but by me.**

Joh 14:6b.

While Jesus is the way he is also the Word of God manifested in the flesh. *(Joh 1:1-2, 14)* Therefore, within the Word of God mankind is enabled to find his way back to the Lord God, the Father, through Christ Jesus. For, even the words of Christ are spirit and life. As he said,

> **It is the spirit that quickeneth; the flesh profiteth nothing: the words that I speak unto you, they are spirit, and they are life.**

Joh 6:63.

Since the celestial angels, in Genesis 3:24, were given the job and duty of protecting the way of the tree of life, which was the way to life eternal, the angels were responsible for delivering the divine messages from the Lord God, whose throne is in heaven *(Ac 7:49),* to man on earth, up until the coming of the Christ. *(Ac 51-53; Ga 3:19)* For, when he came he fulfilled the Word of God that was written on the leaves *(pages)* of the volume of the book that was written about him. *(Ps 40:7; Heb 10:7)* For, he was and is the way that the angels kept until the fullness of time had come. *(Ge 49:10; Ga 4:4; Eph 1:10)* As Apostle Paul declared,

> **4 But when the fullness of time was come, God sent forth his Son, made of a woman, made under the law,**

5 To redeem them that were under the law, that we might receive the adoption of sons.

6 And because ye are sons, God hath sent forth the Spirit of his Son into your hearts, crying Abba, Father.

7 Wherefore thou art no more a servant, but a son; and if a son, then an heir of God through Christ.

Ga 4:4-7.

So, the tree of life possessed life within itself and possessed the power of God to give eternal life to whoever would eat from it, as was described by the Lord God. For,

22 ... the Lord God said, Behold, the man is become as one of us, to know good and evil: and now, lest he put forth his hand, and take also of the tree of life, and eat, and live for ever:

23 Therefore the Lord God sent him forth from the garden of Eden, to till the ground from whence he was taken.

24 So he drove out the man; and he placed at the east of the garden of Eden Cherubims, and a flaming sword which turned every way, to keep the way of the tree of life.

Ge 3:22-24.

The above passages of scripture reveal that man had acquired the knowledge of what was good and what was evil. *(Ge 3:6-7, 22)* Genesis 3:22 also reveals that man had the ability to 'freely eat' from the life sustaining tree of life, as he had been commanded to do in Genesis 2:16. However, during the time that the Genesis 3:22 through 24 events took place man no longer lived and existed within the image and likeness of God. For, he had begun eating from the forbidden tree. *(Ge 3:6-7)* And once he had begun eating and therefore obeying the forbidden tree Adam and Eve became servants of the same. Because,

> **...to whom ye yield yourselves servants to obey, his servants ye are to whom ye obey; whether of sin unto death, or of obedience unto righteousness...**

Ro 6:16.

And so, as servants of the forbidden tree of the knowledge of good and evil, through the sin of disobedience, mankind entered into death. For the Apostle Paul declared,

> **10 And the commandment, which was ordained to life, I found to be unto death.**
> **11 For sin, taking occasion by the commandment, deceived me, and by it slew me.**

Ro 7:10-11.

With sin came death, and death began to reign in man's flesh from Adam to Moses. *(Ro 5:12-14)* Knowing that sin would reign and rule within fallen man the Lord God prophesied, in Genesis 3:15, the coming of the deliverer *(Mt 1:21)* and the repairer of the breach *(Isa 58:12),* who is the Lord Jesus Christ the way of the tree of life. *(Joh 14:6)* And now, having announced his plan to rescue, save, and redeem man, from a life forever in sin, God made sure that life forever, eternal and/or abundant could be obtained only in him. And, in agreement, years later this same Lord God, that was manifested in the flesh *(1Ti 3:16)*, stated,

> **The thief cometh not, but for to steal, and to kill, and to destroy: I am come that they might have life, and that they might have it more abundantly.**

Joh 10:10.

Knowing this beforehand, before He was manifested in the flesh, and while man was still in the garden of Eden, God prevented man from acquiring the ability to live forever while leading a life of sin, by driving man out of the garden of Eden. *(Ge 3:23-24)* For, had Adam eaten of the tree of life and acquired life forever in a carnal state he would have prevented the coming of the Christ, whose birth, death and resurrection had been foreordained before the foundation of the world *(Re 13:8b),* and hidden within the Lord God himself as the hidden wisdom. *(1Co 2:7-8)* There still would have been a Hell, but not a Hell to redeem man from. For, death of the physical body would have been prevented and therefore no human souls would have been suffering in a tormenting Hell.

Furthermore, with man having become unfit to perform his duties as God's watchman, God chose another means of protection by placing

> **...at the east of the garden of Eden Cherubims, and a flaming sword which turned every way, to keep the way of the tree of life.**

Ge 3:24.

And so, from Adam's fall into sin and the driving out of Adam to Moses to the birth of Jesus Christ, the prophesied deliverer *(Read Genesis 3:15),* the Lord God used angels, dispatched from heaven, to deliver the word of God to man. And that

> **...word spoken by angels was stedfast, and every transgression and disobedience received a just recompence of reward...**

Heb 2:2.

But later, on the day of Pentecost, with the way to the tree of life having been opened again that all of mankind might receive eternal life by re-acquiring the neshamah (breath) of life from God through Jesus Christ—which is the indwelling Holy Ghost—man again became God's sole watchman with the duty of preserving, guarding and keeping the way of the tree of life. For, sometime after the Day of Pentecost whereon the one hundred twenty (120) souls *(Ac 1:12-15)* received the indwelling Holy Ghost *(Ac 2:1-4)*, the writer commented saying,

6 And again, when he bringeth in the firstbegotten into the world, he saith, AND LET ALL THE ANGELS OF GOD WORSHIP HIM.

7 And of the angels he saith, WHO MAKETH HIS ANGELS SPIRITS, AND HIS MINISTERS A FLAME OF FIRE.

Heb 1:6-7.

Here, in the Hebrews 1:7 passage we learn that God made his ministers a flame of fire. The ministers of God replaces the flaming sword and the Cherubim angels as the keepers of *'the way of the tree of life'*. Also, the Apostle Paul warned,

8 ...though we, or an angel from heaven, preach any other gospel unto you than that which we have preached unto you, let him be accursed.

9 As we said before, so say I now again, If any man preach any other gospel unto you than that ye have received, let him be accursed.

Ga 1:8-9.

And in further agreement, the Apostle John stated,

10 If there come any unto you, and bring not this doctrine, receive him not into your house, neither bid him God speed:

11 For he that biddeth him God speed is partaker of his evil deeds.

2Jo 10-11.

Man Re-Acquires The Keys of the Kingdom of Heaven

Not only are the Cherubim angels of heaven no longer in control of the means of keeping the way of the tree of life, but through the last Adam, who is the Lord Jesus Christ *(1Co 15:45; Read 1Co 15:45-50),* mankind reacquired the keys to the kingdom of God and the means to entering into the kingdom of God. With the keys and the means to enter into the kingdom of heaven, in hand, man thereby reacquired the right to the tree of life. *(Re 22:14-15)* For, Jesus said unto the Apostle Peter,

> **18 And I say also unto thee, That thou art Peter, and upon this rock I will build my church; and the gates of hell shall not prevail against it.**
>
> **19 And I will give unto thee the keys of the kingdom of heaven: and whatsoever thou shalt bind on earth shall be bound in heaven: and whatsoever thou shalt loose on earth shall be loosed in heaven.**

Mt 16:18-19.

And, just as the Apostle Peter was given the keys to the kingdom of heaven, he used them for the first time on the Day of Pentecost fifty days after the resurrection of Jesus Christ. For, after he and the other one hundred nineteen (119) souls received the Holy Ghost *(Ac 1:15; Ac 2:1-4)* Peter stood up with the other eleven Apostles and preached the gospel—the death, burial and resurrection of Jesus Christ *(Read Ac 2:14-36)*—unto the men of Judaea who thought that the one hundred twenty (120) Spirit filled souls were drunk. *(Ac 2:14-15).*

While preaching, the Judean men asked Peter and the other Apostles that stood with him,

...Men and brethren, what shall we do?
Ac 2:37b.

Having witnessed the effect of the indwelling Holy Ghost upon their fellow countrymen *(Read Ac 2:5-15)* and after having received an anointed explanation as to why these things had occurred, the listening men wanted to know, 'What did they have to do to receive the same power of the Holy Ghost as the one hundred twenty (120) had received?' And having been asked, Peter used the keys to unlock the door of the kingdom of God for all mankind. For, the **'anyman'** had been locked out of the kingdom of heaven and from the way to the tree of life since Adam's sin *(See Ge 3:22-24),* but

37 In the last day, that great day of the feast, Jesus stood and cried, saying, If *any man* thirst, let him come unto me, and drink.
38 He that believeth on me, as the scripture hath said, out of his belly shall flow rivers of living water.
39 (But this spake he of the Spirit, which they that believe on him should receive: for the Holy Ghost was not yet given; because that Jesus was not yet glorified.)
Joh 7:37-39 *(Emphasis added).*

In this John 7:39 passage the word **glorified** *(glōr'ə-fied)* is translated from the Greek word **doxazo** *(dox-ad'-zo).* **Doxazo** means to render or esteem glorious, full of glory, honour, magnify; to make glorious, glorify. **Glorify** *(glōr'ə-fi')* means to make glorious or give glory to; to exalt in worship; to honor, to make or make seem better, larger or more beautiful. And **glory** *(glō'ri)* means great honor and admiration, fame, renown, or, anything that brings great honor, admiration, fame and/or renown. It also means worship, adoration, and, the condition of highest achievement. And so, we learn from this passage that the people had not yet begun to give Jesus, the Son of God, the honor, adoration, admiration and fame that was necessary for them to worship him. For, as the Prophet Isaiah foretold of his coming birth and life,

> **2 ...[H]e shall grow up before him as a tender plant, and as a root out of a dry ground: he hath no form nor comeliness; and when we shall see him, there is no beauty that we should desire him.**
>
> **3 He is despised and rejected of men; a man of sorrows, and acquainted with grief: and we hid as it were our faces from him; he was despised, and we esteemed him not.**

Isa 53:2-3.

And since the people despised him and failed to esteem him glorious by giving him the honor, adoration and admiration due unto the Son of God, they were not able to worship him. But, as unrepentant sinners, if they wanted to be delivered, blessed or to receive salvation that comes only through belief in Jesus Christ, it was necessary for the people to learn to worship Christ. For, the Lord God will not hear an unrepentant sinner's prayer. *(Pr 1:24-33; Pr 28:9; Pr 15:8)* He must first become a worshipper of God *(Zec 7:13; Joh 9:31; Isa 1:15-20),* because sin separates man from God. *(Isa 59:1-15)* And, God can be worshipped only in Spirit and in truth. As the Lord Jesus declared,

> **23 But the hour cometh, and now is, when the true worshippers shall worship the Father in spirit and in truth: for the Father seeketh such to worship him.**
>
> **24 God is a Spirit: and they that worship him must worship him in spirit and in truth.**

Joh 4:23-24.

The Mystery of the Blindness of Israel

But the failure of the Jews to highly esteem Jesus and to worship him as a nation was in part due to their disobedience and to the act and will of the Lord God to insure that the Jews and not the Gentiles would cause Christ to be crucified. For, the scriptures declare,

> **36 While ye have light, believe in the light, that ye may be the children of light. These things spake Jesus, and departed, and did hide himself from them.**
>
> **37 But though he had done so many miracles before them, yet they believed not on him:**
>
> **38 That the saying of Esa'ias the prophet might be fulfilled, which he spake, LORD, WHO HATH BELIEVED OUR REPORT? AND TO WHOM HATH THE ARM OF THE LORD BEEN REVEALED?**
>
> **39 Therefore they could not believe, because that Esa'ias said again,**
>
> **40 HE HATH BLINDED THEIR EYES, AND HARDENED THEIR HEART; THAT THEY SHOULD NOT SEE WITH THEIR EYES, NOR UNDERSTAND WITH THEIR HEART, AND BE CONVERTED, AND I SHOULD HEAL THEM.**

Joh 12:36-40.

We learn from the above John 12:36-40 passage of scripture that first, the Lord Jesus would teach the Jews and then hide himself from them. This was necessary so that the Prophet Isaiah's prophecy found in verse forty (40) would come to pass. Because, if the people as a nation would see and believe that Jesus was the Christ—the Messiah—that they had been waiting for *(Joh 4:25, 42; Ac 3:22-23; De 18:15, 18-19)* and then worship him—there would be no one to cause him to be crucified. Because, if they would hear, believe and repent, then God would hear and heal them. *(Joh 12:40)* Therefore, it was necessary that the people should reject Christ so that he would have an opportunity to die for the sins of the world.

The Breaking of Beauty and Bands

For this reason the Lord God broke Beauty and Bands. The Breaking of Beauty and Bands is the process by which the Jews, which were God's first chosen and beloved people, being made to be last, and the Gentiles who were without God in the world *(Eph 2:12)*—being made to be first. And, as mentioned above in the John 12:36-40 passage, God accomplished part of this by blinding and hardening the hearts of the Jewish nation against Christ, at a time when they should have believed in him, after having witnessed so many miracles performed by him. *(Joh 12:37)* And with their hearts hardened against him, they rejected their deliverance and their salvation, which is only in Christ. For, the writer wrote,

> **And I took my staff, even Beauty, and cut it asunder, that I might break my covenant which I had made with all the people.**

Zec 11:10.

The covenant that was broken here is the covenant found under the Law of Moses. And with the coming of Jesus Christ,

> **9 Then said he, Lo, I come to do thy will, O God. He taketh away the first, that he may establish the second.**
>
> **10 By the which will we are sanctified through the offering of the body of Jesus Christ once for all.**

Heb 10:9-10.

For the prophets had foretold of the breaking of Beauty, which is the first covenant God made with the Fathers of Israel. For the writer recorded,

31 Behold, the days come, saith the LORD, that I will make a new covenant with the house of Israel, and with the house of Judah:

32 Not according to the covenant that I made with their fathers in the day that I took them by the hand to bring them out of the land of Egypt; which my covenant they brake, although I was an husband unto them, saith the LORD:

33 But this shall be the covenant that I will make with the house of Israel; After those days, saith the LORD, I will put my law in their inward parts, and write it in their hearts; and will be their God, and they shall be my people.

Jer 31:31-33.

When we review the above, Jeremiah 31:31-33 passage, we learn that God made a **covenant** with the Israelites, but it was the Israelites who first broke the **covenant** with God. For, a **covenant** *(kuv'ə-nənt)* is a binding agreement made between two or more persons to do or to keep from doing a specified thing, a compact. And when one person to the **covenant** brakes the **covenant** by not performing the act or task that was promised under the **covenant**, then the other person, who did not violate the **covenant**, has no further obligation to perform under or to honor the **covenant.** For, the word **covenant** *(kuv'ə-nənt)* here is translated from the Hebrew word **beriyth** *(ber-eeth')*, which means a compact, a confederacy, a league.

Furthermore, when we consider the meaning of a **confederacy** *(kən-fed' ẽr-ə-si)* we acquire an even greater understanding of the covenant entered into between God and the Israelites. For, a **confederacy** is a people or nations united for some common purpose. So, the Israelites were a confederacy of people, a confederacy of twelve tribes made into a nation by God for the specific purpose of being his chosen people to serve God in righteousness. *(De 7:6-11)* And in exchange for the Israelites' promise to serve God by obeying his commandments and to put no other gods before the Lord God, God promised the Israelites a land that was flowing with milk and honey *(Ex 13:5);* a land that had already been cultivated, farmed, prepared *(De 6:7-9)* and inhabited by the Gentiles *(De 7:1-5)*, who, at that time, lived in the world without God on their side. *(Eph 2:12)* But, after the Israelites received the blessings of God they turned from serving the Lord God and began serving other gods, thereby breaking the covenant and the confederacy that they had made with God. For, putting other gods before the Lord God is sin. *(Ex 20:3)* And sin is what separated the Israelites from God and from the promises bound up within the covenant made with God. *(Read Isa 59:1-2; De 28:1-68)*

But God remembered his promise made in the beginning when he declared,

> **And I will put enmity between thee and the woman, and between thy seed and her seed; it shall bruise thy head, and thou shalt bruise his heel.**

Ge 3:15.

For God, desirous of receiving praise from his creation called man, broke the covenant by blinding the Jews and hardening their hearts after he appeared in the likeness of sinful flesh *(Ro 8:3),* leading to the crucifixion of his own body, the only begotten Son of God. *(Joh 1:14; Joh 3:16)* For, by his crucifixion, which was a direct result of his breaking of Beauty, the writer declared

> **For God so loved the world, that he gave his only begotten Son, that whosoever believeth in him should not perish, but have everlasting life.**

Joh 3:16.

And so with God reconciling the world back to himself through Christ Jesus, the Jews as a nation shall be the last to accept Christ as the savior. For, before they condemned him to death, the Lord Jesus declared to the Jewish leaders of his day, that

> **28 There shall be weeping and gnashing of teeth, when ye shall see Abraham, and Isaac, and Jacob, and all the prophets, in the kingdom of God, and you yourselves thrust out.**
>
> **29 And they shall come from the east, and from the west, and from the north, and from the south, and shall sit down in the kingdom of God.**
>
> **30 And, behold, there are last which shall be first, and there are first which shall be last.**

Lu 13:28-30.

After Adam's fall and separation from God, in the garden of Eden, the Jews were God's first chosen people or nation. *(De 7:6-9; Isa 44:1)* Therefore, the Gospel was to the Jews first, beginning at Jerusalem and then to the Gentiles. *(Lu 24:47)* But, Christ being rejected by the Jews, as a nation *(Ro 11:11),* opened the way and the door for the Gentiles, who spiritually were like a wild olive tree *(Ro 11:17),* to be engrafted into the body of Christ. *(Ro 11:11-16, 22-25)* For, as the Apostle Paul admonished the non-Israelite Gentiles, saying,

> **11 Wherefore remember, that ye being in time past Gentiles in the flesh, who are Uncircumcision by that which is called the Circumcision in the flesh made by hands;**
>
> **12 That at that time ye were without Christ, being aliens from the commonwealth of Israel, and strangers from the covenants of promise, having no hope, and without God in the world:**

Eph 2:11-12.

Without the crucifixion of Christ, there could be no salvation from sins or eternal life for the common **'anyman'**, because Christ would not have been glorified. *(Joh 7:39)* And it was necessary that the Jews be responsible for crucifying Jesus, because Jesus had done no wrong, no sin and committed no crime. Therefore, the Gentile Romans would not have crucified him because he had not violated any law.

> **For rulers are not a terror to good works, but to the evil…**

Ro 13:3a.

And so, after Pilate had questioned and examined Christ during his trial,

> **38 Pilatc saith unto him, What is truth? And when he had said this, he went out again unto the Jews, and saith unto them, I find in him no fault at all.**
>
> **39 But ye have a custom, that I should release unto you one at the passover: will ye therefore that I release unto you the King of the Jews?**
>
> **40 Then cried they all again, saying, Not this man, but Barab'bas. Now Barab'bas was a robber.**

Joh 18:38-40.

Respect of Persons (Politics) in the Death Penalty

In this above, John 18:38-40, passage we learn that Pilate, a ruler of the Romans over the Jews, found no fault in Jesus. *(Joh 18:38)* And, because no fault was in Christ, after having lived a sinless life *(Heb 4:15; 1Pe 2:21-23; Isa 53:9; 1Jo 3:5),* Pilate, a Gentile ruler, tried to set Jesus free through the Jewish Passover custom of one prisoner release. However, the Jews refused to agree to the release of Jesus. *(Joh 18:39-40)* For, they preferred and requested the release of the criminal and robber Barab'bas rather than the release of Jesus who possessed no fault in him. But Pilate, having found no fault in Christ began using his governmental power in an attempt to release Jesus. *(Joh 19:12)* However, when he was accused by the Jews of not being Caesar's friend *(Joh 19:12)*, Pilate gave in to the political pressure and chose to remain a friend of the world rather than to become a friend of God. Because, he was like many of the Jewish Pharisees who believed Jesus, but refused to publicly confess their belief in him. *(Joh 12:42)*

> **For they loved the praise of men more than the praise of God.**

Joh 12:43.

And therefore, seeking the honor and praise of men, Pilate became unable to administer righteous judgment. For, as the scriptures declare,

> **...He that ruleth over men must be just, ruling in the fear of God.**

2Sa 23:3b.

Once Pilate turned his heart towards seeking and receiving honor from the Jewish leaders and the approval of the supreme ruler of Rome, Caesar, he was rendered incapable of believing in truth or in God. *(Joh 5:44)* And not being able to believe in God prevented Pilate from ruling in the fear of God. For, Jesus said,

> **How can ye believe, which receive honour one of another, and seek not the honour that cometh from God only?**

Joh 5:44.

And Pilate's actions proved that he loved the honor and praise of men and respected their persons more than the honor and praise of God or the respect of God. For, although he had been warned by his wife, due to a dream *(Mt 27:19),* Pilate loved his job more than he loved righteous judgment. For,

> **When he was set down on the judgment seat, his wife sent unto him, saying, Have thou nothing to do with**

that just man: for I have suffered many things this day in a dream because of him.
Mt 27:19.

But, after the Jews falsely accused him of not being Caesar's friend, Pilate

14 … saith unto the Jews, Behold your King!
15 But they cried out, Away with him, away with him, crucify him. Pilate saith unto them, Shall I crucify your King? The chief priests answered, We have no king but Caesar.
16 Then delivered he him therefore unto them to be crucified. And they took Jesus, and led him away.
John 19:14b-16.

Again, if the Jews had not crucified Jesus there would not have been anyone to crucify him. For, the only way the Gentile Romans would have crucified him was for Jesus to have violated their law. And the violation needed to have been a capital crime worthy of death. This capital crime would have been sin. And now with sin in his life and in his body he would have been just another sinful man and not the perfect, sinless sacrifice of the Lord God given for the sins of the world.

Furthermore, with sin in his body he would not have risen on the third day morning. And he would not have been able to take from Lucifer the power of death, because he would have become a servant of Satan worthy of death. Because the scriptures declare, that

The soul that sinneth, it shall die.
Eze 18:20a.

Therefore, it was necessary for Christ to die *(Joh 3:16)* and it was necessary for the Jews to do Satan's work. As the Apostle Paul stated,

For I would not, brethren, that ye should be ignorant of this mystery, lest ye should be wise in your own conceits; that blindness in part is happened to Israel, until the fullness of the Gentiles be come in.

Ro 11:25.

And to be sure that Satan was behind the work of crucifying the Christ, the scriptures declare further that,

7 But we speak the wisdom of God in a mystery, even the hidden wisdom, which God ordained before the world unto our glory:

8 Which none of the princes of this world knew: for had they known it, they would not have crucified the Lord of glory.

1Co 2:7-8.

And so, Jesus would have been a dead soul in hell. And as a result Satan would still possess the keys to hell and the grave along with the power of death.

Apostle Peter Uses the Keys of the Kingdom of Heaven

After Adam's sin in the garden of Eden *(Ge 3:6-7)* and before the day of Pentecost *(Ac 2:1-4)*, receiving the Holy Ghost and reacquiring the image of God had been closed to all but the prophets and leaders of God's people, since Adam was driven out of the garden of Eden. But on the day of Pentecost Peter stood up with the other eleven apostles *(Ac 2:14)* and,

...said unto them, Repent, and be baptized every one of you in the name of Jesus Christ for the remission of sins, and ye shall receive the gift of the Holy Ghost.

Ac 2:38.

In this Acts 2:38 passage Peter informs the men that they must first repent of their sins.

> **For all have sinned, and come short of the glory of God;**

Ro 3:23.

And also, when man repents he repents of those sins that he committed knowingly and willfully and for those sins that were imputed unto him because of the first Adam's *(1Co 15:45)* original sin *(Ge 3:6-7),* even if he has not committed the same sins of disobedience that Adam had committed. For, the scriptures have declared,

> **12 Wherefore, as by one man sin entered into the world, and death by sin; and so death passed upon all men, for that all have sinned:**
>
> **...**
>
> **14 Nevertheless death reigned from Adam to Moses, even over them that had not sinned after the similitude of Adam's transgression...**

Ro 5:12, 14a.

Peter further commanded the men to put on the name of Jesus by being baptized into his name—the name Jesus Christ. Because,

> **Neither is there salvation in any other: for there is none other name under heaven given among men, whereby we must be saved.**

Ac 4:12.

And after obeying the commands of repenting and being baptized in the name of Jesus Christ, Peter promised them the same neshamah (breath) of life that Adam possessed in the beginning—the indwelling Holy Ghost. And hereby is the means by which every man must enter into the kingdom of God and reacquire the right to the tree of life. For, Jesus said,

> **3 ...Verily, verily, I say unto thee, Except a man be born again *(repent)*, he cannot see the kingdom of God.**
>
> **4 ...Verily, verily, I say unto thee, Except a man be born of water *(water baptism in the name of Jesus)* and of the Spirit *(filled with the indwelling Holy Ghost)*, he cannot enter into the kingdom of God.**

Joh 3:5b *(Underlined words in italics added).*

After opening the door to the kingdom of God to his fellow countrymen, because the gospel must have been preached unto the Jews first *(Ac 1:8),* Peter went on to inform everyone listening and everyone who should ever read or hear his message that the promise of the indwelling Holy Ghost and the means and the way back into the kingdom of God and to the tree of life is for all that the Lord God should ever call. For he declared,

> **For the promise is unto you and to your children, and to all that are afar off, even as many as the Lord our God shall call.**

Ac 2:39.

And so, we know that the promise of the indwelling Holy Ghost includes all mankind because,

> **30 And the times of this ignorance God winked at; but now commandeth all men every where to repent:**
>
> **31 Because he hath appointed a day, in the which he will judge the world in righteousness by that man whom he hath ordained; whereof he hath given assurance unto all men, in that he hath raised him from the dead.**

Ac 17:30-31.

And later, the Apostle declared,

> **13 For whosoever shall call upon the name of the Lord shall be saved.**
> **14 How then shall they call on him in whom they have not believed? and how shall they believe in him of whom they have not heard? and how shall they hear without a preacher?**
> **15 And how shall they preach, except they be sent? as it is written, How beautiful are the feet of them that preach the gospel of peace, and bring glad tidings of good things!**

Ro 10:13-15.

Furthermore, after the Day of Pentecost when the one hundred twenty (120) received the indwelling Spirit of the Lord God, the angels of heaven were rendered incapable of future protection and keeping of the way of the tree of life. This is so because the plan of salvation, which includes the means and the way to access the tree of life, was part of the hidden wisdom hidden in God. For the writer declared,

> **7 But we speak the wisdom of God in a mystery, even the hidden wisdom, which God ordained before the world unto our glory:**
> **8 Which none of the princes of this world knew: for had they known it, they would not have crucified the Lord of glory.**

1Co 2:7-8.

And even the angels in heaven desire to look into the plan of salvation, that leads mankind back to life. In agreement, the Apostle Peter wrote,

> **10 Of which salvation the prophets have enquired and searched diligently, who prophesied of the grace that should come unto you;**
>
> **...**
>
> **12 Unto whom it was revealed, that not unto themselves, but unto us they did minister the things, which are now reported unto you by them that have preached the gospel unto you with the Holy Ghost sent down from heaven; which things the angels desire to look into.**

1Pe 1:10, 12.

So, the watchman's diet was required to consist of the natural trees that were good for food for the natural man and the tree of life which was good for food for the spirit man. For, by eating from the tree of life Adam would have tended to his spiritual life in the Lord God. As we know that righteousness tendeth to life and delivereth from death *(Pr 11:19; Pr 10:2),* we also realize that Adam had to have a means of feeding his spirit man and thereby grow in the righteousness of God, after he was given the neshamah (breath) of life. *(Ge 2:7)* For, the neshamah (breath) of life is the same as the water of life as Jesus promised in the scriptures. For, there he said unto the Samaritan woman at Jacob's well,

> **10 Jesus answered and said unto her, If thou knewest the gift of God, and who it is that saith to thee, Give me to drink; thou wouldest have asked of him, and he would have given thee living water.**
>
> **...**
>
> **13 Jesus answered and said unto her, Whosoever drinketh of this water shall thirst again:**
>
> **14 But whosoever drinketh of the water that I shall give him shall never thirst; but the water that I shall give him shall be in him a well of water springing up into everlasting life.**

Joh 4:10, 13-14.

And later he said,

37 ...If any man thirst, let him come unto me, and drink.

38 He that believeth on me, as the scripture hath said, out of his belly shall flow rivers of living water.

39 (But this spake he of the Spirit, which they that believe on him should receive: for the Holy Ghost was not yet given because that Jesus was not yet glorified.)

Joh 7:37b-39.

As it was with Adam in the garden of Eden the watchmen's diet must include the flesh of Jesus, which is the word of God. For Jesus, the Word that was made flesh *(Joh 1:14),* stated,

...the words that I speak unto you, they are spirit, and they are life.

Joh 6:63b.

And He also said,

Whoso eateth my flesh, and drinketh my blood, hath eternal life...

Joh 6:54a.

As the writer wrote earlier,

1 In the beginning was the Word, and the Word was with God, and the Word was God.

2 The same was in the beginning with God.

3 All things were made by him; and without him was not any thing made that was made.

4 In him was life; and the life was the light of men.

Joh 1:1-4.

And we are admonished by the scriptures that righteousness tends to life *(Pr 11:19),* as does the fear of the Lord. *(Pr 19:23)* Therefore we see the Lord God commanding the man to eat freely from all of the trees in the garden of Eden, including the tree of life, except one tree whether natural or spiritual. For we know that

> **...out of the ground made the Lord God to grow every tree that is pleasant to the sight, and good for food; the tree of life also in the midst of the garden, and the tree of knowledge of good and evil.**

Ge 2:9.

When we compare the Genesis 2:16 passage with the Genesis 2:9 passage above we learn that the Lord God commanded the man to eat freely from every tree in the garden of Eden including the tree of life, but he was not to eat from the tree of the knowledge of good and evil. And from this command to eat from the tree of life we understand that Adam was required to eat the righteousness of God, which tends to life. And the righteousness of God is found in the Word of God, that many centuries later was made flesh. For,

> **...the Word was made flesh, and dwelt among us, (and we beheld his glory, the glory as of the only begotten of the Father,) full of grace and truth.**

Joh 1:14.

The Carnal Diet

After reading the Genesis 3:22 passage wherein

> **...the Lord God said, Behold, the man is become as one of us, to know good and evil: and now, lest he put forth his hand, and take also of the tree of life, and eat, and live for ever...**

...the question arises, *'Why did Adam not try to eat from the tree of life right after he had sinned against God and fell from life into death?'*

The simple answer is that Adam had gone carnal and was blinded by the darkness of death. For, the writer wrote that

> **1 In the beginning was the Word, and the Word was with God, and the Word was God.**
> **2 The same was in the beginning with God.**
> **3 All things were made by him; and without him was not any thing made that was made.**
> **4 In him was life; and the life was the light of men.**

Joh 1:1-4.

This Word that was in the beginning was the tree of life. And it was this Word that gave man life and this life was the light of man. Thus when Adam left life and began fellowshipping with darkness he was blinded and could not see clear enough to understand that if he had eaten of the tree of life he would have acquired for his new master, which was the tree of the knowledge of good and evil, the ability to live forever. With his mind set on earthly and fleshly things Adam had acquired a carnal mind, and he therefore was not mindful of the righteous things found in the Word of God, that is the tree of life. And commenting on the subject, the writer declared

> **5 For they that are after the flesh do mind the things of the flesh; but they that are after the Spirit the things of the Spirit.**
> **6 For to be carnally minded is death; but to be spiritually minded is life and peace.**
> **7 Because the carnal mind is enmity against God: for it is not subject to the law of God, neither indeed can be.**
> **8 So then they that are in the flesh cannot please God.**

Ro 8:5-8.

And so, when a watchman consumes only the natural bread and the worldly ways of living he is unable, and unfit to be God's watchman within the kingdom of God. For, it is written,

> **...[M]an doth not live by bread only, but by every word that proceedeth out of the mouth of the Lord doth man live.**

De 8:3b *(See also Mt 4:4; Lu 4:4).*

And this was the Word, the tree of life that was in the garden of Eden, which is the righteousness of God.

The Temptations Of Eve & Jesus Christ Contrasted

Eve **(Ge 3:6)**	Jesus Christ **(Mt 4:1-10; Luke 4:1-12)**
1. The Lust of the Flesh (1John 2:16)	
The woman saw that the tree was good for food...	2 And when he had fasted forty days and forty nights, he was afterward an hungred. 3 And when the tempter came to him, he said, If thou be the Son of God, command that these stones be made bread. 4 But he answered and said, It is written, Man shall not live by bread alone, But by every word that proceedeth out of the mouth of God. **Mt 4:2**-4.
2. The Lust of the Eyes (1John 2:16)	
The woman saw that the tree was... pleasant to the eyes...	8 Again, the devil taketh him up into an exceeding high mountain, and sheweth him all the kingdoms of the world, and the glory of them; 9 And saith unto him, All these things will I give thee, if thou wilt fall down and worship me. 10 Then saith Jesus unto him, Get thee hence, Satan: for it is written, Thou shalt worship the Lord thy God, and him only shalt thou serve. **Mt 4:8**-10.

3. The Pride of Life (1John 2:16)	
The woman saw that the tree was... a tree to be desired to make one wise...	5 Then the devil taketh him up into the holy city, and setteth him on a pinnacle of the temple, 6 And saith unto him, If thou be the Son of God, cast thyself down: for it is written, He shall give his angels charge concerning thee: and in their hands they shall bear thee up, lest at any time thou dash thy foot against a stone. 7 Jesus said unto him, It is written again, Thou shalt not tempt the Lord thy God. **Mt 4:5-7.**

Seeking the Counsel of God

When we compare the temptation of Eve with the temptation of Jesus we immediately see and learn that Eve did not consult her husband, who was with her *(Ge 3:6),* for counsel which is of God. *(Isa 11:2; Pr 8:14)* For, God had instructed Adam concerning the prohibition to not eat from the tree of the knowledge of good and evil before He created Eve. *(Read Ge 2:7-9, 15-18, 19-23)* And therefore, with God as his teacher Adam acquired the wisdom, knowledge and understanding concerning the prohibition. For, even though he received and accepted the forbidden fruit from his wife and did eat *(Ge 3:6-7),* Adam was not tricked or beguiled into eating, or as to the truth of the matter. *(1Ti 2:13-14)* But Eve, the woman, was deceived and beguiled. *(Ge 3:13; 1Ti 2:13-14)* And as a direct consequence of Eve not seeking God's counsel, through her husband, she was easily beguiled and tricked by the serpent to violate the word of God. Because, without counsel she had nothing but the darkened, lying counsel of the devil *(Joh 8:44),* the serpent and the understanding of her flesh to lead and guide her in the decisions of life. And, so she fell from life into the darkness of death, by not obeying the word of God to

5 Trust in the Lord with all thine heart; and lean not unto thine own understanding.

6 In all thy ways acknowledge him, and he shall direct thy paths.

7 Be not wise in thine own eyes: fear the Lord, and depart from evil.

Pr 3:5-7.

Eve failed God and her husband because of a lack of righteous counsel. And, without possessing the righteous counsel of God she also lacked the knowledge of God that she would have acquired from the counsel. As a result of her ignorance, caused by her failure to seek counsel, Eve was led captive and her life within the light and righteousness of God was destroyed, as the word declares,

Therefore my people are gone into captivity, because they have no knowledge: and their honourable men are famished, and their multitude dried up with thirst.

Isa 5:13.

And,

My people are destroyed for lack of knowledge; because thou hast rejected knowledge, I will also reject thee, that thou shalt be no priest to me: seeing thou hast forgotten the law of thy God, I will also forget thy children.

Ho 4:6.

For,

Where no counsel is, the people fall: but in the multitude of counselors there is safety.

Pr 11:14.

Eve's refusal and failure to seek righteous counsel directly from God, from the tree of life or from Adam, God's representative on Earth in the garden of Eden, removed her from the safety of life to the danger and darkness of death. For, we know that when *"...she took of the fruit thereof, and did eat, and gave also unto her husband with her..." (Ge 3:6),* at that point, Eve had demonstrated the use of her body in obedience to and acceptance of the serpent's counsel. As a result she became Lucifer, the serpent's *(Re 12:9),* servant unto death. And in agreement, Apostle Paul wrote,

> **Know ye not, that to whom ye yield yourselves servants to obey, his servants ye are to whom ye obey; whether of sin unto death, or of obedience unto righteousness?**

Ro 6:16.

In contrast, during every temptation suffered by Jesus, he immediately sought counsel from God by consulting the word of God. As a result he reacted to the temptations in the manner in which the word required him to act. For, each time he stated, "*It is written..." (See Mt 4:4, 7, 10)* Jesus did not do as Eve did by following the darkened counsel of Satan, the serpent *(Re 12:9)* and consulting her fleshly desires and needs. For, Eve considered all of the carnal benefits of eating from the tree, such as the tree *'was good for food, pleasant to the eyes and a tree to be desired to make one wise.' (Ge 3:6)*

Counsel Not Sought After

And, being initially counseled by the serpent *(Ge 3:1-5)* about whether she should obey the commandment of God *(Ge 2:16-17)* to not eat from the tree of the knowledge of good and evil *(Ge 3:1-5)* Eve did not reconsider that the word of God forbade mankind's eating from the tree for any purpose. She totally rejected and ignored the counsel of the Lord present in her husband and bound up in the tree of life that was there in the midst. *(Ge 2:9)*

However, although Eve was initially counseled by the serpent, we learn from the scriptures *(Read Ge 3:1-5)* that she did not seek out his counsel. But rather, he tricked her into receiving the serpent's counsel by engaging her in a conversation about things of God that she did not fully understand. For, later, after she had acted upon the serpent's counsel, it is written that,

...[T]he Lord God said unto the woman, What is this that thou hast done? And the woman said, The serpent beguiled me, and I did eat.
Ge 3:13.

For, the serpent had counseled her earlier saying,

> **4 ...unto the woman, Ye shall not surely die:**
> **5 For God doth know that in the day ye eat thereof, then your eyes shall be opened, and ye shall be as gods, knowing good and evil.**

Ge 3:4-5.

Yet, the serpent's counsel was not sought after. The serpent knew that Eve did not fully understand the mystery regarding the commandment to not eat from the tree of the knowledge of good and evil. For, even in her attempt to explain the commandment to the serpent, Eve added to the commandment, to the word of God things that God did not say. God did not say,

> **...neither shall ye touch it, lest ye die.**

Ge 3:3.

So, not having a full understanding of the word of God Eve's adding to the word of God made her more easily tricked by the serpent, because by doing what God did not say, that is, touching the tree of the knowledge of good and evil, she actually would not surely die. And, by not surely dying when she touched him, as she had believed in error, it made it appear that the serpent's counsel was true. Therefore, if the serpent's counsel was true, then that made God's word to not be true. Thus, we realize the necessity of the commandment to all who would set out to be a watchman for the Lord God, that they should,

> **Study to shew thyself approved unto God, a workman that needeth not to be ashamed, rightly dividing the word of truth.**

2Ti 2:15.

For, Adam was so ashamed of his acts that he blamed his help mate, Eve, for his failure saying,

> **...The woman whom thou gavest to be with me, she gave me of the tree, and I did eat.**

Ge 3:12.

And the woman, Eve, was so ashamed of her part in causing the man to sin that she blamed the serpent for her failure, saying,

> **...The serpent beguiled me, and I did eat.**

Ge 3:13.

Therefore, as a watchman for the Lord God, man should always seek the counsel of the Lord first by consulting God in prayer, by studying the word of God and by consulting the brethren within the kingdom of God. However, the watchman should be careful of counsel that is not sought after. He should lay the unsought after counsel beside the counsel of God that is found in the word of God. For, the Lord God will never give or sponsor counsel that is contrary to his word. Thus, when counsel comes that is not sought out the watchman should ask himself: **(1)** Is the unsought out counsel a confirmation of the word and, or the purposes for which God has already put within my path? If yes, then the watchman must take heed and obey the counsel. For, we are admonished that *"In the mouth of two or three witnesses shall every word be established." (2Co 13:1; Mt 18:16b),* and that, *"Every purpose is established by counsel:..." (Pr 20:18);* **(2)** Next, does the unsought out counsel contradict the word of God? If the counsel contradicts the word of God, the watchman should avoid and denounce the unrighteous counsel. **(3)** And finally, does the unsought out counsel confirm the word of God, but contradict, modify or correct the purposes for which God has already put within my path? If yes, then the watchman should obey the confirmed word of God by modifying and correcting the purpose for which God has put within his path. Because,

> **16 All scripture is given by inspiration of God, and is profitable for doctrine, for reproof, for correction, for instruction in righteousness:**
>
> **17 That the man of God may be perfect, throughly furnished unto all good works.**

2Ti 3:16-17.

So, by using the word of God to correct the mistakes made within his life and the work of the ministry the seed planted within the watchman is brought closer to perfection, in Christ, being thoroughly furnished unto all good works. And by doing this the watchman continues to acknowledge God in all his ways. In return the Lord God, through this counsel and by his obedience, will continue to direct his paths and lead him into all truth. *(Pr 3:6)* This counsel, although it was not sought out, is a witness of the Lord God's will. For, the watchman remains at war with the enemy of Christ, and so

> **...by wise counsel thou shalt make thy war: and in multitude of counselors there is safety.**

Pr 24:6 *(Read also Pr 20:18).*

Chapter 13

No. 3: The Commandment to Freely Eat

And the LORD God commanded the man, saying, Of every tree of the garden thou mayest freely eat...
Ge 2:16.

Although the fourth commandment, *'to not eat from the tree of the knowledge of good and evil'*, concerns the spirit man's diet, the third commandment addresses the natural man's diet, declaring,

And the LORD God commanded the man, saying, Of every tree of the garden thou mayest freely eat...
Ge 2:16.

We learn by reviewing the third commandment above, that it is also important to God that the natural man's diet be healthy, full of life and without cost. As the scripture sayeth,

1 Ho, every one that thirsteth, come ye to the waters, And he that hath no money; come ye, buy, and eat; yea, come buy wine and milk without money and without price.

2 Wherefore do ye spend money for that which is not bread? And your labor for that which satisfieth not? Hearken diligently unto me, and eat ye that which is good, and let your soul delight itself in fatness.

Isa 55:1-2.

For, it is important to God that we, as sons of God, take proper care of the natural man as well as the spirit man. For, God desires a house and a place to indwell. And so, he made himself a house and a temple and called it Adam. For Adam was God's first temple built and formed from the dirt, right here on earth—seeing that *"...God formed man of the dust of the ground, and breathed into his nostrils the breath of life; and man became a living soul. (Ge 2:7)* That is, after God formed the temple that he called Adam, he then went into the temple and dwelled therein as the 'breath of life', the 'neshamah of life'. And, in the same fashion, the writer admonishes us, saying

16 Know ye not that ye are the temple of God, and that the Spirit of God dwelleth in you?

17 If any man defile the temple of God, him shall God destroy; for the temple of God is holy, which temple ye are.

1Co 3:16-17.

And again he said,

19 What? Know ye not that your body is the temple of the Holy Ghost which is in you, which ye have of God, and ye are not your own?

20 For ye are bought with a price: therefore glorify God in your body, and in your spirit, which are God's.

1Co 6:19-20.

...[F]or ye are the temple of the living God; as God hath said, I will dwell in them, and walk in them; and I will be their God, and they shall be my people.
2Co 6:16.

Even the Lord Jesus, when responding to questions posed by the Jews, said, concerning his own body,

Destroy this temple, and in three days I will raise it up.
Joh 2:19.

THE word **freely** *(frē'li)* in the Genesis 2:16 passage of the third commandment is translated from the Greek **chinnâm** *(khin-nawm').* **Chinnâm** means gratis, that is devoid of cost, reason or advantage; without a cause, cost or wages; causeless; to cost nothing, free, freely, innocent, for nothing, for naught; in vain. And, **chinnâm** is derived from the Greek **chên** *(khane)* which means graciousness; subjective kindness, favor or objective beauty; favor, grace, gracious, pleasant, precious, well-favored.

Therefore, when the Prophet Isaiah wrote in Isaiah 55:1, that *"...every one that thirsteth, come ye to the waters, and he that hath no money; come ye, buy, and eat; yea, come buy wine and milk without money and without price...",* he was actually describing the conditions that had already existed in the Garden of Eden. Here, we see that the LORD God, through the prophet was informing the people of God that this same condition and situation could and would exist again, if they would

...Hearken diligently unto me, and eat ye that which is good, and let your soul delight itself in fatness.
Isa 55:2.

This point is made clearer when we consider Isaiah 55:13, because, there, the Lord promises to remove the power of the ground's curse to bring forth thorns and thistles. *(Read Ge 3:17-19)* For, the Lord promised,

> **Instead of the thorn shall come up the fir tree, and instead of the brier shall come up the myrtle tree:...**

Isa 55:13.

If we consider the third and fourth commandments together, along with the Isaiah 55:1-2 passage, we are made to see and understand that the promises of freely eating without cost or money was conditional and dependent upon Adam's continued obedience to the fourth commandment *"to not eat of the tree of the knowledge of good and evil"*. Because, the scriptures inform us that after Adam disobeyed the fourth commandment, the promise of freely eating was changed to a curse. The narrative states that, after the woman "*... took of the fruit thereof, and did eat, and gave also unto her husband with her; and he did eat..., (Ge 3:6),* the LORD God came looking for Adam. But Adam had left his place in God, while trying to hide from the presence of the LORD God. *(Ge 3:8-9)* After God questioned Adam, saying

> **9 ...Where art thou?**
>
> **10 And he said, I heard thy voice in the garden, and I was afraid, because I was naked; and I hid myself.**
>
> **11 And he said, Who told thee that thou wast naked? Has thou eaten of the tree, whereof I commanded thee that thou shouldest not eat?**

Ge 3:9-11.

Realizing that he was caught and could not run from or hide from God, Adam confessed his sins unto God, saying,

> **...The woman whom thou gavest to be with me, she gave me of the tree, and I did eat.**

Ge 3:12.

17 And unto Adam he said, Because thou hast hearkened unto the voice of thy wife, and hast eaten of the tree, of which I commanded thee, saying, Thou shalt not eat of it: cursed is the ground for thy sake; in sorrow shalt thou eat of it all the days of thy life;

18 Thorns also and thistles shall it bring forth to thee; and thou shalt eat the herb of the field:

19 In the sweat of thy face shalt thou eat bread, till thou return unto the ground; for out of it wast thou taken: for dust thou art, and unto dust shalt thou return.

Ge 3:17-19.

Before Adam sinned his food variety consisted only of plant life and was determined as

...God, said, Behold, I have given you every herb bearing seed, which is upon the face of all the earth, and every tree, in the which is the fruit of a tree yielding seed; to you it shall be for meat.

Ge 1:29.

After Adam's sin, which eventually resulted in the Lord God's chastisement of the disobedient with the flood, God modified and added to man's variety of food, declaring,

3 Every moving thing that liveth shall be meat for you; even as the green herb have I given you all things.

4 But flesh with the life thereof, which is the blood thereof, shall ye not eat.

Ge 9:3-4.

Therefore, sin brought about a new and changed diet for the natural man. For, with the ground now being cursed *(Ge 3:17),* it brought forth the thorns and the thistles with the herbs and the eatable crops. *(Ge 3:18).* In addition to the weeds of thorns and thistles that would now grow up with man's food crops, it would be hard work just to harvest the wheat that would be needed to make the bread to eat. Because, before Adam sinned, the thorns and thistles did not grow up with the food crops in an attempt to prevent them from growing. For, the Lord God, himself, tended to the crops and caused the herbs and food crops to grow. He even watered them. For the writer wrote,

> **11 And God said. Let the earth bring forth grass, the herb yielding seed, and the fruit tree yielding fruit after his kind, whose seed is in itself, upon the earth: and it was so.**
>
> **12 And the earth brought forth grass, and herb yielding seed after his kind, and the tree yielding fruit, whose seed was in itself, after his kind: and God saw that it was good.**

Ge 1:11-12.

And,

> **5 …the Lord God had not caused it to rain upon the earth, and there was not a man to till the ground.**
>
> **6 But there went up a mist from the earth, and watered the whole face of the ground.**

Ge 2:5b-6.

Furthermore, the seeded food crops and seeded fruit trees, themselves, had no choice but to come forth and grow from the ground because, as seen in Genesis 1:11-12 above, God commanded the earth to bring forth the seeded food crops and fruit trees. And later, although God cursed the ground and gave the ground another commandment, 'to bring forth harmful and useless thorns and thistles', God did not change the commandment or remove the power within the ground to bring forth the seeded food crops and the seeded fruit trees.

Thus, as punishment for man's sin, God cursed the ground for man's sake and within the curse, caused the thorns and thistles to grow up with the seeded food crops that would automatically grow pursuant to the commandment and, or that would be planted by man. For, the Lord God said unto the man,

> **17 ...[C]ursed is the ground for thy sake; in sorrow shalt thou eat of it all the days of thy life;**
> **18 Thorns also and thistles shall it bring forth to thee; and thou shalt eat the herb of the field:**
> **19 In the sweat of thy face shalt thou eat bread, till thou return unto the ground...**

Ge 3:19.

The word **thorns** *('thó(ə)rn)* is translated from **qots** *(kotse)* which means a pricking, a thorn. A **thorn** is a woody plant bearing sharp, impeding processes such as briers, prickles or spines; something that causes distress or irritation. And **thistle** *('this-əl)* is translated from the word **dardar** *(dar-dar').* A **dardar** is a thorn, a thistle. A **thistle** is a thorny, prickly plant with showy heads of mostly tubular flowers. Since thorns and thistles were created as a result of man's sin pursuant to a curse of the ground, they are not eatable plants. For, the prickly, thorny parts of the plant causes distress and are irritating to the flesh of man when they are touched. As a consequence, thorns and thistles brings about sorrow in the planter or sower of seeds because they must be cut out and pulled up least they choke and stunt the growth of the eatable crops. For, the word **sorrow** *('sär-ōw)* in the Genesis 3:17 passage, is translated from the Hebrew word **`itstsabown** *(its-tsaw-bone')* which means worrisomeness, labor, pain, toil, sorrow. And when we have sorrow we possess deep distress and regret (as over the loss of something loved). That which we lost was the act of the Lord God, himself, growing and watering the crops, with no need for man to cut, till and pull up thorns and thistles that causes man's work to be harder, more irritating, distressful, painful and worrisome. **Worrisomeness** *('wər-ē-səm)* is something that causes distress, causing one to worry; causes one to be inclined to worry or to fret. **Toil** *('tói(ə)l)* is to struggle, battle; long strenuous fatiguing labor. **Pain** *('pān)* is punishment, localized physical suffering; a basic bodily sensation induced by a noxious stimulus, received by naked nerve endings, characterized by physical discomfort as pricking, throbbing or aching. **Labor** *('lā-bər)* is expenditure of physical or mental effort while accomplishing a difficult or compulsory task.

Consuming Food from Cursed Ground

When man began to eat the herbs and plant life provided by God in the beginning, there was no curse, no sickness, and no disease. The food that man ate tended to the life of the flesh, because the digestive system of man caused the nutrients needed to sustain life to be absorbed into man's blood stream. And through the blood stream the flesh of man was maintained in life. For, after man sinned the Lord God commanded in one place, that

> **3 Every moving thing that liveth shall be meat for you; even as the green herb have I given you all things.**
>
> **4 But the flesh with the life thereof, which is the blood thereof, shall ye not eat.**

Ge 9:3-4.

And later, in another place the Lord God reminded man that,

> **...it is the life of all flesh; the blood of it is for the life thereof:...Ye shall eat the blood of no manner of flesh: for the life of all flesh is the blood thereof: whosoever eateth it shall be cut off.**

Le 17:14.

The curse and its affects which results in sickness and disease came about due to man's original sin *(Ge 3:6-7),* and negatively affects the body and its organs through the blood stream—wherein lies the life of the flesh. For, the word **cursed** *('kər-səd)* as used in Genesis

3:17, by the Lord God is taken from **`arar** *(aw-rar')* meaning to execrate, to bitterly curse. Furthermore, the word **curse** means to call upon divine or supernatural power to send injury upon; a prayer or invocation for harm or injury to come upon something. **Execrate** *('ek-sə-krāt)* means to put under a curse; to declare to be evil or detestable; denounce; to detest utterly. And, **bitterly** *('bit-ərlē)* means characterized as being peculiarly acrid, astringent or disagreeable; distasteful, or distressful to the mind.

And so, the Lord God's *'curse of the ground'*, that was first heard in Eden, remains upon the ground even to this day, bringing about sickness, disease and death. For, the writers wrote,

> **The curse of the Lord is in the house of the wicked: but he blesseth the habitation of the just.**

Pr 3:33.

> **For we know that the whole creation groaneth and travaileth in pain together until now.**

Ro 8:22.

And, the prophet Jeremiah asked,

> **How long shall the land mourn, and the herbs of every field wither for the wickedness of them that dwell therein? the beasts are consumed and the birds; ...**

Jer 12:4.

From these prophets we are reminded that the land is cursed and remains cursed because of the sin of its inhabitants. For, the Prophet Hosea exclaimed,

> **1 Hear the word of the Lord, ye children of Israel: for the Lord hath a controversy with the inhabitants of the land, because there is no truth, nor mercy, nor knowledge of God in the land.**

2 By swearing, and lying, and killing, and stealing, and committing adultery, they break out, and blood toucheth blood.

3 Therefore shall the land mourn, and every one that dwelleth therein shall languish, with the beasts of the field, and with the fowls of heaven; yea, the fishes of the sea also shall be taken away.

Hos 4:1-3.

And Zechariah reported,

1 Then I turned, and lifted up mine eyes, and looked, and behold a flying roll.

2 And he said unto me, What seest thou? And I answered, I see a flying roll…

3 Then said he unto me, This is the curse that goeth forth over the face of the whole earth: for every one that stealeth shall be cut off as on this side according to it; and every one that sweareth shall be cut off as on that side according to it.

4 I will bring it forth, saith the Lord of hosts, and it shall enter into the house of the thief, and into the house of him that sweareth falsely by my name: and it shall remain in the midst of his house, and shall consume it with the timber thereof and the stones thereof.

Zec 5:1-4.

If the curse flys over the earth like a flying roll or scroll and can enter into the houses of the wicked, then it can be removed from his house when the just takes ownership and occupies it.

Sanctifying Food Taken From Cursed Ground

Removal of the curse from our daily consumption of food by sanctifying it is accomplished by blessing the food by prayer and reciting a scriptural verse over the food before it is eaten. As the Apostle admonishes us,

> **1 Now the Spirit speaketh expressly, that in the latter times some shall depart from the faith, giving heed to seducing spirits, and doctrines of devils;**
> **2 Speaking lies in hypocrisy; having their conscience seared with a hot iron;**
> **3 Forbidding to marry, and commanding to abstain from meats, which God hath created to be received with thanksgiving of them which believe and know the truth.**
> **4 For every creature of God is good, and nothing to be refused, if it be received with thanksgiving:**
> **5 For it is sanctified by the word of God and prayer.**

1Ti 4:1-5.

To **sanctify** *(sank'tə-fī')* means to cleanse and prepare for God's use. And so, if the food that is produced from a cursed ground is thereafter cleansed before eaten, then the curse has no effect upon the consumer, the eater.

Man did not begin to pray and call on the name of the Lord, and therefore use prayer to cleanse and sanctify his food until after Adam's grandson, Enos, was born to Seth. For the writer declared,

> **And to Seth, to him also there was born a son; and he called his name E'-nos: then began men to call upon the name of the Lord.**

Ge 4:26.

The word **call** *('kól)* in this Genesis 4:26 passage is translated from **qara** *(kaw-raw')* to call out to, to address by name, call (for, upon, forth), cry unto, invite, mention, preach, proclaim, make proclamation, pronounce, publish, say. And, the word **prayer** *('pra(ə)r)* in the 1Timothy 4:5 passage is taken from the Greek word **enteuxis** *(ent'-yook-sis)* meaning an interview, supplication, intercession, prayer.

And **enteuxis** is taken from **entugchano** *(en-toong-khan'-o)* which means to chance upon, to confer with, to entreat (in favor or against); deal with, make intercession.

Therefore, from the words **call** and **prayer**, we learn that man did not began to use prayer to call upon God to bless and sanctify man's food until after Enos was born, which was two generations of living outside of the Garden of Eden. And, with the food that was consumed by man being corrupted and contaminated by the ground's curse, man's physical body began to decay and age; because for two generations the food that man consumed was not clean and was not sanctified. This decaying and aging process eventually led to the death of man's physical body. For Adam lived 900 years after they sinned, and he died, according to the commandment of God. For, the writer declared,

> **10 And the commandment, which was ordained to life, I found to be unto death.**
> **11 For sin, taking occasion by the commandment, deceived me, and by it slew me.**

Ro 7:10-11.

Therefore, to slow the curse's decaying processes and to maintain a healthy and productive lifestyle it is important for man to bless and sanctify his food before he eats it, otherwise he actually consumes pieces of the curse with every bite, and with every bite he dies a little every day.

Healing the Land (the Ground) To Prevent Sickness and Disease

As was mentioned before, by the time man began to call upon the name of the Lord and bless his food by prayer, after Enos' birth, the curse had already begun to work within man's physical body, through the food that he ate.

One means of preventing sickness and disease that comes from the curse of the ground is for the ground to be healed. This can be done by removing the power and the operation of the curse upon the ground. This healing of the ground occurs when man turns from his wicked ways and seeks the face of God. For, God said,

> **If my people, which are called by my name, shall humble themselves, and pray, and seek my face, and turn from their wicked ways; then will I hear from heaven, and will heal their land.**

2 Ch 7:14.

In this passage we notice the Lord promising a 'healing of the land', and not a healing of the flesh of man. A healing of the land is necessary because the land, the ground, is cursed and all food items, including water, comes out of the ground, out of and off of the land. The food that man consumes enters his blood stream through the digestive system. If the land and thus the ground is in need of healing, then that means the land is not well, but it is sick and diseased, corrupted. And so, anything that comes out of a sick, diseased and corrupted land will also be sick, diseased and corrupted. For, after Adam sinned,

> **The earth also was corrupt before God, and the earth was filled with violence.**

Ge 6:11.

And the Lord said in a different place,

> **17 Even so every good tree bringeth forth good fruit; but a corrupt tree bringeth forth evil fruit.**
>
> **18 A good tree cannot bring forth evil fruit, neither can a corrupt tree bring forth good fruit.**

Mt 7:17-18.

For every tree is known by his own fruit. For of thorns men do not gather figs, nor of a bramble bush gather they grapes.

Lu 6:44.

Thus, by healing the land from the operation of the curse which corrupts the ground, the sicknesses and diseases that were causing man's illnesses are eliminated and done away with. And man's flesh is then allowed to heal. For, man's flesh began to age, decay and die because of the commandment *(Read Ge 2:17)* that resulted in a curse *(Ge 3:17-19)* after Adam sinned. *(Ge 2:6-7, 11-12)* The curse which resulted from the divine and supernatural power of God brings about sorrow, pain and slow death in man.

Another means of being healed from the ravages, sicknesses and diseases of the flesh that comes from the land is taking advantage of the healing that comes from the stripes of the beating that Jesus endured right before his execution, by crucifixion on the cross. For, the Lord God declared in his word, that

...he was wounded for our transgressions, he was bruised for our iniquities: the chastisement of our peace was upon him; and with his stripes we are healed.

Isa 53:5.

24 Who his own self bare our sins in his own body on the tree, that we, being dead to sins, should live unto righteousness: by whose stripes ye were healed.

25 For ye were as sheep going astray; but are now returned unto the Shepherd and Bishop of your souls.

1Pe 2:24-25.

When we humble ourselves, and seek the face of God by seeking first the Kingdom of God and his righteousness, the Lord will heal the land and ground that we possess for the growing of crops and the raising of livestock for food. And he will also heal our physical bodies through the shed blood and suffering that came from his wrongful beating. And we will no longer have to toil, struggle and worry about whether the land will produce adequate food stuffs for us to eat. Because, he said,

> **31 Therefore take no thought, saying, What shall we eat? or, What shall we drink? or, Wherewithal shall we be clothed?**
>
> **32 (For after all these things do the Gentiles seek:) for your heavenly Father knoweth that ye have need of all these things.**
>
> **33 But seek ye first the kingdom of God, and his righteousness; and all these things shall be added unto you.**
>
> **34 Take therefore no thought for the morrow:...**

Mt 6:31-34a.

Thus, when we review the 2 Chronicles 7:14, 1Peter 2:24-25, and the St. Mathew 6:31-34a passages of scripture we learn that it is the Lord's intent to return man back to the place, in Him, that man stood before he sinned, both spiritually and naturally. Herein we get a glimpse of how the Lord God fulfills the Mystery of his Will—by bringing back together all things in Christ. *(Eph 1:10)* For, as the first Adam did not have to toil, struggle, worry or earn his bread by the sweat of his brow, the Lord has also promised those who seek first his kingdom and his righteousness the same thing. Also, the first Adam did not have to worry about what clothes he would have to wear, and so shall it be, in this life, for those who, with a pure heart, seek the kingdom of God and his righteousness.

For, here, in the Mathew 6:32 passage above, the Gentiles represent the unrepentant, un-reconciled men and women of the world, that stand in the same place that Adam and Eve stood in with God after they sinned. *(Read Ge 3:6-7, 16-19)* For, after they sinned, they toiled, struggled and worried about what they would eat, drink and wear as clothing, because of the ground's curse. Adam had much regret after he sinned, because he did not eat 'freely' without cost from then on—it cost him to eat by hard, strenuous labor, by the sweat of his brow. And so, as the Gentiles do, Adam and Eve had to seek out those things for their own good, because they had left God, his kingdom and his righteousness *(Ge 3:6-7)* for the false doctrine and false righteousness of the serpent. *(Ge 3:7-13)* And, having become servants of the serpent *(Ro 6:16; Ge 3:1-13)* and therefore of the world, they had to seek their livelihood in the world. *(Ge 3:17-19, 23-24)* But, they who will seek to be reconciled back to God and fulfill the Will of God in their personal lives need not fear hunger, nakedness, thirst, sickness, death or disease.

Protection from Pestilence, Plagues and Deadly Poisons

Furthermore, with our healing comes added protection from unknown threats to our physical health and well being. For, the Lord has promised that,

> **16 He that believeth and is baptized shall be saved; but he that believeth not shall be damned.**
>
> **17 And these signs shall follow them that believe; In my name shall they cast out devils; they shall speak with new tongues;**
>
> **18 They shall take up serpents; and if they drink any deadly thing, it shall not hurt them; they shall lay hands on the sick, and they shall recover.**

Mk 16:16a-18.

This protection is so great that we are admonished to

> **25 Whatsoever is sold in the shambles, that eat, asking no question for conscience sake:**

26 For the earth is the Lord's, and the fullness thereof.

27 If any of them that believe not bid you to a feast, and ye be disposed to go; whatsoever is set before you, eat, asking no question for conscience sake.

1Co 10:25-27.

And in agreement, the prophet and psalmist wrote,

1 He that dwelleth in the secret place of the most High shall abide under the shadow of the Almighty.

...

3 Surely he shall deliver thee from the snare of the fowler, and from the noisome pestilence.

...

5 Thou shalt not be afraid for the terror by night; nor for the arrow that flieth by day;

6 Nor for the pestilence that walketh in darkness; nor for the destruction that wasteth at noonday.

7 A thousand shall fall at thy side, and ten thousand at thy right hand; but it shall not come nigh thee.

...

9 Because thou hast made the Lord, which is my refuge, even the most High, thy habitation;

10 There shall no evil befall thee, neither shall any plague come nigh thy dwelling.

...

16 With long life will I satisfy him, and shew him my salvation.

Ps 91:1, 3, 5-7, 9-10, 16.

Chapter 14

No. 4: The Commandment to Not Eat: Do Not Worship Lucifer

> ***But of the tree of the knowledge of good and evil, thou shalt not eat of it: for in the day that thou eatest thereof thou shalt surely die.***

Ge 2:17.

Of all the commandments given to man in the beginning, the one many misinterpret, paraphrase and misunderstand is the fourth commandment which says:

> **But of the tree of the knowledge of good and evil, thou shalt not eat of it: for in the day that thou eatest thereof thou shalt surely die.**

Ge 2:17.

This fourth commandment to man addresses the spirit man's diet. God desired for man's spiritual diet to remain healthy with abundant life. For, bound up in the violation of this fourth commandment is death, first of the spirit man and then later of the physical man. Because, when man was created he was created both human—a natural man, and divine—a spirit man in God's image. In agreement, the scripture declares,

And God said, Let us make man in our image, after our likeness…

Ge 1:26:

And the LORD God formed man of the dust of the ground, and breathed into his nostrils the breath of life; and man became a living soul.

Ge 2:7

But we all…are changed into the same image…by the Spirit of the Lord.

2Co 3:18.

So God created man in his own image, in the image of God created he him; male and female created he them.

Ge 1:27.

…In the day that thou eatest thereof
thou shalt surely die. (Ge 2:17)

When Adam and Eve ate, of the tree of the knowledge of good and evil *(Ge 3:6-7),* they did not immediately die a full, natural death of the flesh, but they did die on the same day, that is, '*in the day that they ate from the bidden tree'. (Ge 2:17)* We see this when we review the scriptures wherein it said,

3 And Adam lived an hundred and thirty years, and begat a son in his own likeness, after his image; and called his name Seth:

4 And the days of Adam after he had begotten Seth were eight hundred years: and he begat sons and daughters:

5 And all the days that Adam lived were nine hundred and thirty years and he died.

Ge 5:3-5.

From the time that Adam and Eve violated the fourth commandment and ate of the forbidden tree they lived one hundred and thirty years and they had their third son, Seth. Adam lived another eight hundred years after Seth was born and died at an aged and decayed life of 930 years. Thus, he died within the day that he violated the fourth commandment, because the writers wrote that a thousand years is but a day unto the Lord. But a full day has both 1000 years of daylight and 1000 years of nighttime, because the times in the day and in the night are equal.

The process of death and decay took hold of Adam and Eve's physical bodies. And, gradually, their bodies grew old from eating things cursed from the ground. Because, they did not begin to bless or sanctify their food by prayer until after their grandson Enos was born, which was 235 years *(Ge 5:3, 6)* after they had violated the fourth commandment and 105 years after their third son Seth was born. *(Ge 5:6)*

Eating and Worshipping

Now the question is, *"How does eating of the tree of the knowledge of good and evil relate to worshipping Lucifer?"* To answer this question we must determine first, *"Is eating, worshipping?"*, and second, *"Is Lucifer the tree of the knowledge of good and evil."* If we determine that eating is worshipping and that Lucifer is the tree of the knowledge of good and evil, then we will see plainly that eating of the tree of the knowledge of good and evil is actually worshipping Lucifer. So, now, let us search the scriptures for the truth.

Is Eating the Same as Worshipping?

First let us review the commandment again. It says,

But of the tree of the knowledge of good and evil, thou shalt not eat of it: for in the day that thou eatest thereof thou shalt surely die.

Ge 2:17.

Notice that the scripture does not say *'thou shalt not eat **from** the tree'*, but rather it says *'thou shalt not eat **of** the tree'*. The words used to relay the meaning of the commandment is significant here. Because, the word **of** *(uv)* means produced by, included among, located at, about or concerning, possessing, belonging to, coming from, pertaining to, and relating to. And, the word **from** *(frum)* means starting at, with—as the origin, out of, out of the totality of. The point here is that man was commanded not to eat anything that was produced by the tree, coming from the tree, belonging to the tree, pertaining to the tree, relating to the tree, possessed by the tree, located at the tree, that was about or concerning the tree or that was included among the tree, least he would surely die. The word **of** includes the point that the things forbidden did not have to have begun with or had its origin with or at the tree, which means the fruit or the thing would have been **from** the tree. That is, the tree did not have to 'create' the thing or cause the thing to come into existence. The commandment goes further to include anything that the tree transforms or changes from the Lord God's created and intended purpose to another purpose that violates the righteousness of God, takes away the Lord God's glory or that draws man away from the Lord God.

The Temptation of Jesus Christ

Thus, being that the tree of the knowledge of good and evil was **the** one, particular tree in the Garden of Eden that possessed the knowledge of what was good and what was evil, he therefore possessed the ability, the power and the knowledge of how to take a thing that is meant to be good and cause it to be used in such a way that it becomes an instrument of evil. We are able to see this clearer when we study the temptation of Jesus by Satan, the devil. There, the scriptures record, that

> **1 Then was Jesus led up of the spirit into the wilderness to be tempted of the devil.**
>
> **2 And when he had fasted forty days and forty nights, he was afterward an hungred.**
>
> **3 And when the tempter came to him, he said, If thou be the Son of God, command that these stones be made bread.**
>
> **4 But he answered and said, It is written, Man shall not live by bread alone, but by every word that proceedeth out of the mouth of God.**
>
> **5 Then the devil taketh him up into the holy city, and setteth him on a pinnacle of the temple,**
>
> **6 And saith unto him, If thou be the Son of God, cast thyself down: for it is written, He shall give his angels charge concerning thee: and in their hands they shall bear thee up, lest at any time thou dash thy foot against a stone.**
>
> **7 Jesus said unto him, It is written again, Thou shalt not tempt the Lord thy God.**
>
> **8 Again, the devil taketh him up into an exceeding high mountain, and sheweth him all the kingdoms of the world, and the glory of them;**
>
> **9 And saith unto him, All these things will I give thee, if thou wilt fall down and worship me.**

10 Then saith Jesus unto him, Get thee hence, Satan: for it is written, Thou shalt worship the Lord the God, and him only shalt thou serve.
Mt 4:1-10 *(Read also Lk 4:1-12).*

The First Temptation: Lust of the Flesh

After Jesus had fasted forty days and forty nights *(Mt 4:2)* without food *(Lu 4:2)* he was hungry. *(Mt 4:2; Lu 4:2)* Therefore, his flesh had been weakened in this area of his life. And while in this weakened state Satan was able to tempt him first with the thought of immediately eating food. For, the scriptures declare that,

14 [E]very man is tempted, when he is drawn away of his own lust, and enticed.
15 Then when lust hath conceived, it bringeth forth sin: and sin, when it is finished, bringeth forth death.
Jas 1:14-15.

Thus we see that Jesus, after having fasted without food for forty days and nights, had a desire to eat food to satisfy the hunger pains that he was experiencing from the lack of consuming food for forty days and nights. Satan understood that Jesus was in need of food and desired to eat and so he set out to use this desire and need for food against Jesus. For, the purpose of the fast was so that he would be weakened and that Satan would have an opportunity to test and tempt Jesus in a state of weakness in the flesh. As the scripture declared,

Then was Jesus led up of the spirit into the wilderness to be tempted of the devil.
Mt 4:1.

During this first temptation Satan tested Jesus by trying to persuade Jesus to use the power of his person, as the Son of God, to change a stone into bread in order to satisfy his forty day hunger. In his testing of Jesus, Satan said unto him,

> **...If thou be the Son of God, command that these stones be made bread.**

Mt 4:3b.

We know that Jesus desired to eat because the scriptures say that he was hungry. And we know that the desire to eat was a strong desire because he had been without food for forty days. *(Mt 4:2; Lu 4:2)* Therefore, this desire was a lust for food. Because, the word **lust** *(lust),* used in the James 1:14-15 passage above, is translated from the Greek **epithumia** *(ep-ee-thoo-mee'ah).* **Epithumia** means a longing (especially for what is forbidden), concupiscence, desire, lust after. **Lust** means an abnormally strong or overwhelming desire. And since Jesus was on a fast he was forbidden to eat during the fast. So, his desire to eat while he was fasting was his flesh lusting after food. It was a lusting after that which is forbidden during a fast. Could he just break the fast? No, not and remain the Sun of Righteousness! *(Mal 4:2; Ro 5:18-21; 1Co 1:30)* Jesus could not just break the fast and began eating, because he had been led into the wilderness by the Spirit of God to be tested and tempted by Satan. *(Mt 4:1; Lu 4:1-2)* The fast and the trying temptations were tests of Jesus' obedience to the Spirit of God while his flesh was weak. So, if Jesus had broken the fast and failed Satan's test it would have been sin and therefore unrighteousness. And with sin in his body he could not have become the perfect sacrifice for the sins of the world. *(Heb 10:9-14; Heb 9:26-28)* Had he sinned there would have been no resurrection, no conquering of death and no hope of salvation for mankind. Because, with sin in his body, Jesus would have become a servant of Satan, as did the first Adam, and that sin within his body would have held his body down in the grave.

But, now, when we reconsider the James 1:14-15 passage we can learn from the manner that Jesus overcame the devil's temptation.

Because, he was indeed tempted in the same areas of human life as is all of mankind.

> **For we have not an high priest which cannot be touched with the feeling of our infirmities; but was in all points tempted like as we are, yet without sin.**

Heb 4:15 *(Read also Lu 22:28; Heb 2:18).*

While considering Jesus' temptation by the devil we need also to review the words **entice** *(en`tīs)* and **conceive** *(kən-`seev)* as used in the James 1:14-15 passage above. For, the word **entice** is taken from **deleazo** *(del-eh-ad'-zo)* which means to entrap, to delude, allure, beguile and entice. We are **enticed** when opportunity brings about arousal; or, the hope of pleasure or profit in having the desire or need satisfied. And we are **allured** *(ə'luur)* by or to a thing when we are attracted, enticed, fascinated or charmed by it. The word **conceive** *(kən-`seev)* is taken from **sullambanō** *(sool-lam-ban'-o)* which means to clasp; seize (arrest or capture); to aid; catch; help; take; to conceive. Lust conceives when one forms a mental image of the desire fulfilled; think of, think with; or become pregnant with the thought; carrying the thought around.

Now, let us consider Jesus. First, the desire was in Jesus to eat because it had become a forty day need for food. And because the need for food was so great it became an abnormally strong desire for food, which is lust. Second, the lust for food enticed, allured and attracted his attention when Satan pointed out to him the opportunity to eat by turning the stones into bread for immediate consumption. This aroused the hope of pleasure or profit in having the desire and need for food satisfied. But, Jesus did not go any further. Jesus did not allow the opportunity, the attraction and the enticement to lead to conception. Instead of thinking about the food that he desired and needed; instead of forming a mental image of the desire fulfilled, or becoming pregnant with the thought, he began thinking upon what the word of God says about the enticement and the opportunity to satisfy a forbidden desire. And so, before the lust was able to conceive and cause him to become pregnant with the thought of eating bread made from a stone, Jesus began eating from his own flesh, which was the Word of God. This in turn removed the pleasure from the thought and the arousal died in him.

So, to overcome Satan, the devil's enticement, Jesus, himself being the Word of God manifested in the flesh *(Joh 1:1-3, 14),* remembered the Word of God and caused his spirit man and not his flesh to take control and the lead in responding to the devil's temptation. For, in his response he said,

> **It is written, Man shall not live by bread alone, but by every word that proceedeth out of the mouth of God. Mt 4:4.**

The Second Temptation: Pride of Life — Suicide

Now, that Jesus had set the standard of how he would respond to Satan's temptation, by way of causing his spirit man to eat from the Word of God, Satan changed his attack and began using random passages of the Word of God within his temptation events. He used the word of God to make it appear that there was no sin involved in the event. And, had Jesus been inexperienced or young in the handling of the Word of God as was Eve during her Eden temptations he would have been beguiled or tricked as Eve had been. *(Read Ge 3:14)* Also, during this second temptation Satan appealed to the pride of Jesus' person—that of being the Son of God—in tempting Jesus to commit suicide. For, the scriptures, recorded that,

> **5 ...the devil taketh him up into the holy city, and setteth him on a pinnacle of the temple,**
>
> **6 And saith unto him, If thou be the Son of God, cast thyself down: for it is written, He shall give his angels**

> **charge concerning thee: and in their hands they shall bear thee up, lest at any time thou dash thy foot against a stone.**

Mt 4:5-6 *(Read also Luke 4:9-11).*

The **pinnacle** *(pin ə kəl)* of the temple was the highest point or place on the temple; a wiglet; the extremity; the top corner, being translated from **pterugion** *(pter-oog'-ee-on).* And it was from this high point, in the air above the ground, that Satan tried to entice Jesus to jump from. For, he said,

> **…cast thyself down.**

Mt 4:6a.

Although Satan did not use the words commit suicide or kill yourself, it was the point of the temptation to entice Jesus to do so. Because, it was obvious that if Jesus jumped down from the temple's highest peak, the pinnacle, he would kill himself if no one else came to his aid to break his fall. So, Satan quoted portions of Psalms 91:11-12, in an attempt to give Jesus false confidence that the Lord God would protect him even from intentional, knowing, self injury. For, in his attempt to hide the sin that would come from self-murder he said,

> **…He shall give his angels charge concerning thee: and in their hands they shall bear thee up, lest at any time thou dash thy foot against a stone.**

Mt 4:6b *(Read Ps 91:11-12).*

Here, we see Satan trying to entice Jesus into depending on a promise, written in the Word of God, of guardian angels watching over him to ensure his safety and protection against physical harm and injury. And to be sure, this passage of scripture and the entire Psalms 91 does promise protection from hurt and harm, dangers seen and unseen. But, Satan did not mention that the promise and protection of guardian angels is conditional. He failed to mention that these protections are only for those who continue to dwell in the secret place of the most High, by obeying the Word of God. For, Psalms 91 begins with the words,

> **1 He that dwelleth in the secret place of the most High shall abide under the shadow of the Almighty.**
>
> **2 I will say of the Lord, He is my refuge and my fortress: my God; in him will I trust.**

Ps 91:1-2.

Therefore, if Jesus had jumped down from the pinnacle of the temple he would have done so out of the pride of his person. That is, he was the Son of God, and he would have been tempting God to see if he would keep his promise of protection, because of his person, because of who he was born as, although he would have now been in sin. But the scripture says that,

> **...God is no respecter of persons:**

Ac 10:34.

And that,

> **Pride goeth before destruction, and an haughty spirit before a fall.**

Pr 16:18.

If he had jumped, at the moment that he decided to jump, lust would have conceived in his heart and he would have possessed sin in his physical body. The sin of pride would have begun to reign within his physical body. And, at the moment that sin began to reign in his mortal body, he no longer would have been dwelling in the secret place of the most High. So, he would have lost the power of the promised protection from the guardian angels. And his casting himself down from the pinnacle would have been suicide, self murder. And in turn self murder would have been a direct violation of the law wherein it admonishes everyone saying,

Thou shalt not kill.
Ex 20:13 *(Read also Ro 13:9).*

Jesus was not beguiled by the devil. For he knew that the word **kill** *(kil)* which is translated from **ratsach** *(raw-tsakh')* in Exodus 20:13 above meant to dash in pieces; that is, to kill a human being as to murder him; put to death; kill; manslay, manslayer; murder, murderer. Just as the word **kill** in Romans 13:9 is translated from **phoeuo** *(fon-yoo'-o)* means to be a murderer; to kill, do murder, slay. Because, Jesus said, himself,

...Thou shalt do no murder...
Mt. 19:18.

For, **murder** *(mur dər)* is the unlawful, intentional killing of a human being. And **suicide** *(soo ə sid)* is defined as the intentional taking of one's own life; killing one's self intentionally. Thus suicide is the unlawful and intentional killing of a human being—one's self. And, it violates the commandment wherein we are admonished,

16 Know ye not that ye are the temple of God, and that the Spirit of God dwelleth in you?
17 If any man defile the temple of God, him shall God destroy; for the temple of God is holy, which temple are ye.
1Co 3:16-17.

Knowing this and being aware of Satan's deception, Jesus, being the Son of God, began to eat from his own flesh, the Word of God, again. For, he, knowing who he was, had no desire to boast of his person or to make for himself a reputation. *(Php 2:7)* So,

Jesus said unto him, It is written again, Thou shalt not tempt the Lord thy God.
Mt 4:7.

Jesus overcame the devil's temptation by eating more Word that qualified and limited the scripture that Satan used, saying, *"...Thou shalt not tempt the Lord thy God"*. This means that if you intentionally take your life God is not obligated to step in and save you. Thus, Jesus did not eat from Satan's tree of false doctrine and half truths. He rejected everything that Satan proposed to him, by eating from his own flesh which was the manifested Word of God. *(Joh 1:1-2, 14)*

The Third Temptation: Lust of the Eyes

During the third temptation event Satan appealed to Jesus' desire, goal and mission to build the kingdom of God on earth. For, the Word of God said about him,

> **Then said I, Lo, I come (in the volume of the book it is written of me,) to do thy will, O God.**

Heb 10:7 *(Read also Ps 40:7-8).*

It was the Father's will for Jesus to be tempted *(Mt 4:1; Lu 4:1-2)* and it was also His will for Jesus to overcome the temptation. For the scripture promises, saying,

> **There hath no temptation taken you but such as is common to man: but God is faithful, who will not suffer you to be tempted above that ye are able; but will with the temptation also make a way to escape, that ye may be able to bear it.**

1Co 10:13.

So, if Jesus had failed the temptation test he would have been unable to do the will of God the Father. But if he would overcome the temptation set before him the writer would latter declare,

> **And the seventh angel sounded; and there were great voices in heaven, saying,** THE KINGDOMS OF THIS

WORLD ARE BECOME THE KINGDOMS OF OUR LORD, AND OF HIS CHRIST; AND HE SHALL REIGN FOREVER AND EVER.

Re 11:15.

So, to make it appear that he was helping and being a blessing to Jesus, by assisting in accomplishing the goal of building Jesus' kingdom on earth, Satan offered him a short cut. This short cut was a way of acquiring a worldwide kingdom that was not of God. The scriptures recorded the temptation event saying,

5 And the devil, taking him up into an high mountain, shewed unto him all the kingdoms of the world in a moment of time.

6 And the devil said unto him, All this power will I give thee, and the glory of them: for that is delivered unto me; and to whomsoever I will I give it.

7 If thou therefore wilt worship me, all shall be thine.

Lu 4:5-7 *(Read also Mt 4:8-9).*

Thus, in the above passage of scripture Satan attempted to entice and persuade Jesus to accomplish Jesus' goal of building the kingdom of God on earth by taking the short cut of leaving the righteousness of God and worshipping the devil. Had Jesus failed the temptation he would have violated the same fourth commandment that Eve and Adam violated, which is

But of the tree of the knowledge of good and evil, thou shalt not eat of it: for in the day that thou eatest thereof thou shalt surely die.

Ge 2:17.

And while worshipping the devil, Jesus would have been running to build his kingdom with zeal but not according to the knowledge of God. Because, he would have been like the unbelieving Israelites of Apostle Paul's day wherein he commented, saying,

2 For I bear them record that they have a zeal of God, but not according to knowledge.

3 For they being ignorant of God's righteousness, and going about to establish their own righteousness, have not submitted themselves unto the righteousness of God. Ro 10:2-3.

The Zeal of God

To possess a zeal of God is a good thing to have, because it causes one to be enthusiastic, excited and eager to start, do and continue a work for God. For, the word **zeal** *(zeel)* is translated from **zelos** *(dsay'-los)* which means heat, zeal in a favorable sense, ardor, emulation, and fervent mind. And further, the word **ardor** *(ahr'-der)* means warmth or intensity of feelings; eagerness; zeal; great heat.

Again, it is a great thing to have a zeal of God, the initiative to get up and go do for God, but the zeal must be tempered, limited and controlled by knowledge of the righteousness of God and its practical application in our everyday lives while we work for Him. For, it is by the righteousness of God through Christ that we possess life *(Pr 11:19; Pr 12:28)*, are protected in life and are established in life. *(Isa 54:14-17)* As it is written,

14 In righteousness shalt thou be established: thou shalt be far from oppression; for thou shalt not fear; and from terror; for it shall not come near thee.

15 Behold, they shall surely gather together, but not by me: whosoever shall gather together against thee shall fall for thy sake.

...

17 No weapon that is formed against thee shall prosper; and every tongue that shall rise against thee in judgment thou shalt condemn. This is the heritage of the

servants of the Lord, and their righteousness is of me, saith the Lord.

Isa 54:14-15, 17.

The zealous, they who have a zeal of God, declare that they are servants of God because they believe that the works they are engaged in are for the benefit of God and His kingdom. But, they do not understand that when they are running, working and building with a zeal that is not according to the knowledge of God they work iniquity within their works. *(Mt 7:21-23)* And as such, they and their works will not be accepted by God in the same manner as Cain and his works were rejected and not accepted by God in Genesis 4:3-7. In agreement, the Lord Jesus said,

21 Not everyone that saith unto me, Lord, Lord, shall enter into the kingdom of heaven; but he that doeth the will of my Father which is in heaven.

22 Many will say to me in that day, Lord, Lord, have we not prophesied in thy name? and in thy name have cast out devils? And in thy name done many wonderful works?

23 And then will I profess unto them, I never knew you: depart from me, ye that work iniquity.

Mt 7:21-23.

It is never God's will for you to work outside of His will. Furthermore, even when we discuss the things that we desire to do, the scriptures require us to condition our intentions upon the will of the Lord. For, we are admonished by them saying,

For that ye ought to say, If the Lord will, we shall live, and do this, or that.

Jas 4:15.

So, when one possesses only a zeal of God and not the knowledge of His righteousness he creates his own situational righteousness to justify his actions and his works which are not of God, because he *went* forth to do a work outside of the will of God.

It is the righteousness of God that tendeth to life. *(Pr 11:19)* And the righteousness of God informs the zealous of *How, Where, When and Why* we should engage ourselves in the work of the Lord. For, the ways of God and the thoughts of God are higher than our ways and higher than our thoughts. *(Isa 55:8-9)* Therefore, the zealous must add knowledge of the righteousness of God to their excited and heated passion and desire to perform a work for God. He can add this knowledge by searching and studying the Word of God and applying what he learns to his life and his work. For, it is written

> **Ye do err, not knowing the scriptures, nor the power of God.**

Mt 22:29.

Here, in this passage, the scriptures are the written Word of God and the power of God is the living Word of God that lives in us and guides us as the Holy Ghost. For Jesus Christ, to us who believe, is the wisdom of God and the power of God. *(1Co 1:24)* And again we are admonished to,

> **Search the scriptures; for in them ye think ye have eternal life: and they are they which testify of me.**

Joh 5:39.

So, if we are running with a zeal of God, **(1)** We should *"... seek ye first the kingdom of God, and his righteousness; and all these things shall be added unto you." (Mt 6:33);* **(2)** We should make sure that our ministry, our mission, our assignment, our work and *"Every purpose is established by counsel:..." (Pr 20:18);* **(3)** We should do nothing out of vain glory. *(Ga 5:26; Php 2:3)* For, the glory belongs to God and he will not give his glory unto another. *(Isa 42:8; Isa 48:11);*

(4) Before we begin our specific work assignment we are required to obtain at least two or three witnesses confirming that now is God's timing for us to begin. For, *"...in the mouth of two or three witnesses shall every word be established." (2Co 13:1; Mt 18:16b);* **(5)** In all of our getting we must get an understanding. *(Pr 4:7)* For, we must *"Trust in the Lord with all thine heart; and lean not unto thine own understanding." (Pr 3:5);* **(6)** We should do all things decent and in order *(1Co 14:40),* and with love. *(Mt 5:44; Joh 15:12; Ro 13:8)*; **(7)** All of our work should be done either for the perfecting of the saints or the edifying of the body *(Eph 4:11-12)* that we may save a soul. *(1Co 9:19-22; 1Co 1:21)*; **(8)** In our work we must totally rely upon God directing our paths and our steps. For, it is written, *"In all thy ways acknowledge him, and he shall direct thy paths." (Pr 3:6);* **(9)** We must strive to maintain the unity of the faith. And, in addition to other things, all of our work must assist in building and maintaining the unity of the faith. *(Eph 4:11-13)*

Therefore, if Jesus had accepted Satan's offer of a short cut to acquiring a worldwide kingdom Jesus would have been running and building with a zeal of God, but not according to the knowledge and righteousness of God. Zeal, without the knowledge of God's righteousness, leads to destruction. *(2Pe 3:16)* For, when one is ignorant of God's righteousness he goes about creating his own righteousness through false doctrine in the same manner as Adam and Eve did after they sinned in the garden of Eden. For, it was there that they attempted to cover up their naked and open sin *(Ge 3:6-11)* when,

> **...they sewed fig leaves together, and made themselves aprons.**

Ge 3:7b.

But the Lord God disapproved of clothing that did not cover their whole naked bodies but covered only the front sexual parts of their naked bodies as an apron does. So, to correct Adams' false teaching of covering only the sexual organs the Lord God fully clothed them. For,

> **Unto Adam also and to his wife did the Lord God make coats of skins, and clothed them.**

Ge 3:21.

Also, the use of false doctrine leads to death. As the Apostle Peter commented upon the unlearned, saying

> **16 As also in all his epistles, speaking in them of these things; in which are some things hard to be understood, which they that are unlearned and unstable wrest, as they do also the other scriptures, unto their own destruction.**
>
> **17 Ye therefore, beloved, seeing ye know these things before, beware lest ye also, being led away with the error of the wicked, fall from your own stedfastness.**
>
> **18 But grow in grace, and in the knowledge of our Lord and Saviour Jesus Christ...**

2Pe 3:16-18a.

Furthermore, during this third temptation event, Satan offered to give Jesus the power and the glory of all the kingdoms on earth. It was possible to tempt Jesus with this promise of glory and power because, even from his birth, people beheld his glory as the only son that God the Father *(Joh 1:14),* who is the Holy Ghost, had physically and intentionally implanted the male seed into the woman's womb. *(Read Mt 1:18-25)* This implantation resulted in fertilization and a pregnant womb. For, the writer declared,

> **And the Word was made flesh, and dwelt among us, (and we beheld his glory, the glory as of the only begotten of the Father,) full of grace and truth.**

Joh 1:14.

Glory *(glor-ee)* is taken from **doxa** *(dox'-ah)* which means glory, dignity, glorious, honor, praise and worship. And, the word **glory** means distinguished honor or praise; exalted reputation; worshipful adoration; a state of extreme wellbeing. Thus the devil's offer of power and glory meant that through the ways and vices of Satan and the world the people would have idolized and therefore worshipped Jesus. For, through the ways of sin Satan would have given Jesus an exalted reputation. And, because of this exalted reputation the peoples of the world would have bestowed upon Jesus the world's glory and honor. But, had Jesus sought out the glory and honor that comes from man and the world he would have been rendered unable to do God's will, because he would not have been able to believe God. For, the honor and praise of man would have blocked and prevented his faith in God. *(Joh 5:41-44; 1Thess 2:5-6)* As the devil reminded Jesus, when he made the offer,

> **...All this power will I give thee, and the glory of them: for that is delivered unto me; and to whomsoever I will I give it.**

Lu 4:6.

The world's power and glory, offered to Jesus by Satan, was the same power and glory that the Lord God gave to mankind in the beginning. *(Read Ge 1:28)* Lucifer, as Satan, the devil and the serpent *(Read Re 12:9)* received this dominion, power and glory over the world when Adam chose to follow his wife, Eve, into obeying, serving and thereby, worshipping the serpent. *(Read Ge 3:1-7).* For, all that the servant owns belongs to his master. As the writer declared,

> **Know ye not, that to whom ye yield yourselves servants to obey, his servants ye are to whom ye obey; whether of sin unto death, or of obedience unto righteousness?**

Ro 6:16.

Therefore, if Jesus had sought out the exalted reputation, power and glory, offered by the devil, he would have become a servant of the devil. Because this seeking for an exalted reputation, power and glory would have been seeking vain glory, which is a violation of the scriptures. *(Read Ga 5:26; Php 2:3; Isa 42:8; Isa 48:11)* And, although the world would have worshipped him, their worship and their glorifying him would not have been in spirit nor in truth as required by God the Father. *(Joh 4:23-24)* And therefore, the world's worship would not have come from the righteousness of God. Because, the righteousness of God is not of the world and can only be found in the Word of God. Therefore, through Satan, the worshipping of Jesus by the people found in the kingdoms of the world would have been as mere filthy rags. For,

> **...we are all as an unclean thing, and all our righteousness are as filthy rags; and we all do fade as a leaf; and our iniquities, like the wind, have taken us away.**

Isa 64:6.

Also, it is written,

> **23 Thus saith the Lord, Let not the wise man glory in his wisdom, neither let the mighty man glory in his might, let not the rich man glory in his riches:**
>
> **24 But let him that glorieth glory in this, that he understandeth and knoweth me, that I am the Lord which exercise lovingkindness, judgment, and righteousness, in the earth: for in these things I delight, saith the Lord.**

Jer 9:23-24.

For, we are further admonished that

> **27 ...God hath chosen the foolish things of the world to confound the wise; and God hath chosen the**

weak things of the world to confound the things which are mighty;

28 And base things of the world, and things which are despised, hath God chosen, yea, and things which are not, to bring to nought things that are:

29 That no flesh should glory in his presence.

30 But of him are ye in Christ Jesus, who of God is made unto us wisdom, and righteousness, and sanctification, and redemption:

31 That, according as it is written, He that glorieth, let him glory in the Lord.

1Co 1:27-31.

After reviewing the above passages of scripture we understand better why Jesus responded to the devil's temptation, to worship Satan, as he did. For,

...Jesus answered and said unto him, Get thee behind me, Satan: for it is written, Thou shalt worship the Lord thy God, and him only shalt thou serve.

Lu 4:8.

But today, many do not understand that when a person believes in false doctrine, obeys it and follows it, they are eating and consuming that doctrine spiritually. And so, they are engaged in worshipping. And now in this endtime, when they worship the beast, the image of the beast or his number they are eating of the beast spiritually *(See Re 14:9-11)* as Eve did, in the beginning. For, she sinned by taking of the tree of the knowledge of good and evil. And after she took of the tree by believing the lie that the serpent had told her *(Ge 3:15)* she obeyed it and thereby she spiritually ate of it. Thus, she worshipped the tree.

In contrast, when we review all of Jesus' temptation events, we learn that he ate from the Word of God and not from the tree,

Lucifer. And, this eating was in spirit and in the truth of God which is found only in the Word of God. Therefore, when Jesus ate, he worshipped God the Father in spirit and in truth. And so we conclude that eating is worshipping.

Is Lucifer the Tree of the Knowledge of Good and Evil?

The second question that we must consider is *"What or who is the tree of the knowledge of good and evil?"* This question is similar to asking, *"What or who, other than the Lord God, is the library or the book that possesses the knowledge or knows what is good and what is evil?"*

The scriptures declare that,

> **The Lord is good...**

Nah 1:7a *(Read also Jer 33:11).*

> **18 And a certain ruler asked him, saying, Good Master, what shall I do to inherit eternal life?**
> **19 And Jesus said unto him, Why callest thou me good? none is good, save one, that is God.**

Lu 18:18-19 *(Read also Mk 10:17-18; Mt 19:16-17).*

Therefore, if God is good and there is none other that is good, but God, as Jesus declared, then all that is good must pertain to God and, or pertain to the ways of God. For, all of the ways of God are good, righteous and judgment. *(Ps 145:17; De 32:4; Da 4:37; Ho 14:9; Pr 8:20)* So, in order for a tree, person or thing to possess the knowledge of or to know what is good and what is evil the tree, the person or thing is therefore required to possess knowledge about God and his ways. Because, since good can only come from or because of God, then, God is the only resource for good. In addition, the thing could not be a natural, wood tree because of the requirement to possess knowledge of what is good and what is evil, which is a requirement to know who God is. This requirement is beyond a natural tree's ability. Furthermore, God is a spirit. *(Joh 4:24)* So for one to acquire knowledge of what is good and what is evil the knowledge must be acquired and maintained in a spiritual manner. And natural trees do not possess a soul or a spirit. Therefore, the writer used the word tree in the Genesis 2:17 passage in a symbolic manner. Likewise, many other writers of the scriptures symbolically referred to men as trees *(Lu 3:7-10; Mt 3:8-10; Da 4:10-27; Jer 17:7-8)*, as cedar trees *(Job 40-15-19; Ps 92:12-14)*, as green trees *(Lu 23:28-31; Ho 14:8),* as dry trees *(Lu 23:28-31),* as wild olive trees *(Ro 11:17),* as olive trees *(Ho 14:4-7),* as good trees *(Lu 6:43-45; Mt 7:15-20; Mt 12:33-35),* as corrupt trees *(Lu 6:43-45; Mt 7:15-20; Mt 12:33-35),* as branches *(Ro 11:16-21),* as vines *(Joh 15:1-8; Jer 2:20-21; Eze 15:1-8),* as palm trees *(Ps 92:12-14),* as a root *(Isa 53:3)*, and as a tender plant. *(Isa 53:2)* Therefore, the tree of the knowledge of good and evil was a person that possessed the required knowledge of God and the knowledge of what is good and evil based upon understanding the ways of God.

The scriptures declare that Lucifer was the chief of the ways of God. *(Job 40:19)* And in another place the prophet said of him,

> **Thou wast perfect in thy ways from the day that thou wast created…**

Eze 28:15a.

Therefore, as the chief of the ways of God, no one else knew more about the ways of God than Lucifer did, except God himself. Furthermore, the writer also wrote that when Lucifer was created,

> **…Thou sealest up the sum, full of wisdom…**

Eze 28:12b.

And the prophet Isaiah, when speaking of him, stated that Lucifer was '*cut down to the ground'*. Trees are 'cut down to the ground' when their usefulness as a standing, living tree has passed. For, Isaiah stated,

> **How art thou fallen from heaven, O Lucifer, son of the morning! how art thou cut down to the ground, which didst weaken the nations!**

Isa 14:12.

In this Isaiah 14:12 passage the word **cut** *(kut)* is taken from the Hebrew word **gada'** *(gaw-dah')* which means to fell a tree; to destroy anything, to cut asunder, to cut down, cut off and to hew down. So, from Isaiah's use of the word **gada'** we learn that the prophet referred to Lucifer symbolically as a tree that had been cut down to the ground. And the word **ground** *(graund)* in this passage is taken from **`erets** *(eh'-rets)* which means to be firm, the earth at large; earth, field, ground, land, nations, wilderness and world. Thus, Lucifer's being cut down to the ground means that after he fell from heaven, the earth at large, the world became his new home. He lost his place in heaven and was no longer allowed to stay in heaven. For, another writer, while discussing Lucifer's fall from heaven, declared,

> **7 And there was war in heaven: Michael and his angels fought against the dragon; and the dragon fought and his angels,**
>
> **8 And prevailed not; neither was their place found any more in heaven.**
>
> **9 And the great dragon was cast out, that old serpent, called the Devil, and Satan, which deceiveth the whole world: he was cast out into the earth, and his angels were cast out with him.**

Re 12:7-9.

And before Lucifer, that old serpent was cast out into the earth, we see the Lord God proclaiming and announcing where Lucifer's future home would be after he had lied *(Ge 3:1-5; Joh 8:44),* beguiled the woman, Eve, and thereby caused her to sin. *(Ge 3:1-6, 13-14)* For, the Lord God said unto

> **...the serpent, Because thou hast done this, thou art cursed above all cattle, and above every beast of the field; upon thy belly shalt thou go, and dust shalt thou eat all the days of thy life:**

Ge 3:14.

So, Lucifer is now a fallen angel that once stood upright as a righteous tree, possessing the knowledge of what is good and what is evil. For, in his creation he was perfect in his ways *(Eze 28:15),* being anointed and set aside by the Lord God. *(Eze 28:14)* But, after creating and fathering the lie *(Joh 8:44; Ge 3:1-5)* he became cunning and took on the characteristics of a snake, a serpent. *(Ge 3:1)* For, the writer said of him,

> **Now the serpent was more subtil than any beast of the field which the Lord God had made....**

Ge 3:1a.

Likewise and in comparison, the writer said of Lucifer, the anointed cherubim angel of God

> **3 Behold, thou art wiser than Daniel; there is no secret that they can hide from thee:**
>
> **...**
>
> **12 ...Thus saith the Lord God; Thou sealest up the sum, full of wisdom, and perfect in beauty.**
>
> **13Thou hast been in Eden the garden of God; every precious stone was thy covering, the sardius, topaz, and the diamond, the beryl, the onyx, and the jasper, the sapphire, the emerald, and the carbuncle, and gold: the workmanship of thy tabrets and of thy pipes was prepared in thee in the day that thou wast created,**

14 Thou art the anointed cherub that covereth; and I have set thee so: thou wast upon the holy mountain of God; thou hast walked up and down in the midst of the stones of fire.

15 Thou wast perfect in thy ways from the day that thou wast created, till iniquity was found in thee.

Eze 28:3, 12b-15.

The word **subtil** *(sut' l)* in the Genesis 3:1 passage above is taken from the word **aruwm** *(aw-room).* **Aruwm** means cunning (usually in a bad sense), crafty, prudent, subtil. **Subtil** means fine, precise, capable of making or noticing fine distinctions in meaning; marked by or requiring mental keenness; delicately skillful or clever; deft or ingenious; not open or direct; crafty; sly; delicately suggestive; not grossly obvious; not easily detected. So, like the serpent was more subtil, crafty, prudent and cunning than any of the land animals (beasts) that the Lord God created on the sixth day, Lucifer, the anointed angel of God, possessed more wisdom, power and beauty than any man or angel that the Lord God had made. And, it was his being full of wisdom that made him subtil and capable of making or noticing fine distinctions in meaning and that gave him his mental keenness. For the word **wisdom** *(wiz'dəm)* in the Ezekiel 28:12 passage is taken from **chokmah** *(khok-maw')* which means wisdom (in a good sense), skilful, wisely, wit.

Moreover, not only was Lucifer in Eden, the garden of God *(Eze 28:13),* but he was created on the sixth day of creation, after Adam, the man, was created and before Eve, the woman, was created. As Ezekiel stated, he was created 'in the day'. *(Eze 28:13)* Time and therefore the days did not begin to exist until after the Lord God had created heaven and earth, and after He divided the light from the darkness. For, the writer wrote,

1 In the beginning God created the heaven and the earth.

> **2 And the earth was without form, and void; and darkness was upon the face of the deep. And the Spirit of God moved upon the face of the waters.**
>
> **3 And God said, Let there be light: and there was light.**
>
> **4 And God saw the light, that it was good: and God divided the light from the darkness.**
>
> **5 And God called the light Day, and the darkness he called Night. And the evening and the morning were the first day.**

Ge 1:1-5.

In the above passages of scripture we learn that time, the morning and the evening *(Ge 1:5)* did not begin until the Lord God separated light from darkness. And the first day to ever exist did not come into being until after God called light Day and darkness Night. So, Lucifer, having been created 'in the day', was created during the daylight hours of a day during creation, in Eden. As the tree of the knowledge of good and evil he was created from Eden's dirt. For, the scriptures declared,

> **8 And the Lord God planted a garden eastward in Eden; and there he put the man whom he had formed.**
>
> **9 And out of the ground made the Lord God to grow every tree that is pleasant to the sight, and good for food; the tree of life also in the midst of the garden, and the tree of knowledge of good and evil.**

Ge 2:8-9.

Here, in this passage we learn that the tree of knowledge of good and evil was made to grow out of the ground of the dirt of Eden. And to be sure that it was the same dirt and ground that the cherub angel came from that the prophet Ezekiel wrote about, we see the writer confirming Ezekiel's account when he wrote,

11 The name of the first is Pi'son: that is it which compasseth the whole land of Havilah, where there is gold;

12 And the gold of that land is good: there is bdellium and the onyx stone.

Ge 2:11-12.

Here we see the writer of Genesis describing some of the precious stones that were present in the land of Eden, which were some of the same stones worn by the anointed *(Eze 28:14),* perfect in beauty *(Eze 28:12)*, full of wisdom *(Eze 28:12),* cherub angel of God. *(Eze 28:14, 16)* Thus, the precious stones that Lucifer wore upon his person, that was part of his perfection in beauty, as described by the prophet Ezekiel, came from the dirt, the ground of Eden—because, he was created in the day, the sixth day, which is the number of a man, six hundred threescore and six (666). *(Re 13:18)* Adam was created on the first part of the sixth day after the land animals. *(Ge 1:24-31; Ge 2:7)* Lucifer was created during the day light hours of the sixth day after Adam was created. *(Ge 2:8-9)* And, the woman, Eve, was the last thing that God created on the sixth day. *(Ge 2:18-25)* Because, the next day was the seventh day, and God rested from all of his work, and his creation was complete. *(Ge 2:1-3)*

So, as the serpent's home is confined to the earth, and must live on the earth, so is Lucifer's home. Having left the truth, and abode not therein *(Joh 8:44),* he became like as a cunning serpent, and he therefore must live as one. And so, we conclude that Lucifer is the tree of the knowledge of good and evil. And all that worship him, by eating and consuming his false doctrines and teachings, and that worship his perfection in physical, beauty image, and that receiveth the mark of his name shall surely die. *(Ge 2:17; Re 14:9-12)*

Chapter 15

No. 5: The Commandment to Cleave

Therefore shall a man leave his father and his mother, and shall cleave unto his wife: and they shall be one flesh.
_Ge 2:24._

God told Adam to cleave unto his wife and once again live as one flesh. *(Ge 2:24)* Adam and Eve lived, at first, in a state of innocence. They were not innocent because they did not know what sin was, but rather because they had not sinned. They had not violated any of God's commandments. For, the moment they heard the Word of God, the law of God, they understood that to violate those laws would put them in violation of God, which is unrighteousness. *(Ro 3:30)* And, all unrighteousness is sin. *(1Jo 5:17)*

As long as man stayed away from presumptuous sins, that is, sins due to arrogance, and did not become insolent and disrespectful of authority, he remained upright. *(Ps 19:13)* But once man became prideful, it caused him to go against the commandment and authority of God. This pride caused man to seek and to lust after unrighteous things and evil inventions. For, the wise King Solomon commented later, saying,

> **Lo, this only have I found, that God hath made man upright; but they have sought out many inventions.**

Ec 7:29.

And, once the lust conceived it brought forth sin in man. *(Jas 1:15)* Then, sin began to reign within the mortal body of man, thereby acquiring dominion and control over the will, intellect, moral character and emotional state of man. *(Ps 19:13)* For, *"...every imagination of the thoughts of his [man's] heart was only evil continually." (Ge 6:5)* And, sin, once it had run its course rewarded man with death *(Jas 1:15; Ro 6:23)*, as the commandment of God *(Read Ge 2:17)*, which is truth *(Ps 119:151)*, had already decreed. For, the fourth commandment, to the first Adam, declared,

> **But of the tree of the knowledge of good and evil, thou shalt not eat of it: for in the day that thou eatest thereof thou shalt surely die.**

Ge 2:17.

Adam walked with God, served him and worked for God as a dresser and keeper of the garden of God, for quite some time. And God, being mindful of the man he had created *(Heb 2:7)*, brought every beast of the field and every fowl of the air

> **...unto Adam to see what he would call them: and whatsoever Adam called every living creature, that was the name thereof.**

Ge 2:19.

While Adam served God he acquired knowledge and wisdom about his work and duties and about who God is and what his requirements are. This was knowledge that Adam acquired before Eve was created. For,

> **...Adam gave names to all cattle, and to the fowl of the air, and to every beast of the field; but for Adam there was not found an help meet for him.**

Ge 2:20.

The help meet, the woman, was not found, because she had not yet been created. For, the word **found** *(found)* is translated from **matsa′** *(maw-tsaw′)*. **Matsa′** means to come forth, to appear, exist; to attain, find or acquire. The help meet (mate) that would later be created was not supposed to walk behind Adam, nor in front of Adam, but rather she was supposed to walk along beside Adam. For, a man's rib is located and resides within his side.

Adam was not born, but was formed, created. *(Ge 1:27; Ge 2:7)* He had no natural father or mother, and was the beginning and first of all mankind. Latter, out of this man would come mankind and the mother of all other mankind. *(1Co 11:8)* Adam began his existence as a fully developed, adult man and as the only living human being on earth. *(Ge 2:15, 18)* Adam was made in the likeness, manner and shape and after the similitude of God, because he was the figure of him, Jesus Christ, that was to come. *(1Co 11:7; Jas 3:9; Ro 5:14)* Adam, the man, was—is the glory of God. *(1Co 11:7)*

THE MYSTERY OF THE ONE FLESH:

The Separation of the Man from Himself

We find in the book of Genesis that Adam was alone. *(Ge 2:18)* If it had been a good thing for Adam to be alone, and to attend to God's work by himself, then, no other human being would have been created. But, we see that Adam was alone, and it was the great, all wise God, Adam's father and his creator, who saw, understood and declared that,

> **It is not good that the man should be alone; I will make him an help meet for him.**

Ge 2:18.

God, being the great law giver and the judge of all things *(Isa 33:22; Jas 4:12)* passed judgment upon Adam's condition of loneliness and his situation of working alone. After the judgment was declared it was necessary for God to provide a means, a way to correct the only situation not good in all of his, God's, creation work.

All of Adam's crown of honor and glory *(Heb 2:7)* could not fix the problem God observed in Adam's lonesome condition and lonely work. The word **alone** *(a-lōn')* is translated from the Hebrew word **bad** *(bad)* which means lonely, single, to be solitary and by one's self.

Solomon declared that working alone is vanity and a **sore** *(sôr)* **travail** *(tra-vāl').* That is, the Hebrew word **ra'** *(rah)*, meaning sore, misery, bad, wicked and great grief, and the Hebrew word **inyan** *(in-yawn')*, meaning travail, employment, job or business—lets us know that working alone is a bad, miserable, and unsatisfactory working environment and job situation. And because it is vanity and vain, **habel** *(hab-ale')*, being alone lacks usefulness, is hollow and worthless. In light of this, we understand why God declared that Adam's being alone was not good. Adam's job performance, alone, was not pleasing to God, and extremely distressful for Adam. A person's best work is not accomplished when he is under great grief and stress, and the work leaves an emptiness in the worker.

This theme, that it is not good for mankind to attempt to perform God's work alone is vividly demonstrated when Jesus,

> **[C]alled unto him the twelve, and began to send them forth by two and two; and gave them power over unclean spirits.**

Mk 6:7.

Again I say unto you, That if two of you shall agree on earth as touching any thing that they shall ask, it shall be done for them of my Father which is in heaven.
Mt 18:19.

As a further warning to those who would try making it alone, the wise King Solomon wrote,

8 There is one alone, and there is not a second; yea, he hath neither child nor brother: yet is there no end of all his labour; neither is his eye satisfied with riches; neither saith he, For whom do I labour, and bereave my soul of good? This is also vanity, yea, it is a sore travail.
9 Two are better than one; because they have a good reward for their labour.
10 For if they fall, the one will lift up his fellow: but woe to him that is alone when he falleth; for he hath not another to help him up.
11 Again, if two lie together, then they have heat: but how can one be warm alone?
12 And if one prevail against him, two shall withstand him; and a threefold cord is not quickly broken.
Ec 4:8-12.

Solomon's two and threefold cord is highlighted again when Jesus declares,

For where two or three are gathered together in my name, there am I in the midst of them.
Mt 18:20.

Moreover, King Solomon's father, King David, the psalmist, wrote,

God setteth the solitary in families:..
Ps 68:6.

The Hebrew word **yachiyd** *(yaw-kheed')* means lonely, desolate, **solitary** *(sŏl'a-tĕr'ē)*. That is, it is God who places those who are alone and lonely into families. Why? Because being alone is empty and hollow. And working alone is miserable, strenuous mental and physical labor without a good reward.

Thus, we see why the Apostles sent the brethren out in pairs of two, during the ministry of the first church. For sure it is safer to send more than one. Also, the Apostles were hoping for a greater reward and return for their labors than what one person could produce and earn. *(See Acts 8:14; Ac 11:29-30; Ac 12:25; Ac 13:2-3; Ac 14:19-20; Ac 15:35, 39-40; Ac 16:19-26; Ac 17:10-15; Ac 19:21-22)*

So, God decided to place the solitary, lonely man named Adam in a family. To do this, God caused a deep sleep to come upon Adam. God operated on Adam and changed him. He changed Adam by taking part of Adam's flesh away, namely a rib. After God took the rib from Adam he would never be the same again. Using the part of Adam that God took from Adam, God made a woman. *(Ge 2:20-22)*

When God made Adam he formed and shaped him in God's own image and likeness. *(Ge 1:26)* And he was equipped with every ability necessary to perform the work and Will of God. *(Ge 2:15)* When God divided Adams flesh and formed a woman from the part taken away, bound up therein was part of Adam, and therefore part of God's image and likeness from which comes mankind's ability to do the work and Will of God. With Adam's rib came gifts to the woman. For, Adam had been changed from the created lonesome Adam, into the Adam family. If the family, the help mate, was provided to assist him, then it was necessary for the man to share the gifts with the family. For, God had crowned Adam with honor and glory *(Heb 2:7)*, thereby making the man God's glory. *(1Co 11:7)* When God took away part of Adam's flesh and made the woman, with the separated flesh came part of Adam's honor and glory. God took this flesh, the rib, along with the honor and glory that came with it and made a woman. *(Ge 2:22)* Since this honor and glory was taken out of Adam, the woman became, Adam's, the man's glory. *(1Co 11:7-9)* For the woman was taken out of the man *(Ge 2:23)*, and was created for the man. *(1Co 11:9)*

> **7 For a man indeed ought not to cover his head, forasmuch as he is the image and glory of God: but the woman is the glory of the man.**
> **8 For the man is not of the woman; but the woman of the man.**
> **9 Neither was the man created for the woman; but the woman for the man.**

1Co 11:7-9.

And the woman, if she *"...have long hair, it is a glory to her: for her hair is given her for a covering." (1Co 11:15)*

Reconciliation of the One Flesh:

Adam was first one, whole man whose one flesh was housed and existed within one, physical body called a man. With the separation of man came the need and requirement to reconcile the two separated pieces of the one flesh, spiritually, physically and legally. To accomplish this task the LORD God began what is known as the institution of marriage.

Marriage:
Legal Reconciliation of the One Flesh

Marriage is the legal reconciliation of the two pieces of the one flesh. It is an open, public acknowledgement of the two pieces coming together for the same purpose, the same cause. This is so because marriage is an institution ordained by the law of God for a particular cause. For, Jesus Christ, the Word of God made Flesh *(Joh 1:1-2, 14)*, declared,

> **4 ...Have ye not read, that he which made them at the beginning made them male and female,**
>
> **5 And said, *For this cause* shall a man leave father and mother, and shall cleave to his wife: and they twain, shall be one flesh?**
>
> **6 Wherefore they are no more twain, but one flesh. What therefore God hath joined together, let not man put asunder.**

Mt 19:4-6 *(Emphasis added).*

The word **cause** *(kôz)* in the above passage is translated from the Greek word **heneka** *(hen'-ek-ah)*, which means on account of, because, by reason of. Thus, we see that the institution of marriage, the man rejoining his missing piece, his rib, his wife is because of the fact that the man began his existence as one, single piece of flesh, with a singleness of spirit and purpose. And so, marriage is designed and intended to be the vehicle by which the two pieces are reunited and rejoined legally as one, in spirit, in authority, in body, and in purpose. In the first marriage in Genesis 2:22-25, we see the LORD God himself bringing the two pieces together as husband and wife. For, the scriptures saith,

> **22 And the rib, which the LORD God had taken from man, made he a woman, and brought her unto the man.**
>
> **23 And Adam said, This is now bone of my bones, and flesh of my flesh: she shall be called Woman, because she was taken out of Man.**
>
> **24 Therefore shall a man leave his father and his mother, and shall cleave unto his wife: and they shall be one flesh.**

25 And they were both naked, the man and his wife, and were not ashamed.

Ge 2:22-25.

We see in the above passage that God, who is a spirit *(Joh 4:24; 2Co 3:17)*, made the rib into what Adam named woman. That is, God made the woman what she was. She was totally subject to the will and purpose of God. For the clay could not say to the potter,

...Why hast thou made me thus?

Ro 9:20 *(Read also Isa 29:16; Isa 45:9-10).*

After God created the man He knew exactly what type of woman this particular man needed in order to be successful in his work for God and to be pleased with his personal, home life. So, when God fashioned the woman, for the man, God then brought the woman to the man to be his wife. *(Ge 2:22)* Adam's creator, his father, chose his wife for him. The fact that God had been a faithful father to Adam in times past gave Adam the confidence and trust in God to believe that God knew what was best for him and what type of wife he needed. This is shown in the fact that it was not Adam that discovered that he needed a wife and that being and working alone was not good. But, it was his father, the creator God, who determined and declared,

...It is not good that the man should be alone; I will make him an help meet for him.

Ge 2:18.

Before God made man, God had already declared on six occasions during his creation work that all his other creations and the manner in which they were situated was good. In every instance where the word **good** *(good)* appears in Genesis chapter one through Genesis chapter 19, it is always translated from the Hebrew word **towb** *(tobe),* including the Psalmist's declaration that God is **good** in Psalms 107:1.

The word **towb** means good, a good thing, well, beautiful, best, better, bountiful, cheerful.

Therefore, the fact that Adam's condition was not good meant that the situation, his condition was not of God. Because, God is good. *(Lu 18:19; Mt 19:17; Ps 107:1)* Even the word **good**, taken from the Greek word **agathos** *(ag-ath-os')*, as it relates to God's essence in Matthew 19:17, means benefit, good things, good, well.

Thus, the essence of the God of Adam and Abraham is the same as the God of Peter and Paul, **good**, **towb**, **agathos**. So, we understand that Adam's condition was not a benefit to him; was not well with him or for him. And, as for the fact that Adam was alone, we discussed earlier that King Solomon said,

> **There is one alone, and there is not a second; yea, he hath neither child nor brother: yet is there no end of all his labour; neither is his eye satisfied with riches; neither saith he, For whom do I labour, and bereave my soul of good? This is also vanity, yea, it is a sore travail.**

Ec 4:8.

The question arises then, why did God create Adam's situation since he knew that working alone was not good. The answer is found in the scripture, wherein the writer declared,

> **And we know that all things work together for good to them that love God, to them who are the called according to his purpose.**

Ro 8:28 *(Emphasis added).*

The word **good** in the Romans 8:28 passage is the same **agathos** as used in the Luke 18:19 passage in reference to the essence of God. Therefore, we must come to the conclusion that since God is all-knowing, God knew and understood Adam's condition before it occurred in time. But, Adam did not know or understand that his condition was not good. Adam had absolutely no knowledge or even a thought of the possibility of a thing or situation being good or not good, which is evil. The concept of good was a concept that God, himself, would teach his son Adam, in time, as he would reveal himself to Adam. For, God, who is a spirit, desired to and would have taught Adam all things, as he teaches us today through the anointing of the Holy Ghost. *(Joh 14:26; 1Jo 2:27)* This is another reason why God commanded Adam not to eat from the tree of the knowledge of good and evil. *(Ge 2:17)*

Now, let us return to answering the immediate question. God allowed Adam's condition to come into existence, into time to begin teaching him the difference between good and evil. God set out to teach Adam a foundational concept. That concept is that when the LORD God is on your side he is greater than your situation and—or the world against you and this truth is a benefit to you, because God is good. And therefore, although man's condition in life may not be the best, the good will of God toward man *(Lu 2:14)* has set the events in time in motion to work together, in concert for the good, to benefit mankind that love God, who are called according to God's purpose.

After the creation of the woman and she becoming his wife, Adam learned many things. ***First***, he learned the evil involved in working and being alone.

> **8 There is one alone, and there is not a second; yea, he hath neither child nor brother: yet is there no end of all his labour; neither is his eye satisfied with riches; neither saith he, For whom do I labour, and bereave my soul of good? This is also vanity, yea, it is a sore travail.**
>
> **9 Two are better than one; because they have a good reward for their labour.**

Ec 4:8-9.

Second, he acquired the wisdom and learned how the evil is removed from lonesome conditions and situations. As Apostle James admonishes us

If any of you lack wisdom, let him ask of God, that giveth to all men liberally, and upbraideth not; and it shall be given him.

Jas 1:5.

For, God is good, yet he also creates evil. For, he declared,

I form the light, and create darkness: I make peace, and create evil: I the LORD do all these things.

Isa 45:7.

Thirdly, Adam learned that in due time God will cause all things pertaining to us to become good for us.

And we know that all things work together for good to them that love God, to them who are the called according to his purpose.

Ro 8:28.

Fourth, Adam learned that with God nothing is too hard *(Ge 18:14)*, all things are possible *(Mt 19:26; Mk 14:36; Lu 18:27)*, and that God is able to make a way out of no way.

And Jesus looking upon them saith, With men it is impossible, but not with God: for with God all things are possible.

Mk 10:27.

And ***fifth***, Adam learned that men should

8 ...praise the LORD for his goodness, and for his wonderful works to the children of men!

9 For he satisfieth *the longing soul*, and filleth the hungry soul with goodness.

Ps 107:8-9 *(Emphasis added).*

Later, Adam would learn, after his fall from God, that although God knew that his changing Adam's condition and giving him help would lead to God's lost of his glory through the help, God's love *(Eph 2:4),* mercy *(Ps 57:10; Ps 86:13; Ps 103:11; Ps 108:4; Ps 117:2; Ps 119:156; Ps 145:8; Isa 54:7-10; Da 9:18; Joe 2:13; Jon 4:2; Lu 1:58),* goodness *(Ps 31:19; Ps 145:7; Isa 63:7)* and faithfulness *(La 3:22-23)* towards man remained great.

> **For God so loved the world, that he gave his only begotten Son, that whosoever believeth in him should not perish, but have everlasting life.**

Joh 3:16.

As the Son of God stated,

> **Greater love hath no man than this, that a man lay down his life for his friends.**

Joh 15:13.

This so great act of love by God, was as a result and in preparation of the fulfillment of the promise, to Adam and Eve, of the way out of the bondage of sin in which they later became slaves to. For the LORD God promised,

> **And I will put enmity between thee and the woman, and between thy seed and her seed; it shall bruise thy head, and thou shalt bruise his heel.**

Ge 3:15.

For Jesus, pointing towards his coming three-day death *(Read Joh 2:19-22) (three-day heel bruise—wherein he could not walk upon the face of the earth)* and his taking from the serpent, Lucifer, the power of death *(Read Heb 2:14; 2Ti 1:10; Col 2:15) (which was the bruising of his headship—his authority and power of reigning over men through death)*—the Lord stated,

> **Greater love hath no man than this, that a man lay down his life for his friends.**

Joh 15:13.

For, they did not take his life, but rather, Jesus laid down his life for the sins of the world, and picked it back up again. *(Joh 10:11, 15, 17-18)*

Now that we have determined 'why' the institution of marriage became necessary, let us look into God's role in making sure the institution was successful. First, the writer declared,

> **And the rib, which the LORD God had taken from man, made he a woman, and brought her unto the man.**

Ge 2:22.

The fact that God fashioned and made the woman from Adam's rib, means that God considered Adam's needs while he made the woman. God made the woman in such a way that she would be of benefit and a help mate to Adam. God did not make the woman **contentious**, for then Adam could not have lived with her, because his home would have been filled with **contests of contention**, **confusion**, **quarrels**, *(Pr 19:13; Pr 21:9, 19; Pr 27:15)*, **strife**, and **pride**. For, *"Only by pride cometh contention..." (Pr 13:10)* Neither did he fashion her as a **strange** woman, *"For her house inclineth unto death, and her paths unto the dead." (Pr 2:16-19); "...her steps take hold on hell." (Pr 5:3-20; Pr 6:23-29, 32-33; Pr 7:4-27)*; and she is a narrow **pit**, lying in wait as for a prey, and increaseth the transgressors among men. *(Pr 23:27b, 28)* God did not make the wife a **whorish** woman, because by her means Adam would have been brought to a piece of bread. *(Pr 6:26)* For, she is a deep ditch. *(Pr 23:27)* A **loud** and **stubborn** woman God did not fashion as a wife, because she would have left and not remained a wife in the home *(Pr 7:10-11).* For, stubbornness is as **iniquity** and **idolatry**. *(1Sa 15:23)* Nor did God create a **foolish** woman to be Adam's wife, because she is **clamorous**, **simple** and knoweth nothing and her guests are in the depths of hell. *(Pr 9:13-18)* God did not give Adam a **beautiful**, **fair** woman who had **no discretion**, for then she would have been worthless like a jewel of gold in a pig's nose. *(Pr 11:22)* An **adulterous** woman God did not make to wife because *"...she eateth, and wipeth her mouth, and saith, I have done no wickedness." (Pr 30:20)* An **odious**, that is, a **hateful** woman God did not fashion to be a wife, for the marriage would have been without love and the earth would have been disquieted, and quivered with violent emotion. *(Pr 30:21-23)* God did not create the woman with a heart that is **snares** and **nets** and hands that are **bands**, because this type woman is bitterer than death. *(Ec 7:26)* And finally, God did not provide Adam a **brawling** woman for a wife, because then his home would have been full of **discord** and **strife**, and Adam would have had no help, having to dwell in a section of the garden far away from his wife, just to have peace. *(Pr 25:24)*

> **For where envying and strife is, there is confusion and every evil work.**

Jas 3:16.

And, we know that

> **...God is not the author of confusion, but of peace...**

1Co 14:33.

When a man and woman are in Christ and are married, then their joining together is of the LORD God, and no man is allowed to put asunder they whom God have joined.

Sex:
Spiritual, Physical & Emotional Reconciliation Of The One Flesh

After God separated the man into two pieces of the one flesh, there arose another concern. Now, God had to cause each part of the one flesh, just separated, to desire to be with, belong to and be rejoined to the opposite, separated part. God accomplished this by placing in both pieces, male and female, a strong and powerful urge and attraction to physically and emotionally want, need and to desire each other. This urge is that desire within the flesh to be rejoined to the missing piece. For, the rib, which God took out of Adam, had always been with Adam. Wherever Adam went, laid down or sat down, that rib was always there and was always in communion with Adam. They had never been separated. Through a natural process, God placed this urge in both the man and the woman and caused their physical bodies to actually respond and react to their emotional needs. This strong attraction and urge is physically manifested within the sexual relationship between a man and a woman.

Fornication: Heterosexual and Same Sex Partners

Fornication, which is sex between two people who are not joined together pursuant to God's will, in marriage, is extremely destructive to the human body. It is also detrimental to God's plans of reconciliation, both of man to himself and of man back to God. This is so because, in fornication, there is only the temporary joining together of lustful desires and not a permanent joining together of the two pieces into the one flesh. For, the only sin that is committed against one's own body is the sin of fornication. *(1Co 6:18)* This destruction against the body is partly to blame for impotence in the man after periods of fornication, and sexually transmitted diseases.

Fornication is performed between a man and a woman who are not married to each other; between a man with another man, called homosexual sex; and—or between a woman and another woman, called lesbian sex. There can never be a holy, blessed and proper reconciliation of the one flesh through the act of fornication. The flesh of mankind can only be reconciled through the institution of marriage between a man and a woman.

Same sex partners, that is, homosexualism and lesbianism is an attempt to imitate the marriage relationship which is honored by God only when it is between a man and a woman. Heterosexual fornication, homosexual and lesbian sex and relationships are enemies of the institution of marriage, and are abominations before the Lord. *(Le 18:22; Le 20:13)* Lesbian and homosexual partnerships represent mankind's attempts to rejoin and reconcile the two pieces of the one flesh, outside of nature and the natural order of things *(Ro 1:26-27; Jude 10)*, and outside of the will and law of God.

The sexual urge is naturally directed towards and inclined to be reunited with that opposite piece of the one flesh that God took away. *(Ro 1:26-27; Ge 2:21-23)* The homosexual and lesbian desire and inclination is not only sin, but is also set against nature. *(Ro 1:26-27)* Same sex partnerships are a corruption of those persons involved. *(Jude 10)*

The sexual relationship between a man and his female wife is so fundamental and important to the will and plan of God that God severely punishes those who misuse the relationship. Death is the ultimate punishment from God for sins involving sex. *(Le 18:22, 29; Le 20:10, 13)*

Secondly, God also turns the participants of homosexual and lesbian relationships over to a reprobate mind. *(Ro 1:24-28)* The word **reprobate** *(rĕp'ra-bāt')* taken from the Greek word **adokimos** *(ad-ok'ee-mos)*, means to be worthless, a castaway, rejected and unapproved. Therefore, the same sex partners, if they fail to repent, are given up, by God, to vile affections. The problem here with reprobateness is the notion of a person's inability to change and to renew their minds in a manner pleasing and acceptable to God, leading to salvation.

Thirdly, fornicators, adulterers, those who are effeminate and same sex partners shall not inherit the kingdom of God. And, fourthly all who have sex outside of marriage sins against their own body. *(1Co 6:18)* Sin brings death. *(Jas 1:15)*

Therefore the body and its sexual functions begin to die and decay. This internal destruction leads to impotence in men and what is known as sexually transmitted diseases, all representing the fruit harvest of the various sex related sins previously sown.

God decided that the sexual relationship should exist only between those men and women whose opposite parts are being reconciled, rejoined with their missing, opposite, gender partner. God accomplishes this reconciling of both pieces of man back to himself, through and by the institution of marriage. God calls the reconciled two pieces the one flesh. *(Mt 19:5-6; Eph 5:31)*

Therefore, in order for Adam to regain that part of his flesh in which he lost, and thereby becoming once again, one flesh, he had to cleave to, or rejoin his flesh with his flesh, his new wife, the woman. The word **cleave** *(klēv)* comes from the Hebrew word **dabaq** *(daw-bak'),* which means to be joined, keep, to stick to, take. The woman possessed within herself, all that Adam had lost. So, in order to regain the lost part, Adam would have to find it within his newly created help mate and 'stick to' her through and by the institution of marriage. *(Ge 2:23-24)*

Sex within the institution of marriage between a man and a woman is the only safe, protected sex, because marriage is honorable in all, and the marriage bed is undefiled. *(Heb 13:4)* **Undefiled** *(ŭn'dĭ-fīl')* is translated from the Greek word **amiantos** *(am-ee'-an-tos),* which means pure and unsoiled. Thus, sex in marriage is good and not harmful to the body of the one flesh.

After the woman was created, God brought her and presented her as the bride unto Adam, the bridegroom. *(Ge 2:22)* Adam was pleased, excited and thankful and declared,

This is now bone of my bones, and flesh of my flesh: she shall be called Woman, because she was taken out of Man.

Ge 2:23.

The scripture goes on to say that,

24 Therefore shall a man leave his father and his mother, and shall cleave unto his wife: and they shall be one flesh.

25 And they were both naked, the man and his wife, and were not ashamed.

Ge 2:24-25.

Centuries later Jesus declared, in a discussion of marriage with the Pharisees that,

5 ...For this cause shall a man leave father and mother, and shall cleave to his wife: and they twain, *[two]*, shall be one flesh?

6 Wherefore they are no more twain, [two], but one flesh. What therefore God hath joined together, let not man put asunder, *[separate]*.

Mt 19:5-6 *(Words in brackets added).*

Before the making of Eve and before the marriage of Adam and Eve, humans did not have sex. Before the woman, Eve's, creation sex had no place with Adam, because there was no human to desire sexually or to cleave to. Humanly speaking, Adam was alone. Adam possessed the male's physical, sexual body parts, but the apparatus was used only for waste disposal. This is understood by the fact that the self-same event occurs in a man during waste disposal as well as during the presence of the active, aroused, sexual urge.

We find in the Word of God that the sexual relationship between a husband and wife is very important to the institution of marriage and therefore, to the reconciliation efforts of the one flesh. The sexual desire and urge within the marriage must be fed, or problems will arise within the marriage. Sex represents the physical and emotional coming together of the one flesh. It is so important to the relationship that the Apostle Paul wrote that,

> **4 The wife hath not power of her own body, but the husband: and likewise also the husband hath not power of his own body, but the wife.**
>
> **5 Defraud ye not one the other, except it be with consent for a time, that ye may give yourselves to fasting and prayer; and come together again, that Satan tempt you not for your incontinency.**

1Co 7:4-5.

We are taught several important lessons in the above passage of scripture concerning sex in marriage. ***First,*** we learn that, since the husband and the wife are one flesh, neither husband nor wife is master of the piece of the one flesh in which their individual soul's dwell. Taken further we see also, why the law that says a woman has a right to an abortion, the killing of an unborn child, without her husband having a voice, is a direct assault and enemy of and against the one flesh and the institution of marriage.

Thus, abortion is against God. For, the abortionist says that the wife's body belongs to her and only she has a voice in whether the child that she carries should live or die. However, the wife does not have power over her own body. *(1Co 7:4)* And since the wife is not able to give life, nor determine when her womb shall conceive, she has no right, power or authority to destroy the life that God, himself, has given and allowed her womb to bear.

Secondly, we learn that the marriage partners are not to defraud the other partner without consent. The word **defraud** *(dĭ-frôd')* is translated from the Greek word **apostereo** *(ap-os-ter-eh-o)*, which means to deprive or to keep back by fraud. In other words, the husband or the wife should always be willing to come together for sexual relations. They are not to deprive the other part of the one flesh of the enjoyment of their body except by consent from the other partner. The practice carried on by some wives and husbands wherein they deprive their spouses of the opportunity for sex as punishment for some disagreement is sinful and against the institution of marriage, and against the will of God.

Third, the only justifiable reasons to ask for consent for a time, to not engage in sex, is that the spouse may give him, or herself a chance to fast and pray. And, ***finally***, even with consent granted, the husband and wife are commanded to come back together again and enjoy one another's body so that Satan will not be able to tempt either of them for a lack of self control. Many married couples who deprive their spouses of the opportunity for sexual relations wonder why the marriage falls apart and the deprived spouse finds a more willing partner outside the marriage. Herein is part of the problem. Your deprivation of what was theirs brought about a lack of self control and Satan's temptation was able to overcome them. Your sin of defrauding resulted in his or her sin of adultery. Adultery is sex between a married person with another person who is not his wife, or her husband.

The partners of the one flesh should take heed to King Solomon's command when he wrote,

> **15 Drink waters out of thine own cistern, and running waters out of thine own well.**
>
> **16 Let thy fountains be dispersed abroad, and rivers of waters in the streets.**
>
> **17 Let them be only thine own, and not strangers' with thee.**
>
> **18 Let thy fountain be blessed: and rejoice with the wife of thy youth.**
>
> **19 Let her be as the loving hind and pleasant roe; let her breasts satisfy thee at all times; and be thou ravished** ***[exhilarated]*** **always with her love.**

20 And why wilt thou, my son, be ravished with a strange woman, and embrace the bosom of a stranger?
Pr 5:15-20 *(Word in brackets added).*

Moreover, God commanded Adam and Eve to have sex, while in the Garden of Eden, before they sinned. The command to engage in sexual relations came when

...God blessed them, and God said unto them, Be fruitful, and multiply, and replenish the earth, and subdue it:...
Ge 1:28.

The only way to be fruitful and multiply, which is a command to bear children, was for the one flesh to come together in sexual relations. Enough said.

Amen.

The Name:
Reconciliation Of The One Flesh In Authority

Adam being first in the family, the whole family of Adam took on the man's name and became known as Adam. It was Adam's creator, the LORD God that instituted the use of the man's sir name as the name to be used by the whole family of the man. *(Ge 5:2)* For, Adam declared that his family was all bone of his bone and flesh of his flesh. *(Ge 2:23)* This is why the whole family of God, and the bride of Jesus is in his name, baptizes in his name *(Read Mt 28:19; Joh 5:43; Mt 1:20; Joh 14:26; Ac 2:38)*, and is commanded to perform every deed or act and speak every word in the name of Jesus. *(Col 3:17; Lu 10:17; Lu*

24:47; Mk 16:17-18) By accepting, putting on and using the name of the bridegroom, the husbandman *(Joh 15:1; Joh 5:43)*, we give honor, praise, thanks and reverence to him. *(Col 3:17)* For, Jesus, being the last Adam, has allowed us to become bone of his bones and flesh of his flesh. *(Eph 5:30)*

Partners In Leadership Authority

We discussed earlier how God looked upon the man's lonely condition and situation and declared that it was not good. Also, we find that after God had created Eve, the help mate for Adam, it was only then that God

> **[S]aw every thing that he had made, and behold, it was very good.**

Ge 1:31.

On the sixth and final day of God's creation work, he looked upon and over what he had completed. *(Ge 1:31)* Adams situation went from being 'not good' being alone, to 'very good' while being in a family *(Ge 2:18; Ge 1:31)*, only after the addition of his wife. As the psalmist wrote, it is God who places the solitary, the lonely, in families. *(Ps 68:6)* And here, we see that God created a family for the solitary, lonely Adam to belong to.

It is important to note at this point, that a help meet (mate) was needed, but the help mate was not made to be Adam's slave, nor his servant. Nor was Adam's permission required before the woman could assist him in the work of God. *(Ge 2:15, 18; Ge 1:26-29)*

The woman was at liberty to take her place at the seat of leadership in God's work, because she was necessary for Adam to accomplish the work that he had performed, alone, for God and that God now had commanded both of them to perform together. If God had desired and intended that only men perform his work, then he would have made Steve rather than Eve. That is to say, God would have made another man rather than a woman.

Furthermore, if God had made Adam another man, to be his help mate, there would have been no means for mankind to multiply. Nor would there have been a way for the saviour to come forth in the fullness of times, to reconcile mankind back to God, at a latter time.

> **27 So God created man in his own image, in the image of God created he him; male and female created he them.**
>
> **28 And God blessed them, and God said unto them, Be fruitful, and multiply, and replenish the earth, and subdue it: and have dominion over the fish of the sea, and over the fowl of the air, and over every living thing that moveth upon the earth.**

Ge 1:27-28.

In the above passage we see God saying to 'them', both the man and the woman, to be fruitful, multiply, replenish, subdue, and have dominion over the earth and all they and it that dwell therein. Because Adam had lost part of himself, but had regained himself in the physical, separate body of his wife, Eve, it was mandatory that the woman, Eve, work along side of him.

Moreover, we know that the reason the woman was created from man was because God was not satisfied with the man working alone. The responsibilities given to both the man and the woman were commandments of God and not the desires and aspirations of the man nor the woman. And, as commandments of God, neither the man nor the woman were then nor are they now required to seek permission from man to do what thus saith the Lord. Centuries latter, even the holy Apostles would answer the rulers, by declaring,

> **...We ought to obey God rather than men.**

Ac 5:29.

Adam and his wife, Eve, lived and enjoyed each other as adults, in a state of innocence and without sin. They existed as two necessary parts required to make up the whole, the one flesh, serving God. The record contained in the Word of God reveals no problem with or within the marriage between Adam and Eve as long as they walked along beside each other as one flesh. The problem showed up only after the second part of the one flesh, Eve, the woman, began walking in front of the man, Adam. *(Ge 3:1-6)* In Genesis 3:6, Eve the second part of the one flesh, makes a unilateral decision that profoundly and negatively impacts upon the complete one flesh. The one flesh consisted of both Adam and Eve, the husband and the wife. Eve was made to help the one flesh that had once resided within one, physical body, in Adam. *(Ge 2:18, 24)* She could not help Adam and therefore, the one flesh, unless there was communication between them, as to what was needed, required and desired. As discussed earlier, before Eve was created, Adam possessed all of the abilities within himself and had no other human being to communicate with. With Eve, he still possessed all of the abilities, not within himself, but within the one flesh.

Therefore, bound up and part of the one flesh is the need and requirement of communication between the two parts, husband and wife, Adam and Eve. Communication was—is required because, when the one flesh resided within the one, single body of Adam, every time Adam made a decision all of him was present, knew the decision made and took part in performing whatever task was required. The rib that God took out of Adam *(Ge 2:21-23)*, and later made into a woman, was always with Adam, even from his creation. Every time Adam sat down, the rib sat with him. When he fed himself, the rib was fed and nourished also. When Adam lay down to sleep, the rib laid down with him. He never said any word or performed any act that resulted in hurt or harm to the rib, because the rib was part of his own flesh.

> **29 For no man ever yet hated his own flesh; but nourisheth and cherisheth it, even as the Lord the church:**
>
> **30 For we are members of his body of his flesh, and of his bones.**

> **31 For this cause shall a man leave his father and mother, and shall be joined unto his wife, and they two shall be one flesh.**
>
> **32 This is a great mystery...**

Eph 5:29-32.

The Word of God teaches us that Eve was beguiled *(Ge 3:13; 2Co 11:3)* by the serpent. That is, she was tricked and deceived. For, the serpent said unto Eve,

> **4 ...Ye shall not surely die:**
>
> **5 For God doth know that in the day ye eat thereof, then your eyes shall be opened, and ye shall be as gods, knowing good and evil.**

Ge 3:4-5.

The part of the one flesh that Eve possessed did not see or understand the trick, the play on words, the half truth and half lie, that the serpent had put before her. Eve did not understand because she had not yet acquired the wisdom needed to deal with the serpent, one on one. Eve had not walked with God as long as Adam had and therefore she was weaker, both in physical body strength and as well as in the strength of spiritual understanding. *(1Pe 3:7; Ge 2:19-20)*

Although Adam and Eve were created on the same numbered day of creation, Day 6, they were not created at the same time. When we consider the fact that time today is not counted as time was counted during the days of the creation; and, that, a thousand years to God is like one day *(Ps 90:4; 2Pe 3:8)*, then, it is easily understood that a very a large amount of time passed between the time Adam began working for God and the time Eve was presented to Adam as his wife.

Before Eve was formed from Adam's rib, Adam had been keeping and dressing the Garden of Eden. *(Ge 2:8, 15)* He also had been naming all of the animals of the world, as God brought them to him, before the woman was created. *(Ge 2:19-20)*

It was during the time that Adam worked alone for God, that God became unsatisfied with the man's solitary, lonely work. God, desiring more praise than one man, Adam, could provide, determined that it was not a good thing for the man to be alone. *(Ge 2:18)* God decided that Adam needed help with the proper performance of the work for which he had been called to do.

Therefore, God separated man, his talents and abilities. Using the separated part, taken by God from the man, he formed the woman. The woman became a necessary part of the whole, the one flesh, which now resided in two physical bodies. The separation of man was the end result of God's determination that the man, Adam, would be required to share the leadership role and the work of replenishing and subduing the earth and exercising dominion and control over all animal life and all other life that moved upon the earth.

We discover in the Word of God, that Adam ruled, that is, he exercised dominion over every living creature on the earth. However, he did not acquire the authority, or the power to rule over or exercise dominion over the woman until after she sinned. *(Ge 2:18-20; Ge 1:28; Ge 3:16)* The scripture is clear on this point. For it says,

> **And God blessed them, and God said unto them, Be fruitful, and multiply, and replenish the earth, and subdue** it: **and have dominion over the fish of the sea, and over the fowl of the air, and over every living thing that moveth upon the earth.**

Ge 1:28.

From this passage of scripture we see that the ruling and exercising of dominion, which is leadership, was a joint power and responsibility, equally engaged in by husband, Adam, and wife, Eve. This joint leadership was for the benefit of, and in praise of God.

Of course, Eve possessed a natural limit of wisdom, knowledge and understanding, because she had not walked with nor worked for God as long as Adam had. Because of her newness in the job, Eve was, by nature required to depend upon and seek out her husband's counsel. And, eventually as time would pass, she would grow into the job. Moreover, since Eve was only the second part of the one flesh, and not the whole, she was required to communicate with the first part about what she was about to do. For her decisions affected not only herself, but the whole of the one flesh. Had she discussed it first with her husband, he could have shared with her, his understanding.

Adam was not tricked or deceived about whether it was good or evil to eat from the tree of the knowledge of good and evil. He knew the complete truth of the matter and had an obligation to inform his wife, Eve, about the truth. *(1Ti 2:14)* Had Eve communicated with Adam before eating from the forbidden tree, she would not have acted upon half truth and half lie. If she would have acted and eaten at all, it would have been with full knowledge and disclosure.

Therefore, we see here, that Eve was first in the transgression against the union of the one flesh, which led to the transgression of God's law and the fall of the man and eventually all of mankind. For the writer declared,

> **13 For Adam was first formed, then Eve.**
> **14 And Adam was not deceived, but the woman being deceived was in the transgression.**

1Ti 2:13-14.

Chapter 16

No. 6: The Commandment to Be Fruitful

And God blessed them, and God said unto them, Be fruitful...
Ge 1:28.

Within the sixth commandment given to mankind we find the Lord God requiring them to produce good works, within their daily lives. For, the word **fruitful** *('früt-fəl)* is translated from **parah** *(paw-raw')* which means to bear fruit, bring forth fruit, cause to be fruitful, make fruitful, grow, increase.

When we review the scriptures we learn that God did not give the commandment to be fruitful until after the woman was created. For, at the time that the Lord God gave the first four commandments he had created only the male of the human species. When God gave the fifth and the sixth commandments he had already created the woman and had given her to the man to be the man's wife *(Ge 2:22-25)* and to be the man's help meet. *(Ge 2:18)* Therefore, now that man had someone to help him in the work of the Lord, he could be much more fruitful in that work. For, before the woman's creation the man worked alone and his report was not as great as it could have been. Commenting on his plight, King Solomon wrote,

8 There is one alone, and there is not a second; yea, he hath neither child nor brother: yet is there no end of all

his labour; neither is his eye satisfied with riches; neither saith he, For whom do I labour, and bereave my soul of good? This is also vanity, yea, it is a sore travail.

9 Two are better than one; because they have a good reward for their labour.

Ec 4:8-9.

Now that there were two sanctified, Spirit filled humans doing the work of the Lord, God was able to obtain more glory and more praise through their spiritual fruitfulness and growth. As the word **fruitful** from the Hebrew **parah** means to grow and increase, we know from the scriptures that the spirit, the inward man grows by using the word of God. As the Apostle admonished the saints centuries later that

As newborn babes, desire the sincere milk of the word, that ye may grow thereby.

1Pe 2:2.

Although Adam was created a grown man, in the flesh, he was yet a newborn babe in the spirit. Because, since he had to ***become*** a living soul *(Ge 2:7),* he could not have been a living soul, or living spirit before he ***became*** it. And therefore, there were things that he had to learn about God and about God's way of holiness that he did not know or understand when he was first created. By desiring and eating the sincere milk of the word of God, which was within the tree of life, man's spirit man grew in the knowledge and understanding of God and his ways. For, the Lord said

8 ... my thoughts are not your thoughts, neither are your ways my ways, saith the Lord.

9 For as the heavens are higher than the earth, so are my ways higher than your ways, and my thoughts than your thoughts.

Isa 55:8-9.

Because of this higher standard in his ways and his thoughts, God set out to teach his son Adam. For, it was necessary to wean Adam off the milk if he was to become an effective keeper and watchman for the Lord God. As the prophet Isaiah stated,

> **9 Whom shall he teach knowledge? And whom shall he make to understand doctrine? Them that are weaned from the milk, and drawn from the breasts.**
>
> **10 For precept must be upon precept, precept upon precept; line upon line, line upon line; here a little, and there a little:**

Isa 28:9-10.

It was necessary that God should teach Adam so that he would be able to eat the strong meat of the tree of life, and thereby be enabled to teach others.

> **13 For every one that useth milk is unskillful in the word of righteousness: for he is a babe.**
>
> **14 But strong meat belongeth to them that are of full age, even those who by reason of use have their senses exercised to discern both good and evil.**

Heb 5:13-14.

Here, we see that a person can discern both good and evil by eating and using the strong meat of the word of God which exercises their senses. Therefore, it was not necessary for Adam to experience good and evil by eating from the tree that possessed its knowledge in order to know what it was. It was only necessary for Adam to discern what was good and evil by eating the strong meat of the word. For, the word **discern** *(dĭ-sûrn'),* taken from the Greek **diakrisis** *(dee-ak'-ree-sis)* means judicial estimation; discern, disputation. This word **diakrisis** is taken from the word **diakrino** *(dee-ak-ree'-no)* which means to separate thoroughly; to withdraw from or oppose; to discriminate, decide, hesitate; contend, make difference, discern, doubt, judge, be partial. Finally, the English word, **discern** means to perceive with the eyes or mind; to recognize as separate and different; to distinguish or discriminate something.

The Challenge in Life

So, when we reconsider the fourth commandment to not eat of the tree of the knowledge of good and evil *(Ge 2:17),* and the commandment to eat from every other tree that was in the garden of Eden, including the tree of life *(Ge 2:9, 16),* we have a clearer picture of the why. Because, God, being Adams creator and father wanted to teach Adam himself what was good and what was evil. This teaching started with Adam's receiving the neshamah (breath) of life *(Ge 2:7)* and Adam becoming a living soul. *(Ge 2:7)* The teaching continued with Adam's maintenance and tending to life by his eating from life, which was bound up in a tree that was in the midst of the garden of Eden, called the tree of life. *(Ge 2:9)* For, within the tree of life was the wisdom, knowledge and understanding of the Word of God. Because, we know that

> **1 In the beginning was the Word, and the Word was with God, and the Word was God.**
> **2 The same was in the beginning with God.**
> **3 All things were made by him; and without him was not any thing made that was made.**
> **4 In him was life; and the life was the light of men. Joh 1:1-4.**

Therefore, within this tree was the power of God, life itself. And, for man to be fruitful in God, in his spirit, inward man, it was necessary for man to grow up in him *"...unto a perfect man, unto the measure of the stature of the fullness of Christ". (Eph 4:13b)* For, life is in Christ, and it was Christ, as the power of God, the wisdom of God *(1Co 1:24)* that would allow man to maintain life. And so, man's challenge was to be fruitful by growing up into a perfect man into the fullness of

Christ, by learning to discern and to discriminate between good and evil. Man would learn to do this by eating from the word of God, found within the tree of life, rather than by experiencing it carnally in the flesh by eating from the tree of the knowledge of good and evil.

Learn to live by eating from the tree of life or learn to live by eating from the tree of the knowledge of good and evil—this was man's test—the challenge in life.

For, knowledge gained from the forbidden tree would cause man to become spiritually carnal and the enmity of God, not subject to the commandment or the law of God. *(Ro 8:6-7)* And knowledge gained from the tree of life through the thirst for righteousness *(Mt 5:6)* would cause out of his belly to *'...flow rivers of living water..."* tending to life. *(Joh 7:37-39.* ***Read also*** *Re 22:1-2, 17; Joh:4:10, 13-14; Re 21:6; Isa 12:3; Isa 43:18-21; Isa 55:1-13)* Therefore, knowledge gained from the tree of the knowledge of good and evil is carnal knowledge leading to death. *(Ro 8:6)*

Thus, as long as man continued in the Spirit and maintained life the fruit that he would produce would be fruit of the Spirit, which is

22 ...love, joy, peace, longsuffering, gentleness, goodness, faith,

23 Meekness, temperance: against such there is no law.

Ga 5:22-23.

However, on the day that man would stop tending to life and decide to experience good and evil by eating from the tree of the knowledge of good and evil, then he would become carnal, walking in spiritual death, being mindful only of the things of the flesh. *(Ro 8:5)*

For to be carnally minded is death...

Ro 8:6a.

And so, the fruit that man would produce by his works while walking in the flesh, would all be in death. For,

19 ...the works of the flesh are manifest, which are these; Adultery, fornication, uncleanness, lasciviousness,

20 Idolatry, witchcraft, hatred, variance, emulations, wrath, strife, seditions, heresies,

21 Envyings, murders, drunkenness, revellings, and such like...

Ga 5:19-21a.

The Mystery Of Fruitfulness

To get a clearer understanding of what it means to be fruitful in God and to grow up in him, we can review the *Mysteries of the Kingdom of God (Lu 8:9-10)*, relating to fruitfulness, as they were taught by Jesus Christ. For, he said,

Fruit of the Lips

33 Either make the tree good, and his fruit good; or else make the tree corrupt, and his fruit corrupt: for the tree is known by his fruit.

34 O generation of vipers, how can ye, being evil, speak good things? for out of the abundance of the heart the mouth speaketh.

35 A good man out of the good treasure of the heart bringeth forth good things: and an evil man out of the evil treasure bringeth forth evil things.

> **36 But I say unto you, That every idle word that men shall speak, they shall give account thereof in the day of judgment.**

Mt 12:33-36 *(Read also Lu 6:43-45).*

Here, in this Matthew 12:33-36 passage, the Lord lets us know that what is in a man's heart shall come out of his mouth. If what he has placed in his heart is good then his mouth will speak good things and if his heart is full of evil things, then, the fruit of his lips will be evil things. But regardless of whether the fruit of the lips is good or evil, the speaking fruit bearer shall give an account for his fruit. For the word **account** *(ə-kount')*, here, is translated from the Greek **logos** *(log'-os).* **Logos** means something said (including the thought); a topic or subject of discourse; reasoning or motive; a computation, account. The word **account** means to provide a reckoning; give a rational explanation (with, for); answer, be responsible; a narrative or record of events.

Therefore, if man's lips shall bear fruit, he shall be responsible for giving a reason for the words used—whether they were for good or for evil.

False Prophets and Leaders

> **15 Beware of false prophets, which come to you in sheep's clothing, but inwardly they are ravening wolves.**
>
> **16 Ye shall know them by their fruits. Do men gather grapes of thorns, or figs of thistles?**
>
> **17 Even so every good tree bringeth forth good fruit; but a corrupt tree bringeth forth evil fruit.**
>
> **18 A good tree cannot bring forth evil fruit, neither can a corrupt tree bring forth good fruit.**
>
> **19 Every tree that bringeth not forth good fruit is hewn down, and cast into the fire.**
>
> **20 Wherefore by their fruits ye shall know them.**

21 Not every one that saith unto me Lord, Lord, shall enter into the kingdom of heaven; but he that doeth the will of my Father which is in heaven.

22 Many will say to me on that day, Lord, Lord, have we not prophesied in thy name? and in thy name have cast out devils? And in thy name done many wonderful works?

23 And then will I profess unto them, I never knew you: depart from me, ye that work iniquity.

Mt 7:15-23.

In this Matthew 7:15-23 passage Jesus discusses the fruit of the leaders of the church. This passage teaches that if a leader fails to do the will of the Father, then Jesus does not know him and that all of his works, his fruit produced for the kingdom of God are works and the fruit of iniquity. This is so, even if the works involved casting out devils and preaching and prophesying in the name of Jesus. Because, without receiving the indwelling Spirit of Christ within you, which is the will of the Father, you are none of his. *(Ro 8:9)* For, the Father announced his will for man in the beginning when he said, *"...Let us make man in our image, after our likeness..." (Ge 1:26a)*

So God created man in his own image, in the image of God created he him; male and female created he them.

Ge 1:27.

And the Lord God formed man of the dust of the ground, and breathed into his nostrils the breath of life; and man became a living soul.

Ge 2:7.

Thus, we see the will of God the Father, for man, is to live and exist in God's image and after his likeness. For, when God breathed the neshamah (breath) of life into the man he became a living soul which is *a* living spirit as God is *the* living Spirit. *(Joh 4:24)* Therefore, the church leaders discussed in the Matthew 7:15-23 passage above, although they had performed many wonderful works on behalf of the kingdom of God, they themselves never did become a part of the kingdom of God, because Jesus said that he 'never **knew**' them. Of course the word **knew**, here, is not knowing like one knows a fact or knows that a thing exist. But rather, this knowing is as a husband, Jesus, knows his bride, the bride of Christ, the Church. For, the writer declared

> **But ye are not in the flesh, but in the Spirit, if so be that the Spirit of God dwell in you. Now if any man have not the Spirit of Christ, he is none of his.**

Ro 8:9.

Thus, without having received, within his physical body, the neshamah (breath) of life *(Read Ac 2:38),* which is the Spirit of Christ that changes us into the image of the Lord *(2Co 3:18),* a leader has not done the will of the Father in his own life, and he has not entered into the kingdom of God. The bridegroom, Jesus, has not entered the bride—the leader—and consummated the marriage. That is, if Jesus has not entered the leader as the Comforter, the indwelling Holy Ghost *(Read Joh 14:26),* then the leader has not entered into the kingdom of God. In agreement, the Lord

> **5 Jesus answered, Verily, verily I say unto thee, Except a man be born of water and of the Spirit, he cannot enter into the kingdom of God.**
>
> **6 That which is born of the flesh is flesh; and that which is born of the Spirit is spirit.**

Joh 3:5-6.

Being born of the Spirit is the act or event of receiving the Holy Ghost into one's physical body. For, Jesus, after he breathed on his disciples, including the Apostle Peter, commanded them to *'...Receive ye the Holy Ghost'. (Joh 20:22)* And, on the day of Pentecost, after he had obeyed Jesus' command to receive the indwelling Holy Ghost himself *(Read Acts 2:1-4, 5-37),*

> **Then Peter said unto them, Repent, and be baptized every one of you in the name of Jesus Christ for the remission of sins, and ye shall receive the gift of the Holy Ghost.**

Ac 2:38.

And, after Peter told the people how to enter into the kingdom of God, into the church, we learn later that some obeyed because,

> **41 Then they that gladly received his word were baptized: and the same day there were** *added unto them about three thousand souls.*
>
> **...**
>
> **44 And all that believed were together, and had all things common;**
>
> **...**
>
> **47 Praising God, and having favour with all the people. And the Lord** *added to the church daily such as should be saved.*

Ac 2:44, 47 *(Emphasis added).*

Thus we see from the Acts 2:38, 41, 44 and 47 passages of scripture above, that when we grow spiritually God increases our spiritual oversight and work by drawing more people (souls) to Him. For, surely no one can come to Christ except the Father draws him. As Jesus said,

> **No man can come to me, except the Father which hath sent me draw him:...**

Joh 6:44a.

And when He draws the souls to Him he gives us someone to pastor, to perfect, to build up and to edify. *(See Eph 4:11-15)* But, except we remain in Jesus we can do nothing. And so, the fruit that is added in our fruitfulness is spiritual fruit. That is, they are added to the spiritual church, the kingdom of God, the body of Christ; and not just to the membership roll or attendance roster belonging to the local church building. While discussing fruitfulness, the Lord Jesus declared,

> **1 I am the true vine, and my Father is the husbandman.**
>
> **...**
>
> **4 Abide in me, and I in you. As the branch cannot bear fruit of itself, except it abide in the vine; no more can ye, except ye abide in me.**
>
> **5 I am the vine, ye are the branches: He that abideth in me, and I in him, the same bringeth forth much fruit: for without me ye can do nothing.**
>
> **...**
>
> **7 If ye abide in me, and my words abide in you, ye shall ask what ye will, and it shall be done unto you.**
>
> **8 Herein is my Father glorified, that ye bear much fruit; so shall ye be my disciples.**

Joh 15:1, 4-5, 7-8.

Meeting the Challenge

When we review the scriptures, we learn that no one was added to the church until after the apostles **(1)** abided, **(2)** remained in Christ and **(3)** grew in Him on the day of Pentecost after they received the indwelling gift of the Holy Ghost. For, Peter stood up with the eleven other apostles and preached to the people *(Read Ac 2:14-40)* after they had received the Holy Ghost. *(Ac 2:1-13)* And, after Peter had said many things to them,

Now when they heard this, they were pricked in their heart, and said unto Peter and to the rest of the apostles, Men and brethren, what shall we do?

Ac 2:37.

Then Peter said unto them, Repent, and be baptized every one of you in the name of Jesus Christ for the remission of sins, and ye shall receive the gift of the Holy Ghost.

Ac 2:38.

Then they that gladly received his word were baptized: and the same day there were added unto them about three thousand souls.

Ac 2:41.

So, we see from the above scriptures that as the apostles grew in Christ spiritually, their fruitfulness increased. And the fruit was spiritual fruit because the scripture did not say three thousand people were added to their number, but that three thousand souls were added. The soul is a spirit and therefore spiritual. So their fruit was spiritual fruit.

The Sower's Four Fruitfulness Types

5 A sower went out to sow his seed: and as he sowed, some fell by the way side; and it was trodden down, and the fowls of the air devoured it.

6 And some fell upon a rock; and soon as it was sprung up, it withered away, because it lacked moisture.

7 And some fell among thorns; and the thorns sprang up with it, and choked it.

8 And other fell on good ground, and sprang up, and bare fruit an hundredfold...

9 And his disciples asked him, saying, What might this parable be?

10 And he said, Unto you it is given to know the mysteries of the kingdom of God: but to others in parables; THAT SEEING THEY MIGHT NOT SEE, AND HEARING THEY MIGHT NOT UNDERSTAND.

11 Now the parable is this: The seed is the word of God.

12 Those by the way side are they that hear; then cometh the devil, and taketh away the word out of their hearts, lest they should believe and be saved.

13 They on the rock are they, which, when they hear, receive the word with joy; and these have no root, which for a while believe, and in time of temptation fall away.

14 And that which fell among thorns are they, which, when they have heard, go forth, and are choked with cares and riches and pleasures of this life, and bring no fruit to perfection.

15 But that on the good ground are they, which in an honest and good heart, having heard the word, keep it, and bring forth fruit with patience.

Lu 8:5-15.

In this Luke 8:5-15 passage, the Lord Jesus reveals a portion of the Mysteries of the Kingdom of God relating to being fruitful. This Mystery of Fruitfulness is divided into four different areas, namely: **(1)** The Wayside Seed; **(2)** The Rocky, No Root, No Moisture Seed; **(3)** The Seed Among Thorns; and **(4)** The Good Ground Seed.

The Wayside Seed

Jesus said,

> **5 A sower went out to sow his seed: and as he sowed, some fell by the way side; and it was trodden down, and the fowls of the air devoured it.**
>
> …
>
> **12 Those by the way side are they that hear; then cometh the devil, and taketh away the word out of their hearts, lest they should believe and be saved.**

Lu 8:5, 12.

The wayside seed reveals the mystery behind why it is difficult for the preacher, the sower of the word of God, to produce much fruit in his hometown, due to the attitudes of the towns people and kinfolk who know of him and his life from birth, before he became a preacher. For, many will set out to kill his influence by slander. As Jesus said on another occasion,

> **…A prophet is not without honour, but in his own country, and among his own kin, and in his own house.**

Mk 6:4 *(Read Mt 13:57; Joh 4:44).*

The Lord said that while the sower sowed, some of the seed, which is the word of God, fell by the wayside. When we consider this point we realize that the sower, who is a preacher planting the word of God, had to leave his home to travel to the place that possessed the good ground. From his home to the good ground the preacher had to pass by the wayside ground, the rocky ground and the thorny ground. The problem with the wayside ground was that someone who knew of the preacher took the word of God that the wayside soul had heard and received—out of the wayside soul's heart. The important question here is,

"How is it possible that the devil, a person, is able to take the word of God out of a person's heart?"

The answer is hidden in the phrase **'the devil'**. The phrase 'the devil' in Luke 8:12 does not refer to a demon, but rather it refers to a specific weapon of warfare used by Lucifer against God and against the kingdom of God. For, the word **devil** *(dĕv'əl),* here, is translated from the Greek word **diabolos** *(dee-ab'-ol-os).* **Diabolos** means a traducer; false accuser, devil, slanderer. The word **traducer** *(tre-doos'-er)* means one who defames, disgraces, slanders and vilifies the name and—or character of another person. To **slander** *(slăn'dər)* means to speak defamatory statements injurious to the reputation or well being of a person; a malicious statement or report. For, we know that

> **Death and life are in the power of the tongue: and they that love it shall eat the fruit thereof.**

Pr 18:21.

The goal of the traducing Devil in Jesus' parable about the wayside fruit was to kill the influence, name and character of the sower, preacher. If the preacher's character is destroyed, then, the wayside soul, the unbeliever, that received the word without understanding *(Mt 13:19),* could not believe the word of God and be saved. We know this is the traducing Devil's purpose because Jesus said,

> **...then cometh the devil** *(the traducer, the slanderer)*, **and taketh away the word out of their hearts, lest they should believe and be saved."**

Lu 8:12 *(Words in brackets added).*

The way and manner by which the traducing, slandering devil was able to take the word out of the wayside soul's heart was by causing the wayside soul to think negatively about the preacher that gave (sowed) him the word. And the member of the body that he, the devil, the slanderer, uses is hell's tongue. *(Jas 3:5-6)* For,

> **...the tongue is a fire, a world of iniquity: so is the tongue among our members, that it defileth the whole body, and setteth on fire the course of nature; and it is set on fire of hell.**

Jas 3:6.

For

> **8 ...the tongue can no man tame; it is an unruly evil, full of deadly poison.**
>
> **9 Therewith bless we God, even the Father; and therewith curse we men, which are made after the similitude of God.**
>
> **10 Out of the same mouth proceedeth blessing and cursing. My brethren, these things ought not so to be.**

Jas 3:8-10.

Thus, the wayside soul was prevented from believing the Word of God, because, due to the preacher's name, or character being slandered, the wayside soul was prevented from believing in the preacher, or to even seek the preacher out and ask the preacher what the Word of God meant that had been sowed—as the Ethiopian eunuch had done in Acts chapter 8, verses 26 through 39. *(Read Acts 8:26-39)* For, there, the Ethiopian Eunuch was returning from a worship service in Jerusalem *(Ac 8:27-28),* where he had heard the Word of God. But, in hearing he did not get an understanding of the Word that had been sowed into his heart. *(Ac 8:30-31)* So, the Ethiopian eunuch stopped along the wayside, beside the road and was reading the sowed Word *(Ac 8:28),* as written in Isaiah chapter 53, verses 7 and 8. *(Ac 8:32-33)* Before the devil could take the sowed Word out of his heart the Lord Jesus 'rescued' the Word through another sower, harvester, teacher, preacher. For,

29 Then the Spirit said unto Philip, Go near, and join thyself to this chariot.

30 And Philip ran thither to him, and heard him read the prophet E-sa'-ias, and said, Understandest thou what thou readest?

31 And he said, How can I, except some man should guide me? And he desired Philip that he would come up and sit with him.

Ac 8:29-31.

So, here, we learn that the Ethiopian eunuch, even though he was a man *"...of great authority under Candace queen of the Ethiopians, who had the charge of all her treasure..." (Ac 8:27),* he had not understood the Word when it was sowed and when he heard it. He realized that he needed someone to teach and guide him in the Word of God, so he asked the preacher, the evangelist, Philip *(Ac 21:8)* to get up in the chariot to teach and explain the Word of God to him. Because, the word **desired** *(di-zīr′d)* in the phrase *"he desired Philip that he would come up and sit with him" (Ac 8:31),* means to invite, invoke, intreat, having been translated from the Greek word **parakaleo** *(par-ak-al-eh'-o).*

So, after the Ethiopian eunuch heard the Word from the first sower without receiving the understanding, the Lord Jesus allowed him to get out of town and out into the desert *(Ac 8:26-28)* where no one else was and where no one could traduce the first sower. Then the Lord sent a second labourer to water the seeds that had been sowed, because, he that planted and sowed the seed and he that latter watered the planted seed were both labourers together with God. *(1Co 3:8-9)* For, the writer declared in agreement, in another place, that one planted, and another watered, but it is God that giveth the increase. *(1Co 3:6-7; Read also 1Co 3:8-10)*

Philip's presence gave the Ethiopian eunuch the opportunity to ask for assistance in understanding the sowed seed. And when asked, by the Ethiopian Eunuch *(Ac 8:30-31),* Philip watered the sowed seed with understanding *(Read Ac 8:32-35)* which caused the

Ethiopian eunuch to believe the Word of God unto salvation. *(Ac 8:36-39)* Now, that the Ethiopian had acquired an understanding of the sowed and planted Word the devil, Satan was not able to take the Word out of his heart. For,

> **36 ...as they went on their way, they came unto a certain water: and the eunuch said, See, here is water; what doth hinder me to be baptized?**
>
> **37 And Philip said, If thou believest with all thine heart, thou mayest. And he answered and said, I believe that Jesus Christ is the Son of God.**
>
> **38 And he commanded the chariot to stand still: and they went down both into the water, both Philip and the eunuch; and he baptized him.**
>
> **39 And when they were come up out of the water, the Spirit of the Lord caught away Philip, that the eunuch saw him no more: and he went on his way rejoicing.**

Ac 8:36-39.

Now, when we compare the Ethiopian eunuch, sitting on the wayside reading the sowed word, with the wayside soul in Jesus' parable we learn that, unlike the wayside soul in the parable, Satan did not get an opportunity to withstand the Word heard by the eunuch. And, the devil did not get an opportunity to traduce the sower, the preacher that planted and sowed the Word into the eunuch's hearing. But, with the wayside soul seed planting, we see how that the wayside soul was prevented from acquiring an understanding of the Word because he could not believe the Word of God coming from the mouth of a disgraced and defamed preacher. For, Satan, as the traducing devil, had traduced him. And as such, this traducing prevented the wayside soul from asking for guidance from the traduced preacher in order to acquire an understanding of the Word, sowed and planted into his hearing. So, as the word **hear** *(hîr)* in the Luke 8:12 verse is translated from **akouo** *(ak-oo'-o)* which means to hear; give audience; come to the ears, the wayside soul did indeed hear the Word with his fleshly, natural ears. But, he never received an understanding of that Word. And thus, the wayside soul seed planting was unfruitful and unprofitable to the kingdom of heaven.

Partnering With a Word Stealing Thief

Thus, as a thief, the devil can steal and take away the hearer's joy of the Word when he kills the preacher's influence by slandering his name, reputation and character. In doing so, Satan thereby destroys the hearer's chance, at that time, to receive salvation and deliverance from the bondage of sin. Because, Satan knows that the hearer cannot be saved without the preacher. As it is written,

> **13 For whosoever shall call upon the name of the Lord shall be saved.**
>
> **14 How then shall they call on him in whom they have not believed? and how shall they believe in him of whom they have not heard? and how shall they hear without a preacher?**

Ro 10:13-14.

> **For…it pleased God by the foolishness of preaching to save them that believe.**

1Co 1:21b.

So, the enemy, Satan, realizes that if he can neutralize and make irrelevant the preacher in the lives, hearts and minds of men then he can keep those unbelieving souls from leaving the power of his worldwide kingdom of iniquity. Therefore, Satan seeks out partners to become the devil, diabolos the traducer, to partner with him in using their vocal chords and their tongues to become busybodies, talebearers and whisperers, knowing that God has commanded us saying,

> **Thou shalt not go up and down as a talebearer among thy people...**

Le 19:16a.

And that,

> **He that goeth about as a talebearer revealeth secrets: therefore meddle not with him that flattereth with his lips.**

Pr 20:19.

> **A talebearer revealeth secrets: but he that is of a faithful spirit concealeth the matter.**

Pr 11:13.

Thus, our enemy partners with various members of mankind to assist him in maintaining the captivity of mankind. For, the word **talebearer** *(tāl-ber´-ər)* in Leviticus 19:16a, Proverbs 20:19 and Proverbs 11:13 is translated from **rakiyl** *(raw-keel'),* which means a scandal-monger (as traveling about); slander, carry tales, talebearer. Therefore, the admonition from the Lord is that we should not become a person that travels about carrying and repeating slanders, tales and scandals about our neighbors. But, rather we should be found of a faithful spirit by concealing the matter *(Pr 11:13; Pr 19:11; Pr 29:11)*, that we might win a soul. For, we are to love our neighbor as we love ourselves. *(Mt 19:19)* And we would not spread scandals or slanderous tales about ourselves to others.

When we use our tongue to utter a slander to defame and diminish the name, character and reputation of another person we have partnered with Satan and have become a diabolos, traducer, and a fool that hates his own soul. For,

> **Whoso is partner with a thief hateth his own soul: he heareth cursing, and bewrayeth it not.**

Pr 29:24.

And,

He that hideth hatred with lying lips, and he that uttereth a slander, is a fool.

Pr 10:18.

Here, to **partner** *(pärt′-nər)* with Satan, the thief, in Proverbs 29:24 is to **chalaq** *(khaw-lak')* in the Hebrew, meaning to be smooth; to apportion or separate; deal, distribute, divide, flatter, give, have part, have partner; take away a portion, receive, separate self, be smooth (er). Thus, the person who becomes a traducing devil with Satan actually thinks he is a smooth dealer and flatterer, because he refuses to reveal or bewray the truth that he has traduced and slandered his fellow man in the hearing of another. For, to **bewray**, taken from **nagad** *(naw-gad),* means to front, to stand boldly out opposite; to manifest; to announce (always by word of mouth to one present); to expose, predict, explain, praise; bewray, certify, declare, denounce, expound, messenger, profess, rehearse, report, shew (forth), speak, tell, utter. Thus, the partnering talebearer, traducer and slanderer does not reveal to the hearer the truth concerning the thief's intent to kill, steal and destroy the preacher's influence when he slanders and traduces the preacher.

Furthermore, a talebearer brings and maintains strife in the body of Christ thereby hindering the saving and deliverance of souls out of the kingdom of Satan. As it is written,

For where envying and strife is, there is confusion and every evil work

Jas 3:16.

And,

Where no wood is, there the fire goeth out: so where there is no talebearer, the strife ceaseth.

Pr 26:20.

Because,

The words of a talebearer are as wounds, and they go down into the innermost parts of the belly.

Pr 18:8 *(Read also Pr 26:22-28).*

And here, in the Proverbs 18:8 and the Proverbs 26:20 passages, the word **talebearer** is derived from **nirgan** *(neer-gawn)* meaning to roll to pieces, a slanderer; a talebearer, whisperer. Whispering, so that others with truth cannot hear, is a very effective method of name, reputation and character assassination used by the strife bringing talebearer. For, King David said,

All that hate me whisper together against me: against me do they devise my hurt.

Ps 41:7.

And his son, King Solomon, wrote

...a whisperer separateth chief friends.

Pr 16:28b.

And,

He that covereth a transgression seeketh love; but he that repeateth a matter separateth very friends.

Pr 17:9.

And finally, as it was with the Hebrews, so it is with the church wherein the apostles, on occasion, had to admonish the wrongdoing talebearers, busybodies and tattlers within the congregations, saying,

But let none of you suffer as a murderer, or as a thief, or as an evildoer, or as a busybody in other men's matters.

1Pe 4:15.

For we hear that there are some which walk among you disorderly, working not at all, but are busybodies. 2Th 3:11.

And withal they learn to be idle, wandering about from house to house; and not only idle, but tattlers also and busybodies, speaking things which they ought not. 1Ti 5:13.

Thus, we learn from 1Peter 4:15 that some of the saints had become a **busybody** *(biz'-ē-bad'-ē)* and in the Greek an **allotriepiskopos** *(allot-ree-ep-is'-kop-os)* overseeing other's affairs; a meddler; a busybody in other men's matters. In 2Thessalonians members in the congregation had hard working **busybodies** as a Greek **periergazomai** *(per-ee-er-gad'-zom-ahee)* working all around; bustling and hurrying about medd-ling and doing the work of a busybody. And in 1Timothy 5:13 some had become Greek **periergos** *(per-ee'-er-gos)* **busybodies** working all around, even engaging in curious arts and magic, and being officiously meddlesome and overbearingly so offering unwanted advice and services to others; all the while being a Greek **phluaros** *(floo'-ar-os)* which is a **tattler** *(tat'-lər),* a prater, a garrulous person that talk much and a lot especially about unimportant things. This ought not to be in the church.

Amen.

The Rocky, No Root, No Moisture Seed

Unlike the wayside soul, the seed that fell upon a rock did spring up with some understanding. But the joy and zeal that the rocky, no root, no moisture soul started out with passed away by and by. For, Jesus said of him,

And some fell upon a rock; and as soon as it was sprung up, it withered away, because it lacked moisture. Lu 8:6.

Explaining further, He said,

5 Some fell upon stony places, where they had not much earth: and forthwith they sprung up, because they had no deepness of earth:

6 And when the sun was up, they were scorched; and because they had no root, they withered away.

Mt 13:5-6 *(Read also Mk 4:5-6).*

This portion of the Sower's parable reveals the mystery behind why many start out with the Lord with joy and great zeal, enduring for a while. But, later they are found to have given up on God and true holiness. They fall away from Christ and the apostolic way because they, having little understanding, no depth or deepness in the mysteries of God and His kingdom, spring up and 'go out—went out to do a work', rather than being 'sent out to do a work', possessing only a zeal that is not according to knowledge. As the Apostle stated, concerning another zealous group,

2 ...I bear them record that they have a zeal of God, but not according to knowledge.

3 For they being ignorant of God's righteousness, and going about to establish their own righteousness, have not submitted themselves unto the righteousness of God. Ro 10:2-3.

So, although they have joy and zeal and are believers in Christ Jesus so that the signs of a believer follow them, yet they are not sent by God to do or perform the work that they are engaged in for the kingdom. Because, as of yet, although they do believe, they have no deepness of earth, of wisdom, knowledge and understanding of God and his ways in them. Therefore, they have no root deep enough into God and his righteousness to maintain the proper moisture needed to lean on and rely on when the sun's tribulation and persecuting heat bears down upon them. For, every man's work must be tried by the fire. *(1Pe 1:7)* And so, the sunrise of trouble, temptation, tribulation and persecution test their steadfastness, their work and their understanding of the ways and will of God. As Jesus said,

> **20 ...[H]e that received the seed into stony places, the same is he that heareth the word, and anon with joy receiveth it;**
>
> **21 Yet hath he not root in himself, but endureth for a while: for when tribulation or persecution ariseth because of the word, by and by he is offended.**

Mt 13:20-21.

Again,

> **They on the rock are they, which, when they hear, receive the word with joy; and these have no root, which for a while believe, and in time of temptation fall away.**

Lu 8:13.

Further,

> **5 And some fell on stony ground, where it had not much earth; and immediately it sprang up, because it had no depth of earth:**
>
> **6 But when the sun was up, it was scorched; and because it had no root, it withered away.**
>
> **...**
>
> **16 And these are they likewise which are sown on stony ground; who when they have heard the word, immediately receive it with gladness;**

17 And have no root in themselves, and so endure but for a time: afterward, when affliction or persecution ariseth for the word's sake, immediately they are offended.
Mk 4:5-6, 16-17.

This group of rocky, no root, no moisture souls are those believers who are impatient and fail to wait on their ministry. For we are admonished

...let us wait on our ministering...
Ro 12:7.

But, since the gifts of the kingdom work within them as believers they, through their zeal and joy, set out to do a work for the Lord God, not according to knowledge, but according to their zeal and joy. As the Lord Jesus stated,

17 And these signs shall follow them that believe; in my name shall they cast out devils; they shall speak with new tongues;
18 They shall take up serpents; and if they drink any deadly thing, it shall not hurt them; they shall lay hands on the sick, and they shall recover.
Mk 16:17-18.

Therefore, armed with the gifts of the kingdom of heaven, as believers, these rocky, no root, no moisture souls turn their zeal towards working the gifts of the kingdom of heaven, rather than towards an effort to gain an understanding of the ways, will and righteousness of God through studying and searching the scriptures. And, by doing so, many believers violate the admonishing commandment that says,

...[W]ith all thy getting get an understanding.
Pr 4:7b.

But, because they do not wait long enough to get an understanding about the hardness of a good soldier, the rocky, no root, no moisture believers do not acquire the wisdom needed to endure offenses, persecutions and hardships that will come about because of the Word. For, "*Wisdom is before him that hath understanding...*" *(Pr 7:24)* Because, *"In the lips of him that hath understanding wisdom is found..." (Pr 10:13a)* And, *"...a man of understanding hath wisdom." (Pr 10:23b)* Therefore, if the rocky, no root, no moisture souls had waited, studied and learned the ways of God, before going out to work, they would not have failed. For,

> **5 ...[A] wise man's heart discerneth both time and judgment.**
>
> **6 Because to every purpose there is time and judgment...**

Ec 8:5b-6a.

Wisdom and understanding would have taught them to wait until the proper timing least they should suffer the judgment of God. For, by studying the Word of God they would have learned, that, after we have sought out the kingdom of God, and entered into it *(Joh 3:5),* next we should seek *"...his righteousness..." (Mt 6:33),* rather than seeking to immediately spring up to operate the gifts of the kingdom. We seek to know and to do the righteousness of God, first, by studying His Word. For, a person cannot do what he is unaware of. And, as a natural man he is unaware of the righteousness of God because he cannot receive the things of God, as the scriptures declare,

> **11 For what man knoweth the things of a man, save the spirit of man which is in him? even so the things of God knoweth no man, but the Spirit of God.**
>
> **12 Now we have received, not the spirit of the world, but the spirit which is of God; that we might know the things that are freely given to us of God.**

13 Which things also we speak, not in the words which man's wisdom teacheth, but which the Holy Ghost teacheth; comparing spiritual things with spiritual.

14 But the natural man receiveth not the things of the Spirit of God: for they are foolishness unto him: neither can he know them, because they are spiritually discerned.

1Co 2:11-14.

And, in addition and in agreement, the Lord God said,

7 Let the wicked forsake his way, and the unrighteous man his thoughts: and let him return unto the Lord, and he will have mercy upon him; and to our God, for he will abundantly pardon.

8 For my thoughts are not your thoughts, neither are your ways my ways, saith the Lord.

9 For as the heavens are higher than the earth, so are my ways higher than your ways, and my thoughts than your thoughts.

Isa 55:7-9.

After we are made aware of God's requirements in righteousness we then must become doers of it. Because we are admonished to

22 …[B]e ye doers of the word, and not hearers only, deceiving your own selves.

23 For if any be a hearer of the word, and not a doer,

he is like unto a man beholding his natural face in a glass:

24 For he beholdeth himself, and goeth his way, and straightway forgetteth what manner of man he was.

25 But whoso looketh into the perfect law of liberty, and continueth therein, he being not a forgetful hearer,

but a doer of the work, this man shall be blessed in his deed.
Jas 1:22-25.

But, when we, as believers, fail to exercise patience to wait on our ministry, as the rocky soil souls did, we lose our souls when we fall away from the apostolic faith and quit the righteousness of God. For, the Lord Jesus instructs us, that,

In your patience possess ye your souls.
Lu 21:19.

Had the rocky, no root, no moisture souls exercised patience in studying the Word of God to learn of his ways, his will and his righteousness, before they sprung up to go out to do a work for God, they would not have been ashamed latter due to their inability to endure hardness as a good soldier. *(Read 2Ti 2:3)* For, the hardness of a good soldier, in the army of the Lord, includes, among other things, trouble, tribulation, persecution, perplexity, being cast down and being falsely accused. *(Read 2Co 4:8-10)* So, by studying, the rocky soil souls would have gained knowledge and understanding concerning the hardships that are encountered and endured by good soldiers. Therefore, armed with the knowledge of the enemy's coming assaults and offenses, ignorance would not have been the cause for them to be offended when the hardships arose. Studying and acquiring an understanding of the ways, will and righteousness of God forewarns us of the trouble that shall come. For, through their studying they would have learned that,

Many are the afflictions of the righteous: but the Lord delivereth him out of them all.
Ps 34:19.

> **Yea, and all that will live godly in Christ Jesus shall suffer persecution.**

2Ti 3:12.

And, as it was said earlier, every man's faith must be tried with fire. *(1Pe 1:7)* For, the Lord Jesus warned us, saying,

> **1 These things have I spoken unto you, that ye should not be offended.**
>
> **2 They shall put you out of the synagogues: yea, the time cometh, that whosoever killeth you will think that he doeth God service.**
>
> **3 And these things will they do unto you, because they have not known the Father, nor me.**
>
> **4 But these things have I told you, that when the time shall come, ye may remember that I told you of them…**

Joh 16:1-4a.

Here, in this St. John 16:1 passage and in the St. Matthew 13:21 and the St. Mark 4:17 passages of scripture above, the word **offended** *(ə fend′d)* is translated from **skandalizo** *(skan-dal-id'-zo).* **Skandalizo** means to scandalize, to entrap, to trip up, to stumble, to entice to sin, apostasy or displeasure; make to offend. Thus, we learn that the rocky, no root, no moisture souls were scandalized, entrapped, tripped up, made to stumble, were tempted and enticed to sin and did sin becoming a displeasure unto the Lord God due to their lack of knowledge and understanding of the will, ways and righteousness of God. For, their lack of depth and deepness in understanding the mysteries of God caused them to spring up and go out too soon. *(Mk 4:5)* That is, rather than being sent by God after learning of His will and ways, as Saul (Paul) and Barnabas did in Acts chapter 13, verses 1 through 5—by their own will the rocky, no root, no moisture souls went.

Failure: Being Led by a Deceitful Heart

For, they obeyed and were led by the deceitfulness of their own hearts rather than being led by the Spirit of God *(See Ro 8:14),* just as the Prophet Jeremiah warned us saying,

> **The heart is deceitful above all things, and desperately wicked: who can know it?**

Jer 17:9.

In this Jeremiah 17:9 passage the word **heart** *(härt)* is taken from the Hebrew **leb** *(labe)* which means the heart; and figuratively it means the feelings, the will, the intellect; the center of anything. Also, the word **deceitful** *(de-sēt' fəl),* here, is taken from **aqob** *(aw-kobe)* meaning a knoll or swelling up; fraudulent, tracked; crooked, deceitful, polluted. Thus, we learn from the words **heart** and **deceitful** that the will, feelings and intellect of man's flesh is more deceitful, crooked, polluted and fraudulent than anything or anybody else that man has a relationship with. For, since Adam's original sin in the garden of Eden *(Ge 3:6-7),* man's soul has dwelt in the midst of sinful flesh. *(Read Ro 5:12-21)* And, in agreement, the Apostle commented saying,

> **For I know that in me (that is, in my flesh,) dwelleth no good thing: for to will is present with me; but how to perform that which is good I find not.**

Ro 7:18.

So, since there is no good thing in man's flesh, without God, man's desire, feelings, will and intellect are all polluted, crooked, deceitful and fraudulent. For, he does not know how to perform that which is good *(Ro 7:18),* because of **1)** the sin that dwells in him *(Ro 7:17, 20),* and **2)** the law of sin that is present in his mortal flesh. *(Ro 7:23)*

These two things prevent man from seeking out Him who is the only good. And that, Him, is the Lord God. For, only

> **The Lord is good...**

Nah 1:7a.

For example, even when the rich young ruler *(Mk 10:17-22; Lu 18:18-23)* came to the Lord Jesus, and while looking upon Jesus' flesh,

> **...said unto him, Good Master, what good things shall I do, that I may have eternal life?**

Mt 19:16b.

Although the young man honored Jesus, Jesus corrected him saying,

> **...Why callest thou me good? there is none good but one, that is, God...**

Mt 19:17a *(Read Mt 19:16-22).*

Jesus answered him in this manner because the rich young ruler called Jesus good because he was a teacher, a master and not because Jesus was God manifested in the flesh. *(Read 1Ti 3:16; Joh 1:1-3, 14; Ge 1:1)* For, the word **master** *(mas'tər)* in Matthew 19:16 comes from the Greek **didaskalos** *(did-as'-kal-os)* meaning an instructor, doctor, master, teacher. In other words, Jesus' answer meant that being a teacher, doctor or instructor does not make a person good. Because, these attributes of a person does not give him understanding of God and his ways, nor will they cause him to seek after God. And, if God is the only one that is good, then to have any thing that is good in you and to consistently do good in your life—you must come to know God by possessing Him within your physical body. In agreement, King David wrote,

> **2 The Lord looked down from heaven upon the children of men, to see if there were any that did understand, and seek God.**

3 They are all gone aside, they are all together become filthy: there is none that doeth good, no, not one.
Ps 14:2-3 *(Read also Ro 3:9-18).*

And centuries later the Apostle Paul quoted King David writing,

9 What then? are we better than they? No, in no wise: for we have before proved both Jews and Gentiles, that they are all under sin;
10 As it is written, There is none righteous, no, not one:
11 There is none that understandeth, there is none that seeketh after God.
12 They are all gone out of the way, they are together become unprofitable; there is none that doeth good, no, not one.
Ro 3:9-12.

Thus, having gained a personal understanding of what King David meant when he wrote *'that no man seeketh after God, none is righteous and none doeth good' (Ps 14:2-3),* the Apostle Paul explained to us why no man is good, saying,

21 I find then a law, that, when I would do good, evil is present with me.
22 For I delight in the law of God after the inward man:
23 But I see another law in my members, warring against the law of my mind, and bringing me into captivity to the law of sin which is in my members.
Ro 7:21-23.

So, now, realizing that there was no good thing in his flesh—the will, intellect and feelings *(Ro 7:18)*—and that he did not possess within his flesh (the will, intellect and feelings) the understanding as to how to perform that which is good *(Ro 7:18),* Apostle Paul then asked the question,

> **O wretched man that I am! who shall deliver me from the body of this death?**

Ro 7:24.

He then answered the question, that we all may know how not to be led by the deceitfulness of our hearts, saying,

> **I thank God through Jesus Christ our Lord. So then with the mind I myself serve the law of God; but with the flesh the law of sin.**

Ro 7:25.

> **There is therefore now no condemnation to them which are in Christ Jesus, who walk not after the flesh, but after the Spirit.**

Ro 8:1.

Being Led By the Heart's Will to Sacrifice Rather Than the Will to Obey the Commandments of God

For many times, because of the zeal of God *(Ro 10:2)* that believers possess, we go out into the world with a mind, the intent, feelings, will and intellect *'to do good'*, and to do a *'good work'* for God and the kingdom of God. And,*'the good'* that comes from our fleshly will, feelings and intellect often include great, personal sacrifices that lead to our own deception. For, we are deceived when we rationally and intellectually feel and believe that the sacrificing and giving of ourselves for the kingdom's sake, alone, is what makes us *'good Christians'* and therefore by our works we are *'doing good'*. But our good works, alone, cannot save us. Yet, the answering of a good conscience, through obedient faith in the Word of God, will save us. *(Read 1Pe 3:21; Ga 2:16, 20)* Thus, we must be careful not to allow the will of our flesh, through a sincere sacrifice for the work of the kingdom of God, lead us into our own righteousness which is never according to the knowledge and righteousness of God. *(Read Ro 10:2-3)* As the prophet Samuel informed King Saul,

> **22 …Behold, to obey is better than sacrifice, and to hearken than the fat of rams.**
>
> **23 For rebellion is as the sin of witchcraft, and stubbornness is as iniquity and idolatry. Because thou hast rejected the word of the Lord, he hath also rejected thee…**

1Sam 15:22b-23a.

To be delivered from the body of this death *(Ro 7:24)* through Jesus Christ as our Lord *(Ro 7:25),* without condemnation, a believer must walk not after the flesh but after the Spirit *(Ro 8:1)* by being obedient to the Word of God *(1Sam 15:22-23)* and to the words of Christ. For, he said,

> **…the words that I speak unto you, they are spirit, and they are life.**

Joh 6:63b.

So, when we obey the Word of God we are walking in the Spirit and not in the flesh (our will, feelings and intellect).

Testing of the Heart—the Will, Intellect and Feelings

Therefore, to show man where his heart (the will, intellect and feelings) stand with God, and whether he's being led by his heart or by the Spirit of God, God warns us saying

> **I the Lord search the heart, I try the reins, even to give every man according to the fruit of his doings.**

Jer 17:10.

Thus, God searches the secrets of our hearts to let us know whether we are being led by our heart (the flesh) or by the Spirit of God. And, He uses the tempter to search us and try us, because there is no secret that we can hide from the tempter, Lucifer, the anointed angel of God. *(Eze 28:3, 12-15)* For, the word **try** *(trī)* here is taken from the Hebrew **bachan** *(baw-khan)* which means to test; to investigate; examine, prove, tempt, try (trial). And likewise, the word **reins** *(rāns)* is translated from the Hebrew **kilyah** *(kil-yaw')* meaning a kidney (as an essential organ); and figuratively the mind (as the interior self); reins.

So, in the same manner that we are tried and tested to prove our hearts (our will, feelings and intellect) today—so were the rocky, no root, no moisture souls tested in Jesus' parable. And, because their hearts loved the gifts of the Kingdom *(Read Mk 16:17-18)* more than the giver of the gifts *(Eph 4:7-8),* when the trials and temptations arose, because of the word of God, they were offended and quit the righteousness of God *(Mk 4:16-17)* thereby forsaking the Lord who is the fountain of living waters. And, because they forsook God and his ways, God rewarded them according to the fruit of their doings. *(Jer 17:10)* For, Jeremiah declared,

> **O Lord, the hope of Israel, all that forsake thee shall be ashamed, and they that depart from me shall be written in the earth, because they have forsaken the Lord, the fountain of living waters.**

Jer 17:13.

Forsaking the Lord, the fountain of living waters, is forsaking the leading of the Holy Ghost by disobeying the Word of God. Because, the Holy Ghost is the living water as Jesus informed the woman at the well when he said unto her,

> **13 ...Whosoever drinketh of this water shall thirst again.**

14 But whosoever drinketh of the water that I shall give him shall never thirst; but the water that I shall give him shall be in him a well of water springing up into everlasting life.
Joh 4:13-14.

And this well of water that springs up into everlasting life is the same

1 ...pure river of water of life, clear as crystal, proceeding out of the throne of God and of the Lamb.
2 In the midst of the street of it, and on either side of the river, was there the tree of life, which bare twelve manner of fruits, and yielded her fruit every month: and the leaves of the tree were for the healing of the nations.
Re 22:1-2.

Furthermore, the scriptures declare

For as many as are led by the Spirit of God, they are the sons of God.
Ro 8:14.

So, it is possible to be led by our heart (the flesh)—the will, intellect and feelings—or, by the Spirit of Christ. *(Ro 7:25)* If we are to be led by the Spirit of Christ then we must drink his blood and eat his flesh. For only then, will we have life. *(Joh 6:53-58)* To eat his flesh we must obey the Word of God and apply it to our lives. For, again we are reminded that Jesus said, *"...the words that I speak unto you, they are spirit, and they are life." (Joh 6:63b)* The flesh of Jesus Christ is the Word of God. For,

1 In the beginning was the Word, and the Word was with God, and the Word was God.
2 The same was in the beginning with God.
...

14 And the Word was made flesh, and dwelt among us, (and we beheld his glory, the glory as of the only begotten of the Father,) full of grace and truth.

Joh 1:1-2, 14.

Who's Leading: the Flesh or the Spirit of Christ (the Moisture)?

To eat the flesh of Christ, so that we may be lead by Him, requires the Word of God to beome a part of our everyday lives. The desire to obey the Word must become our will as it is His will. It must become our delight and our meditation, both night and day. *(Read Ps 1:1-3; Ps 119:15-16, 24, 35, 41-48)* The Word and the commandments of God, relating to life itself, must become how we feel about things and events in our lives. And when we seek to know and understand life the wisdom, knowledge and understanding of the Word must become our intellect—how we see things and how we view life. *(Read Ps 119:125, 127-128, 130, 133)* For, we must take on and possess the mind of Christ *(Php 2:5; Mt 11:29)*, and show his sufferings in our bodies. *(2Co 1:5-7; 1Pe 4:12-13; Php 3:10)* As the word **led** *(led)* in the Romans 8:14 passage above is translated from the Greek **ago** *(ag-o)* meaning to lead; to bring, drive, go, pass (time) or induce; be, bring (forth), carry, (let) go, keep, lead away, be open—as fruit from the seed of the Most High God, we must be driven and led by Christ through an understanding application of his flesh (the Word) to our living existence in this world. For, to possess spiritual moisture in our lives that we may endure hardness as a good soldier *(Read 2Ti 2:3-6),* we must maintain our possession of the fountain of living waters and not forsake the righteousness of God by acknowledging Him as supreme in our everyday lives, in all that we say and do. For,

In all thy ways acknowledge him, and he shall direct thy paths.

Pr 3:6.

So, not only must we seek to enter into the kingdom of God, but after entering we must seek to remain in the kingdom of God *(Mt 6:33)*, taking

> **...heed, brethren, lest there be in any of you an evil heart of unbelief, in departing from the living God.**

Heb 3:12.

For, if we fail to take heed to ourselves and acknowledge the Lord God in all that we do in life in times of distress, persecution, offenses, temptations and tribulation, then we will faint and depart from the living God who is the fountain of living waters. *(Jer 17:13)* And then, having departed from God, the Spirit of Christ which is the living water—will no longer lead us while our minds are carnal and not subject to the law of God. *(Ro 8:6-8)* For, if we will obey and not forsake Christ and drink of him he has promised that,

> **...whosoever drinketh of the water that I shall give him shall never thirst; but the water that I shall give him shall be in him a well of water springing up into everlasting life.**

Joh 4:14.

And furthermore, the scriptures recorded that,

> **37 In the last day, that great day of the feast, Jesus stood and cried, saying, If any man thirst, let him come unto me, and drink.**
>
> **38 He that believeth on me, as the scripture hath said, out of his belly shall flow rivers of living water.**

Joh 7:37-38.

But when we fail to continue believing in Jesus as the way and the life *(Joh 14:6)* that we should live by acknowledging him before we act or speak *(Pr 3:6)*—which is a continuance drinking of him—then, we forsake him by allowing ourselves to be led by the carnality of our flesh—our will, our feelings and our intellect. As a result, as carnally led Christians, we then have no ability to be led by the living waters' moisture which is required to endure the fiery darts *(Eph 6:16)* and scorching heat that accompanies the trying of a Christian's faith. *(Jer 17:10)* And, with no moisture in our lives we become and shall exist as

> **...wells without water, clouds that are carried with a tempest; to whom the mist of darkness is reserved for ever.**

2Pe 2:17 *(Read also 2Pe 2:10-22).*

Then, without repentance, as a carnal Christian in unbelief we shall find that we have become like the seed that

> **... fell upon a rock; and as soon as it was sprung up, it withered away, because it lacked moisture.**

Lu 8:6.

For,

> **They on the rock are they, which, when they hear, receive the word with joy; and these have no root, which for a while believe, and in time of temptation fall away.**

Lu 8:13.

Failure: Having Respect Of One's Person based upon Inheritance, Wealth and Power

The rocky, no root, no moisture souls were new converts unto the Lord, and novices in handling the Word of God. What was needed was a desire for the sincere milk of the Word so that by the Word they could grow *(1Pe 2:2)* their roots deeper into the earth, into the knowledge and understanding of the will, ways and righteousness of God. But, being novices with great zeal and gifts of the kingdom of heaven Jesus said, *"...immediately they sprung up..." (Mk 4:5; Lu 8:8)* Thus, since the word **sprung** *(spruŋ)* means to puff up, blow up or swell up, we further understand that those rocky soil souls' lack of knowledge caused them to think more of themselves than they should have. *(Read Ro 12:3)* For, they thought they were ready to go out, so they went without knowledge. And, without knowing, they were puffed up and swollen in pride. For, they sprung up and went out because they had become believers and sons of God, not because God had sent them out. Thus, they failed the same test that Eve failed in the garden of Eden *(Read Ge 3:1-7),* and the same test that Jesus overcame during the wilderness temptations. For, there,

> **...[W]hen the tempter came to him, he said, If thou be the Son of God, command that these stones be made bread.**

Mt 4:3.

Here, in this Matthew 4:3 passage, Satan, the tempter, tempted Jesus with the idea of satisfying a great, pressing, natural need and desire to feed the hunger pains that had developed within his physical body over a forty (40) day period of time. Jesus had not eaten any food *(Lu 4:2)*, for

> **...[W]hen he had fasted forty days and forty nights, he was afterward an hungred.**

Mt 4:2.

The tempter used this natural, common need to eat and consume food to tempt Jesus into using Jesus' power and position as the Son of God to fulfill the need and desire to eat. For, he did not say, *"If you are hungry command that these stones be made bread."* Because, it would be proper to eat food due to hunger. But, it is sin to be lifted up in the pride of inheritance, power or wealth against the will of God, in an attempt to satisfy this hunger. For, the scriptures declare that the Spirit's expressed purpose for Jesus being in the wilderness was so that Jesus might be tempted of the devil. *(Mt 4:1)* For, it is written that

> **...Jesus [was] led up of the Spirit into the wilderness to be tempted of the devil.**

Mt 4:1 *(Words in brackets added).*

Therefore, the Spirit, who is God, intended for Jesus to suffer the temptations and to overcome them, by obedience to the Word of God, and not by worldly short cuts made available to Him because of His inheritance, power or wealth. So, Jesus' overcoming the temptation and desire to eat by using his power as the Son of God would have been contrary to the Spirit's expressed will for Him, which was to be tempted and to overcome that temptation as a natural man with God, the Spirit, indwelling and leading him, and not as God himself. For, had Jesus taken the short cut and used his power to turn the stones into bread he would have set an impossible standard for those that he came to rescue out of a life of sin. And, being lifted up in pride he would have sinned and this would have made him an imperfect sacrifice.

But, since he possessed the knowledge of God, of His ways, of His will and of His Word, Jesus overcame the temptation by feeding his spirit man with the Word, proclaiming,

> **...It is written, man shall not live by bread alone, but by every word that proceedeth out of the mouth of God.**

Mt 4:4 *(Read also De 8:3).*

By rejecting Satan's offer of food Jesus rejected the pride and power of his inheritance as the Son of God and chose obedience to the Word of God. For,

8 Though he were a Son, yet learned he obedience by the things which he suffered;

9 And being made perfect, he became the author of eternal salvation unto all them that obey him;

Heb 5:8-9.

Now, let us revisit the actions of the rocky, no root, no moisture souls. They sprung up immediately after gladly receiving the Word of God with joy. But, without having depth in the Word of God, as they went they were armed only with the gifts of the kingdom and the knowledge of being believers in Christ. *(Read Mk 16:15-18)* Thus, Satan was able to tempt them in ways that caused them to be offended because of the Word's sake. And, without the knowledge of what the Word had to say about their situation they were not willing to wait on the Lord to fulfill the Word's promise. So, when they sought to overcome the temptations, as believers, they used the wisdom of the world *(See 1Co 2:6)* and not the hidden wisdom *(1Co 2:7)* found only in the Word of God. And so, they failed God by quitting his righteousness and the apostolic way, thereby becoming apostates. An **apostate** *(ə-pas'tat')* is a person that is guilty of apostasy; a renegade.

Failure: Apostasy

After being scandalized, tripped up and entrapped in the sins that were bound up in their temptations, the rocky, no root, no moisture souls became the servants of apostasy. For, **apostasy'** *(ə-pas'tə sē)* means an abandoning of what one has believed in, as a faith, cause or principles. So, when they began suffering tribulations and persecutions, because of the Word, they were offended and quit believing in Christ Jesus and the righteousness of God as found in the apostolic doctrine. And they fell away into apostasy. For all that do so become apostates, even renegades guilty of apostasy. In agreement, the Lord Jesus said,

> **They on the rock are they, which, when they hear, receive the word with joy; and these have no root, which for a while believe, and in time of temptation fall away.**

Lu 8:13.

For,

> **Yet hath he not root in himself, but endureth for a while: for when tribulation or persecution ariseth because of the word, by and by he is offended.**

Mt 13:20-21.

Thus, because they did not understand, before hand, that offenses must come *(Mt 18:7; Lu 17:1),* when they came the rocky, no root, no moisture souls stopped believing in Christ and in his Word and fell away. That is, they left the apostolic doctrine and became apostate unbelievers, living in ignorance as the Apostle Paul warns us concerning the church. *(Read 2Thes 2:3)* For, it was their lack of depth, knowledge and root in the Word and in the righteousness of God that allowed them to be overcome by the enemy through various temptations and offenses. A lack of depth and knowledge is ignorance. And, it was this ignorance that resulted in their stumbling and falling away. As it is written,

> **Therefore my people are gone into captivity, because they have no knowledge: and their honourable men are famished, and their multitude dried up with thirst.**

Isa 5:13.

Here, in Isaiah 5:13, the prophet proclaims that the captivity of the people of God is due to their lack of knowledge, which is ignorance. Their honourable men were famished because their souls were in need of eating the righteousness of God, but they did not eat the righteousness of God. The multitude was dried up with thirst because their souls were in need of drinking the righteousness of God, but their leaders did not give them righteousness to drink. For, had they done so they would have been blessed and not have gone into captivity or hell because Jesus said,

> **Blessed are they which do hunger and thirst after righteousness: for they shall be filled.**

Mt 5:6.

There are no blessings in hell or in captivity. And, when everyone in the family, the group or the congregation is ignorant of the righteousness of God, they all are blind—the leaders and those that are led. For the Lord Jesus, commenting on blind leaders and blind followers, said

> **Let them alone: they be blind leaders of the blind. And if the blind lead the blind, both shall fall into the ditch.**

Mt 15:14.

Furthermore, in agreement with Jesus, the prophet Isaiah proclaimed the future home of the spiritual blind, saying

> **Therefore hell hath enlarged herself, and opened her mouth without measure: and their glory, and their multitude, and their pomp, and he that rejoiceth, shall descend into it.**

Isa 5:14.

Thus, ignorance is a form of captivity that leads the possessor into further captivity. **Captivity** *(kap-tiv′ə-tē),* in the Isaiah 5:13 passage above, is taken from **galah** *(gaw-law′)* meaning to denude in a disgraceful manner; an exile that has been stripped; to reveal; to carry, lead or go captive; to carry, lead or go into captivity; to depart; discover, exile; to remove, publish or reveal shamelessly; to uncover. Therefore, **ignorance** *(ig′nə-rəns),* which is a lack of knowledge, will cause a believer to be lead into captivity, to be exiled and removed from the presence of God; to be uncovered, denuded and revealed in a disgraceful and shamelessly manner. This in turn becomes a scandal, and the believer's name, character and reputation is scandalized and traduced. As a result he is unable to produce any fruit for the Lord God, or to bring any to perfection.

Failure: Rejecting the Word is Rejecting Christ

Also, in another place a different prophet, while addressing the problem of ignorance amongst God's people, wrote for the Lord God, saying,

> **My people are destroyed for lack of knowledge; because thou hast rejected knowledge, I will also reject thee, that thou shalt be no priest to me: seeing thou hast forgotten the law of thy God, I will also forget thy children.**

Ho 4:6.

Here, again, the people of God are forewarned that their hurt, harm and destruction comes about because they lack knowledge. For, the word **lack** *(lak)* in Hosea 4:6 is taken from **beliy** *(bel-ee')* which means failure, nothing, destruction, without, not yet, corruption, ignorantly, none, and, for lack of. If the people of God would

> **Study to shew thyself approved unto God, a workman that needeth not to be ashamed, rightly dividing the word of truth.**

2Ti 2:15.

They would, through their studying, acquire knowledge and thereby not go into captivity *(Isa 5:13)* and not be destroyed *(Ho 4:6)* because of ignorance. For, the Lord Jesus has commanded all to,

> **Search the scriptures; for in them ye think ye have eternal life:...**

Joh 5:39.

Because he loves us, the Lord Jesus desires and commands us to study, that we may learn of Him and of His ways. For, He said

> **28 Come unto me, all ye that labour and are heavy laden, and I will give you rest.**
> **29 Take my yoke upon you, and learn of me; for I am meek and lowly in heart: and ye shall find rest unto your souls.**
> **30 For my yoke is easy, and my burden is light.**

Mt 11:28-30.

The word **learn** *(ˈlərn)*, here, is taken from **manthano** *(man-than'-o).* **Manthao** means to learn in any way; to understand. And **Learn** means to gain knowledge, understanding or skill by study or experience; to find out. So, we see, here, that it is not the Lord's will for his people to lack knowledge and therefore to be and exist in a state of ignorance. *(1Th 4:13; 1Co 10:1)* Error comes about through ignorance as

> **Jesus answered and said unto them. Ye do err, not knowing the scriptures, nor the power of God.**

Mt 22:29 *(Read also Mk 12:24).*

To refuse to study is rejecting knowledge, because by studying a person receives and acquires knowledge. So, if you do not study you do not acquire knowledge and therefore this refusal and failure to study is a rejection of that knowledge that would have been acquired through studying. For, the words **reject** *(rēˈjekt)* and **rejected** *(rēˈ-jekt-dˈ)* in the Hosea 4:6 passage is translated from the Hebrew **ma'ac** *(maw-as').* **Ma'ac** means to spurn, to disappear, to abhor, cast away, cast off, despise, disdain, become loathe (some), melt away, refuse, reject, reprobate, vile person. And later, on another day, the Lord Jesus said,

> **He that rejecteth me, and receiveth not my words, hath one that judgeth him: the word that I have spoken, the same shall judge him in the last day.**

Joh 12:48.

Here, in this John 12:48 passage, the word **reject** *(rē´jekt)* is similar in meaning to the word **reject** in the Hosea 4:6 passage above. For, here, **reject** is taken from the Greek **atheteo** *(ath-et-eh'-o)*, which means to set aside; to disesteem, neutralize or violate: cast off, despise, disannul, frustrate, bring to naught, reject. Thus, when we reject Christ by rejecting his Word that same word that we have rejected shall judge us in the last day. But, even before that Day of Judgment, our refusal to study and lack of knowledge will have caused us to twist the scriptures unto our own destruction. For, ignorance will have led us away with the error of the wicked, causing us to fall from our own steadfastness in the apostles' doctrine. *(Read Ac 2:42)*

> **15 ...[E]ven as our beloved brother Paul also according to the wisdom given unto him hath written unto you;**
>
> **16 As also in all his epistles, speaking in them of these things; in which are some things hard to be understood, which they that are unlearned and unstable wrest, as they do also the other scriptures, unto their own destruction.**
>
> **17 Ye therefore, beloved, seeing ye know these things before, beware lest ye also, being led away with the error of the wicked, fall from your own stedfastness.**
>
> **18 But grow in grace, and in the knowledge of our Lord and Saviour Jesus Christ...**

2Pe 3:15b-18a.

Thus, to be fruitful, believers must cast their nets out into the deep by studying the Word of God and learning of His will and His way. For,

> **Blessed are they which do hunger and thirst after righteousness: for they shall be filled.**

Mt 5:6.

The Seed Among Thorns

With the third type of sown seeds within Jesus' parable of the sower, *the seeds sown among thorns*, we learn another secret of the kingdom of God. *(Mt 13:11)* This mystery concerns the failure and inability of believers to be fruitful within the kingdom of God, although they are in the church, they do study the Word of God and they are working within their calling. For, He said,

> **7 And some fell among thorns and the thorns grew up, and choked it, and it yielded no fruit.**
>
> **....**
>
> **18 And these are they which are sown among thorns; such as hear the word,**
>
> **19 And the cares of this world, and the deceitfulness of riches, and the lusts of other things entering in, choke the word, and it becometh unfruitful.**

Mk 4:7, 18-19 *(Read also Lu 8:7, 14; Mt 13:7).*

In this Mark 4:7, 18-19 passage we learn that although a believer may study the Word of God and possess that Word within himself, there are some things in this life that can choke the Word, making him and the Word unfruitful. For, when a thing is **choked** *(chōk'd)* in the Greek it is **sumpnigo** *(soom-pnee'-go).* **Sumpnigo** means to strangle completely; to drown; to crowd, choke, throng. The Lord Jesus provided us with a categorical list of things that can become spiritual thorns in the believer's life that completely strangles and drowns the Word within him—making him *(Mt 13:22)* and the Word unfruitful. *(Mk 4:19)*

The spiritual thorn categories discussed by the Lord Jesus are: **(1)** ***the cares of the world*** *(Mk 4:7, 19);* **(2)** ***the deceitfulness of riches*** *(Mk 4:7, 19);* **(3)** ***pleasures*** *(Lu 8:7, 14);* and, **(4)** ***the lusts of other things***. *(Mk 4:7-19)* Jesus also said, *"...some fell among thorns; and the thorns sprang up with it..." (Lu 8:7)* If the thorns sprang up with the seeds, then as the believer began to grow in the knowledge of Christ, through and by studying the Word of God, the influence of the spiritual thorns in his life grew also. And this growth of the spiritual thorns was such that it crowded out, thronged, strangled and drowned the effectiveness of the Word in the life of the believer. In agreement, the Apostle exclaimed,

> **3 Thou therefore endure hardness, as a good soldier of Jesus Christ.**
>
> **4 No man that warreth entangleth himself with the affairs of this life; that he may please him who hath chosen him to be a soldier.**
>
> **5 And if a man also strive for masteries, yet is he not crowned, except he strive lawfully.**
>
> **6 The husbandman that laboureth must be first partaker of the fruits.**

2Ti 2:3-6.

One might ask, Where did the thorns come from?

When we review the scriptures we find that the first mention of the thorn, in all of creation, is found in the book of Genesis. There, the Lord God said unto the man,

> **17 ...Because thou hast hearkened unto the voice of thy wife, and hast eaten of the tree, of which I commanded thee saying, Thou shalt not eat of it: cursed is the ground**

for thy sake; in sorrow shalt thou eat of it all the days of thy life;

18 Thorns also and thistles shall it bring forth to thee; and thou shalt eat the herb of the field;

Ge 3:17-18.

Obeying the Wrong Voice Brings Thorns Into Our Lives

Here, in this Genesis 3:17-18 passage we learn that the introduction of the thorn into the life of mankind came from a curse placed upon the ground. And this curse was due to the man's knowing disobedience after listening to the wrong voice.

There are, it may be, so many kinds of voices in the world, and none of them is without significance.

1Co 14:10.

But only one voice will lead us to safety and salvation if we harden not our hearts in disobedience.

7 Wherefore …as the Holy Ghost saith, To day if ye will hear his voice.

8 Harden not your hearts, as in the provocation, in the day of temptation in the wilderness:

Heb 3:7-8.

All disobedience is sin. And this sin came about because of whose voice and counsel the man hearkened to, listened to, and obeyed. After the woman sinned, Adam did not hearken to and continue in obedience to the voice and commandment of God even though God had given him the fourth commandment before the woman was created. *(Read Ge 2:7-9, 16-25)* For, the scriptures recorded the fourth commandment saying,

16 And the Lord God commanded the man, saying, Of every tree of the garden thou mayest freely eat.
17 But of the tree of the knowledge of good and evil, thou shalt not eat of it: for in the day that thou eatest thereof thou shalt surely die.
Ge 2:16-17.

God gave the commandment to the man *(Ge 2:16-17),* and the man taught the commandment to the woman after she was created. But, the woman did not continue to hearken to and obey the commandment that Adam had taught her. She disobeyed the commandment by listening to and obeying the voice *(Ge 3:1-6)* of Lucifer, Satan the serpent. *(Re 12:9)* For,

4 …the serpent said unto the woman, Ye shall not surely die:
5 For God doth know that in the day ye eat thereof, then your eyes shall be opened, and ye shall be as gods, knowing good and evil.
Ge 3:4-5.

Although the serpent, in substance, called God a liar when he said, *"Ye shall not surely die." (Ge 3:4)*, after God had said *"…thou shalt surely die." (Ge 2:17)*, the woman believed the serpent and hearkened unto his voice. And as a result,

…[W]hen the woman saw that the tree was good for food, and that it was pleasant to the eyes, and a tree to be desired to make one wise, she took of the fruit thereof, and did eat…
Ge 3:6a.

So, here, we learn that the woman was the first human to violate and transgress the commandment of God *(1Ti 2:14)* after she was beguiled and tricked by the serpent. *(Ge 3:1-6, 13)* For, while living in a state of confusion, having been beguiled and tricked into disobeying God, the woman obeyed Lucifer. And, at this point in human and world history Lucifer had become Satan, the serpent, the enemy of God and of all righteousness. The serpent's voice was directly against the will, the ways and the commandments of God. And so, the woman now having left God by eating from the forbidden tree *(Ge 3:6),* then allowed herself to be used by Satan as an instrument of unrighteousness *(Read Ro 6:13, 16)* to entice and tempt the man, Adam, to follow her in her disobedience. For, after she ate from the tree she

...gave also unto her husband with her; and he did eat. Ge 3:6b.

But the scriptures admonishes us, saying,

> **13 Neither yield ye your members as instruments of unrighteousness unto sin: but yield yourselves unto God, as those that are alive from the dead, and your members as instruments of righteousness unto God.**
>
> **...**
>
> **16 Know ye not, that to whom ye yield yourselves servants to obey, his servants ye are to whom ye obey; whether of sin unto death, or of obedience unto righteousness?**

Ro 6:13, 16.

Adam failed the temptation of his flesh by eating the fruit from the forbidden tree that his wife, Eve, had given him. *(Ge 3:6-7)* Therefore, Adam obeyed and hearkened unto his wife's voice resulting in Adam's disobedience to the commandment of God. This disobe-dience resulted in man's punishment. Within the punishment is the curse *(Ge 3:17-19),* wherein thorns grow by the operation of the Word of God as the Lord God announced it in Genesis chapter 3, verse 18.

When the Lord said to Adam, *"...Because thou hast hearkened unto the voice of thy wife..",* the reference to 'thy wife' is not just a reference to the fact that she was a woman or a female. But rather, 'thy wife' refers also to Adam's flesh. That is, Adam and Eve had become 'one flesh' as husband and wife. *(Ge 2:24)* One half, Eve, of the 'one flesh' had now sinned and when she *"...gave also unto her husband with her..." (Ge 3:6)* she tempted the other half, Adam, to sin. And Adam did indeed hearken unto the voice of his flesh, that was residing within Eve, because *"...he did eat." (Ge 3:6)* For, after the Lord God created the woman *(Ge 2:21-22)* and brought the woman to him *(Ge 2:22),*

> **...Adam said, This is now bone of my bones, and flesh of my flesh: she shall be called Woman, because she was taken out of Man.**

Ge 2:23.

And the scriptures state further that,

> **Therefore shall a man leave his father and his mother, and shall cleave unto his wife: and they shall be one flesh.**

Ge 2:24.

Thus, after the two, the man and the woman, had become one flesh through the consummation of the marriage *(Ge 2:24),* Adam chose to disobey the voice of the Lord, when confronted with the thought of losing her to the serpent in sin. *(Ge 3:6-7, 8-13)* Unlike Eve the man, Adam, was not beguiled or tricked. He knowingly and willingly disobeyed God. *(1Ti 2:14)* Because, when questioned by God about why he was hiding from God after they had sinned *(Read Ge 3:8-11)*, Adam answered saying,

...The woman whom thou gavest to be with me, she gave me of the tree, and I did eat.
Ge 3:12.

Again, unlike Eve, he did not say that he was tricked or beguiled. *(Read Ge 3:13)* Here, in Genesis 3:12, Adam says, in substance, *"My flesh, my wife, tempted me to eat by giving me the things of the forbidden tree and I gave in to the temptation of my flesh, my wife, and I did eat."* Thus, Adam entered into sin with his flesh so that he might remain with and cleave to his flesh, in Eve. And by doing so, Adam failed to exercise faith in the Lord God that, even after Eve had left him in sin, God was able to renew his flesh, in Eve, and make them whole again.

A Crown of Thorns

Because of Adam's sin his reward was paid with sin's wages, which are death and thorns.

For the wages of sin is death...
Ro 6:23a.

And, since,

...as by one man sin entered into the world, and death by sin; and so death passed upon all men, for that all have sinned;
Ro 5:12.

For as by one man's disobedience many were made sinners...
Ro 5:19a.

Therefore, now that sin and thorns by sin were a part of the life of man, if the Lord God desired to rescue his creation called man he would have to send a savior that could not only deliver man from sin and the thorns but also from death. So, pursuant to this plan the Lord God announced the coming of the repairer of the breach *(Isa 58:12b),* when he said to Satan, the serpent,

> **...I will put enmity between thee and the woman, and between thy seed and her seed; it shall bruise thy head, and thou shalt bruise his heel.**

Ge 3:15.

And seventy-six generations later *(Lu 3:23-38)* the promised, righteous seed of the woman *(Ga 3:16)* appeared, on earth, wearing a crown of thorns on his head representing the sins of the world, past, present, and future. *(Joh 19:2, 5)* For, the thorns are a curse for disobedience. *(Read Heb 6:4-8)* But, through obedience to Christ, man need not remain barren and unfruitful in the knowledge of Christ because of the thorns. For, through Christ, the Lord God removes the curse and heals the land occupied by his people, as he said,

> **If my people, which are called by my name, shall humble themselves, and pray, and seek my face, and turn from their wicked ways; then will I hear from heaven, and will forgive their sin, and will heal their land.**

2Ch 7:14.

The people of the Lord God, mentioned in the above 2Chronicles 7:14 passage, are the water baptized and Spirit baptized *(See Joh 3:5)* believers in the name of Jesus. *(Ac 2:38)* This is so, because the name of the Lord God, the Father, is Jesus. For, Jesus himself said,

> **I am come in my Father's name, and ye receive me not: if another shall come in his own name, him ye will receive.**

Joh 5:43.

And,

9b ...Now if any man have not the Spirit of Christ, he is none of his.

10 And if Christ be in you, the body is dead because of sin; but the Spirit is life because of righteousness.

Ro 8:9b-10.

Furthermore, the life of Christ was and remains a gift from the Lord God to mankind.

For God so loved the world, that he gave his only begotten Son, that whosoever believeth in him should not perish, but have everlasting life.

Joh 3:16.

So,

...if through the offence of one many be dead, much more the grace of God, and the gift by grace, which is by one man, Jesus Christ, hath abounded unto many.

Ro 5:15b *(Read Ro 5:16-19b).*

Jesus Christ is the promised, righteous seed of the woman that will heal the land, rescue man from a life of sin and deliver him from death. And, after he wore the crown of thorns on his head, he also took on the sins of the world *(Joh 1:29; 1Pe 2:24; Heb 9:28)* and was made 'sin' *(2Co 5:21)* for man's deliverance. Thereafter, he died for all of mankind *(Heb 9:26-28)* that should believe in him. *(Joh 3:16)* Because,

Thorns and snares are in the way of the forward: he that doth keep his soul shall be far from them.

Pr 22:5.

We keep our souls in life, by denying the flesh to rule our lives, through obedience to the Word of God. As Jesus said,

> **It is the spirit that quickeneth; the flesh profiteth nothing: the words that I speak unto you, they are spirit, and they are life.**

Joh 6:63.

Thorn Growth: Failure to Exercise Self Control

Now, let us consider thorn growth. For, the Lord Jesus said,

> **And some fell among thorns and the thorns grew up, and choked it, and it yielded no fruit.**

Mk 4:7.

And again,

> **And some fell among thorns; and the thorns sprang up with it, and choked it.**

Lu 8:7.

From these two passages of scripture, from two different writers, we gain a greater understanding about the workings of the thorns against the effectiveness of the seed, which is the Word of God. *(Lu 8:11)* Because, Jesus said that the thorns grew up with the seed that had been planted. Therefore, as the believer grew in the Word the thorns, the things that would and could hinder his growth and fruitfulness in God, also grew up with him to the point that the Word of God working in his life was crowded out and thronged. This is why the Lord God admonished the people of God saying,

> **3 For thus saith the Lord to the men of Judah and Jerusalem, Break up your fallow ground, and sow not among thorns.**

4 Circumcise yourselves to the Lord, and take away the foreskins of your heart, ye men of Judah and inhabitants of Jerusalem…

Jer 4:3-4a.

For, when a believer's seed begins to grow amongst thorns, although he understands the Word, he and the Word are ineffective in producing fruit for the kingdom of God. The ineffectiveness is a direct result of the Word of God being drowned and completely strangled by the believer's over active, all consuming involvement in the thorns. This unbalanced, immoderate thorn involvement results from the believer's failure to exercise self control. And, as he grows without total self control, his involvement in the thorns increases requiring more of his time and therefore more of his life, so that he has no time for unhindered growth in the Word. For, a man's life consists of the total time allowed and allotted to him, to live in this life, by the Lord God. *(Job 7:1; Ec 3:2; Ec 9:12a)*

Many things done in this life are lawful and will not become the choking, strangling thorns, discussed in Jesus' parable, when done in moderation at the proper time, in the proper manner and for the proper purpose. Because,

To every thing there is a season, and a time to every purpose under the heaven:

Ec 3:1.

Season *(sē´zən)* here, is taken from **zeman** *(zem-awn').* **Zeman** means an appointed occasion; season, time. And **time** *(tīm)* is taken from **'eth** *(ayth).* **'Eth** means time, now, when, after, season, etc. Thus, the thorny seed believer never learned, acquired or steadfastly practiced the proper balance of time and, or occasion to engage in the life events that would become thorns in his life as opposed to studying the Word of God, doing the Word of God and performing the soul winning work of the kingdom of God. For, *"...a wise man's heart* *discerneth both time and judgment. Because to every purpose there is time and judgment..." (Ec 8:5b-6a)*

Furthermore, we are commanded to,

Let your moderation be known unto all men. The Lord is at hand.
Php 4:5.

Moderation *(mod'er a'tion)* here, is taken from **epieikes** *(ep-ee-i-kace')*. **Epiekes** means appropriate; mild, gentle, moderation, patient. **Moderation** means avoidance of extremes; calmness. Thus, even those things that are lawful for believers to engage in should be done so in moderation, in mild and appropriate proportions as compared to the believer's present, active engagement in building the kingdom of God. As the Apostle Paul stated,

All things are lawful unto me, but all things are not expedient: all things are lawful for me, but I will not be brought under the power of any.
1Co 6:12.

Expedient *(ek spē'dē ənt)* here, is taken from **sumphero** *(soom-fer'-o)*. **Sumphero** means to bear together, contribute, to collect, to conduce; advantage, be better for, bring together, be expedient (for), be good, be profitable (for). **Expedient** means useful for effecting a desired result; convenient, a means to an end. So, even when the believer is engaged in non-sinful, lawful things he must exercise self control to prevent his coming under the power and influence of that thing. As **lawful** *(lô'fəl)* here, is taken from **exon** *(ex-on')*, **exon** means it is right (the idea of being out in public); be lawful; let; may (est). **Lawful** means in conformity with the law; recognized by law. For, if he engages in the thing only because it is lawful he may find that the lawfulness of it, alone, does not assist him in effecting the desired result of growing and sustaining his fruitfulness in Christ. And, if the desired result is not assisted, then the lawful thing, though lawful, is not expedient and therefore becomes a hindrance, a distraction and a thorn to his fruitfulness.

So in order to prevent, diminish or reverse thorn growth in one's life the believer must strive for a proper balance in his life by being **temperate** *(tem′-pər-it)* in all things. *As*

> **...every man that striveth for the mastery is temperate in all things...**

1Co 9:25a.

Temperance *(tem′-pər-əns)*, being a fruit of the Spirit *(Ga 5:22-23)*, is taken from **egkrateia** *(eng-krat'-i-ah)* which means self-control (especially continence), temperance. And **egkrateia** is derived from the Greek **egkrateuomai** *(eng-krat-yoo'-om-ahee)* from which the word **temperate** is taken from—meaning to exercise self-restraint (in diet and chastity); to contain, to be temperate.

Thus, when believers exercise self restraint, by watching and moderating their daily diet of life's activities to make sure they are leaning towards the cause of Christ—thorn growth is prevented, diminished and, or reversed. For, when we receive the indwelling spirit of God—the Holy Ghost—we receive with it the Spirit's fruit called **temperance**. And, it is from **temperance** that we receive our self control which enables us to maintain a proper balance in our life in Christ. For, that balance must always be tilted in favor of keeping ourselves unspotted in the world *(Read Jas 1:19-27)* and actively engaged in the mission of winning souls for the kingdom of God. As the word **balance** *(bal′əns),* here, means harmonious proportion of elements in a design; a weight, value, etc, that counteracts another; to counteract; offset; to bring into proportion; harmony. For, there is always in the believer a war raging within his mortal body.

> **For the flesh lusteth against the Spirit, and the Spirit against the flesh: and these are contrary to the other: so that ye cannot do the things that ye would.**

Ga 5:17.

22 For I delight in the law of God after the inward man:

23 But I see another law in my members, warring against the law of my mind, and bringing me into captivity to the law of sin which is in my members.

…

25 …So then with the mind I myself serve the law of God; but with the flesh the law of sin.

Ro 7:22-23, 25.

We must always remember that as believers in Christ Jesus, we are in the world, but not of the world *(Joh 15:19; Joh 17:14, 16),* and that a man's life consists not in the abundance of the things that he possesses. *(Lu 12:15)* For, after you have believed in Christ and in his Word towards salvation if you will give all diligence to add

5 …to your faith virtue; and to virtue knowledge;

6 And to knowledge temperance; and to temperance patience; and to patience godliness;

7 And to godliness brotherly kindness; and to brotherly kindness charity.

8 And if these things be in you, and abound, they make you that ye shall neither be barren nor unfruitful in he knowledge of our Lord Jesus Christ.

9 But he that lacketh these things is blind, and cannot see afar off, and hath forgotten that he was purged from his old sins.

10 Wherefore the rather, brethren, give diligence to make your calling and election sure: for if ye do these things, ye shall never fall:

2Pe 1:5b-10.

Thus, the thorns in the believer's life in Jesus' Mark 4:7, 18-19 parable, whether lawful or not, caused the believer to be barren and unfruitful. He was barren and unfruitful because he failed to add to that faith which caused him first to become a believer—virtue, knowledge, temperance, patience, godliness, brotherly kindness and charity. *(2Pe 1:5-10)*

Furthermore, as believers, we are admonished as soldiers and warriors of the Most High to not entangle ourselves with the affairs of this life that we may please God who has chosen us to be soldiers. *(2Ti 2:4)* Because the Lord Jesus said,

> **Ye have not chosen me, but I have chosen you, and ordained you, that ye should go and bring forth fruit, and that your fruit should remain...**

Joh 15:16a.

The Thorn Type Catogories:

Now, let us consider each thorn type category as taught by the Lord Jesus. The first type is called the **cares of the world**. *(Mk 4:7, 19)*

1st Thorn Type: **The Cares Of The World**

Jesus said,

> **18 And these are they which are sown among thorns; such as hear the word,**
>
> **19 And the cares of this world ... entering in, choke the word, and it becometh unfruitful.**

Mk 4:18-19.

Here, the word **cares** *(kerz)* is taken from **merimna** *(mer'-im-nah)* which means solicitude, care; a distraction. Thus, there are concerns in this life that, as saints, we will be passionate about and desire to use our gifts and talents to help solve. But, when these concerns and cares of this life do not directly assist us in the up-building of the kingdom of God, by winning souls, these cares can become a distraction and therefore a hindrance to our work in the Lord. Also, the greater our understanding of the Word of God, the greater will be our sorrow and burden for the plight of the unsaved.

> **For in much wisdom is much grief: and he that increaseth knowledge increaseth sorrow.**

Ec 1:18.

So, we must be extremely careful that we hearken to the voice of the Apostle when he said,

> **4 No man that warreth entangleth himself with the affairs of this life; that he may please him who hath chosen him to be a soldier.**
>
> **5 And if a man also strive for masteries, yet is he not crowned, except he strive lawfully.**
>
> **6 The husbandman that laboureth must be first partaker of the fruits.**

2Ti 2:4-6.

We are not striving lawfully, when, while we are striving and working for God we are more concerned with the cares of the world than with the up-building of the kingdom of God. And therefore we have a growth hindering, fruit preventing thorn in our lives. As a result, except we rid ourselves of the thorn we will not receive our crown. *(2Ti 2:5)* Because, to **strive lawfully** in the Greek is **nomimos** *(nom-im'-oce)* which means to strive legitimately; specially agreeably to the rules of the list. And one of the rules on the list is

> **...[T]thou shalt love the Lord thy God with all thy heart, and with all thy soul, and with all thy mind, and with all thy strength: this is the first commandment.**

Mk 12:30.

So, when our actions show that we are more concerned with the cares of the world and worldly causes than we are with the up-building of the kingdom of God—then we have not loved God with all of our heart, soul, mind and strength. This is a major cause for failure and unfruitfulness in Christ. Another rule on the list of striving lawfully is that

> **...[E]very man that striveth for the mastery is temperate in all things...**

1Co 9:25a.

And, as we learned earlier, to be **temperate** in the Greek is to be **egkrateuomai** *(eng-krat-yoo'-om-ahee)* meaning to exercise self-restraint (in diet and chastity); to contain, be temperate. Therefore, to prevent thorn growth believers must exercise self control in order to maintain a proper balance in their appetite for things that can hinder their fruitfulness and growth in Christ Jesus.

Thus, we must not become entangled with 'the affairs of this life', if we are to become and remain soldiers that please God. Being barren and unfruitful does not please God, even when the cares of this world are worthwhile causes. For, the word **entangleth** *(en taŋ' glf)* is taken from **empleko** *(em-plek'-o).* **Empleko** means to entwine, involve with; entangle (in, self with). **Entangle** means to involve in a tangle; to involve in difficulty; to confuse; to complicate. A **tangle** *(taŋ' gəl)* is to catch as in a snare; trap; to make a snarl of; intertwine; to argue; an intertwined, confused mass; a confused condition or state. And **entwine** *(en twīn')* means to twine together or around. Thus, the Apostle admonishes us, as saints, not to allow the thorns to cause us to become entangled with difficult, confused and complicated, worldly affairs. Because, these passionate causes and affairs can cause us to become tangled and caught in a trap, or in a snare to where our minds are twined around and together with the affair. When our minds twine around and together with the cares and concerns that are not directly intended to assist in winning souls, then we are not loving God with all our mind. And so, the Word in us is drowned, choked and strangled making us unfruitful in the kingdom of God.

Furthermore, when one is overly involved and entangled with the cares of the world he makes himself a friend of the world and therefore an enemy to God, because he has placed the second greatest commandment, which says, *"[T]thou shalt love thy neighbor as thyself", (Mt 22:39b),* in front of the first, greatest commandment thereby making it more important, in his life, than the first and greatest commandment *(Mt 22:37-38)* which says,

> **...[T]thou shalt love the Lord thy God with all thy heart, and with all thy soul, and with all thy mind, and with all thy strength: this is the first commandment.**

Mk 12:30.

For, the scripture says,

> **...[K]now ye not that the friendship of the world is enmity with God? Whosoever therefore will be a friend of the world is the enemy of God.**

Jas 4:4.

Being a friend of the world removes our main focus from building up the kingdom of God, one soul at a time, to building up and improving the systems and institutions of the world. Lucifer, Satan, the Devil is the prince *(Read Eph 2:1-3; Joh 12:31; 2Co 4:4; Joh 14:30; Joh 16:11)* and ruler of this world *(Eph 6:12),* although he has not always been so. For, the Lord God first gave the dominion, power and control over the earth and this world to mankind. *(Read Ge 1:28)* But, when man sinned in the Garden of Eden *(Read Ge 3:1-7)* he willingly gave this dominion, power and control of the earth and the world to Lucifer, Satan, the Devil *(Read Lu 4:5-8)* and thereby man became the servants of sin and of Satan. *(Read Ro 6:13, 16)*

Therefore, believers should not become so tangled up with the affairs and cares of this world to where we are found using the gifts and talents of the kingdom of God to assist Lucifer in making this world appear more attractive to the souls of mankind than the attraction of the kingdom of God. For, to do so sets the believer against God, against his will *(Eph 1:9-10)* and against the purpose of the coming of His Christ. *(Joh 12:47; Mt 9:12-13; Mt 18:11; Lu 9:56)* And so, the believer becomes a friend and lover of the world in violation of the commandment that admonishes us saying,

> **15 Love not the world, neither the things that are in the world. If any man love the world, the love of the Father is not in him.**
>
> **16 For all that is in the world, the lust of the flesh, and the lust of the eyes, and the pride of life, is not of the Father, but it is of the world.**

1Jo 2:15-16.

And to be sure, it was these things of the world: the lust of the flesh, the lust of the eyes and the pride of life, that caught Eve's eye, her attention and her heart and caused her to sin against God, against her soul, against the union of the one flesh *(Ge 2:24)* and against her husband who was with her. *(Read Ge 3:1-7).*

Amen.

2nd Thorn Type: **The Deceitfulness of Riches**

Let us now consider the second type of thorn called the **deceitfulness of riches.** *(Mk 4:7, 19)*

Again, Jesus said

> **18 And these are they which are sown among thorns; such as hear the word,**

> **19 And … the deceitfulness of riches … entering in, choke the word, and it becometh unfruitful.**

Mk 4:18-19.

Here, the word **riches** *(rich′iz)* is taken from **ploutos** *(ploo′-tos)* which means wealth (as fullness), money, possessions, abundance, richness, valuable bestowment; riches. And the word **deceitfulness** *(dē-sēt′fəl-nis)* is taken from **apate** *(ap-at′-ay)* which means delusion; deceit (ful, fullness), deceiving, deceivableness.

Therefore, the St. Mark 4:18-19 parable admonishes us to be careful concerning the use, acquisition and maintenance of wealth, possessions and money, because riches can deceive. And Jesus admonishes us further, that,

> **24 No man can serve two masters: for either he will hate the one, and love the other; or else he will hold to the one, and despise the other. Ye cannot serve God and mammon.**
>
> **25 Therefore I say unto you, Take no thought for your life, what ye shall eat, or what ye shall drink; nor yet for your body, what ye shall put on. Is not the life more than meat, and the body than raiment?**

Mt 6:24-25.

Doctrine of Contentment vs. The Prosperity Doctrine

Riches have the ability to deceive the possessor or the owner into thinking that life and living will be better if he possesses more of them. But,

> **He that trusteth in his riches shall fall…**

Pr 11:28.

And,

He that loveth silver shall not be satisfied with silver; nor he that loveth abundance with increase...
Ec 5:10a.

And,

3 If any man teach otherwise, and consent not to wholesome words, even the words of our Lord Jesus Christ, and to the doctrine which is according to godliness;
4 He is proud, knowing nothing, but doting about questions and strifes of words, whereof cometh envy, strife, railings, evil surmisings,
5 Perverse disputings of men of corrupt minds, and destitute of the truth, supposing that gain is godliness: from such withdraw thyself.
6 But godliness with contentment is great gain.
7 For we brought nothing into this world, and it is certain we can carry nothing out.
8 And having food and raiment let us be therewith content.
1Ti 6:3-8.

The word **contentment** *(kən-tent'-mənt)* in this passage is taken from **autarkeia** *(ow-tar'-ki-ah).* **Autarkeia** means self-satisfaction, contentedness, a competence, sufficiency, contentment. **Contentment** means living in a state of satisfaction and happiness with one's station in life. Prophet Agur gave us a word picture of contentment when he wrote,

7 Two things have I required of thee; deny me them not before I die:

8 Remove far from me vanity and lies: give me neither poverty nor riches; feed me with food convenient for me:

9 Lest I be full, and deny thee, and say, Who is the Lord? or lest I be poor, and steal; and take the name of my God in vain.

Pr 30:7-9.

In this passage Prophet Agur is concerned with ensuring that he is not blessed with too many riches or too little wealth. For, he desires to possess an adequate amount so that he is not ungratefully rich *(Ec 6:2)* or doubtfully poor. *(Pr 30:8-9)* In this passage he asked the Lord God for a middle ground, for a balanced amount of things in his life such as wealth and food. For, he understood that too much wealth could cause him to desire nothing from the Lord God for his soul, for his spirit man, as King Solomon informs us that,

1 There is an evil which I have seen under the sun, and it is common among men:

2 A man to whom God hath given riches, wealth, and honour, so that he wanteth nothing for his soul of all that he desireth, yet God giveth him not power to eat thereof, but a stranger eateth it: this is vanity, and it is an evil disease.

Ec 6:1-2.

For, we know that

...the wealth of the sinner is laid up for the just.

Pr 13:22b.

Discontentment Opens One's Heart To Temptations

When a person is not content and lives in a state of discontentment he opens his heart to various temptations relating to covetousness and unrighteous mammon. This in turn, places him in danger of serving unrighteous mammon rather than obeying the commandments of St. Matthew 6:33 and serving God. So, when he begins serving unrighteous mammon, by placing his confidence in money and wealth, this act removes his trust from God and places it in the unrighteous mammon that he now seek. And since unrighteous mammon is of the world, then, while serving unrighteous mammon he is actually serving the ruler and prince of this world, Lucifer *(1Co 2:6, 8; Eph 6:12; Joh 12:31; Joh 14:30; Joh 16:11; Eph 2:2; Mt 12:24),* rather than serving God.

Thus, when we compare the Apostle Paul's admonishment of contentment and being content in 1Timothy 6:3-8 with Prophet Agur's request for convenient food and wealth as found in the Proverbs 30:7-9 passage we learn that to be content is to desire and to be satisfied with the wealth, food and worldly possessions that are convenient for your station, calling and abilities in life. For, the word **convenient** *(kən-vēn′-yənt)* in the Proverbs 30:8 passage above is translated from the Hebrew **choq** *(khoke).* **Choq** means an enactment; an appointment (of time, space, quantity, labor or usage); appointed, bound, commandment, convenient, custom, decree, due, law, measure, necessary, ordinance (-nary), portion, set time, statute, task.

Therefore, if the scriptures are right, and we believe they are, then, even before we pray our heavenly father knows what we are in need of even before we ask. *(Mt 6:32; Lu 12:28-30)* So, believers must learn to be content and satisfied with the portion and allotment of gifts, talents, calling, money, food, time, wealth and abilities that our heavenly father, God, has appointed and provided for us to use and to be responsible for. Because,

> **Every good gift and every perfect gift is from above, and cometh down from the Father of lights...**

Jas 1:17a.

And, as the Apostle stated,

> **10 As every man hath received the gift, even so minister the same one to another, as good stewards of the manifold grace of God.**
>
> **11 If any man speak, let him speak as the oracles of God; if any man minister, let him do it as of the ability which God giveth: that God in all things may be glorified through Jesus Christ, to whom be praise and dominion for ever and ever. Amen.**

1Pe 4:10-11.

Here, in this 1Peter 4:11 verse, the word **ability** *(ə-bil'ə-tē)* is taken from **hikanoo** *(hik-an-ŏ'-o)* which means to enable, that is to qualify; make able. Thus, the gift and the ability, which is the power and the qualification to perform and operate the gift, are two separate endowments from the Lord. For, the word **gift** *(gift),* here, means a divine gratuity; deliverance; specifically a spiritual endowment, religious qualification, miraculous faculty, or a free gift, it having been translated from the Greek **charisma** *(khar'-is-mah).* So, in addition to the gift *(Eph 4:8)* the Lord freely gives us a measured amount of ability to operate the divine gift. For, God, as a faithful father, knows what blessings to bless us with and what gifts and abilities to ordain us with so that we will not fail, but that we may be successful in our daily lives and work in Him. Because, every person is given a certain measure of faith *(Ro 12:3),* talents, gifts and grace. *(1Pe 4:10-11)* We, as believers, being many members within the same body are not given the same degree of gifts, talents and grace.

Neither are we given the same measure of ability within the same gift or talent. Because, the amount of grace received from the Lord determines the measure of the ability within the gift or talent. For,

> **...unto every one of us is given grace according to the measure of the gift of Christ.**

Eph 4:7.

And, here, by **measure** *(mezh'ər)* we mean in the Greek a **metron** *(met'-ron),* a limited portion; a limited degree; a measure; the extent, dimensions and capacity of anything. Thus, the amount of grace is limited by what is necessary to operate and to be fruitful in the degree and level of the gift received and possessed.

> **4 For as we have many members in one body, and all members have not the same office:**
> **5 So we, being many, are one body in Christ, and every one members one of another.**
> **6 Having then gifts differing according to the grace that is given to us...**

Ro 12:4-6.

Here, in the above Romans 12:4-6 passage, the writer compares and relates the believers in Christ to the members of the human body with each member (believer) possessing a gift that differs from the other members (believers) within the body of Christ based upon (according to) the grace that is given to each individual member.

Favour Illustrated: Right Side vs. Left Side

To explain this doctrine of giving of gifts according to the receiver's ability *(Read Eph 4:7-16; Ps 68:18-19),* we can consider the human body further. For, although the human body has a left side and a right side that includes hands, arms, legs and feet, the physical body of the majority of all human beings favors either the right side or the left side of their body over the other side.

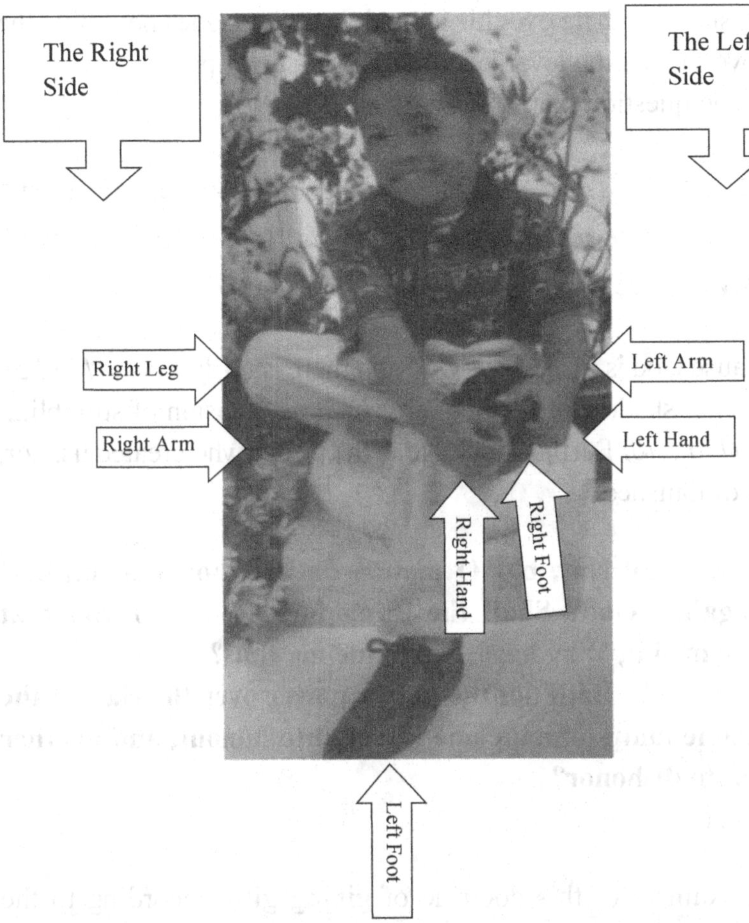

In the above illustration the little boy shows favor towards his right side over his left side by requiring his left leg to act as a stool to support his right leg. However, although the left leg is being used to support the favored right leg the little boy loves both legs the same. His favoring the right side actually means that the right side will be called upon to perform work more often than the left side will. However, at the end of the day both legs will receive the same reward: washing, care and nourishment.

That is, a right handed person possesses more talent, ability and power in his right arm, right hand and right leg than he does his left hand, arm and leg. Thus, the favored side of the body is more dominant than the less-favored side. However, the right handed person's favoring his right side members over his left side members does not affect the equal love that the believer has for all of his body parts.

The question that arises now is,

Does this doctrine of giving unequal gifts according to the receiver's ability violate the doctrine that 'God is not a respecter of persons'?

No. Because God is a righteous God and there is no darkness *(1Jo 1:5),* sin *(1Jo 3:5),* shadow of turning *(Jas 1:17)* or occasion of stumbling in Him. *(1Jo 2:10)* Furthermore, He is the potter who created us. For, we are admonished,

> **20 Nay, but O man, who art thou that repliest against God? Shall the thing formed say to him that formed it, Why hast thou made me thus?**
>
> **21 Hath not the potter power over the clay, of the same lump to make one vessel unto honour, and another unto dishonor?**

Ro 9:20-21.

A good example of this doctrine of giving gifts according to the receiver's ability is where,

> **11 ...God wrought special miracles by the hands of Paul:**
>
> **12 So that from his body were brought unto the sick handkerchiefs or aprons, and the diseases departed from them, and the evil spirits went out of them.**

Ac 19:11-12.

And another:

> **10 ...[N]ot only this; but when Rebecca also had conceived by one, even by our father Isaac;**
>
> **11 (For the children being not yet born, neither having done any good or evil, that the purpose of God according to election might stand, not of works, but of him that calleth;)**
>
> **12 It was said unto her, THE ELDER SHALL SERVE THE YOUNGER.**
>
> **13 As it is written, JACOB HAVE I LOVED, BUT ESAU HAVE I HATED.**
>
> **14 What shall we say then? Is there unrighteousness with God? God forbid.**
>
> **15 For he saith to Moses, I WILL HAVE MERCY ON WHOM I WILL HAVE MERCY, AND I WILL HAVE COMPASSION ON WHOM I WILL HAVE COMPASSION.**
>
> **16 So then it is not of him that willeth, nor of him that runneth, but of God that sheweth mercy.**

Ro 9:10-16.

So, we learn after reviewing Acts 19:11-12 and the Romans 9:10-16 passages that the unequal giving of gifts, whether it be ability, grace, mercy or compassion does not violate the doctrine that 'God is not a respecter of persons'. For, to have respect of persons is sin. *(Jas 2:9)* And as stated above, there is no sin in Him *(1Jo 3:5),* and He doeth no sin. *(1Pe 2:22; Heb 4:15)*

Now, here in this discussion and in Romans 12:4-6, Ephesians 4:7 and in the 1Peter 4:10-11 passages above, the word **grace** *(grās)* is instructive. For, **grace** is translated from the Greek **charis** *(khar'-ece)* which means graciousness (as gratifying) of manner or act (spiritually especially the divine influence upon the heart, and its reflection in the life; including gratitude); acceptable, benefit, favour, gift, grace (-ious), joy, liberality, pleasure, thank (-s, worthy). Thus, with **grace** comes the **favour** *(fā'-vər)* of God. And we know by the scriptures that we are able to grow and increase in **favour** with God like Christ Jesus did. For,

> **... Jesus increased in wisdom and stature, and in favour with God and man.**

Lu 2:52.

And, we are commanded to

> **...grow in grace, and in the knowledge of our Lord and Saviour Jesus Christ...**

2Pe 3:18a.

So, when we delight ourselves in God and in His law *(Ps 1:1-3; Ps 37:4; Ps 40:8; Ps 119:16, 24, 35, 47, 77, 174)* and grow in the knowledge of our Lord and Saviour Jesus Christ thereby increasing the level of His divine influence upon our hearts with a corresponding reflection of His influence showing in our lives—we will increase in wisdom, stature and in favour with God.

Furthermore, the word **favour,** here in Luke 2:52, is translated from the same Greek **charis** as was the word **grace** in Romans 12:6. And, to grow in **favour** with God refers to a friendly regard, partiality, a kind or obliging act; to approve or like; to be partial to; to support; advocate; to make easier; help; to do a kindness for; to resemble. Thus, when a believer increases in **favour** with God, God as a friend makes his way and the work and vision that he sets out to do and perform—easier. For, when a man's ways pleases God, then

> **2 ...his delight is in the law of the Lord; and in his law doth he meditate day and night.**
>
> **3 And he shall be like a tree planted by the rivers of water, that bringeth forth his fruit in his season; and**

his leaf also shall not wither; and whatsoever he doeth shall prosper.

Ps 1:2-3.

An example of differing gifts and abilities amongst fellow members within the body of Christ is found in the Lord's parable of the three servants wherein he taught the people saying,

> **14 For the kingdom of heaven is as a man travelling into a far country, who called his own servants, and delivered unto them his goods.**
>
> **15 And unto one he gave five talents, to another two, and to another one; to every man according to his several ability; and straightway took his journey.**

Mt 25:14-15 *(e.g. Read also 2Pe 3:15-17).*

Again, in this Matthew 25:15 verse the word **ability** is used. However, this is a different word **ability** than the **ability** that is used in the 1Peter 4:11 verse above, which is translated from the Greek word **hikanoo** meaning to make able; to qualify. The word **ability** in this Matthew 25:15 verse is taken from the Greek **dunamis** *(doo'-nam-is).* **Dunamis** means force, specifically miraculous power (usually a miracle itself); ability, abundance, might (-ily, -y, -y deed) (worker of) miracle (-s), power, strength, violence, mighty (wonderful) work.

So, we learn that within the kingdom of heaven, the Church, everyone gets a gift or talent, but not in the same amount. The number and amount of talents received by each servant is determined in advance by the owner of the talents, who is Christ Jesus. *(Mt 25:15)* And the owner, Christ Jesus, makes his determination based upon each servant's present ability, power, or strength to operate or handle the talents given. *(Mt 25:15)* For, it is not the owner's, the intent of Christ to give his servants more than they can presently handle and cause them to fail.

So, each member is **hikanoo**—qualified (ability) to perform certain gifts and talents in the kingdom of heaven. *(1Pe 4:11)* The number and amount of gifts and talents received for the kingdom of heaven, from Christ Jesus, is based upon the level of the **dunamis—ability** power presently possessed. *(Mt 25:15)* The amount of the **dunamis** power presently possessed depends upon the amount of **charis—grace** received from the Lord. *(Eph 4:7; Ro 12:6a)*

Furthermore, even if a believer starts out with the **hikanoo** to perform only two types of gifts and he receives five talents within the two gift types, if he is faithful in the performance of the five talents and produce fruit for the kingdom of God he will grow in **favour** with God. And when he grows in **favour** with God he acquires more **charis—grace** and will receive more **dunamis—ability** power to perform and operate more gifts and talents within the kingdom of God. *(Mt 25:15; Lu 2:52)*

To assist us in further understanding the gifts and talents in the kingdom of heaven the Apostle Paul instructs us saying,

> **4 Now there are diversities of gifts, but the same Spirit.**
>
> **5 And there are differences of administrations, but the same Lord.**
>
> **6 And there are diversities of operations, but it is the same God which worketh all in all.**
>
> **7 But the manifestation of the Spirit is given to every man to profit withal.**
>
> **8 For to one is given by the Spirit the word of wisdom; to another the word of knowledge by the same Spirit;**
>
> **9 To another faith by the same Spirit; to another the gifts of healing by the same Spirit;**
>
> **10 To another the working of miracles; to another prophecy; to another discerning of spirits; to another divers kinds of tongues; to another the interpretation of tongues:**

11 But all these worketh that one and the selfsame Spirit, dividing to every man severally as he will.

12 For as the body is one, and hath many members, and all the members of that one body, being many, are one body: so also is Christ.

13 For by one Spirit are we all baptized into one body, whether we be Jews or Gentiles, whether we be bond or free; and have been all made to drink into one Spirit.

14 For the body is not one member, but many.

15 If the foot shall say, Because I am not the hand, I am not of the body; is it therefore not of the body?

16 And if the ear shall say, Because I am not the eye, I am not of the body; is it therefore not of the body?

17 If the whole body were an eye, where were the hearing? If the whole were hearing, where were the smelling?

18 But now hath God set the members every one of them in the body, as it hath pleased him.

19 And if they were all one member, where were the body?

20 But now are they many members, yet but one body.

21 And the eye cannot say unto the hand, I have no need of thee: nor again the head to the feet, I have no need of you.

22 Nay, much more those members of the body, which seem to be more feeble, are necessary:

23 And those members of the body, which we think to be less honourable, upon these we bestow more abundant honour; and our uncomely parts have more abundant comeliness.

24 For our comely parts have no need: but God hath tempered the body together, having given more abundant honour to that part which lacked:

25 That there should be no schism in the body; but that the members should have the same care one for another.

26 And whether one member suffer, all the members suffer with it; or one member be honoured, all the members rejoice with it.

27 Now ye are the body of Christ, and members in particular.

28 And God hath set some in the church, first apostles, secondarily prophets, thirdly teachers, after that miracles, then gifts of healings, helps, governments, diversities of tongues.

1Co 12:4-28.

In this 1Corinthians 12:4-28 passage a further review of four phrases will assist us in a further understanding of the doctrine of giving unequal gifts and abilities to the members of the body of Christ. They are: **(1)** diversities of gifts; **(2)** differences of administrations; **(3)** diversities of operations; and, **(4)** the manifestation of the Spirit is given to every man to profit withal.

First, the word **diversities** *(dī-vũr′sə-tis)*, in 'diversities of gifts', is translated from **diairesis** *(dee-ah'ee-res-is)* which means a distinction, variety, difference, diversities. Therefore, the gifts given unto men are of a variety and different; not all the same. **Secondly**, the word **administrations** *(ad-min′ə-strā′-shəns)* in 'differences of administra-tions' is taken from **diakonia** *(dee-ak-on-ee'-ah)* meaning attendance as a servant, aid, official service especially as a teacher or the diaconate—the rank, office or tenure of a deacon; administration, minister (ing), office, relief, service. So, even if a member has the same gift as another member the degree, level or dunamis power possessed to operate the gift will be different and will depend upon their office, rank, tenure (length of service) and type of ministry engaged in. **Thirdly**, the word **operation** *(op′ə-rā′shən)* in diversities of operations comes from **energema** *(en-erg′-ay-mah)* meaning an effect, operation, working. **Operation** means the act, process, or method of operating. Thus, even if two members have the same gift and the same amount of dunamis power, within the same office, the manner, act, process and method of operating those gifts will be different, distinct and varied. But, **finally** the word **manifestation** *(man′ə-fes-tā′shən)* in 'the manifestation of the Spirit is given to every man to profit withal' is taken from **phanerosis** *(fan-er′-o-sis)* which means an exhibition, expression; a bestowment, manifestation. Therefore, regardless as to how and to what degree the Spirit of God manifest Himself through the working of a member's gift—it is all done to profit the one body of Christ as a whole. And, because of this, we are admonished

> **For I say, through the grace given unto me, to every man that is among you, not to think of himself more highly than he ought to think; but to think soberly, according as God hath dealt to every man the measure of faith.**

Ro 12:3.

Furthermore, even if a believer starts out with the **hikanoo** to perform only two types of gifts and he receives five talents within the two gift types, if he is faithful in the performance of the five talents and produce fruit for the kingdom of God he will grow in **favour** with God. And when he grows in **favour** with God he acquires more **charis—grace** and will receive more **dunamis—ability.**

A Believer's Station in the Life of Christ

So, the food and wealth that is convenient for a particular member—believer depends upon his station in life. And his station in life includes, among other things, his gifts, talents and offices, the **hikanoo**—qualifications (ability) to operate and perform those gifts, talents and offices within the body of Christ *(1Pe 4:11);* the number of gifts, talents and offices presently possessed and the **dunamis—ability** power, grace and favor—which is the provision provided for by God—to help him succeed in bringing forth fruit into the kingdom of heaven.

Also, in all of the work of the kingdom of heaven there is a need for another ability. That ability is the ability to gain wealth for the kingdoms use. For, the scriptures declare

> **...[T]hou shalt remember the Lord thy God: for it is he that giveth thee power to get wealth, that he may establish his covenant which he sware unto thy fathers, as it is this day.**

De 8:18.

Thus, we learn here that God gives us power to get wealth for the purpose of establishing his covenant and therefore his kingdom with his chosen people—those who believe in Christ Jesus. *(1Pe 2:9-10; 2Th 2:13; Eph 1:3-6; Ro 2:28-29; Ro 9:6-8, 24-26)* And, we can see this doctrine in action in the early church wherein the writer wrote,

> **Then the disciples, every man according to his ability, determined to send relief unto the brethren which dwelt in Judaea.**

Ac 11:29.

Here, in this Acts 11:29 passage we see the word **ability** once again. But, this **ability** is translated from the Greek **euporeo** *(yoo-por-eh'-o),* which means to be good for; have pecuniary means, ability. So, it is necessary for believers to have the ability to acquire wealth so that they can assist in providing relief within the kingdom of God to assist God with establishing his new covenant with all that should believe in Him and in his name. For,

> **The blessing of the Lord, it maketh rich, and he addeth no sorrow with it.**

Pr 10:22.

For, the Lord God is he that *"...hath pleasure in the prosperity of his servant." (Ps 35:27b)*

Planting Seeds Of Discontentment: A doorway to homosexuality and other temptations

Therefore, when leaders and shepherds within the kingdom of God teach, preach, live and, or showcase a doctrine of godliness based upon worldly prosperity *'supposing that gain is godliness' (1Ti 6:5)* rather than a doctrine of godliness based upon righteousness, patience, contentment and faith in God, they do not plant seeds of contentment. Instead, they plant seeds of discontentment amongst the believers. **Discontentment** *(dis'kən-tent'-mənt)* means being unhappy, and not satisfied with one's station in life, to the point of complaining, murmuring and wanting something more or different. But we are admonished,

> **10 Neither murmur ye, as some of them also murmured, and were destroyed of the destroyer.**
> **11 Now all these things happened unto them for ensamples: and they are written for our admonition, upon whom the ends of the world are come.**
> **12 Wherefore let him that thinketh he standeth take heed lest he fall.**

1Co 10:10-12.

Here, in this passage the word **murmur** *(mur'mər)* is taken from the Greek **gogguzo** *(gong-good'-zo)* meaning to grumble, murmur. **Murmur** means a low steady sound; a mumbled complaint. So, when we reconsider the 1Corinthians 10:10-12 passage above we learn that discontentment and murmuring brings about destruction and a loss of those blessings that the Lord God has promised us. For, sustainable prosperity from the Lord God comes only through obedience to His Word. Because he said,

> **...[S]eek ye first the kingdom of God, and his righteousness; and all these things shall be added unto you.**

Mt 6:33.

That is, a believer must seek and enter the kingdom of God by obeying Acts 2:38; seek to know, understand and apply the righteousness of God, to our everyday lives by obeying 2Timothy 2:15, James 1:22-25, St. John 5:39, Hebrews 5:11-14 and Hebrews 6:1-3; and then will all of these things be added unto him by the Lord God.

Also, a spirit or disposition of discontentment, unthankfulness and murmuring, if not repented of, will cause one to fall into a general state and mindset of unthankfulness. And, although we normally direct our unthankful and ungrateful comments to people and things that we can see, feel, hear and taste, the truth is our ungrateful and unthankful attitude and comments are actually against the Lord God. For, it was *"...he that hath made us, and not we ourselves..." (Ps 100:3)* As the writer wrote,

> **And God said, Let us make man in our image, after our likeness:...**

Ge 1:26a.

To accomplish this,

> **...the Lord God formed man of the dust of the ground, and breathed into his nostrils the breath of life; and man became a living soul.**

Ge 2:7.

> **So God created man in his own image, in the image of God created he him; male and female created he them.**

Ge 1:27.

For, after Adam was created and had worked for God,

> **21 …the Lord God caused a deep sleep to fall upon Adam, and he slept: and he took one of his ribs, and closed up the flesh instead thereof;**
>
> **22 And the rib, which the Lord God had taken from man, made he a woman, and brought her unto the man.**
>
> **23 And Adam said, This is now bone of my bones, and flesh of my flesh: she shall be called Woman, because she was taken out of Man.**
>
> **24 Therefore shall a man leave his father and his mother, and shall cleave unto his wife: and they shall be one flesh.**

Ge 2:21-24.

Adam and his wife Eve did well until the serpent found a place of discontentment down in her heart, her mind, her life. For, until then, mankind had not sinned and was worshipping God. But, after

> **4 … the serpent said unto the woman, Ye shall not surely die:**
>
> **5 For God doth know that in the day ye eat thereof, then your eyes shall be opened, and ye shall be as gods, knowing good and evil.**

Ge 3:4-5.

Adam's wife, Eve, became dissatisfied with her station in life as a help meet *(Ge 2:18-25)* and as a wife and ungrateful that the Lord had made her second (as a woman) and not first as a man. For, the food *(Read Ge 3:6)* and the beautiful and pleasant things *(Read Ge 3:6)* did not bother her as much as not having the wisdom, knowledge and understanding of her husband who was created before her. For, Adam had been working for the Lord God long before Eve was created. *(Read Ge 2:15-23)* Thus, because wisdom and understanding comes in length of days *(Job 12:12)*, the only way Eve knew and understood that she could acquire the wisdom, knowledge and understanding that Adam possessed was to have been created first—and therefore to have been created as a male person, a man. For, Adam did in fact possess more wisdom, knowledge and understanding than Eve. This is so, because he had already been working for a while naming all living creatures for the Lord before Eve was created and brought forth. *(Ge 2:7, 15-22)*

> **20 And Adam gave names to all cattle, and to the fowl of the air; and to every beast of the field; but for Adam there was not found an help meet for him.**
> **21 And the Lord God caused a deep sleep to fall upon Adam, and he slept: and he took one of his ribs, and closed up the flesh instead thereof;**
> **22 And the rib, which the Lord God had taken from man, made he a woman, and brought her unto the man.**
> **23 And Adam said, This is now bone of my bones, and flesh of my flesh: she shall be called Woman, because she was taken out of Man.**

Ge 2:20-23.

But now, while living in a state of unthankfulness, the serpent was able to cause Eve's heart to deceive her. For, although Eve had been warned not to eat of the tree *(Ge 2:17; Ge 3:1-3)* she was persuaded in her heart that the tree of the knowledge of good and evil had become

> **...a tree to be desired to make one wise...**

Ge 3:6.

For, if Eve could not turn back time and be recreated as the male of the species, she could now take a shortcut revealed to her by the serpent that would make her *'first'* in acquiring Lucifer's—the forbidden tree's knowledge. In this shortcut Eve would use her station in life to lead and cause Adam, the man, to follow her into sin. For, her flesh included her station in life as a wife which was also Adam's weakness in his flesh. And, in her new station in life—transgressing the commandment of God by eating from the tree of the knowledge of good and evil—she was first. As, the writer wrote,

> **13 For Adam was first formed, then Eve.**
> **14 And Adam was not deceived, but the woman being deceived was in the transgression.**

1Ti 2:13-14.

For, the serpent had showed Eve a shortcut to acquiring knowledge *(Ge 3:1-6, 22)*—by eating and thereby worshipping the forbidden tree that possessed the knowledge of good and evil. *(Ge 2:17)* By eating from the forbidden tree of the knowledge of good and evil and thereby begin worshipping Lucifer, the son of the morning *(Isa 14:12),* the anointed cherub angel *(Eze 28:14)* that was created perfect in beauty *(Eze 28:12)* and full of wisdom *(Eze 28:12)*—Eve would be able to acquire some of the knowledge and wisdom possessed by Lucifer. Adam did not possess the knowledge and wisdom that Lucifer possessed, at this time, because the anointed angel of God's wisdom had become carnal and he had already began planning a war in heaven against God. For, during his preparation the writer wrote about him saying,

> **3 And there appeared another wonder in heaven; and behold a great red dragon, having seven heads and ten horns, and seven crowns upon his heads.**
> **4 And his tail drew the third part of the stars of heaven, and did cast them to the earth:...**

Re 12:3-4.

Because Lucifer refused to remain in the truth of God *(Joh 8:44)* and created and fathered the deception called the 'lie'. *(Joh 8:44)* As a result his wisdom became carnal and not subject to the law and wisdom of God. *(Ro 8:6-7)* Being carnal, his wisdom consisted of the wisdom of man *(1Co 2:4-5),* the wisdom of the world *(1Co 2:6),* and the wisdom of the princes of this world *(1Co 2:6),* but not the hidden wisdom of God *(1Co 2:7)* which Lucifer did not know existed. *(1Co 2:7-8)*

So, although Eve could acquire, through worshipping Lucifer, the wisdoms of man, the world and the princes of this world, she would not and could not acquire the hidden wisdom of God that Adam had been acquiring through his obedience to God's commandments, even though she stole him from God for Lucifer when

> **...she took of the fruit thereof and did eat, and gave also unto her husband with her; and he did eat.**

Ge 3:6b.

For, although Lucifer and Eve joined together to steal Adam from God *(Isa 54:15),* and did acquire his physical body and his worldly power and authority *(Lu 4:5-7),* they did not acquire the wisdom and power of God that Adam once possessed. Because, having left God, Adam lost the power of the wisdom that he once possessed. This is so because, having sinned against God he became carnal and his

> **...carnal mind is enmity against God: for it is not subject to the law of God, neither indeed can be.**

Ro 8:7.

Because,

> **...to be carnally minded is death...**

Ro 8:6.

So, Eve became someone else, something that she had not been before she ate and began worshipping the forbidden tree. She became a woman walking in death. As the Apostle Paul explained,

> **10 And the commandment which was ordained to life, I found to be unto death.**

11 For sin, taking occasion by the commandment, deceived me, and by it slew me.
Ro 7:10-11.

Thus, while nursing this secret desire to be something or somebody that she was not and had not been created to be, Eve became vain in her imaginations and her foolish heart was thereby darkened from the light of the truth that *'...thou shalt surely die...' (Ge 2:16-17)* And, as a result, Eve refused to glorify God in her obedience to his commandment not to eat of the forbidden tree and so

...she took of the fruit thereof, and did eat, and gave also unto her husband with her; and he did eat.
Ge 3:6.

And now as the Apostle Paul stated,

21 Because that, when they knew God, they glorified him not as God, neither were thankful; but became vain in their imaginations, and their foolish heart was darkened.

22 Professing themselves to be wise, they became fools,

...

24 Wherefore God also gave them up to uncleanness through the lusts of their own hearts, to dishonour their own bodies between themselves:

25 Who changed the truth of God into a lie, and worshipped and served the creature more than the Creator, who is blessed for ever. Amen.
Ro 1:21-22, 24-25.

The truth of God that the serpent and Eve changed into a lie was the commandment where the Lord God said,

But of the tree of the knowledge of good and evil, thou shalt not eat of it: for in the day that thou eatest thereof thou shalt surely die.

Ge 2:17.

The serpent changed the truth of God into a lie when he

...said unto the woman, Ye shall not surely die:

Ge 3:4.

Both, the serpent's words and the Lord God's words, could not be truth because they were exact opposites. But, because the Woman was now dissatisfied with her station in life as a wife and help meet—that did not know and understand as much as her husband—she allowed her heart and her secret desire to be as wise as her husband to deceive her into believing that the truth of God was a lie and that the words of the serpent were the truth. And, having thereby rejected the word of the Lord she became carnal possessing a darkened and rebellious heart residing in death.

6 For to be carnally minded is death...

7 Because the carnal mind is enmity against God: for it is not subject to the law of God, neither indeed can be.

Ro 8:6a-7.

Seek, First

Now, let us return to the St. Matthew 6:33 passage above. For, by reviewing that scripture we learn that the things of prosperity, that are of this world, are added to us *after* we have sought out and entered into the kingdom of God; and, *after* we have sought out, learned and began applying the righteousness of God to our lives. For, the words which hold the key to our blessings in all scripture, here, are *'seek, first'*. When we *seek first* to enter into a divine relationship with Christ we seek to obey the greatest commandment which says,

> **37 …Thou shalt love the Lord thy God with all thy heart, and with all thy soul, and with all thy mind.**
> **38 This is the first and great commandment.**

Mt 22:37-38 *(Read also Mk 12:28-30).*

For, the word **seek** *(sēk)* in Matthew 6:33 is taken from **zeteo** *(dsay-the´-o)*. **Zeteo** means to seek; to worship (God); or in a bad sense to plot (against life); to desire, endeavour, enquire (for), require, seek after. And the word **first** *(furst)* is taken from **proton** *(pro´-ton),* which means firstly (in time, place, order, or importance); before, at the beginning, chiefly, (at, at the) first (of all). Therefore, if one is to possess worldly prosperity that is sustainable and that will not hinder his relationship with God, he must place the worshipping of God, in spirit and in truth *(Joh 4:24; Joh 6:63),* as the first and most important thing in his life, before the pursuit of acquiring things and worldly prosperity. For, Jesus promised,

> **29 …Verily I say unto you, There is no man that hath left house, or brethren, or sisters, or father, or mother, or wife, or children, or lands, for my sake, and the gospel's,**
> **30 But he shall receive an hundredfold now in this time, houses, and brethren, and sisters, and mothers, and children, and lands, with persecutions; and in the world to come eternal life.**

Mk 10:29-30.

But, after *seeking first* to enter into the kingdom of God (*Read Joh 3:5; Ac 2:38)* the believer must then search the scriptures *(Joh 5:39)* that he may learn to apply God's righteousness within his new life. For,

> **Butter and honey shall he eat, that he may know to refuse the evil, and choose the good.**

Isa 7:15.

And thereby, he is enabled to keep the Lord God first in his life.

Storing and Laying Up Wealth

In addition, take notice that in Matthew 6:33b Jesus said, "*... all these things shall be added unto you." (Mt 6:33b)* Here, the word **added** *(ad-ed)* is taken from the Greek word **prostithemi** *(pros-tith'-ay-mee),* which means to place additionally; lay beside, annex, repeat; add, again, give, more, increase, lay unto and proceed further. Thus, we have no true need to labor to be rich *(Pr 23:4),* because Jesus promised that *'these things shall be added'.* And, if these things are added to us by our heavenly Father, then our sustained increase and prosperity, as sons of God, does not come because of our labor or our power, but by the favor *(Pr 3:3-4)* and the fulfillment of the promises of God. Otherwise, the wealth, riches and honor received and acquired come as an evil disease sent by God. *(Ec 6:1-2)* For, our heavenly Father has given the sinners and unbelievers the worldly job of working to lay up and store wealth and treasures for our benefit as believers who are just. *(Pr 13:22b)* For, the Lord has determined, said and confirmed, by his Word, declaring through the writing Prophet,

> **For God giveth to a man that is good in his sight wisdom and knowledge, and joy: but to the sinner he giveth travail, to gather and to heap up, that he may give to him that is good before God...**

Ec 2:26a.

So, when a person seeks first and does enter into the kingdom of God *(Joh 3:5; Ac 2:37-39)* and thereafter seek to apply the righteousness of God to his life through studying, the Lord God then takes the wealth and the things accumulated by the unbeliever and gives it—adds the wealth and the things belonging to the unbeliever to the life and possessions of the just that is good in his sight. *(Mk 10:28-31)* And, because He has set in motion the process of prosperity *(Ro 8:28)* by which wealth and things are added to the just, without the just working and paying for them like the world does, He has warned every Believer to

Labour not to be rich...

Pr 23:4.

And here, the word **labour** *(la′-bər)* is taken from **yaga′** *(yaw-gah′)* meaning to gasp; to be exhausted, to tire, to toil; faint, (make to) labour, (be) weary. So, when we tire ourselves out, by over working, trying to get ahead in life or to become rich the deceitfulness of the riches that we labour for become thorns in our lives, choking and strangling the Word of God that is in us. For, *"...he that maketh haste to be rich hath an evil eye..." (Pr 28:22),* and *"...shall not be innocent..." (Pr 28:20b)* Because,

9 ...they that will be rich fall into temptation and a snare, and into many foolish and hurtful lusts, which drown men in destruction and perdition.

10 For the love of money is the root of all evil: which while some coveted after, they have erred from the faith, and pierced themselves through with many sorrows.

1Ti 6:9-10.

And the Lord Jesus commented, saying

For what is a man profited, if he shall gain the whole world, and lose his own soul? or what shall a man give in exchange for his soul?

Mt 16:26 *(Read also Mk 8:36; Lu 9:25).*

Furthermore, the Lord God said to Joshua, a leader of His people,

> **This book of the law shall not depart out of thy mouth; but thou shalt meditate therein day and night, that thou mayest observe to do according to all that is written therein: for then thou shalt make thy way prosperous, and then thou shalt have good success.**

Jos 1:8.

In agreement, in another place, the Psalmist wrote,

> **1 Blessed is the man that walketh not in the counsel of the ungodly, nor standeth in the way of sinners, nor sitteth in the seat of the scornful.**
>
> **2 But his delight is in the law of the Lord; and in his law doth he meditate day and night.**
>
> **3 And he shall be like a tree planted by the rivers of water, that bringeth forth his fruit in his season; his leaf also shall not wither; and whatsoever he doeth shall prosper.**

Ps 1:1-3.

Here, the word **prosperous** *(präs′-pər-əs)* and **prosper** *(präs′pər),* both, are taken from the Hebrew **tsaleach** *(tsaw-lay′-akh).* **Tsaleach** means to push forward, break out, come mightily, be good, be meet, be profitable, cause to prosper, make to prosper. **Prosperous** means successful; wealthy. And **prosper** means fortunately; to succeed; thrive.

So, if they nurse a desire for more and different and to be prosperous in obtaining the things of the world rather than the things of Christ, the people will become discontented with their stations and conditions in life. That is, if a leader is flamboyant and lusts after money and worldly prosperity so will the flock that he leads. For, they will follow and imitate the type of Christ that they see in him in the same manner as the Apostle Paul admonished the people of God in his day. For, there, he said,

Be ye followers of me, even as I also am of Christ. 1Co 11:1.

So, Apostle Paul admonished the believers to follow him as he follows Christ. Thus, the manner by which Paul represented Christ would be the manner by which the believers would follow and represent Christ. And again he said to the Philippian brethren,

17 Brethren, be followers together of me, and mark them which walk so as ye have us for an ensample.
18 (For many walk, of whom I have told you often, and now tell you even weeping, that they are the enemies of the cross of Christ:
19 Whose end is destruction, whose God is their belly, and whose glory is in their shame, who mind earthly things.)
Php 3:17-19 *(Read also 1Co 4:16; 1Th 1:6).*

Therefore, the people will desire and strive to be like their leaders in whatever state of godliness or lack thereof that he expresses—be it godliness by righteousness or godliness by worldly gain. So, a doctrine of godliness based upon worldly gain grows discontentment which prepares the soul to receive the seeds of covetousness. Thereby, out of ignorance, the people will begin coveting after the wealth, money and—or possessions that others have. As Brother James stated, when they go to God with their petitions and their requests, they

2 …lust, and have not: ye kill, and desire to have, and cannot obtain: ye fight and war, yet ye have not, because ye ask not.

3 Ye ask, and receive not, because ye ask amiss, that ye may consume it upon your lusts.

Jas 4:2-3.

For, if gain, wealth and abundance were the standard for godliness and being more Christ-like, then the poor—those who are not successful with wealth and abundance in life—will think that God is not with them, or that their lives are not pleasing to God because they lack wealth in abundance. In turn, their poverty of mind and spirit and their lack of wisdom, knowledge and understanding in the ways of God will cause them to lust and seek after the things of the world rather than the things of God.

So, the prosperity doctrine which teaches that gain is godliness, *(1Ti 6:3-5)* leads the people astray making them prime subjects and fertile thorn ground for being tempted and falling into a snare that was caused by and grown up within the deceitfulness of riches. Knowing this the leaders and shepherds, through covetousness, are able to turn their flocks into merchandise for the shepherds' own personal gain. *(2Pe 2:5)* Commenting on the same subject the Apostle Peter wrote,

1 But there were false prophets also among the people, even as there shall be false teachers among you, who privily shall bring in damnable heresies, even denying the Lord that bought them, and bring upon themselves swift destruction.

2 And many shall follow their pernicious ways; by reason of whom the way of truth shall be evil spoken of.

3 And through covetousness shall they with feigned words make merchandise of you: whose judgment now of a long time lingereth not, and their damnation slumbereth not.

2Pe 2:1-3.

These leaders and teachers spoken of by Apostle Peter are the same type of preachers and teachers spoken of by Prophet Isaiah when he said,

> **10 His watchmen are blind: they are all ignorant, they are all dumb dogs, they cannot bark; sleeping, lying down, loving to slumber.**
> **11 Yea, they are greedy dogs which can never have enough, and they are shepherds that cannot understand: they all look to their own way, every one for his gain, from his quarter.**
> **12 Come ye, say they, I will fetch wine, and we will fill ourselves with strong drink; and to morrow shall be as this day, and much more abundant.**

Isa 56:10-12.

They also, take the Word of God and twist it. For example, they use 3John, verse 2 to teach the people that God wants them to prosper and be in health, without teaching them that their souls must prosper, in spiritual things, first. Thereby, they cause the people to seek after the things of the world, first, rather than the things of God, which results in failure and disappointment. Thus, the 'prosperity-first' preaching leaders fail and refuse to teach the understanding of the whole verse where it says,

> **Beloved, I wish above all things that thou mayest prosper and be in health, even as thy soul prospereth.**

3Jo 2.

The truth that the blind, dumb and greedy dogs *(Read Isa 56:10-12)* refuse to teach is that God requires the believer's soul to prosper in His righteousness, first, before the believer prospers with worldly gain. As a witness, the Lord Jesus said

> **...seek ye first the kingdom of God, and his righteousness; and all these things shall be added unto you.**

Mt 6:33.

In the above 3John verse 2 passage the words **prosper** and **prospereth** are both translated from the Greek word **euodoo** *(yoo-od-ŏ΄-ō)* which means to help on the road; succeed in reaching; to succeed in business affairs; to have a prosperous journey; prosper. So, the secret to success in life and in our business affairs is seeking first to obey God by seeking and becoming a part of the kingdom of God—the body of Christ—and to seek to know and do the righteousness of God in our daily lives, by studying, meditating on, and applying the Word of God to our flesh. *(Jos 1:8; 1Ki 2:3; Ps 1:2-3)* And, hereby are we enabled to show the suffering of Christ in our physical bodies. *(Php 3:9-10; 1Pe 4:12-13; 2Co 1:5-7)* For, the psalmist wrote,

> **...Let the Lord be magnified, which hath pleasure in the prosperity of his servant.**

Ps 35:27b.

For, he also admonished us saying,

> **Delight thyself also in the Lord; and he shall give thee the desires of thine heart.**

Ps 37:4.

Covetousness

The Lord Jesus taught contentment by avoiding covetousness when he

> **...said unto them, Take heed, and beware of covetousness: for a man's life consisteth not in the abundance of the things which he possesseth.**

Lu 12:15.

Here, this idea of **covetousness** *(kuv′i-təs-nis)* warned against by the Lord Jesus comes from the word **pleonexia** *(pleh-on-ex-ee′ah).* **Pleonexia** means avarice; fraudulency, extortion; covetous (ness) practices, greediness. **Covetousness** means being and living in a state of greediness and possessing an intense desire to want a thing, especially something that another person has. And **avarice** *(av′-ə-ris)* means to desire and be greedy for money. Thus, we are to **beware** *(bē-wer′),* as translated from **phulasso** *(foo-las'-so)* which means to watch, be on guard; to avoid, keep self, observe, to preserve and save ourselves from becoming a person seeking with intense desire wealth, riches, and money. For, when we become greedy for riches we fall in love with those riches, having forgotten that,

> **...the love of money is the root of all evil: which while some coveted after, they have erred from the faith, and pierced themselves through with many sorrows.**

1Ti 6:10.

And having been warned,

> **But thou, O man of God, flee these things; and follow after righteousness, godliness, faith, love, patience, meekness.**

1Ti 6:11.

The believers that refuse to flee the thought of using the gifts of the kingdom of heaven to strive to become rich fall into a snare and a trap making them barren and unfruitful seeds. And as the Lord God said unto the prophet Ezekiel,

> **...they come unto thee as the people cometh, and they sit before thee as my people, and they hear thy words, but they will not do them: for with their mouth they shew much love, but their heart goeth after their covetousness.**

Eze 33:31.

For, a believer cannot serve, both, the pursuit of unrighteous gain and the pursuit of a righteous God of the universe. *(Mt 6:24)* For, **covetousness** *(kuv′i-təs-nis)* in the Hebrew is taken from **betsa'** *(beh'-tsah)* which means plunder; gain (usually unjust); covetousness, (dishonest) gain, lucre or profit. For, the delusion of riches can cause the possessor to believe that wealth and not God is who he should entrust his future, his physical health and his wellbeing. Because of this, the Apostle Paul instructs us saying,

> **17 Charge them that are rich in this world, that they be not highminded, nor trust in uncertain riches, but in the living God, who giveth us richly all things to enjoy;**
> **18 That they do good, that they be rich in good works, ready to distribute, willing to communicate;**
> **19 Laying up in store for themselves a good foundation against the time to come, that they may lay hold on eternal life.**

1Ti 6:17-19.

And in another place the Lord Jesus warned, saying

> **19 Lay not up for yourselves treasures upon earth, where moth and rust doth corrupt, and where thieves break through and steal:**
> **20 But lay up for yourselves treasures in heaven, where neither moth nor rust doth corrupt, and where thieves do not break through nor steal:**
> **21 For where your treasure is, there will your heart be also.**

Mt 6:19-21.

To demonstrate and teach by example the principles of the deceitfulness of riches, Jesus

16 ...spake a parable unto them, saying, The ground of a certain rich man brought forth plentifully:

17 And he thought within himself saying, What shall I do, because I have no room where to bestow my fruits?

18 And he said, This will I do: I will pull down my barns, and build greater; and there will I bestow all my fruits and my goods.

19 And I will say to my soul, Soul, thou hast much goods laid up for many years; take thine ease, eat, drink, and be merry.

20 But God said unto him, Thou fool, this night thy soul shall be required of thee: then whose shall those things be, which thou hast provided?

21 So is he that layeth up treasure for himself, and is not rich toward God.

Lu 12:16-21.

Amen.

Sound, Physical Health

Follows Prosperity of the Soul

There are many sick and chronically ill saints in the kingdom of God. And there is always a 'reason' and a 'why' this is. For, we are promised by the scriptures that,

5 ...[H]e was wounded for our transgressions, he was bruised for our iniquities: the chastisement of our peace was upon him; and with his stripes we are healed.

6 All we like sheep have gone astray; we have turned every one to his own way; and the Lord hath laid on him the iniquity of us all.

Isa 53:5-6.

Here, in this Isaiah 53:5 passage the word **stripes** *(strīp-s)* is taken from the Hebrew word **chaburah** *(khab-oo-raw').* **Chaburah** means to bound (with stripes), that is a weal (or black-and-blue mark itself); blueness, bruise, hurt, stripe, wound. And a **stripe** is a long, narrow band differing from the surrounding area of the skin. Thus, the sinner that repents of his sins benefits from the black-and-blue, weal marks that Jesus received before he was crucified on the tree. *(1Pe 2:24)* For, Apostle Peter, also, stated in agreement saying,

24 Who his own self bare our sins in his own body on the tree, that we, being dead to sins, should live unto righteousness: by whose stripes ye were healed.

25 For ye were as sheep going astray; but are now returned unto the Shepherd and Bishop of your souls.

1Pe 2:24.

And, just as **stripes** in the Isaiah 53:5 passage means a long, narrow blue and black wound or mark so does **stripes** in 1Pe 2:24 mean a mole, a black eye, blue mark or blow mark—it having been translated from the Greek **molopes** *(mo'-lopes).* For, Jesus received the stripes from the Roman style beating or scourging that he received from Pilate. *(Joh 19:1).* Pilate used the scourging to accomplish several purposes, namely: **(1)** as chastisement for the accusations brought against Jesus by the Jewish Chief priests, elders, scribes and rulers *(Lu 23:13-22; Mk 15:1-15; Mt 27:1-2, 11-26);* **(2)** to satisfy the desire for punishment of the righteous man, Jesus, by his Jewish false accusers *(Mk 15:1-15);* and, **(3)** to content and gratify the crowd *(Mk 15:15)* of people because he knew that the Jewish leaders wanted Jesus put to death *(Mt 27:1-2, 15-25; Mk 15:61-15)* only because they envied him. *(Mt 27:18; Mk 15:10)* For Pilate, the governor *(Mt 27:2,*

14), had examined Jesus *(Lu 23:13-15; Mt 27:11-14)* and found no fault in Him *(Lu 23:4; 13-14; Joh 19:4),* nor any evil and nothing worthy of a crucifixion. *(Lu 23:13-15)* So, after publicly beating and scourging Jesus, Pilate's intent was to release Jesus. *(Lu 23:16; Joh 19:1, 12)* And so he looked for political, correct ways to release him *(Joh 19:12),* but found none. Therefore, the Roman scourging was intended to save Jesus' life and to keep him from the death of a cross, in the same manner as when the Lord *"...scourgeth every son whom he receiveth." (Heb 12:6)*

Although the scourging did not prevent the death of Christ it does assist believers in their healing from sin when they repent and live unto righteousness. For, Christ committed no sin and no unrighteousness to merit a beating of stripes within his own life, but

> **4 Surely he hath borne our griefs, and carried our sorrows: yet we did esteem him stricken, smitten of God, and afflicted.**
>
> **5 But he was wounded for our transgressions, he was bruised for our iniquities: the chastisement of our peace was upon him; and with his stripes we are healed.**
>
> **6 All we like sheep have gone astray; we have turned every one to his own way; and the Lord hath laid on him the iniquity of us all.**

Isa 53:4-6.

So, since *"...it pleased the Lord to bruise him..." (Isa 53:10)* for our transgressions and our iniquities, God uses the unjustness of the bruising and scourging of a righteous man, Jesus, to heal the sicknesses of the unrighteous who believe in him by repenting and obeying his command-ments.

Furthermore, the scriptures also inform us that some of our healing shall come through the faith of others believing in Christ Jesus. For, Jesus said,

17 And these signs shall follow them that believe; In my name shall they cast out devils; they shall speak with new tongues;

18 They shall take up serpents; and if they drink any deadly thing, it shall not hurt them; they shall lay hands on the sick, and they shall recover.

Mk 16:17-18.

But, the question arises, if all of the above scriptures are true, and they are, then

'Why are many saints chronically ill and never healed?'

One reason why the chronically ill saints are not healed is due to the operation of the Word of God found in 3John, verse 2, where it says

Beloved, I wish above all things that thou mayest prosper and be in health, even as thy soul prospereth.

3Jo 2.

In the above 3John verse 2 passage the word **health** *(helth)* is taken from **hugiainō** *(hoog-ee-ah'ee-no).* **Hugiainō** means to have sound health; be well in body; to be uncorrupt and true in doctrine; be in health; be safe and sound; be whole (-some). Here, we learn that our wellness in body, and our sound health comes about and is maintained after our soul prospers. *(3Jo 2)* That is, the healing of our physical man follows the healing of our spirit man (our soul). And, our soul cannot be healed or prosper except in Christ Jesus. For in Him we have life *(1Jo 5:12; Joh 1:4; Joh 3:16, 36; Joh 6:33, 47, 53-54; Joh 11:25; Joh 14:6; Col 3:4)* and even that more abundantly. *(Joh 10:10)* So, we must first be in Christ and Christ in us in order for our soul to begin prospering in Him. *(Ro 8:9-11)* And, to maintain the prosperity of our soul we must search the scriptures *(Joh 5:39),* study the scriptures *(2Ti 2:15),* and meditate on the Word day and night *(Ps 1:2)* until we begin delighting in the Word of God and in God himself. For, it is a promise,

> **Delight thyself also in the Lord; and he shall give thee the desires of thine heart.**

Ps 37:4.

So, if one is sick and his heart's desire is to be well in his physical body and possess sound health, when he is found delighting in the Lord by studying *(2Ti 2:15)* and obeying His commandments as he study—the Lord shall give him his heart's desire to be well and in sound health. Because, God already knows what the believer is in need of. And He knows that the believer needs sound, physical health to do a work for him, even before he makes the request. *(Mt 6:8; Ro 8:26)* Yet, God still desires for the believer to seek and ask him for his healing. For, He said, ask and it shall be given unto you. *(Lu 11:9)* And the scripture records,

> **Blessed are they which do hunger and thirst after righteousness: for they shall be filled.**

Mt 5:6.

By reviewing the Psalms 37:4 passage with the Matthew 5:6 passage we learn that delighting in the Lord is to hunger and thirst after righteousness, because God is righteous *(Ezr 9:15; Da 9:14; Ps 11:7; Ps 116:5; 1Jo 2:1; Re 16:5)*, all of his ways are righteousness *(Ps 145:17; Ho 14:9),* he leads in righteousness *(Pr 8:20; Ps 23:3),* and he speaks in righteousness. *(Isa 45:19, 23)* For, we hunger and thirst after those things that we enjoy, things that pleases us. And the word **delight** *(di-līt')* means to give great pleasure; rejoice; to be highly pleased; great pleasure; something giving great pleasure. So, if the chronically ill believers will cause their souls to prosper, *first*, by delighting in the righteousness of God and not in the spiritual thorns,

God will answer their prayers and give them their hearts' desire—healing, and sound health. For Jesus said,

> **...If any man thirst, let him come unto me, and drink.**

Joh 7:37b.

We are healed by Our Faith

For, we are healed by our faith. *(Mt 9:22; Mk 10:52)* Therefore, when we ask the Lord for healing or when we access other kingdom of God remedies for healing such as,

> **13 Is any among you afflicted? let him pray. Is any merry? let him sing psalms.**
>
> **14 Is any sick among you? let him call for the elders of the church; and let them pray over him, anointing him with oil in the name of the Lord:**
>
> **15 And the prayer of faith shall save the sick, and the Lord shall raise him up; and if he have committed sins, they shall be forgiven him.**

Jas 5:13-15.

We must exercise our faith and believe that we are healed. For, if we think that we will not be healed then we doubt the Lord, which makes us a double minded person. As we are admonished,

> **6 But let him ask in faith, nothing wavering. For he that wavereth is like a wave of the sea driven with the wind and tossed.**
>
> **7 For let not that man think that he shall receive any thing of the Lord.**
>
> **8 A double minded man is unstable in all his ways.**

Jas 1:6-8.

And, further in agreement,

> **22 … Jesus answering saith unto them, Have faith in God.**
>
> **23 For verily I say unto you, That whosoever shall say unto this mountain, Be thou removed, and be thou cast into the sea; and shall not doubt in his heart, but shall believe that those things which he saith shall come to pass; he shall have whatsoever he saith.**
>
> **24 Therefore I say unto you, What things soever ye desire, when ye pray, believe that ye receive them, and ye shall have them.**

Mk 11:22-24.

Thus, by exercising faith in God we can be healed of our illnesses if we ask and not doubt in our heart. One might ask then,

What is Faith?

The writer wrote,

> **Now faith is the substance of things hoped for, the evidence of things not seen.**

Heb 11:1.

Thus, the believer's request of God for healing or anything else is substantively made up from the faith that he exercises—the depth of his belief in God that God will do what he ask. For, **substance** *(sub′stəns)* is translated from **hupostasis** *(hoop-os′-tas-is)* which means a setting under (support); essence, assurance, confidence, confident, person, substance. And **substance** means the real or essential part of anything; essence; the physical matter of which a thing consists. **Evidence** *(ev′ə-dəns),* in this passage, means something that makes another thing evident; a sign; it having been taken from **elegchos** *(el′-eng-khos)* which means proof, conviction; evidence, reproof.

Therefore, when one ask or petition God for healing, by faith, the assurance that he will be healed is his unwavering faith. His healing actually exist, now, at the moment that he exercises his faith to believe it has taken place. And the sign, the evidence, that he will be healed is his faith: *"Does he live his life like someone that believes they are healed?"* For, if the substance of his faith wavers, then it is not stable and as Apostle James has warned,

> **For let not that man think that he shall receive any thing of the Lord.**

Jas 1:7.

The next important question is,

If our Faith is wavering, How do we Increase our Faith?'

The Apostle Paul exclaimed,

> **So then faith cometh by hearing, and hearing by the word of God.**

Ro 10:17.

If faith comes by hearing the Word of God, then the more Word that we gladly receive and apply to our daily lives the more faith we will have. And one, sure means of acquiring and hearing more Word is by studying and searching the scriptures. And once we have acquired the knowledge of the scriptures if we will meditate on the Word day and night the Lord God will teach us the understanding and the wisdom of the Word studied. For, the Prophet Isaiah asked,

> **9 Whom shall he teach knowledge? And whom shall he make to understand doctrine? Them that are weaned from the milk, and drawn from the breasts.**

> **10 For precept must be upon precept, precept upon precept; line upon line, line upon line; here a little, and there a little.**

Isa 28:9-10.

The Hebrew word **hugiainō,** from which the word **health** *(helth)* is taken from, means not only to have sound health and to be well in body, but it also means to be uncorrupt and true in doctrine. And the only way to ensure that we are uncorrupt and true in doctrine is to live in a state of steadfast studying and being taught knowledge and understanding of the doctrine of Christ. Hereby, are we able to increase our faith in God because we gain knowledge and understand more of Him and His ways through studying.

Therefore, the chronically ill saints can increase their faith for healing by causing their souls to prosper through studying and being taught the Word of God *and* then applying that studied and taught Word to their lives.

A second reason as to why the chronically sick saints are not healed is because of sin remaining in their lives that they have not forsaken and repented of. For, the Apostle James stated,

> **14 Is any sick among you? let him call for the elders of the church; and let them pray over him, anointing him with oil in the name of the Lord:**
>
> **15 And the prayer of faith shall save the sick, and the Lord shall raise him up; and if he have committed sins, they shall be forgiven him.**

Jas 5:14-15.

In this passage Apostle James instructs the sick to **1)** call for the church elders; **2)** let the elders anoint the sick with anointing oil in the name of the Lord Jesus; **3)** let the elders pray over the sick in the name of the Lord Jesus; **4)** let the elders pray in faith believing that the Lord Jesus will heal the sick; and then, **5)** the prayer of faith will save the sick; **6)** the Lord Jesus shall raise the sick up from his sick bed in healing; and **7)** if the sickness was due to sin, then the sick person's sins shall be forgiven him.

Someone to Confess To

Also, James 5:16 instructs us to,

> **Confess your faults one to another, and pray one for another, that ye may be healed. The effectual fervent prayer of a righteous man availeth much.**

The problem, prevalent in the church today, is busybodies going about as talebearers gossiping and telling things about fellow members in the body of Christ that ought not to be spread as gossip.

> **And withal they learn to be idle, wandering about from house to house; and not only idle, but tattlers also and busybodies, speaking things which they ought not.**

1Ti 5:13.

Talebearers cause such strife in the body of Christ *(Pr 26:20)* until they cause believers not to trust one another enough to enable them to confess their faults and their shortcomings to each other. Their fear is that after they have confessed the person that they have confessed to will carry the tale to someone else and scandalize their name, character and reputation. Therefore, they do not confess because,

> **The words of a talebearer are as wounds, and they go down into the innermost parts of the belly.**

Pr 18:8 *(Read also Pr 26:22-28).*

So many believers, not knowing what earthly bound person to trust, long suffer with their conditions because they fail to find someone who: **1)** loves them enough that they can confess to and not hear it again; **2)** lives a righteous life; and, **3)** whose effectual and fervent prayer will avail unto their being healed. For,

> **He that covereth a transgression seeketh love; but he that repeateth a matter separateth very friends.**

Pr 17:9.

The problem of the busybody and the talebearer is so detrimental to the health and prosperity of the church until Apostle Peter placed it on the same level of a murderer, when he admonished us saying

> **But let none of you suffer as a murderer, or as a thief, or as an evildoer, or as a busybody in other men's matters.**

1Pe 4:15.

For, if our talebearing and our busy bodying prevent our members from being healed, then we are opposite of Christ's commandment where he said,

> **This is my commandment, That ye love one another, as I have loved you.**

Joh 15:12.

Jesus loved us so until he was wounded for our transgressions and by his stripes we are healed. *(Isa 53:5)* But, the talebearing busybodies cause others to suffer pain beyond their troubles because their words are as wounds that go down into the innermost parts of the belly. *(Pr 18:8)* Although,

> **Love worketh no ill to his neighbor…**

Ro 13:10.

When the above procedures does not result in the sick being healed the problem is at least one of six things, either: **1)** The elders that are praying over him did not exercise the proper faith in prayer believing that when they laid hands on the sick that God would heal; **2)** the sick person did not exercise the faith to believe that they could be healed; **3)** the sick person failed to confess their sins to a righteous living believer that they trusted was not a talebearer; **4)** the power of God was not present to heal the sickness of that person *(Consider Lu 5:16-25);* **5)** the person participated in communion unworthily, not properly discerning the Lord's body *(1Co 11:23-30);* and—or, **6)** If the sickness came about due to sin, then the believer had not forsaken and repented of his sins before the elders began praying for him. Because, if he has not forsaken his sins, and the sickness is present because of his sins—then God will not remove the chastisement, the punishment, that he has allowed because of his sins. Otherwise, if he is healed while the sin reigns in his mortal body *(Read Ro 6:12-14),* he will not repent. And therefore, the Lord will have to send a greater and worse chastisement upon him to convince him to repent, as he instructed the impotent man that he had healed, saying

> **...Behold, thou art made whole: sin no more, lest a worse thing come unto thee.**

Joh 5:14b *(Read also Joh 5:2-14).*

For, the Lord chastens whom he loves. *(Heb 12:6)* As, the writer exclaimed,

> **5 ...My son, despise not thou the chastening of the Lord, nor faint when thou art rebuked of him:**
>
> **6 For whom the Lord loveth he chasteneth, and scourgeth every son whom he receiveth.**
>
> **7 If ye endure chastening, God dealeth with you as with sons; for what son is he whom the father chasteneth not?**
>
> **8 But if ye be without chastisement, whereof all are partakers, then are ye bastards, and not sons.**

…

11 Now no chastening for the present seemeth to be joyous, but grievous: nevertheless afterward it yieldeth the peaceable fruit of righteousness unto them which are exercised thereby.

12 Wherefore lift up the hands which hang down, and the feeble knees;

13 And make straight paths for your feet, lest that which is lame be turned out of the way; but let it rather be healed.

Heb 12:5-8, 11-13.

Here, in this Hebrews 12:5-8, 11-13 passage we learn that God chastens and chastises those that he loves as his sons. **Chastening** *(chās′-ən-iŋ)* and **chastisement** (*(chas-tīz′-mənt),* both, are translated from the word **paideia** *(pahee-di'-ah).* **Paideia** means tutorage; education or training; disciplinary correction; chastening, chastisement, instruction, nurture. **Chasten** *(chās′-ən)* means to punish so as to correct; to restrain or subdue. And, **chastise** *(chas-tīz′)* means to punish especially by beating; to scold sharply. So, we learn here that the chastisement of the Lord is to help us, to disciple, correct, educate and train us when we do not obey the Word of God. For,

All scripture is given by inspiration of God, and is profitable for doctrine, for reproof, for correction, for instruction in righteousness.

2Ti 3:16.

So, when believers refuse to obey the written Word of God for their discipline, correction, education and training, which is presented to them by brethren in the body of Christ, then the Lord, himself, takes over the discipline and correction, by **scourging** them. Scourging comes when we fail to

Take good heed therefore unto yourselves, that ye love the Lord your God.

Jos 23:11.

And, the degree and extent of our demonstrated love towards God is described in a word picture spoken by the Lord Jesus, when he said

...[T]hou shalt love the Lord thy God with all thy heart, and with all thy soul, and with all thy mind, and with all thy strength: this is the first commandment.

Mk 12:30.

Thus, when we, as believers, fail to love God and therefore refuse to repent we go back and cleave to the worldly, unholy works and desires that we had forsaken when we came to Christ. For, the Apostle said,

...[I]f I build again the things which I destroyed, I make myself a transgressor.

Ga 2:18.

And, the Lord Jesus spoke of those who *'look back'* to rebuild pass sins, saying

...No man, having put his hand to the plough, and looking back, is fit for the kingdom of God.

Lu 9:62b.

While Joshua, the leader God's people, warned of the *'looking back'* believer's plight, admonishing us that

12 Else if ye do in any wise go back, and cleave unto the remnant of these nations, even these that remain among you, and shall make marriages with them, and go in unto them, and they to you:

13 Know for a certainty that the Lord your God will no more drive out any of these nations from before

you; but they shall be snares and traps unto you, and scourges in your sides, and thorns in your eyes, until ye perish from off this good land which the Lord your God hath given you.

Jos 23:12-13.

So, *'looking back'* and rebuilding past sins, once forsaken, brings about a punishing scourging from the Lord God and causes thorns to grow in our lives. And when we fail to repent we fail to bring any fruit to perfection.

When a person is **scourged** *(skurj)* he is whipped or flogged and punished or afflicted severely. For, the word **scourgeth** *(skurj-if),* here, is taken from **mastigoo** *(mas-tig-ŏ′-o)* which means to flog, scourge. And, **mastigoo** comes from the Hebrew word **mastix** *(mas'-tix)* which means a whip, a disease; plague, scourging. Thus, when a believer refuses the chastisement coming from those brethren that he can see and hear naturally and refuses to repent, the Lord himself scourges him by allowing a disease or plague to enter his physical body causing him to become feeble and lame. *(Read Heb 12:25)* To be **lame** *(lām)* means to be crippled, having an injury that makes one limp; stiff, painful; poor; ineffectual; it having been translated from the Greek **cholos** *(kho-los').* And to be **feeble** *(fē′-bəl)* is to be **paraluo** *(par-al-oo'-o)* which means to loosen beside, relax, paralyzed or enfeebled; feebled, sick of the palsy; weak; infirm; without force or effectiveness. So, after we have been chastised locally on earth, and reject the chastisement we are then rebuked from heaven by the Lord God. *(Heb 12:5)* And when we are rebuked by the Lord, we are convicted, reproved of our wrong, and scolded in a sharp way with a plague or disease that makes us feeble, lame, weak and ineffectual in the work of the Lord. For, **rebuked** *(ri-byook'd)* is taken from **elegcho** *(el-eng′-kho)* which means to confute, admonish; convict, convince, tell a fault, rebuke, reprove.

Repentance brings about healing

But, with the chastisement and the rebuking, if we will endure, not faint *(Heb 12:5)* and repent of our sins, by making straight paths for our feet *(Heb 12:13)* thereby forsaking our sins *(Pr 28:13),* the punishment will bring forth our righteousness in Christ Jesus. *(Heb 12:11)* And we will be made whole, cured, healed and made healthy again. For, to be **healed** *((hēl-d),* here, is to be **iaomai** *(ee-ah'-om-ahee).* **Iaomai** means to cure, heal, make whole. As the Psalmist wrote,

> **3 When I kept silence, my bones waxed old through my roaring all the day long.**
>
> **...**
>
> **5 I acknowledged my sin unto thee, and mine iniquity have I not hid. I said, I will confess my transgressions unto the Lord; and thou forgavest the iniquity of my sin. Selah.**
>
> **6 For this shall every one that is godly pray unto thee in a time when thou mayest be found: surely in the floods of great waters they shall not come nigh unto him.**

Ps 32:3, 5-6.

Failure to Repent results in being turned out of the way

After a believer receives in his body, because of his sins, a chronic illness or injury that will not be healed and he refuses to repent and make straight the paths for his feet by forsaking his sins, God will turn him out of the way of Christ and he shall be lost. *(Heb 12:13)* For,

As for such as turn aside unto their crooked ways, the Lord shall lead them forth with the workers of iniquity…

Ps 125:5b.

And he shall not be restored to sound health because, without repentance, his soul cannot prosper and as a result he is corrupt and his doctrine is not true. *(3Jo2)* For, his refusal to repent is an attempt to cover up his sins as if he has no sin to repent of. But we know that,

He that covereth his sins shall not prosper: but whoso confesseth and forsaketh them shall have mercy.

Pr 28:13.

Therefore, as a result of the unrepentant believer despising his trouble and chastisement from the Lord, his sickness shall be unto death. For,

…holiness, without which no man shall see the Lord:

Heb 12:14b.

Those who fail and refuse to repent, after the onset of a chronic, crippling disease or plague that will not be healed, will lose the grace of God and will become a bastard child having no heavenly Father. *(Heb 12:8)* As the Lord said,

20 Again, When a righteous man doth turn from his righteousness, and commit iniquity, and I lay a stumblingblock before him, he shall die: because thou hast not given him warning, he shall die in his sin, and his righteousness which he hath done shall not be remembered; but his blood will I require at thine hand.

21 Nevertheless if thou warn the righteous man, that the righteous sin not, and he doth not sin, he shall

surely live, because he is warned; also thou hast delivered thy soul.

Eze 3:20-21 *(Read also Eze 18:24; Eze 33:12-13)*.

So, after being warned and refusing to repent and now with no heavenly Father the unrepentant believer has no savior to save him. And if he has no savior to save him, then he is in the world without God, and lost. For, we are admonished,

Looking diligently lest any man fail of the grace of God; lest any root of bitterness springing up trouble you, and thereby many be defiled;

Heb 12:15.

Diseases and Plagues Not Due to Sin

There are some diseases and plagues that come upon the people that are not due to sin *(Joh 11:3-4, 39-40; Joh 9:1-3, 6-7),* and are present to test the faith in God of the believer or to show the glory of God within the deliverance and—or miraculous healing process. However, the sicknesses remain and are not healed for one of two reasons. The ***first*** reason is due to a lack of faith that results from a lack of studying the Word of God, as discussed above, which prevents the believer's soul from prospering. When the soul does not prosper the sick cannot be made whole. For, in this instance, because of a lack of knowledge the sick is corrupt and his doctrine not true because of ignorance. So, he does not receive healing and sound health, because to do so would assist him in spreading a false and untrue doctrine—his doctrine not being true. As the prophet wrote

My people are destroyed for lack of knowledge…

Ho 4:6a.

And,

Therefore my people are gone into captivity, because they have no knowledge...

Isa 5:13a.

Healing by Intercessors and Intercessory Prayer

The ***second*** reason that some diseases and plagues remain after the saints have laid hands upon the sick is due to the unpreparedness and lack of faith of those attempting to initiate the miraculous deliverance or healing process.

Some healings and miracles come about only by fasting and praying (Mt 17:19-21)

In this instance it is necessary, for he that shall be used by God to initiate the miracle, to: **(1)** be full of faith in the work that he is about to perform; **(2)** be fasted and prayed up in Christ; and, **(3)** be a student of Christ hungering and thirsting after righteousness. In agreement, the Lord Jesus commented after His disciples were unable to heal a demon possessed, young man. For, there it is recorded,

14 And when they were come to the multitude, there came to him a certain man, kneeling down to him, and saying,

15 Lord, have mercy on my son: for he is lunatic, and sore vexed: for ofttimes he falleth into the fire, and oft into the water.

16 And I brought him to thy disciples, and they could not cure him.

17 Then Jesus answered and said, O faithless and perverse generation, how long shall I be with you? how long shall I suffer you? bring him hither to me.

18 And Jesus rebuked the devil; and he departed out of him: and the child was cured from that very hour.

19 Then came the disciples to Jesus apart, and said, Why could not we cast him out?

20 And Jesus said unto them, Because of your unbelief: for verily I say unto you, If ye have faith as a grain of mustard seed, ye shall say unto this mountain, Remove hence to yonder place; and it shall remove; and nothing shall be impossible unto you.

21 Howbeit this kind goeth not out but by prayer and fasting.

Mt 17:14-21.

Here, in the healing of the child possessed by a demon, the Lord Jesus explained to his disciples who had been laying on hands and healing the sick, the infirm and the demon possessed *(Mt 10:1-8; Mk 6:7, 12-13; Lu 9:1-2, 6; Lu 10:8-9, 17-20)* that it was their unbelief that prevented them from casting out this particular type of demon. Their unbelief was due to a lack of fasting and praying. For, although some demons had come subject to them and they had been able to cast them out, on other occasions *(Mt 10:1; Mk 6:7, 12-13*), this lunatic demon was of a different class, and it required a greater, closer and deeper walk with Christ, the Lord God, to remove the unbelief of those who would command its silence, its rebuke and its unconditional removal from the human host. For, the believer's heart and soul must be humbled enough to believe that God can and will perform his requests even in the midst of the demon's demonic acts and threats. As David said,

> **But as for me, when they were sick, my clothing was sackcloth: I humbled my soul with fasting; and my prayer returned into mine own bosom.**

Ps 35:13.

The Intercessor must be Humble

The word **humbled** *(hum'bəld),* as David used it in Psalms 35:13, is taken from the Hebrew **'anab** *(aw-naw').* **'Anab** means a browbeating, to depress, abase self, afflict self, chasten self, deal hardly with, force, gentleness, humble (self), hurt, weaken, submit self. And, **humble** means having or showing a consciousness of one's short-comings; modest, lowly, unpretentious; to lower in pride. David was a leader of God's people and a fruitful intercessor. He understood God's requirement of self chastening to enable one to properly submit himself in the sight of God *(Jas 4:10)* and under the mighty hand of God. *(1Pe 5:6).* For, even the prophet Micah declared

> **He hath shewed thee, O man, what is good; and what doth the Lord require of thee, but to do justly, and to love mercy, and to walk humbly with thy God?**

Mic 6:8.

When we fast we chastise our flesh and bring it into subjection to the will of the Spirit of Christ that dwells within us so that we may be led by Him as sons. *(Ro 8:14)* Even the Lord Jesus,

> **...being found in fashion as a man, he humbled himself, and became obedient unto death, even the death of the cross.**

Php 2:8.

So, if it required the Lord Jesus, during his earthly ministry, to humble himself so that he was able to become obedient to accepting the death of the cross, then we as intercessors must humble ourselves so that (1) we may become obedient to the suffering life required of an intercessor; and (2) so that we may be successful in our ministries which are assignments of intercession. For, it is through our humbleness that the Lord hears us as David stated,

> **Lord, thou hast heard the desire of the humble: thou wilt prepare his heart, thou wilt cause thine ear to hear.**

Ps. 10:17.

And furthermore, he has also promised, saying

> **If my people, which are called by my name, shall humble themselves, and pray, and seek my face, and turn from their wicked ways; then will I hear from heaven, and will forgive their sin, and will heal their land.**

2Ch 7:14.

> **For thus saith the high and lofty One that inhabiteth eternity, whose name is Holy; I dwell in the high and holy place, with him also that is of a contrite and humble spirit, to revive the spirit of the humble, and to revive the heart of the contrite ones.**

Isa 57:15.

During Jesus' ministry, on earth, his disciples did not fast. *(Lu 5:33-35)* And this lunatic demon, within the child, that is discussed above in St. Matthew 17:14-21, was like a mountain that required unwavering faith the size of a mustard seed. This kind of faith is acquired only through fasting and praying. Although they had been taught to pray *(Read Lu 11:1-4; Mt 6:5-13)* the disciples of Christ were not fasting, even though they also had been taught to fast. For, the Lord Jesus taught them, saying,

> **16 Moreover when ye fast, be not, as the hypocrites, of a sad countenance: for they disfigure their faces, that they may appear unto men to fast. Verily I say unto you, They have their reward.**
>
> **17 But thou, when thou fastest, anoint thine head, and wash thy face;**
>
> **18 That thou appear not unto men to fast, but unto thy Father which is in secret: and thy Father, which seeth in secret, shall reward thee openly.**

Mt 6:16-18.

So, although they had been taught to fast and pray, the disciples' unbelief was due to their souls not being made humble by fasting because they were the children of the bridechamber with the bridegroom physically present with them. And as children of the bridechamber, they stood in a special place, with the Lord, which did not assist them in humbling their souls so that they could believe for greater and impossible things. In like manner, today, many members of the bride of Christ who possess Christ indwelling fail to fast because they believe that Christ will make all things alright, even though they are constantly falling down and failing to be fruitful in the work of the Lord. To justify their barrenness and unfruitful lifestyle they quote Romans 8:28 which says,

> **And we know that all things work together for good to them that love God, to them who are the called according to his purpose.**

Romans 8:28 is true, but the Lord requires all believers to humble themselves, in their everyday lifestyles, so that He can work through them under the mighty hand of God. *(1Pe 5:6)* Romans 8:28 is not a substitute for a believer's steadfast obedience to the commandments of God which limits the periods of barrenness and unfruitful work.

Therefore, with the bridegroom, Jesus, being with them the disciples did not see the need to fast. *(Lu 5:34)* That is, if their belief was not enough they could depend on Jesus, who was physically with them, to use his faith and his power to perform the impossible work of the ministry. And, as a consequence, when they needed the power through unwavering faith, they did not possess enough faith to cast out the lunatic demon. For, the writer wrote,

> **33 And they said unto him, Why do the disciples of John fast often, and make prayers, and likewise the disciples of the Pharisees; but thine eat and drink?**
> **34 And he said unto them, Can ye make the children of the bridechamber fast, while the bridegroom is with them?**
> **35 But the days will come, when the bridegroom shall be taken away from them, and then shall they fast in those days.**

Lu 5:33-35.

Intercessors Must Fast and Pray

Thus, we learn that to be an effective intercessor the believer must engage in fasting and praying; fasting to humble his soul *(Ps 35:13)* and praying to communicate with God—who is the power that heals and performs the miracles and requests of the intercessor. For, the Lord God is He

> **That confirmeth the word of his servant, and performeth the counsel of his messengers...**

Isa 44:26a.

Another question that arises is,

"What are believers to do when diseases and plagues come upon the people who do not have the mental stability or the mental ability to exercise faith to repent of their sins or to ask for help or prayer?"

In these instances an intercessor is necessary to stand in the person's stead utilizing and exercising their obedience and their faith on behalf of the sick person, whether their sicknesses are due because of sin or to show the glory of God. For,

> **We then that are strong ought to bear the infirmities of the weak, and not to please ourselves.**

Ro 15:1 *(Read also Ro 15:2-6).*

And, we should,

> **Bear ye one another's burdens, and so fulfil the law of Christ.**

Ga 6:2.

For, the law of Christ says,

> **12 This is my commandment, That ye love one another, as I have loved you.**
> **13 Greater love hath no man than this, that a man lay down his life for his friends.**

Joh 15:12-13.

And so, the doctrine of interceding on the behalf of another is born out of love. For, Christ interceded on our behalf and gave his life for our sins *(Joh 3:16; Mk 10:45; Joh 10:15-18; Ga 1:3-4; Ga 2:20;1Ti 2:5-6; Tit 2:13-14)* that we may be rescued from the perishing death that results from a life of sin unrepented of and unforgiven by God; and, so that we may be made whole and reconciled back to God through everlasting life that is in Christ. *(1Jo 5:11-13)* As the writer wrote of Him,

> **16 For God so loved the world, that he gave his only begotten Son, that whosoever believeth in him should not perish, but have everlasting life.**

17 For God sent not his Son into the world to condemn the world; but that the world through him might be saved.
Joh 3:16-17.

Furthermore, the whole plan of salvation for man is a plan of intercession by Jesus Christ interceding on behalf of man to defeat Lucifer's, the serpent's, eternal plan to take and rule over God's Genesis creation *(Read Ge 1:1-31; Ge 2:7-25; Isa 14:12-16; Re 12:7-12),* for himself. And, this doctrine of intercession is demonstrated further by the Lord Jesus in the Matthew 17:14-21 passage above where he healed the demon possessed boy. Likewise, even before the coming of the Christ, the writer said of him,

And he saw that there was no man, and wondered that there was no intercessor: therefore his arm brought salvation unto him; and his righteousness, it sustained him.
Isa 59:16.

The Intercessor

The arm of the Lord, mentioned in Isaiah 59:16, is described in Isaiah chapter 53:1-12. For, there the prophet wrote,

1 Who hath believed our report? And to whom is the arm of the Lord revealed?

2 For he shall grow up before him as a tender plant, and as a root out of a dry ground: he hath no form nor comeliness; and when we shall see him, there is no beauty that we should desire him.

3 He is despised and rejected of men; a man of sorrows, and acquainted with grief: and we hid as it were our faces from him; he was despised, and we esteemed him not.

4 Surely he hath borne our griefs, and carried our sorrows: yet we did esteem him stricken, smitten of God, and afflicted.

5 But he was wounded for our transgressions, he was bruised for our iniquities: the chastisement of our peace was upon him; and with his stripes we are healed.

6 All we like sheep have gone astray; we have turned every one to his own way; and the Lord hath laid on him the iniquity of us all.

7 He was oppressed, and he was afflicted, yet he opened not his mouth: he is brought as a lamb to the slaughter, and as a sheep before her shearers is dumb, so he openeth not his mouth.

8 He was taken from prison and from judgment: and who shall declare his generation? For he was cut off out of the land of the living: for the transgression of my people was he stricken.

9 And he made his grave with the wicked, and with the rich in his death; because he had done no violence, neither was any deceit in his mouth.

10 Yet it pleased the Lord to bruise him; he hath put him to grief: when thou shalt make his soul an offering for sin, he shall see his seed, he shall prolong his days, and the pleasure of the Lord shall prosper in his hand.

11 He shall see the travail of his soul, and shall be satisfied: by his knowledge shall my righteous servant justify many; for he shall bear their iniquities.

12 Therefore will I divide him a portion with the great, and he shall divide the spoil with the strong; because he hath poured out his soul unto death: and he was numbered with the transgressors; and he bare the sin of many, and made intercession for the transgresssors.

Isa 53:1-12.

The above Isaiah 53:1-12 passage of scripture is a description of the person, work and suffering of an intercessor. For, the work of the ministry of Christ, His kingdom and His Church is one of intercession—someone standing in the gap for the benefit of another *(Eze 22:30)* at the intercessor's own expense and suffering.

Furthermore, there are times when the diseased and sick person is in their right mind but just does not know what to pray for. Here, again, an intercessor is necessary for their deliverance and prosperity. The words **intercession** *(in′-ter-sesh′ən)* in Isaiah 53:12 and **intercessor** *(in′-ter-ses′ər)* in Isaiah 59:16 are both translated from the same Hebrew **paga** *(paw-gah').* **Paga** means to impinge by violence, accident or importunity; come betwixt, cause to entreat, fall upon, make intercession, intercessor, entreat, light upon, pray, reach, and meet together. For, in agreement, the scripture records that,

> **Likewise the Spirit also helpeth our infirmities: for we know not what we should pray for as we ought: but the Spirit itself maketh intercession for us with groaning which cannot be uttered.**

Ro 8:26.

Here, in this Romans 8:26 passage the Apostle Paul informs us that even those of us who are healthy, and in our right minds need an intercessor to help us. We all need an intercessor, because we do not know what we should be praying for to help us in our infirmities. For, here, when we say **infirmities** *(in-furm′-mə-tēs)* we mean **astheneia** *(as-then′-i-ah)* in the Greek. **Astheneia** means feebleness (of body or mind); malady; frailty; disease, infirmity, sickness and weakness. And, a **malady** *(mal′ə-dē)* is a disease, an illness. **Weakness** *(wēk′-nis)* means an immoderate fondness for something; or, living in a state of: **(1)** the lack of physical strength, feeble; **(2)** the lack of moral strength or willpower; **(3)** lacking mental power; and **(4)** lacking power or authority. And, **frailty** *(frāl′tē)* means a being frail, that is, easily broken or easily tempted due to a moral weakness; a fault arising from a moral weakness. Thus, all believers are weak and infirm in some area of their lives and are in need of an intercessor to assist us in overcoming our physical, mental and moral weaknesses. And, to make intercession for another person demonstrates the greatest love one can have for that person. Because, he that intervenes on behalf of another person will cause his flesh to suffer as is demonstrated in the Isaiah 53:1-12 passage above. And, as Jesus said below,

> **12 This is my commandment, That ye love one another, as I have loved you.**
>
> **13 Greater love hath no man than this, that a man lay down his life for his friends.**
>
> **14 Ye are my friends, if ye do whatsoever I command you.**

Joh 15:12-14.

So, the Isaiah 53:1-12 passage teaches us that Christ, his life and his death, here on earth was that of an intercessor for man, because man was not able to intercede with God on his own behalf *(Read again Isa 59:16),* he having sinned and divorced himself from God in the garden of Eden. *(Ge 3:6-8)* For, it was there, in the garden of Eden, that the Lord God announced and prophesied the coming of the intercessor, the repairer of the breach *(Isa 58:12; Isa 30:26),* when he said,

> **And I will put enmity between thee and the woman, and between thy seed and her seed; it shall bruise thy head, and thou shalt bruise his heel.**

Ge 3:15.

And, by reviewing the Romans 8:26 passage above we learn that after the death, burial, resurrection, ascension and return of Jesus Christ as the Holy Ghost, the Comforter *(Joh 14:16-18, 26)* on the day of Pentecost *(Ac 2:1-4)*—the Spirit of Christ has taken on the unseen role of intercessor for all who will believe on His name and obey His Word. For, if we are to demonstrate our belief in and obedience to the commandment to ***"Let this mind be in you, which was also in Christ Jesus:"*** *(Php 2:5)* we must exercise that same love for the brethren as Christ demonstrated for us. *(Read again Joh 15:12)* In doing so, as intercessors,

> **1 We then that are strong ought to bear the infirmities of the weak, and not to please ourselves.**
>
> **2 Let every one of us please his neighbor for his good to edification.**
>
> **3 For even Christ pleased not himself; but, as it is written, THE REPROACHES OF THEM THAT REPROACHED THEE FELL ON ME.**

Ro 15:1-3.

Intercessory Request

Also, because we are the one body of Christ, it is necessary and expedient for us as fellow laborers and brethren in Christ to make intercessory requests one for another. For, if the natural body helps its members so should the body of Christ as demonstrated by Apostle Paul when he needed assistance in traveling to Rome to meet the saints. For, he said,

> **30 Now I beseech you, brethren, for the Lord Jesus Christ's sake, and for the love of the Spirit, that ye strive together with me in your prayers to God for me;**
>
> **31 That I may be delivered from them that do not believe in Judae'-a; and that my service which I have for Jerusalem may be accepted of the saints;**
>
> **32 That I may come unto you with joy by the will of God, and may with you be refreshed.**

Ro 15:30-32.

Another example of interceding on a brother's behalf before God is discussed here,

> **16 If any man see his brother sin a sin which is not unto death, he shall ask, and he shall give him life for them that sin not unto death. There is a sin unto death: I do not say that he shall pray for it.**
>
> **17 All unrighteousness is sin: and there is a sin not unto death.**

1Jo 5:16-17.

And, as for the sin that is unto death, Jesus said,

> **28 Verily I say unto you, All sins shall be forgiven unto the sons of men, and blasphemies wherewith soever they shall blaspheme:**
>
> **29 But he that shall blaspheme against the Holy Ghost hath never forgiveness, but is in danger of eternal damna-tion:**

Mk 3:28-29.

Thus, when we review the 1John 5:16-17 and Mark 3:28-29 passages together we learn that, as believers in Christ, we can intercede as intercessors, before God, on one another's behalf for our infirmities, our weaknesses and for all of our sins—except for the sin of blasphemy against the Holy Ghost—that we all may be saved and have life in Christ Jesus. For,

> **1 Brethren, if a man be overtaken in a fault, ye which are spiritual, restore such an one in the spirit of meekness; considering thyself, lest thou also be tempted.**
>
> **2 Bear ye one another's burdens, and so fulfill the law of Christ.**

Ga 6:1-2.

Thus, even the law of Christ is one of intercession, to intercede on one another's behalf bearing one another's burdens.

Amen.

3rd Thorn Type: **The Pleasures of this life**

Now, the third type of thorn is called **the pleasures of this life.** *(Lu 8:14)*

The Lord Jesus stated,

> **And that which fell among thorns are they, when they have heard, go forth, and are choked with … pleasures of this life, and bring no fruit to perfection.**

Lu 8:14.

Here, in this Luke 8:14 passage, the word **pleasures** *(plezh'ərs)* is taken from the Greek **hedone** *(hay-don-ay')* which means to please; sensual delight; desire, lust, pleasure. The word **pleasure** *(plezh'ər)* means a pleased feeling; delight; one's wish, will or choice; a thing that gives delight or satisfaction. **Sensual** *(sen'shoo əl)* means of the body and the senses as distinguished from the intellect or spirit; connected or preoccupied with sexual pleasure.

In his letter to Timothy the Apostle Paul also admonished Timothy to turn away from brethren who love pleasures more than they love God. For, he said

1 This know also, that in the last days perilous times shall come.

2 For men shall be lovers of their own selves, covetous, boasters, proud, blasphemers, disobedient to parents, unthankful, unholy,

3 Without natural affection, trucebreakers, false accusers, incontinent, fierce, despisers of those that are good,

4 Traitors, heady, highminded, lovers of pleasures more than lovers of God.

5 Having a form of godliness, but denying the power thereof: from such turn away.

2Ti 3:1-5.

As we discussed earlier, discontentment, dissatisfaction and ungratefulness and not being thankful will open a believer's heart to various temptations. And these temptations may include the pleasures of this life which are things that cause sensations, delight, satisfaction and pleased feelings in and upon our physical bodies such as sexual pleasures, strong drinks like alcoholic beverages, and natural and man-made mood and mind altering substances such as drugs and narcotics. Pleasures also include one's wish, will or choice.

For example, although the marriage bed is undefiled *(Heb 13:4; Pr 5:15-19),* and the husband's body belongs to the wife; and, the wife's body belongs to the husband *(1Co 7:4)* believers still ought to govern their daily lives so that their lives are not preoccupied with sexual pleasures. *(1Co 7:29)* Yet, the husband and wife are not to neglect one another in such a way so as to cause the neglected spouse to become incontinent and thereby tempted to act without self control and temperance in sexual matters playing the harlot. *(1Co 7:5)*

Furthermore, as believers, we should not use strong drinks, drugs or narcotics except for medicinal purposes. As the scriptures admonish us saying,

Drink no longer water, but use a little wine for thy stomach's sake and thine often infirmities.
1Ti 5:23 *(Read also Pr 31:6-7).*

Here, the Apostle confirms our use of *'a little wine'* for medical purposes. However, when believers use wine, strong drink or other mind altering drugs and narcotics for pleasure, delight and the sensations it provide for the physical body they thereby become carnal Christians unable to please God. Because,

Wine is a mocker, strong drink is raging: and whosoever is deceived thereby is not wise.
Pr 20:1.

And,

4 It is not for kings, O Lemuel, it is not for kings to drink wine; nor for princes strong drink:
5 Lest they drink, and forget the law, and pervert the judgment of any of the afflicted.
Pr 31:4-5.

Thus, when we have infirmities and weaknesses in the flesh that involves our use of strong medicinal drinks, drugs or narcotics we must be careful to obtain assistance with our duties in the kingdom of God and his church to guard against the mocking, raging and deceiving effects and affects that these chemical pleasures can have upon our flesh and therefore our minds. More importantly, believers should guard their souls at all cost so that they do not forget the law and commandments of God; and so that they do not *"pervert the judgment of any of the afflicted." (Pr 31:5)* Because, many believers are deceived by the promised wonders of strong drinks, drugs, medicines and physicians to the point that they fail to believe or quit believing in the healing power of the word of God where it says,

13 Is any among you afflicted? let him pray. Is any merry? let him sing psalms.

14 Is any sick among you? let him call for the elders of the church; and let them pray over him, anointing him with oil in the name of the Lord:

15 And the prayer of faith shall save the sick, and the Lord shall raise him up; and if he have committed sins, they shall be forgiven him.

Jas 5:13-15.

Freewill Gives Us a Choice: The Right to Choose

Another area in a believer's life, involving pleasures, is his right to exercise his freewill with regards to the righteousness of God and God's will versus the believer's own will. This right of freewill is given to every man because the Lord God has given all men a measure of faith. *(Ro 12:3)* For, God desires and seeks freewill praise as a sacrifice of a person's right not to praise Him. God desires for man to choose Him and to praise Him freely. For, thereby is he glorified. As Joshua, a leader of God's people commanded,

14 Now therefore fear the LORD, and serve him in sincerity and in truth: and put away the gods which your fathers served on the other side of the flood, and in Egypt; and serve the LORD.

15 And if it seem evil unto you to serve the LORD, choose you this day whom ye will serve; whether the gods which your fathers served that were on the other side of the flood, or the gods of the Amorites, in whose land ye dwell: but as for me and my house, we will serve the LORD.

Jos 24:14-15.

So, when we take the pleasure of exercising our freewill right to choose to satisfy our flesh and please ourselves, rather than pleasing God by faith, righteousness and the commandments of God, as believers, we hereby add on a spiritual, life strangling thorn. And, this thorn of pleasures, if not repented of, will choke the life of Christ *(2Ti 1:1;1Jo 5:11-12)* out of us leaving us barren, unfruitful and not capable of bringing any fruit to perfection.

The Ministry of Perfection

By **perfection** *(pər-fek'shən)* Jesus meant, in the sower's parable above, **telesphoreo** *(tel-es-for-eh'-o).* **Telesphoreo** means to be a bearer to completion, to maturity; to ripen fruit; bring fruit to perfection. **Perfection** means the act of perfecting; a person or thing that is the perfect embodiment of some quality. And, **perfect** means complete in all respects; flawless; excellent as in skill or quality; completely accurate; absolute. The Lord Jesus desires and even commands us to strive and reach for perfection, in all that we do—whether it is in skill while working the gifts, talents and offices of the kingdom of God or in the quality of the righteousness of Christ that is seen in our lifestyle. For, He has commanded all believers to,

> **Be ye therefore perfect, even as your Father which is in heaven is perfect.**

Mt 5:48.

Our Father, God, who art in heaven knows all things *(Joh 16:29-30; Joh 21:17)* and understands all things. Jesus said that He, the Father, God, **is perfect, teleios** *(tel'-i-os),* complete in labor, growth, mental and moral character; completeness, of full age. Therefore, if the Father, God, is complete and perfect the completeness and perfection must be in all that He knows and understands—which is in all things. So, if the Lord Jesus commands us to be *"perfect, even as your Father which is in heaven is perfect",* then to be like the Father in perfection we must be complete and righteous in all that we know and understand. In addition we must strive to know and understand more of His ways by studying the Word of God *(2Ti 2:15),* and searching the scriptures. *(Joh 5:39; Mt 22:29; La 3:40)*

Moreover, our increase in growing up in Christ to the full stature of a man in perfection is so important to God that he gave us gifts to assist the kingdom in this ministry of perfection. For, it was recorded that

> **7 ...[U]nto every one of us is given grace according to the measure of the gift of Christ.**
>
> **8 Wherefore he saith, When he ascended up on high, he led captivity captive, and gave gifts unto men.**
>
> **...**
>
> **11 And he gave some, apostles; and some, prophets; and some evangelists; and some, pastors and teachers;**
>
> **12 For the perfecting of the saints, for the work of the ministry, for the edifying of the body of Christ:**
>
> **13 Till we all come in the unity of the faith, and of the knowledge of the Son of God, unto a perfect man, unto the measure of the stature of the fullness of Christ:**
>
> **14 That we henceforth be no more children, tossed to and fro, and carried about with every wind of doctrine, by the sleight of men, and cunning craftiness, whereby they lie in wait to deceive;**
>
> **15 But speaking the truth in love, may grow up into him in all things, which is the head, even Christ.**

Eph 4:7-8, 11-15.

And, to be sure that we are to continue to strive for perfection as our Father which art in heaven is perfect, the Apostle, using the gift, instructed us saying,

> **Therefore leaving the principles of the doctrine of Christ, let us go on unto perfection...**

Heb 6:1a.

And,

...[B]e not conformed to this world: but be ye transformed by the renewing of your mind, that ye may prove what is that good, and acceptable, and perfect, will of God.

Ro 12:2.

Whom we preach, warning every man, and teaching every man in all wisdom; that we may present every man perfect in Christ Jesus.

Col 1:28 *(Read also Col 4:12; Heb 6:1; 2Co 13:9; Joh 17:23; 2Co 13:11; 1Th 3:10).*

For, we are made perfect when we choose to suffer in order to obey the Word of God, as

16 All scripture is given by inspiration of God, and is profitable for doctrine, for reproof, for correction, for instruction in righteousness:

17 That the man of God may be perfect, throughly furnished unto all good works.

2Ti 3:16-17.

Because, perfection comes through suffering and enduring tribulation *(1Pe 5:10; Heb 13:20-21; Ro 5:3)* by which we gain patience *(Jas 1:2-4)* to continue in the life of Christ Jesus by possessing our souls. As Jesus warned,

In your patience possess ye your souls.

Lu 21:19.

For, even the flesh of the Lord Jesus, before he completed his work on earth, did not want to die the death of the cross,

39 And he went a little farther, and fell on his face, and prayed, saying, O my Father, if it be possible, let this

cup pass from me: nevertheless not as I will, but as thou wilt.

...

42 He went away again the second time, and prayed, saying, O my Father, if this cup may not pass away from me, except I drink it, thy will be done.

Mt 26:39, 42 *(Read also Mk 14:36; Lu 22:42).*

From Matthew 26:39 we learn that the will of Jesus' flesh was not to drink the cup of death which would cause him to die upon the cross, as he said to the Father, *"...not as I will, but as thou wilt." (Mt 26:39)* This lets us know that the will of the flesh and the will of the Father, the Spirit, are not the same which is a result of our freewill choice. For,

47 The first man is of the earth, earthy: the second man is the Lord from heaven.

48 As is the earthy, such are they also that are earthy: and as is the heavenly, such are they also that are heavenly.

1Co 15:47-48.

Therefore, it is necessary that we study the Word of God *(2Ti 2:15)* that we may know and understand what God's will is. When we come to know and understand God's will only then can we apply it to our life in Christ—and thereby be made *'perfect, throughly furnished unto all good works'*. For, then shall we be able, to,

2 My brethren, count it all joy when ye fall into divers temptations;

3 Knowing this, that the trying of your faith worketh patience.

4 But let patience have her perfect work, that ye may be perfect and entire, wanting nothing.

Jas 1:2-4.

For, to be fruitful and to maintain good works for necessary uses we must possess the mind of Christ. So,

> **5 Let this mind be in you, which was also in Christ Jesus:**
>
> **6 Who, being in the form of God, thought it not robbery to be equal with God:**
>
> **7 But made himself of no reputation, and took upon him the form of a servant, and was made in the likeness of men:**
>
> **8 And being found in fashion as a man, he humbled himself, and became obedient unto death, even the death of the cross.**

Php 2:5-8.

It was Jesus' patience and obedience that gave him the victory,

> **7 Who in the days of his flesh, when he had offered up prayers and supplications with strong crying and tears unto him that was able to save him from death, and was heard in that he feared;**
>
> **8 Though he were a Son, yet learned he obedience by the things which he suffered;**
>
> **9 And being made perfect, he became the author of eternal salvation unto all them that obey him;**

Heb 5:7-9.

Therefore, a person's exercise of his freewill right to choose will either lead him to life in Christ by the obedience of faith through suffering for righteousness' sake or to the ruins and pains of death by leaning on his own understanding *(Pr 3:5)* through following his heart *(Jer 17:9)* to do his own will. As Solomon admonished the young man, saying

20 My son, keep thy father's commandment, and forsake not the law of thy mother,

21 Bind them continually upon thine heart, and tie them about thy neck.

22 When thou goest, it shall lead thee; when thou sleepest, it shall keep thee; and when thou awakest, it shall talk with thee.

23 For the commandment is a lamp; and the law is light; and reproofs of instruction are the way of life:

24 To keep thee from the evil woman, from the flattery of the tongue of a strange woman.

25 Lust not after her beauty in thine heart; neither let her take thee with her eyelids.

26 For by means of a whorish woman a man is brought to a piece of bread: and the adulteress will hunt for the precious life.

27 Can a man take fire in his bosom, and his clothes not be burned?

Pr 6:20-27.

Thus, when a believer becomes preoccupied with the pleasures of this life those pleasures will cause him to forget the law of God. And now, having become a Carnal Christian, preoccupied with life's pleasures, his mind is no longer subject to the law of God. *(Ro 8:6-7)*

Moreover, as men and women of God, believers should only be preoccupied with pleasing the Lord God at all times, and not become lovers of pleasures more than lovers of God. *(2Ti 3:4)* For, the word **preoccupy** *(prē-äk'yōō-pī')* means to wholly occupy the thoughts of; to engross. When a believer's thoughts, and therefore his mind, are wholly occupied by the pleasures of this life he violates the first commandment wherein we are admonished

> **And thou shalt love the Lord thy God with all thy heart, and with all thy soul, and with all thy mind, and with all thy strength: this is the first commandment.**

Mk 12:30.

And, when a believer is in violation of this first commandment he has thereby become like as the people of Noah's day wherein the writer said of them,

> **And God saw that the wickedness of man was great in the earth, and that every imagination of the thoughts of his heart was only evil continually.**

Ge 6:5.

For, if a believer's heart, mind, soul and strength are preoccupied with pleasing and satisfying his flesh, then he is being led by his flesh and not by the Spirit of God. Therefore, his preoccupation with satisfying and pleasing his flesh will choke the life from him and cause his thoughts to become sinful and evil. Because,

> **...they that are after the flesh do mind the things of the flesh...**

Ro 8:5a.

And, the preoccupation of things sensual and things pleasing and satisfying to the physical body of man brings about carnality of the mind, resulting in spiritual death through the choking and strangulation of life.

> **For to be carnally minded is death...**

Ro 8:6.

So, with his heart and mind preoccupied with the things pertaining to death the believer becomes **unfruitful** *(un-frōōt′-fəl)* and unable to please God because he is incapable of bringing fruit to perfection. For,

...they that are in the flesh cannot please God.

Ro 8:8.

Because the carnal mind is enmity against God: for it is not subject to the law of God, neither indeed can be.

Ro 8:7.

Be Careful To Maintain Good Works

Therefore, as a carnal Christian possessing a carnal mindset because of his preoccupation with pleasures, the believer cannot obey the command to

...let ours also learn to maintain good works for necessary uses, that they be not unfruitful.

Ti 3:14.

Here, the concern with believers learning to **maintain** *(mān-tān')* good works is taken from the Greek word **proistemi** *(pro-is'-tay-mee)* meaning to stand before, in rank to preside; or to practice; maintain, be over, rule. Furthermore, the word **maintain** means to keep or keep up; to keep in continuance or in a certain state, as of repair; to support by providing what is needed.

So, when we become preoccupied with the pleasures of this life we quit trying to please God in our support, practice and concern for the maintainance and continued survival of good works by our walk of faith. And without faith we attempt to live for God and maintain the kingdom's work like the world which is impossible and unfruitful. Because,

...without faith it is impossible to please him: for he that cometh to God must believe that he is, and that he is a rewarder of them that diligently seek him.

Heb 11:6.

And so now, while possessing a thorn of pleasures in our daily lives, having left and abandoned the faith that we once received, we shall become unfruitful in the work of Christ and his kingdom. For, when we fail in faith, we forsake His cause, His purpose and His deliverance.

> **3 For we ourselves also were sometimes foolish, disobedient, deceived, serving divers lusts and pleasures, living in malice and envy, hateful, and hating one another.**
> **4 But after that the kindness and love of God our Saviour toward man appeared,**
> **5 Not by works of righteousness which we have done, but according to his mercy he saved us, by the washing of regeneration, and renewing of the Holy Ghost;**
> **6 Which he shed on us abundantly through Jesus Christ our Saviour;**
> **7 That being justified by his grace, we should be made heirs according to the hope of eternal life.**

Tit 3:3-7.

And again, because our carnal mind causes us to become preoccupied with life's pleasures we also forget that

> **This is a faithful saying, and these things I will that thou affirm constantly, that they which have believed in God might be careful to maintain good works. These things are good and profitable unto men.**

Tit 3:8.

Not being careful to maintain good works puts a believer at a greater risk of his righteous lifestyle being choked out of him by the spiritual thorns taught by Jesus in the Parable of the Sower. *(See Lu 8:4-15)* For,

This know also, that in the last days perilous times shall come.
2Ti 3:1.

Here, the word **perilous** *(per'-ə-ləs)* is translated from the Greek **chalepos** *(khal-ep-os').* **Chalepos** means reducing the strength; difficult, dangerous, furious; fierce, perilous. **Perilous** means involving peril or risk; dangerous. **Peril** *(per'əl)* means exposure to harm or injury; something that may cause harm.

Thus, in these the last days, the believer shall find it more difficult and dangerous to carry on a holy and sanctified life for Christ while maintaining good works.

Yea, and all that will live godly in Christ Jesus shall suffer persecution.
2Ti 3:12.

For, we find ourselves surrounded by and exposed to harm, injury and evil everywhere in the world. For,

...evil men and seducers shall wax worse and worse, deceiving, and being deceived.
2Ti 3:13.

Because, in these last days there is a falling away from the apostolic doctrine *(2Th 2:3)* and the way called holiness. *(Isa 35:8-9)* For, many believers have become lovers of themselves and of entertainment pleasures rather than lovers of God. The honor that they once sought from God, they now seek from one another resulting in unbelief in God and in his Word. *(Joh 5:41-44)* Even the beauty that they seek after, is no longer the beauty of holiness *(Ps 29:2; 2Ch 20:21; 1Ch 16:29; Ps 90:17; Ps 96:9; Ps 110:3),* or the modest apparel *(1Ti 2:9)* that comes with a quiet and humble spirit *(1Pe 3:4),* with shamefacedness. *(1Ti 2:9)* But rather, they paint their faces and their bodies with tattoo paintings and seek the ornaments of the beauty of Lucifer, the anointed angel *(Eze 28:12-15; 1Pe 3:3; 1Ti 2:9);* of the harlot *(Eze 23:1-49);* and, of a Jezebel spirit *(Re 2:18-23),* all of which steals their strength, and chokes and strangles the life giving power of the Word within them.

So, in these last days the strength that believers could use to witness and reach other souls for Christ, because of the perilous times we live in, they must use more to protect and save themselves from an untoward, perverse and wicked generation. *(Ac 2:40)* For, every believer must strive to learn how to assist in maintaining good works for necessary uses. Here, in the Titus 3:14 passage above, the word **necessary** *(nes′ə-ser′ē)* is taken from **anagkaios** *(an-ang-kah'-yos)* which means near, necessity, necessary, needful. **Necessary** means essential, indispensable, required, inevitable. The good works of the kingdom of God are necessary, required and indispensable for the saving of souls, deliverance, healing the broken hearted, giving sight to the blind, setting the captives free and for sustained, sorrow-free prosperity.

Amen.

Now, the fourth type of thorn is called **the lusts of other things entering in.** *(Mk 4:18-19)*

4th Thorn Type: The Lusts of Other Things Entering In

The Lord Jesus stated,

> **18 And these are they which are sown among thorns; such as hear the word,**
>
> **19 And the ... lusts of other things entering in, choke the word, and it becometh unfruitful.**

Mk 4:18-19 *(Read also Lu 8:7, 14; Mt 13:7, 22).*

Lusts *(lusts),* here, is taken from the Greek **epithumia** *(ep-ee-thoo-mee'-ah)* which means a longing (especially for what is forbidden); concupiscence, desire, to lust after. **Lust** means an overwhelming desire; to feel an intense desire; bodily appetite; especially excessive sexual desire. If we love the world and the things of the world there are two areas in a believer's life that lust will creep in upon him: the lust of the flesh and the lust of the eyes. For, the Apostle John stated,

> **15 Love not the world, neither the things that are in the world. If any man love the world, the love of the Father is not in him.**
>
> **16 For all that is in the world, the lust of the flesh, and the lust of the eyes, and the pride of life, is not of the Father, but is of the world.**

1Joh 2:15-16.

There are some sinful traits that reside in our flesh by which we are tempted. And there are things that we see with our eyes. The temptation, desire and thoughts concerning the visual thing arise because we saw it. Knowing this beforehand and knowing that these lusts and temptations are not of the Father, the Apostle Peter warns us saying,

> **Dearly beloved, I beseech you as strangers and pilgrims, abstain from fleshly lusts, which war against the soul;**

1Pe 2:11.

Apostle Peter's warning is important because, before *'the lusts of other things enters'* into a believer's life, he is first tempted but not by the Lord God. As the Apostle James instructs us saying,

13 Let no man say when he is tempted, I am tempted of God: for God cannot be tempted with evil, neither tempteth he any man:

14 But every man is tempted, when he is drawn away of his own lust, and enticed.

15 Then when lust hath conceived, it bringeth forth sin: and sin, when it is finished, bringeth forth death.

Jas 1:13-15.

To prevent a thorn from entering into his life a believer must exercise his faith in the keeping power of the Holy Ghost by rejecting the initial temptation before it grows and becomes an overwhelming, intense desire and feeling for the thing that is forbidden. Because,

11 ...the grace of God that bringeth salvation hath appeared to all men,

12 Teaching us that, denying ungodliness and worldly lusts, we should live soberly, righteously, and godly, in this present world;

Tit 2:11-12.

A believer is able to reject sin and protect against sin by subduing his flesh *(Ge 1:28);* keeping his flesh under subjection *(1Co 9:27)* and by obeying the command to

7 Submit yourselves therefore to God. Resist the devil, and he will flee from you.

8 Draw nigh to God, and he will draw nigh to you. Cleanse your hands, ye sinners; and purify your hearts, ye double minded.

Jas 4:7-8.

For, if we will submit our ways, our minds and our desires to the light of the Word of God He will direct our paths *(Pr 3:6)* and be a lamp unto our feet. *(Ps 119:105; Pr 6:23)* For

> **There hath no temptation taken you but such as is common to man: but God is faithful, who will not suffer you to be tempted above that ye are able; but will with the temptation also make a way to escape, that ye may be able to bear it.**

1Co 10:13.

Parables of the Forbidden Lust

Many times to avoid temptation it's a matter of not putting ourselves in a position to be tempted, above what we can bear, like the young man in King Solomon's parable. For, there he taught,

> **1 My son, keep my words, and lay up my commandments with thee. 2 Keep my commandments, and live; and my law as the apple of thine eye. 3 Bind them upon thy fingers, write them upon the table of thine heart. 4 Say to wisdom, Thou art my sister; and call understanding thy kinswoman: 5 That they may keep thee from the strange woman, from the stranger which flattereth with her words. 6 For at the window of my house I looked through my casement, 7 And beheld among the simple ones, I discerned among the youths, a young man void of understanding, 8 Passing through the street near her corner; and he went the way to her house, 9 In the twilight, in the evening, in the black and dark night: 10 And, behold, there met him a woman with the attire of an harlot, and subtil of heart. 11 (She is loud and stubborn; her feet abide not in her house: 12 Now is she without, now in the streets, and lieth in wait at every corner.) 13 So she caught him, and kissed him, and with an impudent face said unto him, 14 I have peace offerings with me; this day have I payed my vows. 15 Therefore came I forth to meet thee, diligently to seek thy face, and I have found**

thee. 16 I have decked my bed with coverings of tapestry, with carved works, with fine linen of Egypt. 17 I have perfumed my bed with myrrh, aloes, and cinnamon. 18 Come, let us take our fill of love until the morning: let us solace ourselves with loves. 19 For the goodman is not at home, he is gone a long journey: 20 He hath taken a bag of money with him, and will come home at the day appointed. 21 With her much fair speech she caused him to yield, with the flattering of her lips she forced him. 22 He goeth after her straightway, as an ox goeth to the slaughter, or as a fool to the correction of the stocks; 23 Till a dart strike through his liver; as a bird hasteth to the snare, and knoweth not that it is for his life. 24 Hearken unto me now therefore, O ye children, and attend to the words of my mouth. 25 Let not thine heart decline to her ways, go not astray in her paths. 26 For she hath cast down many wounded: yea, many strong men have been slain by her. 27 Her house is the way to hell, going down to the chambers of death.

Pr 7:1-27.

In this parable, the young man had two problems, no understanding *(Pr 7:7)* and he went to an area where prostitutes and harlots were known to hang on the corner, placing himself in a position to be tempted. Had he kept the wisdom and understanding that had been offered and obeyed it he would not have been tempted. For, the scriptures admonish us saying

Neither give place to the devil.

Eph 4:27.

Here, **place** *(plās)* is translated from the Greek **topos** *(top'-os)* meaning a spot, opportunity, license, room. So the young man gave the devil license to tempt him. And since he gave the license and provided the opportunity when the Lord provided a way to escape *(1Co 10:13)* he refused to take the escape route. For, he was drawn away by his own lust, and was enticed. By giving place to the devil he committed in his heart to engage in the lustful act if and when the devil provided him with the opportunity. Therefore the lust conceived in his heart and brought forth sin, even before he physically committed the act. *(Jas 1:14-15; Mt 5:28)*

In another of King Solomon's parables, he taught,

> **20 My son, keep thy father's commandment, and forsake not the law of thy mother: 21 Bind them continually upon thine heart, and tie them about thy neck. 22 When thou goest, it shall lead thee; when thou sleepest, it shall keep thee; and when thou awakes, it shall talk with thee. 23 For the commandment is a lamp; and the law is light; and reproofs of instruction are the way of life: 24 To keep thee from the evil woman, from the flattery of the tongue of a strange woman. 25 Lust not after her beauty in thine heart; neither let her take thee with her eyelids. 26 For by means of a whorish woman a man is brought to a piece of bread: and the adulteress will hunt for the precious life.**

Pr 6:20-26.

In this parable King Solomon gives advice on how to not be tempted by a beautiful woman. First, he says do not make conversation and allow her to flatter you with the words from her tongue. *(Pr 6:24)* Second, he says do not dwell on her beauty until it is in your heart—that is, you are thinking about her long after you meet her, or you undress her in your mind. *(Pr 6:25)* For, Jesus said,

> **But I say unto you, That whosoever looketh on a woman to lust after her hath committed adultery with her already in his heart.**

Mt 5:28.

And thirdly he warns not to allow her to take you with her eyelids *(Pr 6:25)*—that is do not look into her eyes and hold a gaze. For, in this manner she is able to reach your soul, cause you to desire her and fill you with darkness. Her eyes will talk to you. As the Lord Jesus taught,

> **34 The light of the body is the eye: therefor when thine eye is single, thy whole body also is full of light; but when thine eye is evil, thy body also is full of darkness.**
>
> **35 Take heed therefore that the light which is in thee be not darkness.**
>
> **36 If thy whole body therefore be full of light, having no part dark, the whole shall be full of light, as when the bright shining of a candle doth give thee light.**

Lu 11:34-36 *(Mt 6:22-23).*

The Company We Keep

Sometimes we come subject to various lust because of the company we keep. Jude wrote,

> **10 But these speak evil of those things which they know not: but what they know naturally, as brute beasts, in those things they corrupt themselves.**
>
> **11 Woe unto them! for they have gone in the way of Cain, and ran greedily after the error of Balaam for reward, and perished in the gainsaying of Core.**
>
> **12 These are spots in your feasts of charity, when they feast with you, feeding themselves without fear: clouds they are without water, carried about of winds; trees whose fruit withereth, without fruit, twice dead, plucked up by the roots;**

13 Raging waves of the sea, foaming out their own shame; wandering stars, to whom is reserved the blackness of darkness for ever.

14 And Enoch also, the seventh from Adam, prophesied of these, saying, Behold, the Lord cometh with ten thousands of his saints,

15 To execute judgment upon all, and to convince all that are ungodly among them of all their ungodly deeds which they have ungodly committed, and of all their hard speeches which ungodly sinners have spoken against him.

16 These are murmurers, complainers, walking after their own lusts; and their mouth speaketh great swelling words, having men's persons in admiration because of advantage.

17 But, beloved, remember ye the words which were spoken before of the apostles of our Lord Jesus Christ;

18 How that they told you there should be mockers in the last time, who should walk after their own ungodly lusts.

19 These be they who separate themselves, sensual, having not the Spirit.

20 But ye, beloved, building up yourselves on your most holy faith, praying in the Holy Ghost,

21 Keep yourselves in the love of God…

Jude 10-21.

Here, Jude admonishes the believers that those believers who go around complaining and murmuring are those who walk after their own ungodly lusts, separating themselves, being sensual, having not the Spirit. Thus, the point here is not to fellowship with those who Jude warns about. That way we keep ourselves unspotted from their ways of life. He further says that the believer should build himself up in his holy faith and keep himself in the love of God.

Amen.

The Good Ground Seed

And finally, the last fruitfulness type that Jesus taught with the Parable of the Sower is called the *good ground seed.* For, Jesus said,

> **3 Hearken; Behold, there went out a sower to sow:...**
>
> **4 And it came to pass, as he sowed...**
>
> **8 ...other fell on good ground, and did yield fruit that sprang up and increased; and brought forth, some thirty, and some sixty, and some an hundred.**
>
> **...**
>
> **20 And these are they which are sown on good ground; such as hear the word, and receive it, and bring forth fruit, some thirtyfold, some sixty, and some an hundred.**

Mk 4:3-4, 8, 20.

And again,

> **But that on the good ground are they, which in an honest and good heart, having heard the word, keep it, and bring forth fruit with patience.**

Lu 8:15.

And finally,

> **But he that received seed into the good ground is he that heareth the word, and understandeth it; which also beareth fruit, and bringeth forth, some an hundredfold, some sixty, some thirty.**

Mt 13:23.

Good Ground Seed vs. Wayside Seed

Here, in this portion of the parable of the sower, the good ground seed received the Word of God in an ***honest*** and ***good heart***, with ***understanding***. Then they ***kept*** the Word through ***patience*** and brought forth fruit some thirty, some sixty and some an hundredfold. In contrast, the wayside seed did not get an understanding of the Word of God that they heard. And so, unlike the good ground seed, they could not keep the Word because they did not understand it. Nor did they become followers of the preacher (the sower) in order to acquire a real life example of the Word and righteousness of God, in action, as the Thessalonians did when they began following the apostles and then Christ. For, the writer wrote,

> **5 For our gospel came not unto you in word only, but also in power, and in the Holy Ghost, and in much assurance; as ye know what manner of men we were among you for your sake.**
>
> **6 And ye became followers of us, and of the Lord, having received the word in much affliction, with joy of the Holy Ghost:**
>
> **7 So that we were ensamples to all that believe in Macedonia and Achaia.**
>
> **8 For from you sounded out the word of the Lord not only in Macedonia and Achaia, but also in every place your faith to God-ward is spread abroad; so that we need not to speak any thing.**
>
> **9 For they themselves shew of us what manner of entering in we had unto you, and how ye turned to God from idols to serve the living and true God;**

1Th 1:5-9.

The wayside seed was prevented from learning about the life and righteousness of Jesus Christ, through the life of the preacher, because the sower (the preacher's) life was traduced, defamed and slandered by the devil. And now, with the sower's life destroyed in the wayside seed's mind he lost a real life, living, suffering example of the Word and righteousness of God. And so, the enemy was able to steal the Word out of the wayside soul's heart making him barren and unfruitful. For, without an understanding of the Word of God the wayside seed was not connected to the vine or the root, and therefore he was unable to produce fruit. For, Jesus said,

> **1 I am the true vine, and my Father is the husbandman.**
> **2 Every branch in me that beareth not fruit he taketh away: and every branch that beareth fruit, he purgeth it, that it may bring forth more fruit.**
> **3 Now ye are clean through the word which I have spoken unto you.**
> **4 Abide in me, and I in you. As the branch cannot bear fruit of itself, except it abide in the vine; no more can ye, except ye abide in me.**
> **5 I am the vine, ye are the branches: He that abideth in me, and I in him, the same bringeth forth much fruit: for without me ye can do nothing.**

Joh 15:1-5.

So, after the Word of God was stolen from him, the wayside seed had no connection to Christ who is the vine. *(Joh 15:1)* He was unclean and remained unclean, because the Word of God had been stolen out of his heart and therefore out of his life. Without the Word of God there was nothing else to cleanse him. *(Joh 15:3)* As Jesus declared,

> **Now ye are clean through the word which I have spoken unto you.**

Joh 15:3.

Therefore, the wayside seed abided in himself and not in Christ, living a life that made it impossible for him to bear fruit. For,

> **Those by the way side are they that hear; then cometh the devil, and taketh away the word out of their hearts, lest they should believe and be saved.**

Lu 8:12.

In contrast, the good ground seed received the Word and then got an understanding of that Word by obeying the commands, to

> **...[W]ith all your getting get an understanding.**

Pr 4:7b.

> **Study to shew thyself approved unto God, a workman that needeth not to be ashamed, rightly dividing the word of truth.**

2Ti 2:15.

And,

> **Search the scriptures; for in them ye think ye have eternal life: and they are they which testify of me.**

Joh 5:39.

After getting an understanding of the Word that they had heard and received, the good ground seed then **kept** it. That is, in the Greek they **katecho** *(kat-ekh'-o)* the Word and its understanding. **Katecho** means to hold down, have, hold (fast), keep (in memory), let, make toward, possess, retain, seize on, stay, take, withhold. And, **keep** *(kēp)* means to celebrate, observe, to fulfill (a Promise); to protect; guard; take care of; tend; to preserve; to provide for; support; to maintain in a specified state, position; to hold for the future; retain; to hold and not let go; to stay in or on course; to stay in a specified condition or state; to continue or go on; to stay fresh, not spoiled.

Thus, the good ground seed did, with the Word of God, what the Lord God had commanded Adam to do in the beginning. For, there,

> **...the Lord God took the man, and put him into the garden of Eden to dress it and to keep it.**

Ge 2:15.

Within the garden of Eden stood the tree of life *(Ge 2:9)* which is the Word of God that gives and sustains life. Adam's job was to **keep** *(kēp)* it, that is, in the Hebrew Adam was required to **shâmar** *(shaw-mar')* the garden of Eden and the tree of life that stood in the midst of it. To **shâmar** in the Hebrew and to **katecho** in the Greek one must **keep** it. When the Hebrews **keep** the Word they guard, protect and preserve it in the same manner as the Greeks do. For, **shâmar** means to hedge about; to guard, protect, attend to, beware, be circumspect, take heed to self, keeper, keep self, mark, look narrowly, observe, preserve, regard, reserve, save, save self, sure, watch, watchman. So, by keeping the Word Adam was able to preserve and save himself. Just like Adam was required to keep the garden of Eden and the tree of life by watching, guarding and protecting it, so are believers who profess Christ as their savior. For, by keeping the tree of life, which possesses leaves as does a book with words written on the page *(Re 22:2),* Adam was thereby able to keep himself by obeying the word of God written upon the leaves of it. For it is by man's obedience to the commandments of God that his soul and spirit are preserved and kept in the image and likeness of God. *(Ge 1:26-27)* Because, when God made man he made him upright. *(Ec 7:29)*

Good Ground Seed vs. Rocky, No Root, No Moisture Seed

Furthermore, when we compare the good ground seed to the rocky, no root, no moisture seed we see a great difference in the level of patience exercised by the two seed type believers. For, although the rocky, no root, no moisture seed also received the Word of God gladly *(Mk 4:16; Mt 13:20; Lu 8:13),* as did the good ground seed, when trouble arose in the lives of the rocky, no root, no moisture seeds they did not exercise patience and so they quit the righteousness of God and became unfruitful.

The Suffering Way to Glory

The rocky, no root, no moisture seed did not understand what the good ground seed understood, and that is, that the life of Christ lived in by believers is a suffering way. Suffering in the flesh is required so that the believer may, through the suffering in his life for righteousness' sake, become and remain the praise and glory of God, by showing the sufferings of Christ in his own body. *(1Pe 4:14)* As the Apostle stated,

> **19 What? know ye not that your body is the temple of the Holy Ghost which is in you, which ye have of God, and ye are not your own?**
> **20 For ye are bought with a price: therefore glorify God in your body, and in your spirit, which are God's.**

1Co 6:19-20.

As believers we exist as the Lord's praise and glory only when we continue to live and respond to life in holiness and the righteousness of God. That is, if Jesus was here and this trouble came upon him, 'What would Jesus do in response to the trouble?' We are to respond to our tribulations as Jesus would, because we are commanded to

Let this mind be in you, which was also in Christ Jesus:
Php 2:5.

This is possible through and by the indwelling Holy Ghost *(1Co 6:19; 1Co 3:16-17)* as the Lord God determined in the beginning that His creation called man should exist in His image and His likeness, which is in holiness for He is holy *(1Pe 1:15-16; Le 11:44-45; Le 19:2; Le 20:7),* and in righteousness as He is righteous. *(Ps 119:137; Ps 129:4; Ps 145:17; Ps 11:7; Ps 7:9, 17; Ps 116:5; Jer 12:1; La 1:18; Da 9:14)* For, God declared the state and condition that he had determined man to exist in when he said,

...Let us make man in our image, after our likeness...
Ge 1:26a.

Then God performed what he had determined,

So God created man in his own image, in the image of God created he him; male and female created he them.
Ge 1:27.

And so we see Adam created in the image of God after he was created from the dust of the ground. For, the writer described the process saying,

And the Lord God formed man of the dust of the ground, and breathed into his nostrils the breath of life; and man became a living soul.
Ge 2:7.

So, when a believer chooses to suffer, so that he may be able to obey the Word of God, he proves to the world that it is possible to live a holy and sanctified life while living, here, in this world. This shows the righteousness of God within the believer, and convicts and reproves the unbelievers of their sins lived in within the world. As the Lord Jesus said,

> **7 Nevertheless I tell you the truth; It is expedient for you that I go away: for if I go not away, the Comforter will not come unto you; but if I depart, I will send him unto you.**
>
> **8 And when he is come, he will reprove the world of sin, and of righteousness, and of judgment:**
>
> **9 Of sin, because they believe not on me;**
>
> **10 Of righteousness, because I go to my Father, and ye see me no more;**
>
> **11 Of judgment, because the prince of this world is judged.**

Joh 16: 7-11.

In this St. John 16:7-11 passage we learn that through *"...the Comforter, which is the Holy Ghost..." (Joh 14:26)* whom the Lord sent *(1Pe 1:12)* to indwell all of mankind, that believeth on him *(Joh 1:12),* beginning on the day of Pentecost *(Ac 2:1-4)*, God reproves the world of sin. To **reprove** *(ri-prōōv')*, here is to **elegcho** *(el-eng'-kho)* in the Greek. **Elegcho** means to confute, admonish; convict, convince, tell a fault, rebuke, reprove. And, **reprove** means to rebuke, or express disapproval of something done or said. Therefore, through the indwelling Holy Ghost that leads the believer *(Ro 8:14)* and guides him into all truth *(Joh 16:13),* which enables him to obey and fulfill the righteousness of God, God convicts all unbelievers of sin. *(Joh 16:8-9)* They are convicted of sin as sinners because they refuse to repent unto salvation and believe on Jesus Christ as the answer to the issues, tribulations and sufferings of life. *(Joh 16:8-9)* So, the good ground seed's life of suffering for the cause of Christ was for the saving of his own soul and the convincing, convicting, reproving, rebuking and confuting of all those who heard and refused to believe on Jesus also.

The good ground seed's patient suffering, unto perfection and fruitfulness, also admonished the world's unbelievers of the righteousness of Jesus Christ, thereby telling and showing them their faults, by showing and demonstrating true holiness and righteousness, as a lifestyle, on a daily basis. For, the good ground seed's lifestyle proves that the righteous standard of Christ is real, doable and attainable. Because, although the world does not see the physical body of Jesus anymore *(Joh 16:10),* they do see and behold the righteous standard that His body lived while he was on earth—through and by the righteousness shown in the lives of the good ground seed. For, their bodies are the new temple of God *(1Co 3:16-17; 1Co 6:19-20; 2Co 6:16)*, not made by hands,

> **16 ...as God hath said, I will dwell in them, and walk in them; and I will be their God, and they shall be my people.**
>
> **17 Wherefore come out from among them, and be ye separate, saith the Lord, and touch not the unclean thing; and I will receive you,**
>
> **18 And will be a Father unto you, and ye shall be my sons and daughters, saith the Lord Almighty.**

2Co 6:16-18.

And,

> **Because it is written, Be ye holy; for I am holy.**

1Pe 1:15.

The scripture declared further,

> **And an highway shall be there, and a way, and it shall be called The way of holiness; the unclean shall not pass over it; but it shall be for those: the wayfaring men, though fools, shall not err therein.**

Isa 35:8.

So, the lack of root *(depth [Mk 4:5])* and moisture in the ways and Word of God prevented the rocky, no root, no moisture seeds from knowing and understanding the offenses, persecution and sufferings that accompanies the life of Christ lived in by Christian believers. For, had they gained knowledge and understanding and therefore depth and moisture through studying the Word and the righteousness of God and by being led by the Spirit of God they should not have been offended. For, in His Word Jesus warned all believers saying,

> **Woe unto the world because of offences! for it must needs be that offences come; but woe to that man by whom the offence cometh!**

Mt 18:7.

> **And ye shall be hated of all men for my name's sake: but he that endureth to the end shall be saved.**

Mt 10:22.

But, the problem with the rocky, no root, no moisture seed was that he had no root in himself and therefore, with no root, depth, moisture or patience he was unable to endure to the end. For, he only

> **...dureth for a while: for when tribulation or persecution ariseth because of the word, by and by he is offended.**

Mt 13:21b.

Yet, he should not have been offended, because Jesus said

> **These things have I spoken unto you, that ye should not be offended.**

Joh 16:1.

Overcoming Suffering through Patience

The rocky, no root, no moisture souls fainted in the spirit and withered away when the scorching heat of tribulation and trouble came *(Mt 13:6; Mk 4:6),* into their lives, because of the Word. *(Mt 13:21)* They fainted because they failed to keep the Word of God through obedience and faith. And, their failure to keep the Word was a direct result of their failure to acquire patience that is gained only by enduring, suffering and overcoming temptations, trouble, tribulations and offences.

For, the rocky, no root, no moisture seeded soul did not understand that believers are required to,

> **...glory in tribulations also: knowing that tribulation worketh patience...**

Ro 5:3b.

Nor did he understand that to possess and therefore to maintain his soul, in the righteousness of God, he could only do it through patience. *(Lu 21:19)* In agreement, the Lord Jesus declared,

> **In your patience possess ye your souls.**

Lu 21:19.

For, the word **patience** *(pā'shəns)* in the Luke 21:19 and Luke 8:15 passages above is taken from the Greek **hupomone** *(hoop-om-on-ay').* **Hupomone** means cheerful or hopeful endurance, constancy; enduring, patience, patient continuance; waiting. So, the rocky, no root, no moisture seeded soul lost his soul and withered away because his endurance was not constant, continuing, patient and waiting to the end. *(Mt 10:22)* For, when he was offended, because of the Word, he fell away and lost hope in the life of Christ while in the midst of the troubles and storms of life. That is, he simply stopped praying and waiting for his change to come and fainted in the spirit. *(Read Lu 18:1-8)*

Being Patient Means Not Fainting and Not Fretting To Produce

But the good ground seed did not faint because they obeyed the Word's admonition that says,

> **And let us not be weary in well doing: for in due season we shall reap, if we faint not.**

Ga 6:9.

And the admonition of King Solomon to,

> **Fret not thyself because of evil men, neither be thou envious at the wicked;**

Pr 24:19.

For, the good ground seed stood steadfast in the power of the Holy Ghost *(Ro 15:13)* possessing their souls by keeping the Word active in their lives through a patient understanding of the suffering life of those who choose to believe in and live for Christ. As King Solomon and the apostles heard and obeyed the admonitions of King David, who came before them, so is it required of all who desire to produce as the good ground seed some thirty, some sixty and some an hundredfold. For, King David instructed the saints saying,

> **1 Fret not thyself because of evildoers, neither be thou envious against the workers of iniquity.**
>
> **2 For they shall soon be cut down like the grass, and wither as the green herb.**
>
> **3 Trust in the LORD, and do good; so shalt thou dwell in the land, and verily thou shalt be fed.**
>
> **4 Delight thyself also in the LORD; and he shall give thee the desires of thine heart.**
>
> **5 Commit thy way unto the LORD; trust also in him; and he shall bring it to pass.**

6 And he shall bring forth thy righteousness as the light, and thy judgment as the noonday.

7 Rest in the LORD, and wait patiently for him: fret not thyself because of him who prospereth in his way, because of the man who bringeth wicked devices to pass.

8 Cease from anger, and forsake wrath: fret not thyself in any wise to do evil.

9 For evildoers shall be cut off: but those that wait upon the LORD, they shall inherit the earth.

Ps 37:1-9.

For, as a good ground seed, they learned and understood that,

1 Therefore seeing we have this ministry, as we have received mercy, we faint not;

2 But have renounced the hidden things of dishonesty, not walking in craftiness, nor handling the word of God deceitfully; but by manifestation of the truth commending ourselves to every man's conscience in the sight of God.

2Co 4:1-2.

Because, through hearing, receiving, studying and getting an understanding of the Word of God, with an honest and good heart, the good ground seed brought forth and yielded fruit by patiently enduring hardships, tribulation and persecution. For, they understood that,

Yea, and all that will live godly in Christ Jesus shall suffer persecution.

2Ti 3:12.

Because,

8 We are troubled on every side, yet not distressed; we are perplexed, but not in despair;

9 Persecuted, but not forsaken; cast down, but not destroyed;

10 Always bearing about in the body the dying of the Lord Jesus, that the life also of Jesus might be made manifest in our body.

11 For we which live are always delivered unto death for Jesus' sake, that the life also of Jesus might be made manifest in our mortal flesh.

2Co 4:8-11.

So that, even in the midst of trouble, offenses and persecution the good ground seed was, and now is, required to show the suffering of Christ in their own body *(Php 3:8-10),* by

...continue thou in the things which thou hast learned and hast been assured of...

2Ti 3:14.

Because,

16 All scripture is given by inspiration of God, and is profitable for doctrine, for reproof, for correction, for instruction in righteousness:

17 That the man of God may be perfect, thoroughly furnished unto all good works.

2Ti 3:16-17.

And having been thoroughly furnished we are able to thereby

...bring forth fruit, some thirtyfold, some sixty, and some an hundred.

Mk 4:20b.

Patience Produces Experience and a **Convincing** Testimony of Livable Righteousness

The good ground seed heard, received, understood and kept the Word of God with an honest and good heart, through patience. So the Comforter, which is the Holy Ghost, living within the good ground seed was able to use their lives to produce a convincing witness and testimony of the transforming power of the righteousness of God. Thereby the Comforter, while indwelling the good ground seed, did *"...reprove the world of sin, and of righteousness, and of judgment..." (Joh 16: 7-11)* For, the Greek **elegcho** means to convince as well as to reprove. And, if we are more quick to convince rather than rebuke we should be more successful in our fruitfulness. Because, to **convince** *(kən-vins')* involves persuading by argument or evidence; to make one feel sure, as opposed to **rebuke** *(ri-byōōk')* which means to beat, to scold in a sharp way; reprimand; as does **reprove** which means to rebuke, or express disapproval of something. For when we present evidence of persuasion we must avoid offending least our witness and labor, in the Lord and on his behalf, be in vain. As did Christ, the good ground seed looked beyond the faults of those whom he witnessed to and saw their needs. As did Christ, rather than just verbally reprove those outside of the church, he convinced the unbelievers that the righteousness of God is attainable and doable by presenting his own life as a living sacrifice. *(Ro 12:1-2)* For, it is through **lovingkindness** that the unbeliever is drawn to the righteous life of Christ. And so, even in times of trouble, those who would dare become seeds upon the good ground are required to imitate the Prophet David, when he declared,

> **9 I have preached righteousness in the great congregation: lo, I have not refrained my lips, O Lord, thou knowest.**
>
> **10 I have not hid thy righteousness within my heart; I have declared thy faithfulness and thy salvation:**

I have not concealed thy lovingkindness and thy truth from the great congregation.

11 Withhold not thou thy tender mercies from me, O Lord: let thy lovingkindness and thy truth continually preserve me.

Ps 40:9-11.

Because the word **lovingkindness** *(luv'iŋ-kind'nəs)* is taken from the Hebrew **checed** *(kheh'-sed)* meaning *kindness, beauty, favour, good deed, kindly (loving) kindness, merciful (kindness), mercy, pity, reproach and wicked thing*—it is necessary for the good ground seed to **produce fruit by convincing** rather than rebuking; to use honey rather than vinegar. For,

1 A soft answer turneth away wrath: but grievous words stir up anger.

2 The tongue of the wise useth knowledge aright: but the mouth of fools poureth out foolishness.

…

4 A wholesome tongue is a tree of life: but perverseness therein is a breach in the spirit.

Pr 15:1-2, 4.

For, the good ground seed understood and remembered that,

The Lord hath appeared of old unto me, saying, Yea, I have loved thee with an everlasting love: therefore with lovingkindness have I drawn thee.

Jer 31:3.

And when trouble arose because of righteousness they remembered, that,

12 Beloved, think it not strange concerning the fiery trial which is to try you, as though some strange thing happened unto you:

13 But rejoice, inasmuch as ye are partakers of Christ's sufferings; that, when his glory shall be revealed, ye may be glad also with exceeding joy.
1Pe 4:12-13.

For, they learned through studying and patience that,

If ye be reproached for the name of Christ, happy are ye; for the spirit of glory and of God resteth upon you: on their part he is evil spoken of, but on your part he is glorified.
1Pe 4:14.

Furthermore, as believers desiring to be fruitful and to produce fruit for the Lord, the good ground seed had to,

Be ye also patient; stablish your heart: for the coming of the Lord draweth nigh.
Jas 5:8.

As brethren in the Lord it was necessary for them to,

10Take…the prophets, who have spoken in the name of the Lord, for an example of suffering affliction, and of patience.

11 Behold, we count them happy which endure. Ye have heard of the patience of Job, and have seen the end of the Lord; that the Lord is very pitiful, and of tender mercy.
Jas 5:10-11.

6 Humble yourselves therefore under the mighty hand of God, that he may exalt you in due time:

7 Casting all your care upon him; for he careth for you.

8 Be sober, be vigilant; because your adversary the devil, as a roaring lion, walketh about, seeking whom he may devour:

9 Whom resist stedfast in the faith, knowing that the same afflictions are accomplished in your brethren that are in the world.

10 But the God of all grace, who hath called us unto his eternal glory by Christ Jesus, after that ye have suffered a while, make you perfect, stablish, strengthen, settle you.

1Pe 5:6-10.

Amen.

Good Ground Seed vs. Seed among Thorns

Moreover, in contrast to the seeds that fell among thorns, in Jesus' Parable of the Sower *(Mt 13:3-23; Mk 4:3-20; Lu 8:5-15),* the good ground seed, with an honest and good heart through patience, learned to

Stand fast therefore in the liberty wherewith Christ hath made us free, and be not entangled again with the yoke of bondage.

Ga 5:1.

In the same manner as it was required for the thorny ground seed, the good ground seed had to reject, conquer and overcome the will of the flesh before he could produce and bring forth fruit unto perfection. And, after rejecting, conquering and overcoming the sinful yokes that had once held him captive, in bondage, he had to stand fast and hold on to the freedom and liberty that is found only in Christ Jesus. As the Apostle stated,

Therefore, my beloved brethren, be ye stedfast, unmoveable, always abounding in the work of the Lord… 1Co 15:58a.

Within Jesus' Parable of the Sower *(See Mt 13:3-23; Mk 4:3-20; Lu 8:5-15)* the flesh's will is revealed as **(1)** the cares of this world *(Mt 13:22; Mk 4:19; Lu 8:14);* **(2)** the deceitfulness of riches *(Mt 13:22; Mk 4:19; Lu 8:14)*; **(3)** the pleasures of this life *(Lu 8:14);* and, **(4)** the lusts of other things entering in *(Mk 4:19)*. But, unlike the thorny ground seed the good ground seed continued studying and fellowshipping in the apostles' doctrine. *(See Ac 2:42)* By being stedfast in studying and applying the apostles' doctrine to his life he was able to discover, learn and see spiritual, thorn seedlings (that is, unrighteousness) within his life and his flesh. Then he cleansed his life and his flesh by drinking Jesus' blood and eating Jesus' flesh.

All that we eat and drink is digested and broken down into smaller parts within our body and then absorbed into our blood stream. Our heart then pumps the affected blood to every part of our body to nourish our flesh, and thereby we grow and are healed. So it is also with man's soul and the Word of God. For, the Word is both the blood and the flesh of Jesus Christ. As we are informed,

> 1 In the beginning was the Word, and the Word was with God, and the Word was God.
> 2 The same was in the beginning with God.

Joh 1:1-2.

Here, we learn that the Word was in the beginning with God and He was God. Then, we are told that

> …the Word was made flesh, and dwelt among us, (and we beheld his glory, the glory as of the only begotten of the Father,) full of grace and truth.

John 1:14.

So, by considering John 1:1-2 and verse 14 we learn that the flesh of the only begotten Son of God *(1Jo 4:9)* the Father was made up of and consisted of the Word, which is and who is God. For, **made** *(mād)* is taken from the Greek **ginomai** *(ghin'-om-ahee).* **Ginomai** means to cause to be; to become, come into being; arise, be assembled, be, be brought to pass; be finished, be fulfilled, be made, be ordained to be. Thus, when *'the Word was made flesh' (Joh 1:14)* it was God the Father that caused His Word to become, to be made in the likeness of sinful flesh. *(Ro 8:3)* As the writer wrote,

> **And without controversy great is the mystery of godliness: God was manifest in the flesh, justified in the Spirit, seen of angels, preached unto the Gentiles, believed on in the world, received up into glory.**

1Ti 3:16.

For, the Lord God had already *'ordained it to be'* in the beginning when He said unto Lucifer, Satan, the serpent *(Re 12:9),*

> **And I will put enmity between thee and the woman, and between thy seed and her seed; it shall bruise thy head, and thou shalt bruise his heel.**

Ge 3:15.

The seed of the woman referred to here is Jesus the Christ, the only begotten Son of God. *(1Jo 4:9)* For it was God, who is the Holy Ghost, that planted the seed (the Word) into the womb of the woman. *(Mt 1:18; Lu 1:26-38)* And it was this same Jesus that, thirty-some years later *(Lu 3:23),* went down into the lower parts of the earth *(Eph 4:8-10)* after he was crucified. *(1Co 2:8; Mt 27:26-50; Mt 28:5; Mk 15:15-39; Mk 16:6; Lu 23:33-47; Joh 19:16-23)* With a heel bruise of a three day death Jesus, the seed of the woman, rose the third day morning *(Lu 24:2-8; Mk 16:1-7; Mt 28:1-7; 1Co 15:12-23; 1Th 4:14; Ac 10:38-41; Ro 14:9),* after bruising Lucifer, Satan, the serpent's head by taking from him the power that, as the prince of this world *(1Co*

2:8; Joh 12:31; 2Co 4:4; Joh 14:30; Joh 16:11; Eph 2:2), he held over death and the grave. *(Heb 2:14; 2Ti 1:10; Ac 26:18)*

So, the Word of God was made flesh and we know that Word as Jesus Christ. And His flesh is the meat and the drink necessary to give man life and for man to possess and to maintain that life. For,

> **53 …Jesus said unto them, Verily, verily, I say unto you, Except ye eat the flesh of the Son of man, and drink his blood, ye have no life in you.**
>
> **54 Whoso eateth my flesh, and drinketh my blood, hath eternal life; and I will raise him up at the last day.**
>
> **55 For my flesh is meat indeed, and my blood is drink indeed.**
>
> **56 He that eateth my flesh, and drinketh my blood, dwelleth in me, and I in him.**
>
> **57 As the living Father hath sent me, and I live by the Father: so he that eateth me, even he shall live by me.**

Joh 6:53-57.

Therefore, when we study the Word and apply it to our lives in obedience we eat the flesh of Jesus Christ. And when we do what that Word says we live that Word, by Jesus. *(Joh 6:57)* Because, His flesh is the Word of God *(Joh 1:14)* and it is that Word that empowers us to walk in the newness of life *(Ro 6:4; Ga 6:15-17),* in the Spirit *(Ro 7:6)* that gives us life. *(Joh 6:63)* After we have eaten that Word our spirit man digests that eaten Word into small particles and it is absorbed into our soul's blood stream as the righteous blood of Christ Jesus. Then our spiritual heart pumps that blood all through our body causing us to grow *(1Pe 2:2)* and to be nourished in Christ Jesus, and causing our outer-man to prosper, to be healed *(3Jo 2)* and to reflect the glory and righteousness of God in our everyday lives.

Thus, we drink his blood and eat his flesh when we obey His Word by repenting of our sin—a transgression of His Word—and then eating that Word by continually applying that Word to our flesh and our lives. Hereby are we cleansed of the thorns of life and overcome the will of the flesh, by the blood of Christ *(1Jo 1:7, 9; 2Co 7:1),* through the obedience of our faith in that Word. Because, Jesus said

> **Now ye are clean through the word which I have spoken unto you.**

Joh 15:3.

By being cleansed by that Word that he has heard, studied, understood and kept through patience with an honest and good heart the good ground seed is enabled and empowered to walk, not in the carnality of the flesh through the spiritual thorns, but in the glory of the righteousness of God. *(Read 1Pe 4:12-14; Ro 5:3)* Because, walking in a carnal mind set will cause the fruitful and the faithful to become unfruitful, barren, and unfaithful. For, without that Word he possesses no life while residing on earth in the carnality of a dishonest and deceitful heart.

> **6 For to be carnally minded is death; but to be spiritually minded is life and peace.**
>
> **7 Because the carnal mind is enmity against God: for it is not subject to the law of God, neither indeed can be.**

Ro 8:6-7.

And, *"So then they that are in the flesh cannot please God." (Ro 8:8)* However, the good ground seed was not in the flesh but in the spirit, because the Spirit of God dwelled in him. *(Ro 8:9)* This is how the good ground seed is enabled and empowered to walk in the Spirit of God showing God's righteousness with the spirit of glory upon him. *(1Pe 4:12-13)* For, Jesus did say,

> **It is the spirit that quickeneth; the flesh profiteth nothing: the words that I speak unto you, they are spirit, and they are life.**

Joh 6:63.

Be a Hearer and a Doer

So, through a daily diet (intake) of hearing, studying, understanding and keeping the Word of God, through patient application, the good ground seed became an example of suffering affliction and of patience victorious in conquering and overcoming the will of the flesh, thereby showing and demonstrating the glory and righteousness of God while bearing about in his body the dying of the Lord Jesus that the life of Jesus might be seen in his flesh. *(2Co 4:8-11)* And finally, to become a living sacrifice *(Ro 12:1)* and an example of suffering affliction and of patience the good ground seed became a doer of that Word that he heard, studied and understood by laying,

> **...apart all filthiness and superfluity of naughtiness, and receive with meekness the engrafted word, which is able to save your souls.**

Jas 1:21.

For, the Word of God could cleanse him only if within his heart he determined to do the work by eating, drinking and applying that Word and doing what that Word says he should do. Otherwise, if he seeks to live his life by his own righteousness, running with zeal but not according to knowledge, then that Word that he heard, studied and understood would not cleanse him of his filthiness, because he would not have submitted himself unto the righteousness of God *(Ro 10:2-3),* or, to the cleansing power of that Word which is activated by obedience.

The **filthiness** *(filth'-ē-nəs)* discussed here in the James 1:21 passage is translated from the Greek **rhuparia** *(hroo-par-ee'-ah),* meaning moral dirtiness; turpitude. **Turpitude** *(tur'-pi-tood')* is being baseless and **vile** *(vil')*—which means possessing the quality or existing in a state or condition of being morally evil; wicked; disgusting; degrading; mean; very bad. Now, **filthiness** is possessing the quality, state or condition of being foul dirt; or, **obscenity** *(äb-sēn'ə-tē)*—by existing in a state or condition in life so as to possess the quality of being offensive to modesty or decency; to be lewd or repulsive. Also, the Prophet Isaiah reminds us that

> **...we are all as an unclean thing, and all our righteousnesses are as filthy rags; and we all do fade as a leaf; and our iniquities, like the wind, have taken us away.**

Isa 64:6.

Here, in Isaiah 64:6, the word **filthy** *(filth'-ē)*, is translated from the Hebrew **'ed** *(ayd)* meaning to set a period; the mentrual flux (as periodical); soiling, filthy. So, when a believer fails or quits being a doer of that Word that he has heard, studied and understood he becomes filthy, vile and disgusting to God in the same manner as a woman who leaves her used menstrual cycle rag laying out in clear view for others to see. For, his righteousness, being as a filthy, menstrual cycle rag is put forth to the world as the righteousness of a forgetful hearer *(Read Jas 1:22-25)* who's life is disgusting, and soiled before God. And by living a life of hearing the Word of faith, but not obeying that Word of faith the thorny ground believer has allowed his deceitful heart to deceive him. For,

> **The heart is deceitful above all things, and desperately wicked: who can know it?**

Jer 17:9.

And, without possessing an honest and good heart—cleansed by the Word, the flesh and the blood of Christ—the thorny ground believer is a hearer and not a doer of the Word and thereby he deceives himself by being led by and obeying his own deceitful and wicked heart. *(Jas 1:22; Jer 17:9)*

> **23 For if any be a hearer of the word, and not a doer, he is like unto a man beholding his natural face in a glass:**
>
> **24 For he beholdeth himself, and goeth his way, and straightway forgetteth what manner of man he was.**

Jas 1:23-24.

When a believer hears, studies and understands the Word he is able to see himself, his unrighteousness, spiritual thorns, faults, his short comings and where he stands with God in relation to that Word.

> **For the word of God is quick, and powerful, and sharper than any twoedged sword, piercing even to the dividing asunder of soul and spirit, and of the joints and marrow, and is a discerner of the thoughts and intents of the heart.**

Heb 4:12.

If a believer fails to keep that Word, by applying it to his life, he will soon forget what manner of man he was when he received the understanding. And now, having become a forgetful hearer, he will fail and not obey that Word and thereby he becomes a transgressor of that Word. This failure to be faithful and faint not *(Jas 1:25)* will prevent his blessing and cause his work and his deeds not to prosper. For,

> **...the way of transgressors is hard.**

Pr 13:15b.

And, when a believer looks back and picks up the things that he had repented of he becomes a transgressor unfit for the kingdom of God. *(Lu 9:62)*

> **For if I build again the things which I destroyed, I make myself a transgressor.**

Ga 2:18.

> **But whoso looketh into the perfect law of liberty, and continueth therein, he being not a forgetful hearer, but a doer of the work, this man shall be blessed in his deed.**

Jas 1:25.

So, unlike the thorny ground seed, the good ground seed laid apart and departed from all filthiness of the flesh and superfluity of naughtiness. *(Jas 1:21)* For, to represent Christ and to have the spirit of glory upon him, the good ground seed could not present himself to God or to the world as a used menstrual cycle rag, smelling and stinking even in his own nostrils. Nor, could he convince others that the life and righteousness of Christ was attainable and doable by living a life in superfluity of naughtiness. For, **superfluity** *(soo'pər-floo'ə-tē),* which means excessive or unnecessary, is taken from the Greek **perisseia** *(per-is-si'-ah).* **Perisseia** means superabundance, abundance and superfluity. And, the word **naughtiness** *(nôt'-ē-nəs)* is taken from **kakia**. **Kakia** *(kak-ee'- ah)* means badness, depravity, malignity, trouble, evil, malice, maliousness, naughtiness, wickedness. **Naughtiness** means possessing the quality of or, existing in a state or condition of being **mischievous** *(mis'chə-vəs)*—causing harm or damage through playful teasing, prankish, inclined to annoy with playful tricks; **indelicate** *(in-del'i-kit)*—lacking propriety or modesty, coarse; **disobedience** *(dis'ō-bē'dē-əns)*—refusal to obey, insubordination; and **improper** *(im-präp'ər)*—not suitable, unfit, incorrect, not in good taste.

Thus, a believer who lives a life of excess in being depraved, mischievous, annoying, unfit, not suitable, immodest, insubordinate, malious, wicked, evil, disobedient, trouble and not in good taste has not rejected, conquered or overcome the will of the flesh. And, he therefore will exist as the thorny ground seed unable to bring any fruit to perfection. And as such, he cannot be a true representative of the life and suffering of Christ. For, as a filthy believer living a lifestyle of excess and naughtiness he cannot become an example of suffering affliction and of patience victorious in conquering and overcoming the will of the flesh. And he cannot, by his filthiness and superfluity of naughtiness show or demonstrate the glory and righteousness of God while bearing about in his body the dying of the Lord Jesus. For, the life of Jesus cannot be seen in his filthy and naughty flesh. *(2Co 4:8-11)* As the writer commented, saying,

> **Who is wise, and he shall understand these things? prudent, and he shall know them? for the ways of the Lord are right, and the just shall walk in them: but the transgressors shall fall therein.**

Hos 14:9.

Death in the Menstrual Cycle Rag

A **transgressor** is a person who knows to do right but fails to do right, being a forgetful hearer. *(Jas 4:17)* And as such, by going back into the carnality of death he forgets that he had passed from death to life. For, Jesus said,

> **Verily, verily, I say unto you, He that heareth my word, and believeth on him that sent me, hath everlasting life, and shall not come into condemnation, but is passed from death unto life.**

Joh 5:24.

Death in the menstrual cycle rag is an existence lived in self righteousness outside of the word of righteousness, flesh and blood of Jesus Christ. So Jesus said,

> **...Except ye eat the flesh of the Son of man, and drink his blood, ye have no life in you.**

Joh 6:53.

So there is life in the blood and flesh of Christ, which is the Word of God. And, within the Word of God are found the ways and the righteousness of God. If we eat and live by the Word, then we have life within us because within his blood and his flesh is life. *(Joh 6:53-57, 63)*

On the other hand if we allow our heart to lead us to substitute the blood and flesh of Christ—which are the ways and righteousness of God found in the Word—for our own ways and righteousness—found in the wisdom of man, the wisdom of this world and the wisdom of the princes of this world—then we enter into the death of the menstrual cycle rag. For, during the menstrual cycle there is blood, but there is no life in that blood. Even if the sower sows a seed within the womb, the womb cannot conceive and bring forth life, because no life can occur during the menstrual cycle. During this time the womb is unable to receive or sustain life. Spiritually the filthy, menstrual cycle rag is the carnal righteousness and ways of man talked about by the Prophet Isaiah which causes us to fade away in death as a leaf. *(See Isa 64:6)* As the Apostle stated,

> **For to be carnally minded is death; but to be spiritually minded is life and peace.**

Ro 8:6.

And so, since there is no life in the carnal mind, which results from substituting the ways and righteousness of God with man's righteousness they that are carnal live in death outside of the life that is found only in the Word and law of God—which is the blood and flesh of Jesus Christ.

> **7 Because the carnal mind is enmity against God: for it is not subject to the law of God, neither indeed can be.**
>
> **8 So then they that are in the flesh cannot please God.**

Ro 8:6-8.

Deliverance from the Menstrual Cycle Rag

But, if the forgetful hearer, the backslider, the thorny ground seed has a change of heart to move forward in Christ Jesus to the good ground where there is prosperity of spirit, health and finance, then he can do so. For, the transgressor must humble himself, pray, seek God's face by changing his spiritual diet and turn from his wicked ways. Then God will hear his prayer, forgive his sins and heal his land. *(2Ch 7:14)* For, God is a second chance God and will abundantly pardon. *(Isa 55:6-7)* As the writer declared,

> **For a just man falleth seven times, and riseth up again:...**

Pr 24:16a.

For, when he repents, God will be there to lift him up as he looks up to heaven from which cometh his help. *(Read Ps 121:1-8)* As King David said, after becoming a murderer and an adulterer, God will,

> **Restore unto me the joy of my salvation; and uphold me with thy free spirit.**

Ps 51:12.

And God will go as far as to humble himself and repent of the evil that he had purposed against him. *(Jer 18:8)* As the writer stated,

5 Who is like unto the Lord our God, who dwelleth on high.

6 Who humbleth himself to behold the things that are in heaven, and in the earth!

Ps 113:5-6.

But the restored believer must

Therefore now amend your ways and your doings, and obey the voice of the Lord your God; and the Lord will repent him of the evil that he hath pronounced against you.

Jer 26:13.

The restored believer now must understand that to remain on the good ground he must do the work of the word to become a convincing example of patient, suffering affliction and not be led by his deceitful heart, as Job did when he said,

My righteousness I hold fast, and will not let it go: my heart shall not reproach me so long as I live.

Job 27:6.

The restored believer must allow that Word that he has heard, received and understood to abide, and remain in his spiritual blood stream healing and cleansing his soul. Thereby, the Word will be a light, a lamp and a guide to him in life. By his spirit man's growth in Christ he will be enabled to subdue and replenish the earth *(Ge 1:28)*—the physical body—that his spirit man dwelled in. And by doing so his obedience glorifies God, as Jesus said,

1 I am the true vine, and my Father is the husbandman.

2 Every branch in me that beareth not fruit he taketh away: and every branch that beareth fruit, he purgeth it, that it may bring forth more fruit.

3 Now ye are clean through the word which I have spoken unto you.

4 Abide in me, and I in you. As the branch cannot bear fruit of itself, except it abide in the vine; no more can ye, except ye abide in me.

5 I am the vine, ye are the branches: He that abideth in me, and I in him, the same bringeth forth much fruit: for without me ye can do nothing.

6 If a man abide not in me, he is cast forth as a branch, and is withered; and men gather them, and cast them into the fire, and they are burned.

7 If ye abide in me, and my words abide in you, ye shall ask what ye will, and it shall be done unto you.

8 Herein is my Father glorified, that ye bear much fruit; so shall ye be my disciples.

Joh 15:1-8.

And, after having glorified the Lord God, the Apostle commented, saying

9 For this cause we also, since the day we heard it, do not cease to pray for you, and to desire that ye mght be filled with the knowledge of his will in all wisdom and spiritual understanding;

10 That ye might walk worthy of the Lord unto all pleasing, being fruitful in every good work, and increasing in the knowledge of God;

11 Strengthened with all might, according to his glorious power, unto all patience and longsuffering with joyfulness;

Col 1:9-11.

And, so they of the good ground seed will bring forth fruit unto perfection, some thirty, sixty and a hundredfold as a reward for their righteousness in Christ Jesus as King David did, saying,

> **20 The Lord rewarded me according to my righteousness; according to the cleanness of my hands hath he recompensed me.**
>
> **21 For I have kept the ways of the Lord, and have not wickedly departed from my God.**
>
> **22 For all his judgments were before me, and I did not put away his statutes from me.**
>
> **23 I was also upright before him and I kept myself from mine iniquity.**
>
> **24 Therefore hath the Lord recompensed me according to my righteousness, according to the cleanness of my hands in his eyesight.**

Ps 18:20-24.

Amen.

Chapter 17

No. 7: The Commandment to Multiply

And God blessed them, and God said unto them, ... multiply...
Ge 1:28.

God commanded Adam and his wife, Eve, to multiply. *(Ge 1:28)* This commandment is not only a commandment of procreation, so that God may receive more 'sacrifices of praise' *(Heb 13:15),* but it also involves the act that consummates the marriage between a man and his wife. The consummation of the marriage is the physical reconciliation of the two pieces of the one flesh.

God is the God of procreation, because there is no death or darkness in him *(1Jo 1:5),* and all things were created by him. *(Joh 1:3)* Only the LORD God can create life and therefore give life. *(Ac 17:25)* For, he is the God of life. Even when he, as the Word, became flesh *(Joh 1:1, 14),* he remained the God of life and procreation. For, the Apostle declared,

In him was life; and the life was the light of men.
Joh 1:4.

In another place the Lord himself declared,

> **48 I am that bread of life.**
>
> **…**
>
> **50 This is the bread which cometh down from heaven, that a man may eat thereof, and not die.**
>
> **51 I am the living bread which came down from heaven: If any man eat of this bread, he shall live for ever: and the bread that I shall give is my flesh, which I will give for the life of the world.**
>
> **…**
>
> **53 Then Jesus said unto them, Verily, verily, I say unto you, Except ye eat the flesh of the Son of man, and drink his blood, ye have no life in you.**
>
> **54 Whoso eateth my flesh, and drinketh my blood, hath eternal life; and I will raise him up at the last day.**

Joh 6:48, 50-51, 53-54.

The Beginning Of Human Life

As for the flesh of man, life begins in the womb, at the moment of conception. Conception occurs after the father plants his seed into the earth of the woman, and the woman's earth is united and joined with the man's seed. God, who controls life, decides whether or not the coming together of the man's seed with the woman's earth will become life. If the man's seed germinates in the earth of the woman, then God has made a choice that a life shall come forth, and a life has begun. For the LORD God said in Jeremiah 1:5,

> **Before I formed thee in the belly I knew thee…**

Thus, before the child develops into a fetus, or takes on any shape or form, it possesses life within it. Within the scriptures, we see this process of planting to conception to birth from the womb in action, wherein the writer wrote,

> **13 For thou hast possessed my reins: thou hast covered me in my mother's womb.**
>
> **14 I will praise thee; for I am fearfully and wonderfully made: marvelous are thy works; and that my soul knoweth right well.**
>
> **15 My substance was not hid from thee, when I was made in secret, and curiously wrought in the lowest parts of the earth.**
>
> **16 Thine eyes did see my substance, yet being unperfect; and in thy book all my members were written, which in continuance were fashioned, when as yet there was none of them.**

Ps 139:13-16.

And, in another place it was said,

> **And Adam knew Eve his wife, and she conceived, and bare Cain, and said, I have gotten a man from the Lord.**

Ge 4:1.

Through obedience to the commandment to multiply, came life from God when the two pieces of the one flesh came together, in carnal knowledge. This is why the woman said "I have gotten a man from the Lord," because life comes only from God. Within the woman's statement is a recognition that only God can give life. In the above passage the word **conceived** *(kən-sēvd')*, is taken from the Hebrew **hareh** *(haw-reh').* To be **hareh** is to be pregnant, to be with child, woman with child. **Hareh** is derived from **harah** *(haw-raw')* which means to be pregnant or to become pregnant, to conceive, be with child, conceive, progenitor.

The WOMB: Home of the Potter's House

God is the potter, working in the potter's house *(Isa 64:8; Ro 9:20-21)* who controls, forms and fashions the clay, made from water and the dust of the ground *(Ge 2:7),* into the flesh of man. *(Job 31:15)* As the prophet declared,

But now, O LORD, thou art our father; we are the clay, and thou our potter; and we all are the work of thy hand.

Isa 64:8.

Regardless as to what type of house (womb) the woman provides him with, it is still God who places a life into the womb and fashions it. That is, after God places life into the womb he causes it to grow, forming and fashioning it, making some vessels, vessels of honor and some vessels, vessels of dishonor. *(Ro 9:21)* Only God makes the decision as to which vessel shall be of honor or dishonor. For, after he fashions the vessel, in the potter's house, and brings it forth out of the womb, God then has mercy on whom he chooses *(Ro 9:15)* and shows no mercy on whom he chooses and no man can rightly question God or instruct him. *(1Co 2:16; Isa 40:13-14; Ro 11:34)* As the scripture sayeth,

Therefore hath he mercy on whom he will have mercy, and whom he will he hardeneth.

Ro 9:18.

19 Thou wilt say then unto me, Why doth he yet find fault? For who hath resisted his will?

20 Nay, but, O man, who art thou that repliest against God? Shall the thing formed say to him that formed it, Why hast thou made me thus?

21 Hath not the potter power over the clay, of the same lump to make one vessel unto honor, and another unto dishonor?
Ro 9:19-21.

And, in another place, the Prophet Isaiah commented, saying,

9 Woe unto him that striveth with his Maker! Let the potsherd strive with the potsherds of the earth. Shall the clay say to him that fashioneth it, What makest thou? Or thy work, He hath no hands?
10 Woe unto him that saith unto his father, What begettest thou? Or to the woman, What hast thou brought forth?
Isa 45:9-10.

When the womb has been made holy, by the indwelling Holy Ghost residing in the physical body of the woman, then the fruit of her potter's house—or the product that God produces from her womb, is sanctified. *(See 1Co 7:14; Jer 1:5)* When God places life in the womb he appoints that life to a particular position and service to be performed in this life within the Kingdom of God. This process is known as the Mystery of Election or the Calling of God.

For the gifts and calling of God are without repentance.
Ro 11:29.

The Mystery of Election—Called by God

Within the potter's house—the womb—God calls man to work in his service. We see this as the Apostle Paul discusses his own calling experience, saying,

15 But when it pleased God, who separated me from my mother's womb, and called me by his grace,

16 To reveal his Son in me, that I might preach him among the heathen...

Ga 1:15-16.

The Apostle Paul went on to explain the Mystery of Election as follows,

10 And not only this; but when Rebecca also had conceived by one, even by our father Isaac;

11 (For the children being not yet born, neither having done any good or evil, that the purpose of God according to election might stand, not of works, but of him that calleth;)

12 It was said unto her, The Elder shall serve the younger.

13 As it is written, Jacob have I loved, but Esau have I hated.

14 What shall we say then? Is there unrighteousness with God? God forbid.

15 For he saith to Moses, I will have mercy on whom I will have mercy, and I will have compassion on whom I will have compassion.

16 So then it is not of him that willeth, nor of him that runneth, but of God that showeth mercy.

Ro 9:10-16.

The Hatred of God - Love That Hates

Here, we learn that God goes into the potter's house called the womb of the flesh and chooses one child to perform his righteous will on earth, and then chooses another child, in the same house, the same womb, to demonstrate his power against—thereby showing the glory of God. For the LORD God declared,

> **I form the light, and create darkness: I make peace, and create evil: I the LORD do all these things.**

Isa 45:7.

Therefore, he loved the one (Jacob) that he called, elected and chose to become his servant, and hated the one (Esau) that he called, elected and chose to become his enemy. Although the LORD God is love *(1Jo 4:8),* He also hates. *(Ro 9:13-14; Mal 1:2-3)* Thus, it is Love that hates. Even though the God, who is love, hates, there is no unrighteousness with Him. For, while hating, God also blesses those whom he hates. As the scriptures declare

> **...he maketh his sun to rise on the evil and on the good, and sendeth rain on the just and on the unjust.**

Mt 5:45.

For, he is the potter and we are his clay to do as he pleases. Even though Esau was hated, God still blessed him, and as the sons of God, we are to do the same. For, Christ instructs us to do the same, saying,

> **44 ...Love your enemies, bless them that curse you, do good to them that hate you, and pray for them which despitefully use you, and persecute you;**
>
> **45 That ye may be the children of your Father which is in heaven: for he maketh his sun to rise on the evil and on the good, and sendeth rain on the just and on the unjust.**
>
> **46 For if ye love them which love you, what reward have ye? Do not even the publicans the same?**
>
> **47 And if ye salute your brethren only, what do ye more than others? Do not even the publicans?**

48 Be ye therefore perfect, even as your Father which is in heaven is perfect.
Mt 5:44-48.

We are commanded to be perfect in all our ways, including in the way that we treat our enemies and those that are not with us or who may be against us, because,

As for God, his way is perfect:
Ps 18:30.

We would not understand how God can deliver us from the wicked, if there was no one to perform the part of the wicked. We would not know and understand the power of God if there was no opportunity to show and demonstrate his power. Therefore, there is a part in the affairs of man for the wicked to perform, that God may get the glory. For, the writer wrote,

22 What if God, willing to show his wrath, and to make his power known, endured with much longsuffering the vessels of wrath fitted to destruction:
23 And that he might make known the riches of his glory on the vessels of mercy, which he had afore prepared unto glory.
Ro 9:22-23.

Potter's House Types and Characteristics

The womb is the potter's house. And, there are four different types of wombs that the potter enters to perform his work, namely;

(1) the Barren Womb; **(2)** the Womb of the Morning; **(3)** the Womb of the Flesh; and, **(4)** the Womb of the Bride of Christ. Although, each potter's house type (womb) is different from the others and have different characteristics they all have one thing in common—the Potter. The Lord God is the potter and it is he that performs all of the work withn the womb, molding life in the manner that he sees fit.

I. *The Barren Womb*

There is the *Barren Womb*—where no work is performed by the potter. In the barren womb, the LORD God makes the decision to prevent and restrain the womb from bearing children, as he did Abram's wife Sarai. For,

> **...Sarai was barren; she had no child.**

Ge 11:30.

Because of this,

> **...Sarai said unto Abram, Behold now, the LORD hath restrained me from bearing: I pray thee, go in unto my maid; it may be that I may obtain children by her. And Abram hearkened to the voice of Sarai.**

Ge 16:2.

Here, **restrained** *(ri-strān'd)* is taken from **`atsar** *(aw-tsar')* which means to enclose, hold back, rule, to maintain, detain, keep still, refrain, retain, shut up, stay, stop, withhold. Furthermore, the word **barren** *(bar'ən),* translated from **`aqar** *(aw-kawr')* means sterile, extirpated in the male or female generative organs, barren.

Thus, God, for his own reasons and for his later glory, shut up Sarai's womb and withheld children from entering into her womb, until He decided it was time for a child to come from her womb. For,

> **10 ...he said, I will certainly return unto thee according to the time of life; and, lo, Sarah thy wife shall have a son...**
>
> **11 Now Abraham and Sarah were old and well stricken in age; and it ceased to be with Sarah after the manner of women.**

Ge 18:10-11.

> **1 And the Lord visited Sarah as he had said, and the Lord did unto Sarah as he had spoken.**
>
> **2 For Sarah conceived, and bare Abraham a son in his old age, at the set time of which God had spoken to him.**
>
> **3 And Abraham called the name of his son that was born unto him, whom Sarah bare to him, Isaac.**
>
> **...**
>
> **5 And Abraham was a hundred years old, when his son Isaac was born unto him.**

Ge 21:1-3, 5.

Later, in a *second* example the LORD God would receive glory out of the barren womb of Sarah's daughter-in-law, Rebekah. For,

> **21 ...Isaac entreated the Lord for his wife, because she was barren: and the Lord was entreated of him, and Rebekah his wife conceived.**
>
> **...**
>
> **23 And the LORD said unto her, Two nations are in thy womb, and two manner of people shall be separated from thy bowels; and the one people shall be stronger than the other people; and the elder shall serve the younger.**

...

27 And the boys grew: and Esau was a cunning hunter, a man of the field; and Jacob was a plain man, dwelling in tents.

Ge 25:21, 23, 27.

Here, we see in the barren womb, God does not allow the will of man to decide when and if the womb will conceive, but rather the LORD God maintains control and determines the time and the circumstances of conception and birth. In the Genesis 25:21, 23, 27 passage above, it was the prayer of Isaac and God answering that prayer, according to God's own will, that caused Rebekah to conceive. Later, a whole nation of chosen people called the Israelites would spring forth out of Jacob whose name would become Israel. For, the scripture recorded,

27 And he said unto him, What is thy name? And he said, Jacob.

28 And he said, Thy name shall be called no more Jacob, but Israel: for as a prince hast thou power with God and with men, and hast prevailed.

Ge 32:27-28.

A *third* example of the Lord receiving delayed glory from the barren womb was through Jacob's wife Rachel. For,

...when the LORD saw that Leah was hated, he opened her womb: but Rachel was barren.

Ge 29:31.

1 And when Rachel saw that she bare Jacob no children, Rachel envied her sister; and said unto Jacob, Give me children, or else I die.

2 And Jacob's anger was kindled against Rachel: and he said, Am I in God's stead, who hath withheld from thee the fruit of the womb?

Ge 30:1-2.

22 And God remembered Rachel, and God hearkened to her, and opened her womb.

23 And she conceived, and bare a son; and said, God hath taken away my reproach:

24 And she called his name Joseph; and said, The LORD shall add to me another son.

Ge 30:22-24.

Later, Joseph, the child born from the once barren womb of Rachel, was sold into slavery by his ten older brothers, because of envy and jealousy. *(Ac 7:9; Ge 37:4, 11, 28; Ps 105:17)* But, God being with him delivered him. *(Ac 7:10)*

4 And Joseph said unto his brethren, Come near to me, I pray you. And they came near. And he said, I am Joseph your brother, whom ye sold into Egypt.

5 Now therefore be not grieved, nor angry with yourselves, that ye sold me hither: for God did send me before you to preserve life.

...

7 And God sent me before you to preserve you a posterity in the earth, and to save your lives by a great deliverance.

8 So now it was not you that sent me hither, but God: and he hath made me a father to Pharaoh, and lord of all his house, and a ruler throughout all the land of Egypt.

Ge 45:4-5, 7-8 *(Read also Ps 105:16-22).*

After reviewing the scriptures above we learn that all three of the patriarchs, Abraham, Isaac and Jacob, each married a woman, Sarah, Rebekah and Rachel, whose wombs had been closed and shut up by God. And, we also see that all three wombs were opened later by God and chosen by God to be of great blessings to all of mankind. For, Sarah's womb bore Isaac, the son of the promise. Rebekah's womb bore Jacob, father Israel, who fathered the twelve tribes who became God's chosen people Israel. And, Rachel's womb bore Joseph, whose obedience to God became the salvation of Israel, Egypt and the world, during a seven year world famine. *(Ge 41:25-49; 54-57; Ge 45:3-11; Ge 46:1-7)*

The barren womb is a **reproach** unto a woman *(Ge 30:23),* because in general terms a barren womb represents punishment for disobedience and sin. As the law giver wrote,

> **12 Wherefore it shall come to pass, if ye hearken to these judgments, and keep, and do them, that the Lord thy God shall keep unto thee the covenant and the mercy which he sware unto thy fathers:**
>
> **13 And he will love thee, and bless thee, and multiply thee: he will also bless the fruit of thy womb, and the fruit of thy land, thy corn, and thy wine, and thine oil, the increase of thy kine, and the flocks of thy sheep, in the land which he sware unto thy fathers to give thee.**
>
> **14 Thou shalt be blessed above all people: there shall not be male or female barren among you, or among your cattle.**

De 7:12-14.

Although the word **reproach** *(ri-prōch')* is taken from **cherpah** *(kher-paw')* which means disgrace, rebuke, reproach and shame; the scriptures prove that the Lord is able and willing to remove the disgrace and shame and turn the reproach into a blessing, joy and a source of delayed glory unto God—assisting in the fulfilling of his Will. As Sarah laughed when she heard the promise of her bearing a son in her old age, the response was

> **Is any thing too hard for the Lord? At the time appointed I will return unto thee, according to the time of life, and Sarah shall have a son.**

Ge 18:14.

For, when the once barren womb conceives, due to its being opened by God, then, the child that is conceived is born after the Spirit and not after the will of the flesh. As the Apostle Paul declared,

> **28 Now we, brethren, as Isaac was, are the children of promise.**
>
> **29 But as then he that was born after the flesh persecuted him that was born after the Spirit, even so it is now.**

Ga 4:28-29 *(Read also Ga 4:30-31; Ga 5:1).*

A *fourth* example of the LORD God receiving delayed glory from a once barren womb is found in Hannah, wife of Elkanah.

> **2 And he had two wives; the name of the one was Hannah, and the name of the other Peninnah: and Peninnah had children, but Hannah had no children.**
>
> **...**
>
> **5 But unto Hannah he gave a worthy portion; for he loved Hannah: but the Lord had shut up her womb.**
>
> **6 And her adversary also provoked her sore, for to make her fret, because the LORD had shut up her womb.**
>
> **...**
>
> **8 Then said Elkanah her husband to her, Hannah, why weepest thou? And why is thy heart grieved? Am not I better to thee than ten sons?**
>
> **...**
>
> **10 And she was in bitterness of soul, and prayed unto the LORD, and wept sore.**
>
> **11 And she vowed a vow, and said, O LORD of hosts, if thou wilt indeed look on the affliction of thine handmaid, and remember me, and not forget thine handmaid but wilt give unto thine handmaid a man child, then I will give him unto the LORD all the days of his life, and there shall no razor come upon his head.**

…

19 And they rose up in the morning early, and worshiped before the LORD, and returned, and came to their house to Ramah: and Elkanah knew Hannah his wife; and the LORD remembered her.

20 Wherefore it came to pass, when the time was come about after Hannah had conceived, that she bare a son, and called his name Samuel, saying, Because I have asked him of the LORD.

1Sa 1:2, 5-6, 8, 10-11, 19-20.

After Hannah had weaned her son Samuel, she took him to Shiloh and gave him back to the LORD. *(1Sa 1:24-28)* Hannah was so grateful until she prayed and rejoiced in the LORD, giving God the glory. *(Read 1Sa 2:1-10)* The child Samuel became an instrument of God in the fulfillment of the Will of God. For,

20 … all Israel from Dan even to Beersheba knew that Samuel was established to be a prophet of the LORD.

21 And the LORD appeared again in Shiloh: for the LORD revealed himself to Samuel in Shiloh by the word of the LORD.

1Sa 3:20-21.

A *fifth* example of the LORD God receiving delayed glory from a once barren womb is found in Manoah, whose wife was barren. For,

3 …the angel of the LORD appeared unto the woman, and said unto her, Behold now, thou art barren, and bearest not: but thou shalt conceive, and bear a son.

…

5 For, lo, thou shalt conceive, and bear a son; and no razor shall come on his head: for the child shall be a Nazarite unto God from the womb: and he shall begin to deliver Israel out of the hand of the Philistines.

...

24 And the woman bare a son, and called his name Samson: and the child grew, and the LORD blessed him.

25 And the spirit of the LORD began to move him at times...

Jg 13:3, 5, 24-25.

And he judged Israel in the days of the Philistines twenty years.

Jg 15:20.

28 And Samson called unto the LORD, and said, O LORD God, remember me, I pray thee, and strengthen me, I pray thee, only this once, O God, that I may be at once avenged of the Philistines for my two eyes.

...

30 And Samson said, Let me die with the Philistines, And he bowed himself with all his might; and the house fell upon the lords, and upon all the people that were therein. So the dead which he slew at his death were more than they which he slew in his life.

Jg 16:28, 30.

From the once barren womb of Manoah's wife, by the will of the spirit, God entered the potter's house and shaped and fashioned a judge and deliverer for his people Israel.

A *sixth* and final example of delayed glory unto God coming from the once barren womb is found in Elisabeth, the wife of Zechariah.

7 And they had no child, because that Elisabeth was barren, and they both were now well stricken in years.

...

13 But the angel said unto him, Fear not, Zechariah: for thy prayer is heard; and thy wife Elisabeth shall bear thee a son, and thou shalt call his name John.

…

15 For he shall be great in the sight of the Lord, and shall drink neither wine nor strong drink; and he shall be filled with the Holy Ghost, even from his mother's womb.

16 And many of the children of Israel shall he turn to the Lord their God.

17 And he shall go before him in the spirit and power of Elijah, to turn the hearts of the fathers to the children, and the disobedient to the wisdom of the just; to make ready a people prepared for the Lord.

…

24 And after those days his wife Elisabeth conceived, and hid herself five months, saying,

25 Thus hath the Lord dealt with me in the days wherein he looked on me, to take away my reproach among men.

…

57 Now Elisabeth's full time came that she should be delivered; and she brought forth a son.

…

60 And his mother answered and said, Not so; but he shall be called John.

…

76 And thou, child, shalt be called the prophet of the Highest: for thou shalt go before the face of the Lord to prepare his ways;

77 To give knowledge of salvation unto his people by the remission of their sins,

Luke 1:7, 13, 15-17, 24-25, 57, 60, 76-77.

2 Annas and Caiaphas being the high priests, the word of God came unto John the son of Zechariah in the wilderness.

3 And he came into all the country about Jordan, preaching the baptism of repentance for the remission of sins;

Lu 3:2-3.

Once again, the LORD God obtained great glory from a once barren womb. For, the child born after the will of the Spirit of God, became the forerunner of the Christ—preparing the hearts of the people for the coming salvation of the LORD. As he declared unto his listeners,

I indeed have baptized you with water: but he shall baptize you with the Holy Ghost.

Mk 1:8

Because he is the potter and Lord over the clay, it is God who determines who shall be barren, male or female; man or cattle. *(De 7:14; Jg 13:2-5; Lu 1:24-25, 31)* Like the grave, the fire, and the earth that is not filled with water, the barren womb is never satisfied. *(Pr 30:15-16)* But God, being a kind and merciful God,

...maketh the barren woman to keep house, and to be a joyful mother of children...

Ps 113:9.

God uses the process of removing the shame, disgrace and reproach of the natural, barren woman to foreshadow his desire, will and power to remove our spiritual unfruitfulness, shame, disgrace and reproach because of our sin. While comparing his people, Israel, to a barren, unfruitful woman, the LORD God, speaking through the Prophet Isaiah declared,

1 Sing, O barren, thou that didst not bear; break forth into singing, and cry aloud, thou that didst not travail with child: for more are the children of the desolate than the children of the married wife, saith the LORD.

…

4 Fear not; for thou shalt not be ashamed: neither be thou confounded; for thou shalt not be put to shame: for thou shalt forget the shame of thy youth, and shalt not remember the reproach of thy widowhood any more.

5 For thy Maker is thine husband; the LORD of hosts is his name; and thy Redeemer the Holy One of Israel; The God of the whole earth shall he be called.

6 For the LORD hath called thee as a woman forsaken and grieved in spirit, and a wife of youth, when thou wast refused, saith thy God.

7 For a small moment have I forsaken thee; but with great mercies will I gather thee.

8 In a little wrath I hid my face from thee for a moment; but with everlasting kindness will I have mercy on thee, saith the LORD thy Redeemer.

Isa 54:1, 4-8.

Insurance Against: Falling, Spiritual Barrenness and Unfruitfulness

Many years later, the Apostle Peter compared the unfruitfulness of being barren to our failure to add seven spiritual attributes to our faith in and to our knowledge of Jesus Christ. When these attributes are not present, then we, as believers, shall be barren and unfruitful in the knowledge of Jesus Christ. For, the apostle declared,

5 And beside this, giving all diligence, add to your faith virtue; and to virtue knowledge;

6 And to knowledge temperance; and to temperance patience; and to patience godliness;

7 And to godliness brotherly kindness; and to brotherly kindness charity.

8 For if these things be in you, and abound, they make you that ye shall neither be barren nor unfruitful in the knowledge of our Lord Jesus Christ.

2Pe 1:5-8.

Peter went on to admonish the lutrosis believers that

9 ...he that lacketh these things is blind, and cannot see afar off, and hath forgotten that he was purged from his old sins.

10 Wherefore the rather, brethren, give diligence to make your calling and election sure: for if ye do these things, ye shall never fall.

2Pe 1:9-10.

Here, in the 2Peter 1:9 passage, we are admonished that if we will add to our salvation in Christ, as lutrosis, redeemed, Holy Ghost filled believers these things, namely: virtue to our faith, knowledge to our virtue, temperance to knowledge, patience to temperance, godliness to patience, brotherly kindness to godliness, and charity to brotherly kindness—we shall never fall. For, these things shall keep us in Jesus, and assist us in obeying his command to

Be ye therefore perfect, even as your Father which is in heaven is perfect.

Mt 5:48.

And, if we are kept in Jesus consciously striving for perfection, then we cannot stumble and fall because

...there is none occasion of stumbling in him.

1Jo 2:10.

For,

7 Unto you therefore which believe he is precious: but unto them which be disobedient, the stone which the builders disallowed, the same is made the head of the corner,

8 And a stone of stumbling, and rock of offense, even to them which stumble at the word, being disobedient: whereunto also they were appointed.

1Pe 2:7-8.

It should be noted that we are admonished by 2Peter 1:5, to *'give all diligence'* to accomplishing the task of adding these *'things'* to our faith. When we consider that the word **diligence** *(dil'ə-jəns)* is derived from **spŏudē** *(spoo-day'),* which means speed, dispatch, eagerness, earnestness, business, earnest care, carefulness, diligence, forwardness and haste, then, we realize that Apostle Peter was concerned about the speed and the attitude with which we are possessed while adding these 'things' to our faith. For, **spŏudē** instructs us to proceed with all speed and without delay with: **(1) dispatch** *(di-spach')*—to finish quickly or promptly; to put an end to; kill; to send off or out on a specific errand or official business; **(2) eagerness** *(ē'gẽr-nis)*—the quality or state of keenly desiring, wanting very much, impatient, anxious, ardent, sharp; **(3) earnestness** *(ũr'nist-nis)*—to set oneself in motion, excite, arouse; the quality or state of being serious and intense, not joking or playful, zealous and sincere, deeply convinced, important, not petty or trivial, with determination; **(4) business** *(biz'-nis)*—one's work, occupation, profession, rightful concern or responsibility; **(5) carefulness** *(kâr'fəl-nis)*—the quality or state of caring for; taking care of; watchful; cautious; accurately or thoroughly done or made; painstaking; **(6) forwardness** *(fôr'wẽrd-nis)*—the quality or state of being forward; an advanced state of development or progress, readiness, eagerness, boldness, presumption or pertness; **(7) haste** *(hāst)*—quickness of motion; hurrying; rapidity; in a hurry; **(8) speed** *(spēd)*—the act or state of moving rapidly; swiftness; quick motion. We are admonished to not be slothful. For,

> **He also that is slothful in his work is brother to him that is a great waster.**

Pr 18:9.

We are not to be slothful in business, and especially in the business of the Kingdom of God. *(Ro 12:11)*; and finally, **spǒudē** means **(9) diligence** *(dil'ə-jəns)*—the quality of being diligent—persevering and careful in work; hardworking; done with careful, steady effort; pain-stakingly; constant careful work.

When we consider the phrase 'adding to our faith', the faith here is the faith in Christ Jesus that led and brought us to Him. For we were,

> **Looking unto Jesus the author and finisher of our faith;...**

Heb 12:2.

Our looking unto and coming to Jesus, through obedience to the commands of Acts 2:38, results in the redemption of our soul through the receipt of his indwelling spirit. *(Read Ac 2:38; Ro 8:9)* For, it is by our receiving the Holy Ghost indwelling that we receive his power, as He promised

> **...behold, I send the promise of my Father upon you: but tarry ye in the city of Jerusalem, until ye be endued with power from on high.**

Lu 24:49.

And,

...ye shall receive power, after that the Holy Ghost is come upon you:...

Ac 1:8.

For, it is by the power of the indwelling Holy Ghost that we take on the divine nature of Christ,

3 According as his divine power hath given unto us all things that pertain unto life and godliness, through the knowledge of him that hath called us to glory and virtue:

4 Whereby are given unto us exceeding great and precious promises: that by these ye might be partakers of the divine nature, having escaped the corruption that is in the world through lust.

2Pe 1:3-4.

After we have come into the knowledge of Christ the Lord and have begun to know him as our indwelling saviour through and by our faith in him, then the first thing we must add to our faith in Christ—is virtue. **Virtue** *(vũr'chōō)* is taken from the Greek word Adam **arĕtē** *(ar-et'-ay)* which means manliness, valor, excellence, praise, virtue. **Valor** *(val'ẽr)* means courage, to be strong, to be worth, fearlessness; bravery, especially in battle. And, **excellence** *(ek's'l-ens)* is the condition or fact of excelling; superiority; surpassing goodness, merit. Thus, Apostle Peter admonishes us to be strong and of good courage; fearless and brave in battle within our walk in Christ, in the same manner as the LORD God had admonished Joshua centuries earlier, saying,

5 There shall not any man be able to stand before thee all the days of thy life: as I was with Moses, so I will be with thee: I will not fail thee, nor forsake thee.

6 Be strong and of a good courage:...

7 Only be thou strong and very courageous, that thou mayest observe to do according to all the law, which

Moses my servant commanded thee: turn not from it to the right hand or to the left, that thou mayest prosper whitersoever thou goest.

…

9 Have not I commanded thee? Be strong and of a good courage; be not afraid, neither be thou dismayed: for the Lord thy God is with thee whithersoever thou goest.

Jos 1:5-7, 9.

In essence the LORD God told Joshua, the leader of God's people, to add to Joshua's faith in God, virtue, valor, fearlessness, manliness, ex-cellence. After adding virtue to our faith, we must add knowledge to our virtue if we are to enjoy continued success. **Knowledge** *(nol'ij)* is taken from **gnosis** *(gno'-sis).* **Gnosis** means the act of knowing; knowledge; science. **Science** *(si'ens)* is the state or fact of knowing or possessing knowledge as opposed to belief or intuition; systematized knowledge derived from observation, study, and experimentation carried on in order to determine the nature or principles of what is being studied. Thus, we are admonished by the Lord to

Study to show thyself approved unto God, a workman that needeth not to be ashamed, rightly dividing the word of truth.

2Ti 2:15.

Search the scriptures: for in them ye think ye have eternal life: and they are they which testify of me.

Joh 5:39.

By studying and searching the scriptures we avoid errors and mistakes as

Jesus answered and said unto them, Ye do err, not knowing the scriptures, nor the power of God.

Mt 22:29 *(Read also Mk 12:24).*

For, the question was asked,

> **9 Whom shall he teach knowledge? And whom shall he make to understand doctrine? Them that are weaned from the milk, and drawn from the breasts.**
>
> **10 For precept must be upon precept, precept upon precept; line upon line, line upon line; here a little, and there a little:**

Isa 28:9-10.

Thus, along with our salvation in Christ, through faith, our virtue, courage and bravery in battle, we must add to our virtue knowledge that is more than just a belief. But, we are to know, not only by knowing God indwelling, but also by knowing and understanding the scriptures and the power of God. We are to walk, fight and exist in a state of knowing first-hand beyond emotions, feelings and belief. By knowing as men rather than just believing as children, who are still on the milk and laying on the breast, *(Read Isa 28:9-10; Heb 5:12-14)* we are able to obey the command of the Apostle James when he said,

> **Do not err, my beloved brethren.**

Jas 1:16.

The word **err** *(ûr)* here is taken from **planao** *(plan-ah'-o).* **Planao** means to cause to roam from safety, from truth or from virtue; to go astray, to deceive, err, seduce, wander, be out of the way. Therefore, although we may have been redeemed and received the indwelling spirit of Christ, ignorance brought about due to lack of knowledge of the scriptures and the power of God will cause us to be deceived, be seduced, wander about, go astray, roam from safety, truth and virtue and therefore be out of the way. This is so even though the scripture declares that

> **...a highway shall be there, and a way, and it shall be called The way of holiness; the unclean shall not pass**

over it; but it shall be for those: the wayfaring men, though fools, shall not err therein.
Isa 35:8.

And, when our ignorance causes us to be out of the way, we as the people of God

...are destroyed for lack of knowledge: because thou hast rejected knowledge, I will also reject thee, that thou shalt be no priest to me: seeing thou hast forgotten the law of thy God, I will also forget thy children.
Ho 4:6.

And, in the end, if we fail to repent and to begin acquiring knowledge, the Lord has already declared,

13 Therefore my people are gone into captivity, because they have no knowledge:...
14 Therefore hell hath enlarged herself, and opened her mouth without measure: and their glory, and their multitude, and their pomp, and he that rejoiceth shall descend into it.
Isa 5:13-14.

Once we have added *knowledge* to our *virtue,* then we must add ***temperance*** to our *knowledge.* For, even if we should gain knowledge and understanding of all mysteries and not exercise self-control then we too shall be lost. As the Apostle Paul taught,

24 Know ye not that they which run in a race run all, but one receiveth the prize? So run, that ye nay obtain.
25 And every man that striveth for the mastery is temperate in all things. Now they do it to obtain a corruptible crown; but we an incorruptible.

26 I therefore so run, not as uncertainly; so fight I, not as one that beateth the air:

27 But I keep under my body, and bring it into subjection: lest that by any means, when I have preached to others, I myself should be a castaway.

1Co 9:24-27.

Thus, it is the exercising of **temperance**, a fruit of the Spirit *(Ga 5:22-23),* that assists us in disciplining and controlling our flesh, our heart and our desires that the *knowledge* that we have added to our *virtue* will be fruitful in the kingdom of God. The word **temperance** *(tem'pĕr-əns),* in 2Peter 1:6 above, is translated from the Greek **egkrateia** *(eng-krat'-i-ah)* meaning self-control, especially continence; temperance. **Continence** *(kon'tə-nəns)* means self-restraint; moderation; self-restraint in sexual activity; especially, complete abstinence. For,

He that hath no rule over his own spirit is like a city that is broken down, and without walls.

Pr 25:28.

And,

He that is slow to anger is better than the mighty; and he that ruleth his spirit than he that taketh a city.

Pr 16:32.

In the Proverbs 25:38 passage above the Hebrew word **ma`tsar** *(mah-tsawr')* is translated to mean control, **rule** *(rōōl).* And in the Proverbs 16:32 passage the word **ruleth** *(rōōl'if)* is taken from **mâshal** *(maw-shal')* which means to rule; to have dominion; to make to have dominion; governor, reign, to bear rule, cause to rule, have rule, have power. Therefore, after adding knowledge to our virtue and virtue to our faith, in order to properly utilize the knowledge so to be fruitful and not barren and to keep from falling from the good ground to the thorny ground, we must learn to restrain and control our appetite, our emotions and our spirit. To assist in guarding against a lack of self-control in sexual matters, which is incontinency, the Apostle Paul admonishes the married believers that,

> **4 The wife hath not power of her own body, but the husband: and likewise also the husband hath not power of his own body, but the wife.**
>
> **5 Defraud ye not one the other, except it be with consent for a time, that ye may give yourselves to fasting and prayer; and come together again, that Satan tempt you not for your incontinency.**

1Co 7:4-5.

Incontinency *(in-kon'tə-nən-si)* having been translated from **akrasia** *(ak-ras-ee'-a),* means lack, or want of self-restraint; excess. **Akrasia** is derived from **akratēs** *(ak-rat'-ace)* which means powerless, without self-control, incontinent. Thus, it is necessary for husbands and wives to assist each other in guarding against the lack of temperance in sexual matters. For, this is one of the areas that the enemy will seek to defeat us, and thereby cause us to fall and render us barren and unfruitful in the knowledge of Jesus Christ as in Jesus' Parable of the Sower. For, there, the thorny ground seed was barren because the pleasures of this life, including illicit sex, and lusts of other things entering into the believer's lifestyle actually choked the Word of God that was in him causing him to be unfruitful. *(Lu 8:14; Mk 4:19)*

For this reason, even our fasting, prayers and work for the Lord and his kingdom **are not** to be used as excuses to prevent the husband or the wife from knowing each other in sexual relations. For, it is our being unfruitful and barren that we as members of Christ are working to overcome. Lack of self-control and lack of temperance in sexual matters will cause us to become mindful of the flesh. That is, our minds and thoughts will be pre-occupied and more concerned with taking care of the needs and desires of the fleshly man rather than the needs and desires of the spirit man. When we are more concerned with satisfying of the flesh, rather than the spirit man, then we are walking after the flesh, rather than walking after the Spirit. And,

> **...they that are after the flesh do mind the things of the flesh; but they that are after the Spirit the things of the Spirit.**

Ro 8:5.

When we cause one another to become carnal, due to a lack of self-control in emotions, appetite or spirit we bring about barrenness, unfruitfulness and death as Eve did in the garden of Eden. For, there

> **...[W]hen the woman saw that the tree was good for food, and that it was pleasant to the eyes, and a tree to be desired to make one wise, she took of the fruit thereof, and did eat, and gave also unto her husband with her, and he did eat.**

Ge 3:6.

After listening to the wrong voice of the serpent *(Read Ge 3:1-5, 13),* Eve, the woman's thoughts became pre-occupied and more concerned with taking care of the needs and desires of her fleshly man rather than the needs and desires of her spirit man. Thus, she was now walking after the flesh, in a carnal state of mind, not mindful of life in obedience to the Word or peace with God. And with this carnal mind she enticed Adam and became the object of his carnality leading to his death. For, Adam's appetite was aroused and he did eat. *(Ge 3:6)* As the Apostle wrote,

> **6 For to be carnally minded is death; but to be spiritually minded is life and peace.**
>
> **7 Because the carnal mind is enmity against God: for it is not subject to the law of God, neither indeed can be.**

8 So then they that are in the flesh cannot please God.
Ro 8:6-8.

Therefore, if we fail to add temperance to our knowledge, then we shall fall into the death of the flesh and out of the light and life that is only in Christ Jesus *(Joh 1:4; Joh 8:12; 1Jo 5:11-13)*—becoming thorny ground, barren and unfruitful brides that cannot please their husband. For, in the death of the flesh we cannot please God having left our faith in him, because,

...without faith it is impossible to please him:...
Heb 11:6.

And we know that

...the just shall live by faith: but if any man draw back, my soul shall have no pleasure in him.
Heb 10:38.

But if we are to remain *steadfast, unmovable, always abounding in the work of the Lord (1Co 15:58),* then we must be diligent in working on adding temperance to our knowledge. For,

...we are not of them who draw back unto perdition; but of them that believe to the saving of the soul.
Heb 10:39.

Moreover, temperance and self-control will also assist in the prevention of strife and fighting in the household. For,

It is better to dwell in the wilderness, than with a contentious and an angry woman.
Pr 21:19.

And,

It is better to dwell in a corner of the housetop, than with a brawling woman in a wide house.
Pr 21:9.

Because,

...where envying and strife is, there is confusion and every evil work.
Jas 3:16.

A contentious woman is a woman lacking in temperance in regards to her speech, her conversations and the words that she speak. For, the Lord declared,

Whoso offereth praise glorifieth me: and to him that ordereth his conversation aright will I show the salvation of God.
Ps 50:23.

And, to further impress upon man, the importance of speaking only in praise, without guile, without desire for vainglory, without pride, and without the intent to offend and—or to deceive, the Lord Jesus admonished us, declaring

36 ...That every idle word that men shall speak, they shall give account thereof in the day of judgment.
37 For by thy words thou shalt be justified, and by thy words thou shalt be condemned.
Mt 12:36-37.

Here, the phrase **'idle word'** is concerned with speech, conversations and words spoken without the intent of working together to benefit the cause of Christ or his kingdom. For, in the above passage, the word **idle** *(ī'd'l),* having been translated from the Greek **argŏs** *(ar-gos'),* refers to words that are inactive, unemployed, lazy, useless, barren, and slow. Therefore, when a person uses words in a manner that are not employed or designed with the intent of being a benefit to the cause of Christ or his kingdom, then those words are inactive, useless, barren and unemployed idle words and the speaker shall *'give account thereof in the day of judgment'. (Mt 12:36).*

Thus, when a person is **contentious** as the woman found in Proverbs 21:19, or the man found in Proverbs 26:21, that person is in a **mâdôwn** *(maw-dohn').* **Mâdôwn** means a contest or quarrel; brawling, contention, contentious, discord, strife. Causing discord amongst the brethren, or within the household is not of benefit to the cause of Christ nor his kingdom, because **discord** *(dis'kord)* means lack of concord; disagreement; dissension; conflict; incompatibility. Therefore, where there is discord, contention and strife the brethren will be barren and unfruitful, because the body of Christ cannot bear children without agreement. The members of the kingdom must be in agreement, with one accord, with one mind and with one purpose. *(Read Php 2:2)* For this reason, there is one thing the Lord hates, which is also an abomination unto him, and that is,

> **...he that soweth discord among brethren.**

Pr 6:19.

Thus, rather than engaging in vain, contentious and idle talk, we are admonished, by the Apostle Paul, to

> **...study to be quiet...**

1Th 4:11.

> **...be thou an example of the believers, in word, in conversation, in charity, in spirit, in faith, in purity.**

1Ti 4:12.

> **Only let your conversation be as it becometh the gospel of Christ: that whether I come and see you, or else be absent, I may hear of your affairs, that ye stand fast in**

one spirit, with one mind striving together for the faith of the gospel;
Php 1:27.

Therefore, strife, contention and discord amongst the brethren prevents the church and the brethren from standing *"...in one spirit, with one mind striving together for the faith of the gospel..." (Php 1:27)*

To **study** *(stud'i),* in 1Thessalonians 4:11, means to be **philŏtimĕŏmai** *(fil-ot-im-eh'-om-ahee)* fond of honor, emulous, eager or earnest to do something; strive, labour, study. And to be **quiet** *(kwī'ət),* taken from the Greek **hēsuchazō** *(hay-soo-khad'-zo),* means to keep still; refrain from speech, labor or meddlesomeness; cease, hold peace, be quiet, rest. Therefore, if we are to be fruitful and not barren in the knowledge of Christ we must be eager and earnest in our striving to refrain from idle speaking. To be quiet, we must learn to hold our peace and to be ready to hear and not speak with the sacrifice of fools. For

A fool uttereth all his mind: but a wise man keepeth it in till afterward.
Pr 29:11.

As King Solomon declared,

1 Keep thy foot when thou goest to the house of God, and be more ready to hear, than to give the sacrifice of fools: for they consider not that they do evil.

2 Be not rash with thy mouth, and let not thine heart be hasty to utter any thing before God: for God is in heaven, and thou upon earth: therefore let thy words be few.

3 For a dream cometh through the multitude of business; and a fool's voice is known by multitude of words.

4 When thou vowest a vow unto God, defer not to pay it; for he hath no pleasure in fools: pay that which thou hast vowed.

…

6 Suffer not thy mouth to cause thy flesh to sin;…

7 For in the multitude of dreams and many words there are also divers vanities: but fear thou God.

Ec 5:1-4, 6-7.

And finally, the Apostle Peter instructs us saying,

15 But as he which hath called you is holy, so be ye holy in all manner of conversation;

16 Because it is written, Be ye holy; for I am holy.

1Pe 1:15-16.

A further point, wherein the redeemed believers in Christ must exercise temperance and control, is our appetite for food and drink. Christians must be careful not to destroy the temple of God through over-eating and thereby destroying our health. For when our physical body is sick and afflicted, due to our own mistreatment and lack of self-control, then we will be hindered in our ability to run and not faint.

After we have added temperance to our knowledge, then we must add **patience** to our temperance. For, we are reminded by the Lord Jesus that,

In your patience possess ye your souls.

Lu 21:19.

And, Apostle Peter explained latter that,

20 For what glory is it, if, when ye be buffeted for your faults, ye shall take it patiently? But if, when ye do

well, and suffer for it, ye take it patiently, this is acceptable with God.

21 For even hereunto were ye called: because Christ also suffered for us, leaving us an example, that ye should follow his steps:

22 Who did no sin, neither was guile found in his mouth:

23 Who, when he was reviled, reviled not again; when he suffered, he threatened not; but committed himself to him that judgeth righteously.

1Pe 2:20-23.

Even after we are in the faith, and have virtue added to that faith, along with knowledge to virtue and temperance to knowledge, without patience, which is not a fruit of the spirit *(See and Read Ga 5:22-23),* we will be like the seeds that sprung up amongst the thorns and thistles in Jesus' Parable of the Sower *(Mt 13:7, 22)*—and lose out on apolutrosis, that is, redemption of our physical bodies. *(Read Ro 8:23-24; 1Co 15:51-54)*

20 For if after ...[we] have escaped the pollutions of the world through the knowledge of the Lord and Savior Jesus Christ, ...[we] are again entangled therein, and overcome, the latter end is worse with ...[us] than the beginning.

21 For it had been better for ...[us] not to have known the way of righteousness, than, after ...[we] have known it, to turn from the holy commandment delivered unto ...[us].

22 But it is happened unto them according to the true proverb, The dog is turned to his own vomit again; and the sow that was washed to her wallowing in the mire.

2Pe 2:20-22 *(Words in brackets added).*

The word **patience** in the 2Peter 1:6 passage discussed earlier is translated from the Greek **hupŏmŏnē** *(hoop-om-on-ay').* **Hupŏmŏnē** means cheerful or hopeful endurance, constancy; enduring, patience, patient continuance, waiting. Thus, when a person goes back and quits the Lord, he has stopped waiting on his deliverance and renewed strength. It is necessary to not only strive to be strong in the Lord, with virtue, valor and fearlessness, but it is also necessary to hold on, hold out and endure to the end. For,

> **...the race is not to the swift, nor the battle to the strong...**

Ec 9:11.

And,

> **23 Thus saith the LORD, Let not the wise man glory in his wisdom, neither let the mighty man glory in his might, let not the rich man glory in his riches.**
>
> **24 But let him that glorieth glory in this, that he understandeth and knoweth me, that I am the LORD which exercise lovingkindness, judgment, and righteousness, in the earth: for in these things I delight, saith the LORD.**

Jer 9:23-24.

> **14 Therefore the flight shall perish from the swift, and the strong shall not strengthen his force, neither shall the mighty deliver himself:**
>
> **15 Neither shall he stand that handleth the bow; and he that is swift of foot shall not deliver himself: neither shall he that rideth the horse deliver himself.**
>
> **16 And he that is courageous among the mighty shall flee away naked in that day, saith the Lord.**

Amos 2:14-16.

Our day of temptation is necessary because it is required that our faith be tested so that we may reach perfection in Christ.

3 Knowing this, that the trying of your faith worketh patience.

4 But let patience have her perfect work, that ye may be perfect and entire, wanting nothing.

Jas 1:3-4.

24 For we are saved by hope: but hope that is seen is not hope: for what a man seeth, why doth he yet hope for?

25 But if we hope for that we see not, then do we with patience wait for it.

Ro 8:24-25.

Hope and patience are part of the same perfecting process of active faith. Stated simply, patience is the act and state of waiting on a specific result, because of our faith. And the result that we wait for is our hope. In agreement the Apostle Paul wrote,

3 … [W]e glory in tribulations also: knowing that tribulation worketh patience;

4 And patience, experience; and experience, hope:

5 And hope maketh not ashamed; because the love of God is shed abroad in our hearts by the Holy Ghost which is given unto us.

Ro 5:3-5.

Therefore, the patience that we add to our temperance enables us to exercise temperance and self control for longer, extended periods of suffering, persecution, tribulation and trouble.

To our **patience**, Apostle Peter admonishes us, in 2Peter 1:6, to add **godliness** so that during our waiting patiently and our enduring we are doing it in godliness and holiness according to the word of

God. For the word **godliness** *(gŏd'lē-nĭs)* in 2Pe l:6 is taken from the Greek **eusebeia** *(yoo-seb'-i-ah)* which means piety, specifically as it relates to the gospel scheme or plan; godliness, holiness. To wait and endure and not endure in the godliness of holiness is not being patient. This is a lack of self control; a failure to exercise temperance. And when we lose patience we faint. As the scripture says,

> **16 For which cause we faint not; but though our outward man perish, yet the inward man is renewed day by day.**
>
> **17 For our light affliction, which is but for a moment, worketh for us a far more exceeding and eternal weight of glory;**
>
> **18 While we look not at the things which are seen, but at the things which are not seen: for the things which are seen are temporal; but the things which are not seen are eternal.**

2Co 4:16-18.

Therefore, while we persevere in the patience of godly holiness,

> **9 ...let us not be weary in well doing: for in due season we shall reap, if we faint not.**
>
> **10 As we have therefore opportunity, let us do good unto all men, especially unto them who are of the household of faith.**

Ga 6:9-10.

Faint *(fānt)* in 2Corinthians 4:16, is translated from the Greek **ekkakeo** *(ek-kak-eh'-o)* which means to be bad or weak; to fail in heart, faint, and be weary. And so, while we wait patiently in the midst of our tribulation, persecution and pressure, to insure that we do not go back on God by becoming a carnal Christian, we must follow in the footsteps of Christ. We must remain stedfast in the apostle's doctrine. *(Ac 2:42)* We must not be weak in the faith. *(1Co*

16:13) We must believe that when we do the right thing, although righteousness causes us to suffer,

> **28 … all things work together for good to them that love God, to them who are the called according to his purpose.**
>
> **29 For whom he did foreknow, he also did predestinate to be conformed to the image of his Son, that he might be the first-born among many brethren.**

Ro 8:28-29.

We must not be bad, go bad, act bad, talk bad or do wrong. We must be patient in godliness and holiness. That is, in our trouble, tribulation and trials we must do what Jesus would do. We must act, behave, talk, walk and live as becoming Christ himself.

> **21 For even hereunto were ye called: because Christ also suffered for us, leaving us an example, that ye should follow his steps:**
>
> **22 Who did no sin, neither was guile found in his mouth:**
>
> **23 Who, when he was reviled, reviled not again; when he suffered, he threatened not; but committed himself to him that judgeth righteously.**

1Pe 2:21-23.

Fainting's Effect Upon One's Blessings From God

We must not fall away from the apostle's doctrine *(2Th 2:3),* by becoming so relaxed, in our daily life, that we forget the Christ that we represent. For, the word **faint** *(fānt)* in Galations 6:9 above, is translated from the Greek **ekluo** *(ek-loo'-o)* which means to relax, to faint. And when we review the teachings of Galatians 6:9-10, again we also learn why we are not blessed. For, the Apostle wrote,

> **9 ...let us not be weary in well doing: for in due season we shall reap, if we faint not.**
> **10 As we have therefore opportunity, let us do good unto all men, especially unto them who are of the household of faith.**

Ga 6:9-10.

In this passage, we are promised to reap in due season only *'if we faint not'*. That is, when we fail to *'do good unto all men, especially unto them who are of the household of faith,'* we have fainted and our blessings are either hindered or completely cut off. Therefore, rather than being blessed as Job was after his tribulation *(Job 42:10-15),* because he fainted not *(Jas 5:11; Job 1:13-22; Job 2:1-10),* those who go bad and faint are left being the tail and not the head; a borrower and not a lender; beneath and not above. *(Read De 28:12-44)* Our response to the pressures of this life must be grounded in godliness and holiness, that we may do no sin, nor should guile be found in our mouths. For we are admonished that,

> **15 ...he which hath called you is holy, so be ye holy in all manner of conversation;**
> **16 Because it is written, BE YE HOLY; FOR I AM HOLY.**

1Pe 1:15-16 *(See also Le 11:44-45; Le 19:2; Le 20:7-8).*

Also, we are to

> **Follow peace with all men, and holiness, without which no man shall see the Lord:**

Heb 12:14.

For, the word **holiness** in Hebrews 12:14 is taken from **hagiasmos** *(hag-ee-as-mos').* **Hagiasmos** means purification, the state of purity, being pure; a purifier, holiness, sanctification. And, in 1Peter 1:15-16, the Greek word **hagios** *(hag'-ee-os)* is translated to mean **holy**. **Hagios** also means sacred, physically pure, morally blameless or religious, ceremonially consecrated; most holy, most holy one, most holy thing; saint.

Therefore, to add godliness to our patience is an admonition to endure suffering and trouble in a state of purity and sanctification. In the midst of our tribulations we are to act as saints, by striving to be: physically pure *(Ro 12:1)*; morally blameless *(Ro 12:2-3)*; morally religious *(Jas 1:26-27);* and ceremonially consecrated. When we do these things we have obeyed the Apostle's command to

> **...cleanse ourselves from all filthiness of the flesh and spirit, perfecting holiness in the fear of God.**

2Co 7:1.

For our behavior and actions in time of trouble affects our reward due us after the trouble passes. *(Ga 6:9)* As the aged women are instructed, we all also are to

> **...be in behavior as becometh holiness, not false accusers, not given to much wine, teachers of good things;**

Tit 2:3.

Because, in the end we are admonished that as the servants of Christ we are to *"...do...the will of God from the heart." (Eph 6:6)*

> **7 With good will doing service, as to the Lord, and not to men:**
>
> **8 Knowing that whatsoever good thing any man doeth, the same shall he receive of the Lord, whether he be bond or free.**

Eph 6:7-8.

After adding godliness to our patience Apostle Peter then instructs us to

Add to godliness brotherly kindness…

2Pe 1:7a.

Brotherly *(brŭth′ərlē)* **kindness** *(kīnd′nĭs)* is derived from the Greek word **philadelphia** *(fil-ad-el-fee'-ah)* which means fraternal affection; brotherly love (kindness), love of the brethren. We are admonished: by the writer of Hebrews 13:1 to *"Let brotherly love continue..."*; by the Apostle Paul to *"Be kindly affectioned one to another with brotherly love; in honor preferring one another..." (Ro 12:10),* and; by his instruction, that *"Love worketh no ill to his neighbor: therefore love is the fulfilling of the law..." (Ro 13:10)* All of this is in agreement with the Lord Jesus when he said

37 …THOU SHALT LOVE THE LORD THY GOD WITH ALL THY HEART, AND WITH ALL THY SOUL, AND WITH ALL THY MIND.

38 This is the first and great commandment.

39 And the second is like unto it, THOU SHALT LOVE THY NEIGHBOR AS THYSELF.

40 On these two commandments hang all the law and the prophets.

Mt 22:37-40.

Jesus is the Lord *(Ro 1:3),* and he is the first fruit from the dead. *(1Co 15:20, 23; 1Pe 1:3)* He is our brother and, having risen from the dead first, we are enabled to rise also—through him.

4 Therefore we are buried with him by baptism into death: that like as Christ was raised up from the dead by the glory of the Father, even so we also should walk in newness of life.

5 For if we have been planted together in the likeness of his death, we shall be also in the likeness of his resurrection.

Ro 6:4-5.

And, if we are to exist in the likeness of Christ's resurrection we must strive to

9 Let love be without dissimulation. Abhor that which is evil; cleave to that which is good.

10 Be kindly affectioned one to another with brotherly love; in honour preferring one another;

11 Not slothful in business; fervent in spirit; serving the Lord;

12 Rejoicing in hope; patient in tribulation; continu- ing instant in prayer;

13 Distributing to the necessity of saints; given to hospitality.

14 Bless them which persecute you: bless, and curse not.

15 Rejoice with them that do rejoice, and weep with them that weep.

16 Be of the same mind one toward another. Mind not high things, but condescend to men of low estate. Be not wise in your own conceits.

17 Recompense to no man evil for evil. Provide things honest in the sight of all men.

18 If it be possible, as much as lieth in you, live peaceably with all men.

19 Dearly beloved, avenge not yourselves, but rather give place unto wrath: for it is written, Vengeance is mine; I will repay, saith the Lord.

20 Therefore if thine enemy hunger, feed him; if he thirst, give him drink: for in so doing thou shalt heap coals of fire on his head.

21 Be not overcome of evil, but overcome evil with good.
Ro 12:9-21.

Because,

9 He that saith he is in the light, and hateth his brother, is in darkness even until now.
10 He that loveth his brother abideth in the light, and there is none occasion of stumbling in him.
11 But he that hateth his brother is in darkness, and walketh in darkness, and knoweth not whither he goeth, because that darkness hath blinded his eyes.
1Jo 2:9-11.

And finally, after we have added virtue to our faith, knowledge to our virtue, temperance to knowledge, patience to temperance, godliness to patience and brotherly kindness to godliness—we must make our calling and election sure by insuring that we add

...to brotherly kindness charity.
2Pe 1:7.

Because charity, which is love, is the greatest thing. *(1Co 13:13)* All that we do must be done out of love and not out of vain glory. *(Php 2:3)* For, **charity** *(char'-i-tē)* is taken from the Greek **agape** (*ag-ah'-pay)* meaning love, affection or benevolence; a love feast, feast of charity, dear. Therefore, if we are to be like Christ, charity's agape love must become a part of who we are in thought, actions and walk of life. For God is love *(1Jo 4:7-8),* and Jesus Christ is God. *(Joh 10:30)* And we are admonished to

5 Let this mind be in you, which was also in Christ Jesus:

6 Who, being in the form of God, thought it not robbery to be equal with God:

7 But made himself of no reputation, and took upon him the form of a servant, and was made in the likeness of men:

8 And being found in fashion as a man, he humbled himself, and became obedient unto death, even the death of the cross.

Php 2:5-8.

The brethren of Christ also must become obedient to the death of our personal cross if charity's agape love is to become who we are. For the Lord said,

38 ...he that taketh not his cross, and followeth after me, is not worthy of me.

39 He that findeth his life shall lose it: and he that loseth his life for my sake shall find it.

Mt 10:38-39.

Because, mankind are all born in sin and shaped in iniquity *(Ps 51:5)* after the sin of our father Adam. *(Ge 3:6-7; Ro 5:12-21)* And so, as mere brute beasts we do not know, seek after or understand God or Him as agape Love.

10 As it is written, THERE IS NONE RIGHTEOUS, NO, NOT ONE:

11 THERE IS NONE THAT UNDERSTANDETH, THERE IS NONE THAT SEEKETH AFTER GOD.

12 THEY ARE ALL GONE OUT OF THE WAY, THEY ARE TOGETHER BECOME UNPROFITABLE; THERE IS NONE THAT DOETH GOOD, NO NOT ONE.

Ro 3:10-12.

Therefore, it is necessary that man be taught the ways, actions and thoughts of agape Love. And, rising to the task the Apostle Paul used the entire Chapter 13 of 1Corinthians to teach the New Testament Believers the attributes of the Lord God's Agape Love. He wrote,

> **1Though I speak with the tongues of men and of angels, and have not charity, I am become as sounding brass, or a tinkling cymbal.**

1Co 13:1.

In this verse 1, the Apostle teaches that to be able to speak many different languages (tongues) without God's agape Love the effectiveness of one's speaking will be no more than and accomplish no more than a person hearing sounds coming from a brass instrument or a cymbal. Without the agape Love of God intertwined with the words spoken the words spoken are no more than mere sound to the hearers. And, in another place he said,

> *9 So likewise ye, except ye utter by the tongue words easy to be understood, how shall it be known what is spoken? for ye shall speak into the air. 10 There are, it may be, so many kinds of voices in the world, and none of them is without signification. 11 Therefore if I know not the meaning of the voice, I shall be unto him that speaketh a barbarian, and he that speaketh shall be a barbarian unto me. (1Co 14:9-11)*

> **2 And though I have the gift of prophecy, and understand all mysteries, and all knowledge; and though I have all faith, so that I could remove mountains, and have not charity, I am nothing.**

1Co 13:2.

In this verse 2, he teaches that a brother who does not possess and exercise agape Love is nothing in the body of Christ although he may possess and use great faith to move mountains and do other wonderful works; possess the prophetic gifts to see into the future and preach God's Word; and is wise and studious understanding all of the mysteries and secret things and all knowledge. And, in agreement, the Lord Jesus said,

> *21 Not every one that saith unto me, Lord, Lord, shall enter into the kingdom of heaven; but he that doeth the will of my Father which is in heaven. 22 Many will say to me in that day, Lord, Lord, have we not prophesied in thy name? and in thy name have cast out devils? and in thy name done many wonderful works? 23 And then will I profess unto them, I never knew you: depart from me, ye that work iniquity. (Mt 7:21-23)*

> **3 And though I bestow all my goods to feed the poor, and though I give my body to be burned, and have not charity, it profiteth me nothing.**

1Co 13:3.

Here, in verse 3, the Apostle teaches that even if I give all my worldly possessions to help the poor, the needy and worthy causes; and even if I am an organ donor or give my body to medical science if I do not possess and exercise the agape Love of God all that I do or have done will not benefit me or profit me with my relationship with the savior.

> **4 Charity suffereth long, and is kind; charity envieth not; charity vaunteth not itself, is not puffed up,**

1Co 13:4.

In this verse we learn that: **(1)** Agape Love **suffereth** *(sof'ərif)* long which in the Greek it is **makrothumeo** *(mak-roth-oo-meh'-o)* meaning agape love is long spirited, forbearing, patient; suffers long, is longsuffering, have long patience, is patient and patiently endures. **(2)** Agape Love is **kind** *(kīnd)* which in the Greek it is **chrestenomai** *(khraste-yoo'-om-ahee)* meaning agape love shows oneself useful, acts benevolently, that is, has an inclination to do good and is kind. **(3)** Agape Love **envieth** *(en'vē-if)* **not** and in the Greek it is not **zeloo** *(dzay-lŏ'-o)* meaning agape love does not have warmth of feeling against anyone or for the things of others; does not covet earnestly; does not have desires of envy, is not moved with envy, is not jealous over or zealously affected by a person's gifts, talents, or things. **(4)** Agape Love **vaunteth** *(vônt-if)* **not itself** which in the Greek it is not **perpereuomai** *(per-per-yoo'-om-ahee)* meaning agape love is not a braggart, does not boast about itself, and does not vaunt itself. **(5)** Agape Love is **not puffed** *(puf-ed)* **up** so in the Greek it is not **phusioo** *(foo-see-ŏ'-o)* meaning agape love is not inflated or blown up so as to make one proud, haughty or puffed up.

5 Doth not behave itself unseemly, seeketh not her own, is not easily provoked, thinketh no evil;

1Co 13:5.

Continuing, the Apostle teaches us, in this verse 5, that: **(6)** Agape Love **does not behave** *(bē-hāv')* **itself unseemly** which in the Greek it is not **aschemoneo** *(as-kay-mon-eh'-o)* meaning it is not and it does not act unbecoming, does not behave itself uncomely or unseemly. **(7)** Agape Love **seeketh** *(sek-if)* **not her own** which in the Greek it is not **zeteo** *(dzay-the'-o)* meaning it does not plot against life; does not go about, desire, endeavour, require or seek its own way. **(8)** Agape Love **is not easily provoked** *(prō-vōk'd)* which in the Greek it is not **paroxuno** *(par-ox-oo'-no)* meaning to sharpen alongside; that is, agape love is not easily exasperated, provoked or stirred up. **(9)** Agape Love **thinketh** *(thiŋk-if)* no evil which in the Greek it does not **logizomai** *(log-id'-zom-ahee).* That is, agape love does not take an inventory or an estimate of evil. It does not conclude, account, esteem, impute, lay reason, reckon, or suppose that another person's acts or intent is evil; and agape love does not think on evil.

6 Rejoiceth not in iniquity, but rejoiceth in the truth;
1Co 13:6.

Here, in verse 6, we learn that: **(10)** Agape Love **rejoiceth** *(ri-jois'if)* **not in iniquity** *(i-nik'wi-tē)* which in the Greek it is not **chairo** *(khah'ee-ro).* That is, agape love is not cheerful, does not rejoice in, is not calmly happy, well off, glad, joyful or well in the Greek **adikia** *(ad-ee-kee'-ah)* which is legal injustice, moral wrongfulness whether of character, life or act; unrighteousness, wrong, unjustness or iniquity. **(11)** Agape Love **rejoiceth** *(ri-jois'if)* in the **truth** *(trōōth)* which in the Greek it does **sugchairo** *(soong-khah'ee-ro)* meaning agape love sympathizes in gladness, congratulates and rejoices in or with the Greek **aletheia** *(al-ay'-thi-a)* which is truth, that which is true, truly, and verity.

7 Beareth all things, believeth all things, hopeth all things, endureth all things.
1Co 13:7.

In this verse 7 the Apostle teaches us that: **(12)** Agape Love **beareth** *(ber-if)* **all things** which in the Greek it is **stego** *(steg'-o)* meaning agape love roofs over, covers with silence, endures patiently, bears, forbears and suffers all things. **(13)** Agape Love **believeth** *(bē-lēv'if)* all things which in the Greek it **pisteuo** *(pist-yoo'-o)* meaning agape love has faith in, upon or with respect to a person or thing; credits or entrust one's spiritual well being to Christ; commits to trust, believes and put trust in or with a person or thing. **(14)** Agape Love **hopeth** *(hōp-if)* all things which in the Greek it **elpizo** *(el-pid'-zo)* meaning agape love expects, confides, have hope and trust for and in all things. **(15)** Agape Love **endureth** *(en-door'if)* **all things** which in the Greek it **hupomeno** *(hoop-om-en'-o)* meaning agape love stays under, behind, remain, undergoes and bears all trials, has fortitude, perseveres, abides, takes patiently, suffers and tarry behind all trials and tribulations.

And so, finally, in verses 4, 5, 6 and 7 the Apostle teaches and shows the attributes of agape Love that a believer should possess and demonstrate in his everyday life. The point, here, is that the believer should be more concerned with acquiring, possessing, exercising and demonstrating the various attributes of agape Love rather than the gifts of the kingdom because, in doing so, he will have endeavored to fulfill the second greatest commandment and to fulfill the law and the prophets. As Jesus declared,

> *And the second is like unto it, Thou shalt love thy neighbor as thyself. (Mt 22:39)* And, *Therefore all things whatsoever ye would that men should do to you, do ye even so to them: for this is the law and the prophets. (Mt 7:12)*

---

8 Charity never faileth: but whether there be prophecies, they shall fail; whether there be tongues, they shall cease; whether there be knowledge, it shall vanish away.

1Co 13:8.

Here, in verse 8, the Apostle teaches the superiority of agape Love over the other gifts. For, he says that prophecies shall fail, because many prophecies go out because of what the prophet saw and dreamed while lying on his bed. As Jesus said, *"What I tell you in darkness, that speak ye in light:..." (Mt 10:27).* And, King Solomon stated, *"For a dream cometh through the multitude of business..." (Ec 5:3a).* Apostle Paul taught further that tongues shall stop and come to an end and knowledge shall vanish away and become of no effect. But, agape Love shall never fail.

---

9 For we know in part, and we prophesy in part.
10 But when that which is perfect is come, then that which is in part shall be done away.

1Co 13:9-10.

In verses 9 and 10, he teaches that when we use the gifts of prophecy and of knowledge we already possess some knowledge and understanding about those things that we see and tell about. But, he teaches that when perfection comes then that missing piece that was partial shall be done away with, because the imperfect is replaced with the perfect.

---

11 When I was a child, I spake as a child, I understood as a child, I thought as a child: but when I became a man, I put away childish things.

1Co 13:11.

Here, the Apostle teaches that children, those who possess little knowledge, wisdom and understanding, speak with the tongue of a child and entertain the thoughts and ideas of a child. An example of this is like operating the gifts of the kingdom without considering or engaging in the attributes of agape Love. He further instructs that when he became a man, of full age, he strived for perfection by putting away childish things and a childish way of life. As the writer declared,

> *13 For every one that useth milk is unskillful in the word of righteousness: for he is a babe. 14 But strong meat belongeth to them that are of full age, even those who by reason of use have their senses exercised to discern both good and evil. (Heb 5:13- 14)* For, we are commanded to, *Be ye therefore perfect, even as your Father which is in heaven is perfect. (Mt 5:48)*

> **12 For now we see through a glass, darkly; but then face to face: now I know in part; but then shall I know even as also I am known.**

1Co 13:12.

In this verse 12, we learn that presently our vision is not perfect because even with all that we know it is like looking through a dark glass. But, the day will come when we shall see things as looking face to face and we shall know not in part but we shall know in the same manner by which the Lord knows us.

> **13 And now abideth faith, hope, charity, these three; but the greatest of these is charity.**

1Co 13:13.

And finally, here in this verse 13, we hear the conclusion of the matter. For, we know that, faith is required and necessary *(Eph 2:8; Ro 5:1-2; Ga 3:14, 22, 24-26; Joh 8:24)* for salvation, because without faith a believer cannot please God. *(Heb 11:6)* And that, hope is necessary to maintain our salvation *(Ro 8:24)* it being a product of longsuffering patience *(Ro 5:3-5)*, by which we possess our souls. *(Lu 21:19)* But, even so, the greatest of all these three, faith, hope and agape Love (charity)—is agape Love. This is so, because God is not faith, although we must put our faith in Him and his promises to be blessed, healed, delivered, to overcome and to receive salvation. *(Joh 8:24; 1Jo 5:4-5; Joh 5:24; Joh 11:25-26; Ro 1:16; Mt 21:21-22)* God is not hope, but the hope of glory is Jesus, the Lord God, in us. *(Col 1:27)* However, God is agape Love. *(1Jo 4:8, 16)* Therefore, since no one and nothing is greater than God—then God, who is agape Love, is greater than faith and hope. For, faith points towards Him (agape Love) and hope is desiring and looking to be with Him (agape Love). When we receive Him indwelling as the Spirit of Christ *(See Ro 8:9-11)* we receive the fruit of the Spirit and that fruit includes agape Love. *(Ga 5:22)* And so, now knowing that if we possess Christ indwelling we do indeed possess God in-dwelling *(Ro 8:9, 11)* as agape Love. For,

> **...God is love; and he that dwelleth in love dwelleth in God, and God in him.**

1Jo 4:16b.

And,

> **7 Beloved, let us love one another: for love is of God; and every one that loveth is born of God, and knoweth God.**
>
> **8 He that loveth not knoweth not God; for God is love.**

9 In this was manifested the love of God toward us, because that God sent his only begotten Son into the world, that we might live through him.

10 Herein is love, not that we loved God, but that he loved us, and sent his Son to be the propitiation for our sins.

11 Beloved, if God so loved us, we ought also to love one another.

12 No man hath seen God at any time. If we love one another, God dwelleth in us, and his love is perfected in us.

13 Hereby know we that we dwell in him, and he in us, because he hath given us of his Spirit.

...

20 If a man say, I love God, and hateth his brother, he is a liar: for he that loveth not his brother whom he hath seen, how can he love God whom he hath not seen?

21 And this commandment have we from him, That he who loveth God love his brother also.

1Jo 4:7-13, 20-21.

II. *The Womb of the Morning*

There is the *Womb Of The Morning—(Ps 110:3),* where the potter, having already formed man from the dust of the ground *(Ge 2:7),* and having lost the obedience of his son through the serpent's deception planted, 'in the womb of time' and in the womb of the woman, the seed of the coming salvation of man through Christ. For, the potter declared,

And I will put enmity between thee and the woman, and between thy seed and her seed; it shall bruise thy head, and thou shalt bruise his heel.

Ge 3:15.

And in Psalms 110:3, the psalmist prophesied,

Thy people shall be willing in the day of thy power, in the beauties of holiness from the womb of the morning: thou hast the dew of thy youth.

After the LORD God had endured seventy-five generations of the wrath of Lucifer upon his creation called man, God stood up in the seventy-sixth generation in the day of his power. For, Jesus Christ came into "all power" on the morning of his resurrection. As he said he would *(Read Mt 12:40),* Jesus did in-fact rise from the dead 'out of the womb of the morning'. For, he had been planted the second time in the earth. The first time his seed was planted, by the Holy Ghost, in the womb in the earth of Mary the virgin. *(Read Lu 1:30-35; Mt 1:18, 20)* Jesus, the Christ came out of the womb of the flesh of Mary in Bethlehem. *(Lu 2:4-12; Mt 2:1)* Thirty-some years later, Jesus was planted in the earth the second time, in a borrowed tomb. *(Mt 27:57-60)* He came out of the tomb of the earth on the third day morning—the womb of the morning. *(Mt 28:1, 5-7)*

The death, burial and resurrection of Jesus Christ was the foreshowing of the hidden plan of God for man's salvation and rebirth from the dead and his being reconciled back to God.

4 Therefore we are buried with him by baptism into death: that like as Christ was raised up from the dead by the glory of the Father, even so we also should walk in newness of life.

5 For if we have been planted together in the likeness of his death, we shall be also in the likeness of his resurrection:

Ro 6:4-5.

This plan was so important that had Satan knew and understood its impact upon his kingdom and works, he would not have crucified the Christ. In agreement, the Apostle Paul declared,

> **7 But we speak the wisdom of God in a mystery, even the hidden wisdom, which God ordained before the world unto our glory:**
> **8 Which none of the princes of this world knew: for had they known it. They would not have crucified the Lord of glory.**

1Co 2:7-8.

And, in the person and body of Jesus Christ, the LORD God declared

> **...All power is given unto me in heaven and in earth.**

Mt 28:18.

This same Jesus was the seed of the woman whose heel the serpent bruised, causing him to be in the heart of the earth for three days as Jonah was in the belly of the whale. *(Mt 12:40)*

The word of God, spoken by the LORD God in Genesis 3:15, is the seed planted by the husbandman into the womb of time and the womb of the woman. As Jesus declared,

> **I am the true vine, and my Father is the husbandman.**

Joh 15:1 *(Read also Zec 13:5-6).*

Furthermore, the Lord Jesus, while teaching his disciples the parable of the sower in Matthew 13:18-23, stated,

> **...he that received seed into the good ground is he that heareth the word, and understandeth it; which also beareth fruit, and bringeth forth, some a hundredfold, some sixty, some thirty.**

Mt 13:23.

Here, in the John 15:1 passage and the Matthew 13:23 passage we learn that God the Father is the husbandman and the word of God is the seed that the sower, the husbandman plants or sows.

Therefore, when seed is planted in the womb it causes the womb to conceive life and to grow that life over a period of time. The 'period of time' in the Genesis 3:15 passage is the womb of the morning. That is, 'in the fullness of time' the water would break and the seed that had been planted by the potter, would spring forth as a new born child, after having rode the womb of time for seventy-five generations, beginning with 1. Adam, then with 2. Seth, 3. Enos, 4. Cainan, 5. Mahalaleel, 6. Jared, 7. Enoch, 8. Methuselah, 9. Lamech, 10. Noah, 11. Sem, 12. Arphaxad, 13. Cainan, 14. Salah, 15. Eber, 16. Peleg, 17. Ragau, 18. Serug, 19. Nahor, 20. Terah, 21. Abraham, 22. Isaac, 23. Jacob, 24. Judah, 25. Pharez, 26. Hezron, 27. Ram, 28. Amminadab, 29. Nahshon, 30. Salmon, 31. Boaz, 32. Obed, 33. Jesse, 34. David, 35. Nathan, 36. Mattatha, 37. Menan, 38. Melea, 39. Eliakim, 40. Jonan, 41. Joseph, 42. Judah, 43. Simeon, 44. Levi, 45. Matthat, 46. Jorim, 47. Eliezer, 48. Jose, 49. Er, 50. Elmodam, 51. Cosam, 52. Addi, 53. Melchi, 54. Neri, 55. Salathiel, 56. Zerubbabel, 57. Rhesa, 58. Joanna, 59. Judah, 60. Joseph, 61. Semei, 62. Mattathias, 63. Maath, 64. Naggai, 65. Esli, 66. Nahum, 67. Amos, 68. Mattathias, 69. Joseph, 70. Janna, 71. Melchi, 72. Levi, 73. Mathat, 74. Heli, 75. Joseph, and 76. Jesus stepping out of the womb of the morning and the womb of Mary into the seventy-sixth generation from Adam. *(Read Lu 3:23-38)* For the scriptures declared,

> **4 …when the fullness of the time was come, God sent forth his Son, made of a woman, made under the law,**
> **5 To redeem them that were under the law, that we might receive the adoption of sons.**

Ga 4:4-5.

The Son of God referred to here in Galatians 4:4 is the seed of the woman that God had declared earlier, in Genesis 3:15, that would bruise the head of the serpent. For, it required the wombs of many generations for the word of God to be manifested into flesh from the prophecy of Genesis 3:15 to the declaration of the Apostle John, where he wrote,

> **1 In the beginning was the Word, and the Word was with God, and the Word was God.**
> **2 The same was in the beginning with God.**
> **…**
> **14 And the Word was made flesh, and dwelt among us, (and we beheld his glory, the glory as of the only begotten of the Father,) full of grace and truth.**

Joh 1:1-2, 14.

The sower, being also the giver of life *(2Co 3:6; Joh 6:63; Ac 17:25),* and he that opens and closes the womb *(Ge 16:1-2; Ge 30:1-2, 22-23; 1Sa 1:5-6; Isa 66:9),* began sowing in Genesis from Adam into Eve's womb to bring forth Seth. For,

> **…Adam knew his wife again; and she bare a son, and called his name Seth: For God, said she, hath appointed me another seed instead of Abel, whom Cain slew.**

Ge 4:25.

The Beginning of Man Praying To God

The appointing of 'the seed', here, refers to the generational seed by which the salvation of man would come through as announced in Genesis 3:15. For, it was only after the appointed one, Seth, had had a son named Enos, did man began to pray to God—that is,

And to Seth, to him also there was born a son; and he called his name Enos: then began men to call upon the name of the LORD.
Ge 4:26.

Seth having been **appointed** means that he had been placed and set by God to do his bidding. For, the word **appointed** *(ə-point'd)* in Genesis 4:25 is translated from the Hebrew **shiyth** *(sheeth).* **Shiyth** means to place, apply, appoint, bring, let alone, regard, set, shew. Thus, man having been separated from God, by man's sin, began his attempt to get closer to God through prayer, by calling on his name—after the birth of Enos. These prayers and calling on the name of the LORD by man would result in the manifestation of the Word of God into the promised saviour *(See Joh 1:1-2, 14; Joh 3:16),* walking and possessing the likeness of sinful flesh *(Ro 8:3; Php 2:7)* by the will of the Spirit of God. *(Lu 1:35; Mt 1:18, 20-21)* For, the husbandman declared,

6 I the Lord have called thee in righteousness, and will hold thine hand, and will keep thee, and give thee for a covenant of the people, for a light of the Gentiles;
7 To open the blind eyes, to bring out the prisoners from the prison, and them that sit in darkness out of the prison house.

…

9 Behold, the former things are come to pass, and new things do I declare: before they spring forth I tell you of them.

…

13 The LORD shall go forth as a mighty man, he shall stir up jealousy like a man of war: he shall cry, yea, roar; he shall prevail against his enemies.
14 I have long time holden my peace; I have been still, and refrained myself: now will I cry like a travailing woman; I will destroy and devour at once.
Isa 42:6-7, 9, 13-14.

During the life of Christ on earth, he did stir up jealousy like a man of war. For, even they, which were his brethren and his kindred, conspired and went about to put him to death *(Mt 26:59, 66; Mk 14:55, 64; Lu 23:18-25),* because of his demonstrated works of love.

III. *The Womb of the Flesh*

There is the ***Womb Of The Flesh*** where the life of the flesh has its beginning.

> **For the life of the flesh is in the blood…**

Le 17:11.

Again, in another place the scripture sayeth,

> **Only be sure that thou eat not the blood: for the blood is the life; and thou mayest not eat the life with the flesh.**

De 12:23 *(Read also Le 17:14).*

Therefore, since the life of the flesh is the blood, life for the flesh comes from the womb of the flesh. That is, the blood from the mother's womb provides the life for the flesh of the embryonic child just conceived.

The Children Born In the Garden of Eden

For, it is through the womb of the woman that the life blood of mankind is transferred, making us all of one blood. *(See Ac 17:26)* In agreement, the scripture declared,

And Adam called his wife's name Eve; because she was the mother of all living.
Ge 3:20.

In this passage, the word **mother** *(muth'ĕr),* which means the bond of the family, dam, parting, is translated from the Hebrew **'em** *(ame).* Here, Adam says that she is the mother of all living. This statement concerning the motherhood of the wife, Eve, by Adam her husband was significant because the seventh commandment required Adam and Eve, the husband and wife to *"... multiply..." (Ge 1:28)* However, when we consider the fact that the first son, Cain, was not born until Adam was put out of the garden of Eden *(Ge 3:22-24; Ge 4:1),* the question arises,

"Then who and what was Eve the mother of at the point in time that Adam named her?"

The quick answer to this riddle is that Eve was the mother of all living humans that were alive other than herself and Adam. But, many teach that no children were born before Cain, the firstborn son. However, the scriptures do not teach that. But rather the scriptures let us know that Cain was not the first child born into the first family. There are at least twelve proofs that teaches us that children were born in the garden of Eden before man was put out of the garden.

First, we know that ***Eve was not Adam's mother*** because, she, being the woman, was taken out of Adam, the man. The man, Adam, was first created and later,

21 ...the LORD God caused a deep sleep to fall upon Adam and he slept: and he took one of his ribs, and closed up the flesh instead thereof;
22 And the rib, which the LORD God had taken from man, made he a woman, and brought her unto the man.

> **23 And Adam said, This is now bone of my bones, and flesh of my flesh: she shall be called Woman, because she was taken out of Man.**

Ge 2:21-23.

Secondly, we know that she, ***Eve, was not the mother of all living animals and creatures,*** because as the woman, she was the last thing that God made in creation. Because, all sea life and all flying birds and fowl of the air were created on the fifth day of creation, and Eve was created on the sixth day. For, Moses wrote,

> **20 And God said, Let the waters bring forth abundantly the moving creature that hath life, and fowl that may fly above the earth in the open firmament of heaven.**
>
> **21 And God created great whales, and every living creature that moveth, which the waters brought forth abundantly, after their kind, and every winged fowl after his kind: and God saw that it was good.**
>
> **22 And God blessed them, saying, Be fruitful, and multiply, and fill the waters in the seas, and let fowl multiply in the earth.**
>
> **23 And the evening and the morning were the fifth day.**

Ge 1:20-23.

Moreover, all of the land animals were created on the first part of the sixth day before the man and before the woman. For,

> **24 ...God said, Let the earth bring forth the living creature after his kind, cattle, and creeping thing, and beast of the earth after his kind: and it was so.**
>
> **25 And God made the beast of the earth after his kind, and cattle after their kind, and every thing that**

creepeth upon the earth after his kind: and God saw that it was good.

26 And God said, Let us make man in our image, after our likeness:...

27 So God created man in his own image, in the image of God created he him; male and female created he them.

28 And God blessed them, and God said unto them, Be fruitful and multiply...

...

31 And God saw every thing that he had made, and, behold, it was very good. And the evening and the morning were the sixth day.

Ge 1:24-28, 31.

Therefore, Eve was not the mother of all living sea life, fowl of the air, or land animals.

The ***third proof*** is that the ***seventh commandment to mankind was to "...multiply..."*** *(Ge 1:28)* We know that a commandment is an obligatory thing. That is, one who is subject to the commandment is obligated to obey the commandment. Otherwise, to not obey the commandment is sin, "*[F]or by the law is the knowledge of sin." (Ro 3:20b)*

Because the law worketh wrath: for where no law is, there is no transgression.

Ro 4:15.

In the Genesis 1:28 passage the word **said** *(sĕd)* is translated from the Hebrew word **'amar** *(aw-mar').* **'Amar** means to charge, require, to command, to give a commandment and to declare. So, knowing that God had charged, required and commanded Adam and Eve to multiply we can review the scriptures to determine if they were punished for disobeying the seventh commandment. After reviewing the scriptures we learn that, out of the ten commandments given to mankind, they were punished only for disobeying one of the ten commandments. The commandment that was violated and for which they were punished was the fourth commandment wherein the LORD God commanded the man saying,

> **But of the tree of the knowledge of good and evil, thou shalt not eat of it: for in the day that thou eatest thereof thou shalt surely die.**

Ge 2:17.

If Adam and Eve had disobeyed the seventh commandment, then we would have read about it as we have read about their disobeying the fourth commandment. For, the writer recorded,

> **And when the woman saw that the tree was good for food, and that it was pleasant to the eyes, and a tree to be desired to make one wise, she took of the fruit thereof, and did eat, and gave also unto her husband with her; and he did eat.**

Ge 3:6.

In the above passage we see Adam and Eve disobeying the fourth commandment—not to eat from the tree of the knowledge of good and evil. The following passage of scripture shows the beginning result of the man and his wife disobeying the fourth commandment. For,

> **9 ...the LORD God called unto Adam, and said unto him, Where art thou?**
>
> **10 And he said, I heard thy voice in the garden, and I was afraid, because I was naked; and I hid myself.**
>
> **11 And he said, Who told thee that thou wast naked? Hast thou eaten of the tree, whereof I commanded thee that thou shouldest not eat?**

12 And the man said, The woman whom thou gavest to be with me, she gave me of the tree, and I did eat. Ge 3:9-12.

Within these, Genesis 3:6, and Genesis 3:9-12 passages, we learn that mankind dis-obeyed the fourth commandment of God by eating from the forbidden tree. And from Genesis 3:14 through Genesis 3:19, we learn of the punishment that the serpent, Adam and Eve received for their violation of the fourth commandment. However, there is no mention within the scriptures of mankind ever disobeying any of the remaining nine commandments including the seventh commandment—to multiply. There is no mention, because they were obedient and began having children in the garden of Eden.

The *fourth proof* is the phrase, ***'multiply thy conception'***, found within the punishment received by the woman for her part in violating the fourth commandment—*not to eat from the tree of the knowledge of good and evil. (See Ge 2:16-17)* For,

Unto the woman he said, I will greatly multiply thy sorrow and thy conception; in sorrow thou shalt bring forth children...

Ge 3:16.

Here, the word **multiply** *(mul'tə-plī')* is translated from the Hebrew **rabah** *(raw-baw')* which means to increase, to bring in abundance, enlarge, excel, exceedingly, more in number, much, greater, more, multiply, plenteous. Furthermore, the word **conception** *(kən-sep'shən)* is translated from the Hebrew **herown** *(hay-rone').* **Herown** means pregnancy, conception. So, God said that he would greatly multiply the number of pregnancies that the woman would have. Therefore, if we say that Eve bore no children in the garden of Eden then it would make the phrase 'greatly multiply' thy conception of none effect. For, we know that to multiply zero (none) by any number, you do not get more in number, or an increase, but rather you get zero (none). Therefore, for this passage to be correct and true Eve had to have already borne children in the garden of Eden before she sinned. Then, the number of children that she had already had could be increased or enlarged. For, zero multiplied by any number is zero.

Also, the ***fifth proof*** is the phrase, ***'multiply thy sorrow'***, found within the same sentence of punishment received by the woman for her part in violating the fourth commandment—*not to eat from the tree of the knowledge of good and evil.* *(See Ge 2:16-17)* **Sorrow** is taken from the Hebrew **'etseb** *(eh'-tseb),* meaning usually painful, toil; a pang; grievous, labor, sorrow. Therefore, God informed the woman that he would greatly multiply, increase, and enlarge her pain, labor and toil during her pregnancy, after conception. However, if the woman had never had a child or pregnancy, then she would have no idea about the pain or sorrow involved in childbirth, and again any number times (multiplied by) zero is zero. So, for this passage to be correct and true the woman would have had to have borne children, with little pain and little sorrow, for that pain and sorrow to be greatly multiplied. Furthermore, we see this concept within the punishment scheme used by God throughout. For, in addition to multiplying Eve's conception and sorrow in pregnancy, the Lord also said,

> **...and thy desire shall be to thy husband, and he shall rule over thee.**

Ge 3:16.

This was a punishment to Eve, because before she sinned her desire was not to her husband. That is, she began her existence as a partner in the one-flesh called the Adam family. *(Read Ge 5:1-2)* As a partner, Eve should have communicated with her partner, Adam, before she made a unilateral decision that affected the whole one-flesh. Because her decision caused the one-flesh to sin, Eve is now commanded and required to submit to the will of her husband in those things that she desire for herself. For, the scripture show that when she made the decision to disobey God, it was not a family decision, but rather a selfish, one-sided choice to do wrong. For,

...when the woman saw that the tree was good for food, and that it was pleasant to the eyes, and a tree to be desired to make one wise, she took of the fruit thereof, and did eat...

Ge 3:6.

The woman did not have the understanding necessary to spiritually fight and war with the serpent, concerning the interpretation of the fourth commandment. And, because she was ignorant of his devices, she was tricked and beguiled. As a result, she took it upon herself to become a servant of the serpent, and did eat of him, yielding her members as instruments of unrighteousness unto sin. The woman's unilateral actions were against the will of God and against the marriage of the one flesh. For we are to,

13 Neither yield ye your members as instruments of unrighteousness unto sin: but yield yourselves unto God, as those that are alive from the dead, and your members as instruments of righteousness unto God.

...

16 Know ye not, that to whom ye yield yourselves servants to obey, his servants ye are to whom ye obey; whether of sin unto death, or of obedience unto righteous-ness?

Ro 6:13, 16.

For sin, taking occasion by the commandment, deceived...[Eve], and by it slew...[Eve].

Ro 7:11 *(Words in brackets added).*

The woman, being a part of the one-flesh, was a partner with Adam in authority and dominion. For,

...God blessed them, and God said unto them... have dominion...

Ge 1:28.

Here, the Lord said unto both of them, unto the whole of the one-flesh to have dominion—not just Adam, the man, but to the woman also. The word **dominion** *(də-min'yən)* is taken from the Hebrew **radah** *(raw-daw')* meaning to tread down, to crumble, come to have dominion, make to have dominion, prevail against, reign, bear rule, make rule, rule over, ruler, take. Therefore, when the woman made the decision to go wrong for herself she possessed the authority to do so. For she, herself, was a co-ruler with Adam, the other half of the one-flesh. She possessed a freewill. Being wrong and out of God allowed the woman to step in front of the man. And, rather than walking beside him, being a help mate, she became a hindrance and a stumbling block of offense

> **...and gave also unto her husband with her; and he did eat.**

Ge 3:6.

For,

> **...It is impossible but that offenses will come: but woe unto him, through whom they come!**

Lu 17:1 *(Read also Mt 18:7).*

In the beginning, the woman's desire was not subject to her husband. And he did not rule over her before she sinned. Therefore, she possessed the freewill, the ability and the authority to do as she saw fit, even if it was against God, and against the body and family of the one flesh. And so, the actions of the wife forced the husband to choose between the fifth commandment—*to cleave to his wife* *(Ge 2:24)* and the fourth commandment—*to not eat of the tree of the knowledge of good and evil*. *(Ge 2:16-17)* For, the man was with his wife when she left God. *(Read Ge 3:6)* She began enticing him to leave God and serve the serpent also, by eating from the forbidden tree. For, Adam surmised and rationalized that for him to stay with God would have been leaving and not cleaving to his wife. And so, when the Lord asked Adam had he eaten of the tree that he was told not to eat from, the husband's response was, in substance, *"Yes. You told me not to eat from the tree. But, you also gave me this woman and told me to cleave to her and not leave her. Well, I did cleave to her and while cleaving she left you and then enticed me to cleave to her in sin and leave you."* For, the narrative states,

> **6 And when the woman saw that the tree was good for food, and that it was pleasant to the eyes, and a tree to be desired to make one wise, she took of the fruit thereof, and did eat, and gave also unto her husband with her; and he did eat.**
>
> **...**
>
> **9 And the Lord God called unto Adam, and said unto him, Where art thou?**
>
> **10 And he said, I heard thy voice in the garden, and I was afraid, because I was naked; and I hid myself.**
>
> **11 And he said, Who told thee that thou wast naked? Hast thou eaten of the tree, whereof I commanded thee that thou shouldest not eat?**
>
> **12 And the man said, The woman whom thou gavest to be with me, she gave me of the tree, and I did eat.**

Ge 3:6, 9-12.

Therefore, to prevent the wife from taking advantage of the husband's weakness for her—she having come out of his wound—the LORD God made it a requirement that her desire be subject unto her husband and that he would rule over her. *(Ge 3:16)* The point here, is that had the wife not been free to choose her own way, will and desire, without anyone ruling over her, before she sinned, then after she sinned she would not have understood the chastisement to be punishment for sin. For, a person will never miss or regret the loss of a thing or loss of liberty that they never possessed or never experienced. Had she not had freedom, then subjection would just be the normal way of life. Therefore, the same thing goes with multiplying the conception and sorrow. There had to of been a difference, a past, a history to compare the new rules of life by.

The ***sixth proof*** is that ***Adam lived with his wife for over 2,000 years which is more than 40 generations, before they sinned.*** We get this understanding by considering the words of the writers in different places at different biblical times. The first writer wrote,

> **And on the seventh day God ended his work which he had made; and he rested on the seventh day from all his work which he had made.**

Ge 2:2.

In this Genesis 2:2 passage we see that God rested and did no work on the seventh day. *(Read also Heb 4:4)* If we look further we also learn that mankind, which was called Adam *(Ge 5:1-2),* both male and female, were created on the sixth day of creation *(Ge 1:26-31)* after the birds and fowls of the air *(Ge 1:20-23)* and the fish of the sea which were created on the fifth day of creation *(Ge 1:20-23);* and after the land animals, beasts of the earth, cattle and creeping things which were created on the first part of the sixth day. *(Ge 1:24-25)*

If God rested on the seventh day from all his work and performed no work during the seventh day, then, the punishment and chastisement that God handed out to the serpent *(Ge 3:13-15),* the wife and woman, Eve, *(Ge 3:16, 20),* and Adam the husband *(Ge 3:17-19, 23-24),* were performed sometime during or after the eighth day from the beginning of creation.

Furthermore,

> **Neither was the man created for the woman; but the woman for the man.**

1Co 11:9.

And so, with the husband, Adam, having been encouraged and commanded by his creator, father, the Lord God, to multiply together with the beautiful gift called the woman, Adam set out to obey the Lord's commandment and did so for more than 2000 years. We know this, **first,** because, when

> **...they heard the voice of the Lord God walking in the garden in the cool of the day: and Adam and his wife hid themselves from the presence of the Lord God amongst the trees of the garden.**

Ge 3:8.

They were not hiding because they had disobeyed the commandment to have sex and to have children. *(Ge 1:28).* But they were hiding because they had violated and disobeyed only one of the ten commandments that God had given man, which was not to eat from the tree of the knowledge of good and evil. *(Ge 2:16-17)* For, the writer wrote,

> **11 And he said, Who told thee that thou wast naked? Hast thou eaten of the tree, whereof I commanded thee that thou shouldest not eat?**
>
> **12 And the man said, The woman whom thou gavest to be with me, she gave me of the tree, and I did eat.**

Ge 3:11-12.

The *seventh proof* is that after ***Adam and Eve sinned, they tried to cover up their nakedness with aprons*** made from sewed together fig leaves. *(Ge 3:7)* For, the scripture declares,

> **And the eyes of them both were opened, and they knew that they were naked; and they sewed fig leaves together, and made themselves aprons.**

Ge 3:7.

The point here, is that there is no sin and no problem with a husband and wife, Adam and Eve, seeing and enjoying each other naked without clothes on. For, even the scriptures teaches, that

> **2 … to avoid fornication, let every man have his own wife, and let every woman have her own husband.**
>
> **…**
>
> **4 The wife have not power of her own body, but the husband: and likewise also the husband hath not power of his own body, but the wife.**
>
> **5 Defraud ye not one the other, except it be with consent for a time, that ye may give yourselves to fasting and prayer; and come together again, that Satan tempt you not for your incontinency.**

1Co 7:2, 4-5.

> **Marriage is honourable in all, and the bed undefiled: but whoremongers and adulterers God will judge.**

Heb 13:4.

> **15 Drink waters out of thine own cistern, and running waters out of thine own well.**
>
> **…**
>
> **18 Let thy fountain be blessed: and rejoice with the wife of thy youth.**
>
> **19 Let her be as the loving hind and pleasant roe; let her breasts satisfy thee at all times; and be thou ravished always with her love.**

Pr 5:15, 18-19.

So, from the above passages of scripture, we learn that the word of God instructs the husband and wife to enjoy each other's physical body. And, since God had already commanded the husband and the wife to multiply *(Ge 1:28),* before they sinned, we see, that is, we understand that God promoted, encouraged and commanded the husband and the wife to engage in sexual relations, to know each other carnally—in the flesh. To obey God's command, Adam and Eve had to see, view and enjoy each other's naked, physical body.

The problem arises and therefore sin occurs when a third set of human eyes are allowed to see and view the nakedness of the husband or wife in a sexual manner. The only set of human eyes that could have been watching after Adam and Eve lost their cover of righteousness, which revealed their carnal nakedness to the world to see, were the children born of the marriage inside the garden of Eden. For, we can see that Adam and Eve had knowledge of the fact that they were naked, long before they sinned. Because, they were naked when they got married, as the scripture declared,

23 And Adam said, This is now bone of my bones, and flesh of my flesh: she shall be called Woman, because she was taken out of Man.

24 Therefore shall a man leave his father and his mother, and shall cleave unto his wife: and they shall be one flesh.

25 And they were both naked, the man and his wife, and were not ashamed.

Ge 2:23-25.

Moreover, God was so concerned with Adam and Eve's physical body being viewed by the third set of eyes of the children, born in the garden, until God rejected the fig leaf aprons created by the Adam family *(Ge 3:7)* and,

Unto Adam also and to his wife did the Lord God make coats of skins, and clothed them.

Ge 3:21.

If there were no other third set of eyes able to see and view the nakedness of Adam and Eve, after they sinned, then what was the purpose of God 'clothing them'? For, they already were aware that they were naked and they were not ashamed. *(Ge 2:25)*

But, a person cannot be ashamed of a thing or of a condition if he is not aware or has no knowledge that the thing or the condition exist. For, the word **ashamed** *(ə' shaymd)* in Genesis 2:25 is translated from **buwsh** *(boosh).* **Buwsh** means to pale, to be ashamed, to be dis-appointed, or delayed, be confounded, put to confusion. Also, when we look further into the meaning of the word **ashamed** we find that it means feeling shame. And, **shame** *(shaym)* is a painful sense of guilt or degradation caused by consciousness of guilt or anything degrading, unworthy, or immodest; a state of dishonor or disgrace. Of course, Adam and his wife, Eve, were not ashamed of being naked before they sinned, because it was honorable. For, the writer declared,

> **Marriage is honourable in all; and the bed undefiled.**

Heb 13:4.

Therefore, the fact that Adam and Eve were not ashamed of being naked also means that they were aware that there was no disgrace or dishonor in being naked, as between husband and wife. Also, at this time, they still possessed and wore the covering and garment of righteousness as will the redeemed saints possess and wear to cover their nakedness after the resurrection. *(Re 19:7-8; Re 7:9; Re 3:5, 18; Re 4:4)* And, the knowledge that they possessed about their being naked, before they sinned, was plain, simple and bare. For, the word **naked** in Genesis 2:25 is translated from a different word than the **naked** in Genesis 3:7. The Genesis 2:25 **naked** *(nay'kid)* is translated from **`arom** *(aw-rome').* **Arom** means nude, either partially or totally; naked. In contrast, the Genesis 3:7 **naked** is translated from **erom** *(ay-rome').* **Erom** means nudity, nakedness, and is taken from **`aram** *(aw-ram),* which means to be cunning (usually in a bad sense), beware, take crafty counsel, deal subtly, be prudent.

Therefore, once they sinned, they lost the covering and protection of a righteous, glorified body, which prevented any third set of eyes from seeing their carnal nakedness.

The ***eighth proof*** comes from ***the Genesis 1:28 command to the husband and wife to replenish and subdue the earth***. For the Lord

> **...God blessed them, and God said unto them, Be fruitful, and multiply, and replenish the earth, and subdue it...**

Ge 1:28a.

The point of this proof is that God is a spirit, and his ultimate purpose for creating the earth and placing man over it was for spiritual purposes. Because, the scriptures declare that

> **23 ...true worshippers shall worship the Father in spirit and in truth: for the Father seeketh such to worship him.**
>
> **24 God is a Spirit: and they that worship him must worship him in spirit and in truth.**

Joh 4:23-24.

And we know that before *(Read 1Pe 1:19-20; Re 13:8; lamb slain before the foundation of world)* during and after the creation events *(Ge 1:1-31)*, man was and remains the center of God's attention, so much so that even the Psalmist commented saying,

> **4 What is man, that thou art mindful of him? And the son of man, that thou visitest him?**
>
> **5 For thou hast made him a little lower than the angels, and hast crowned him with glory and honour.**
>
> **6 Thou madest him to have dominion over the works of thy hands; thou hast put all things under his feet:**

7 All sheep and oxen, yea, and the beasts of the field;

8 The fowl of the air, and the fish of the sea, and whatsoever passeth through the paths of the seas.

Ps 8:4-8.

Therefore, God's purpose for giving man the commandments in the beginning *(Read Ge 1:28; Ge 2:15-18, 24),* were so that man would learn and become more like God, and that man would experience a long and prosperous life, in Him. For, the commandments of God tends to life *(Pr 7:2),* and his words of wisdom are a tree of life. *(Read Pr 3:13-18)*

So, when we reconsider the words **replenish** and **subdue** in Genesis 1:28, we learn from their spiritual meaning that God has a primary concern. This primary concern, which is within the perfect will of the Father, is concerned with God's relationship with man being strengthened, as opposed to earthly man's *(1Co 15:47-49)* natural inclination to be more concerned with earthly and carnal things. *(Ro 8:5-9)* Because, the word **replenish** *(rĭ-plĕn′ ĭsh),* in Genesis 1:28, is translated from the Hebrew word **male** *(maw-lay′)*, **Male** means to fill, be full of, confirm, furnish, satisfy, to consecrate. When we **consecrate** *(kŏn′sə-krāt′)* a thing we set it apart as sacred; dedicate it; devote it; make revered; hallow. In addition, when we review the word **subdue**, which is translated from **kabash** *(kaw-bash′),* we get a little more understanding. For, **kabash** means to tread down, to conquer, subjugate, bring into bondage, keep under, subdue, bring under subjection.

Subduing and consecrating is like the process described by the Apostle Paul in another place, where he said,

25 And every man that striveth for the mastery is temperate in all things. Now they do it to obtain a corruptible crown; but we an incorruptible.

26 I therefore so run, not as uncertainly; so fight I, not as one that beateth the air:

27 But I keep under my body, and bring it into subjection: lest that by any means, when I have preached to others, I myself should be a castaway.
1 Co 9:25-27.

Thus, before Adam and Eve could consecrate the earth, they first had to subdue that earth that they sought to consecrate. The question now arises,

What earth were they required to consecrate and subdue, that would assist them in prospering in life; and to be, live and exist on the earth more in the likeness of God? (Read Ge 1:26)

The answer is that God commanded man to subdue and consecrate the earth, the dirt and the dust that is within himself, and that would be a natural part of his children that would be born as a direct result of man walking in the obedience of the seventh commandment *(Ge 1:28)* to multiply. This is so because,

...the Lord God formed man of the dust of the ground...
Ge 2:7a.

And, as discussed earlier, the dust, the dirt and the earth was made by God, but it is not of God and is not a part of God, because God is a Spirit. *(Joh 4:24)* And, the flesh of man, which is made and fashioned from the dirt and dust, cannot inherit the kingdom of God. *(1Co 15:50)*

Adam and Eve were required to bring their fleshly desires under subjection to the will and ways of God by exercising their freewill to choose. And, by and through this process of subduing the desires that naturally come from the dirt and dust of the world, with his freewill empowered by the neshamah (breath) of life *(Ge 2:7),* which is the indwelling Spirit of God, man would be enabled and empowered to consecrate his personal earth, called the flesh, and dedicate it, devote it and set it apart for the work and will of God.

Furthermore, when we review Genesis 2:7 through verse 25 we learn that the first man and woman that were created were not small, physical children. But, they were fully grown adults who were married *(Ge 2:21-25)* and given a job to work. For,

> **...the Lord God took the man, and put him into the garden of Eden to dress it and to keep it.**

Ge 2:15.

But, the children that would later be born to this Adam family *(Ge 5:1-2)* would be newborn babies that would have to be taught and trained up in the ways of the Lord. For, the scriptures admonish man to

> **Train up a child in the way he should go: and when he is old, he will not depart from it.**

Pr 22:6.

Thus, when we review the punishment and chastisement of Adam and Eve, there is no concern or punishment due to the fact that they failed to teach and train up the children that had been born pursuant to their obeying the seventh commandment to multiply. *(Read Ge 1:28; Ge 3:6-24).*

However, we do see punishment meted out to the serpent *(Ge 3:13-15),* the woman *(Ge 3:16)* and the man *(Ge 3:17-24),* for their failure to continue replenishing, that is, consecrating and subduing the dirt and dust that was within themselves. And, it was this failure to subdue and consecrate that led to the woman being first in the transgression *(1Ti 2:14),* and her later being used as an instrument of the serpent to steal the glory of God—the man, Adam. As the writer wrote,

> **Know ye not, that to whom ye yield yourselves servants to obey, his servants ye are to whom ye obey; whether of sin unto death, or of obedience unto righteousness?**

Ro 6:16.

As a further point, the children that were born to Adam and Eve before they sinned were not born as sinners, because sin and death had not yet entered into the world. *(Ro 5:12)* And in order for the children to be born as sinners, their father, Adam, had to first commit sin. For, the writer declared, that

> **Wherefore, as by one man sin entered into the world, and death by sin; and so death passed upon all men, for that all have sinned:**

Ro 5:12.

Therefore, after Adam sinned *(Ge 3:6-7),* sin and death entered into the world and passed upon all mankind, thereby making all of Adam's children, who were born before Adam's original sin, sinners, although they had not sinned after the likeness or similitude of Adam's sin. *(Read Ro 5:12-14).*

The ***ninth proof,*** comes from the point made above that the children born in the garden of Eden before Adam's original sin were not born sinners, but latter became sinners subject to death, although they had not sinned. The point of this proof seeks to show that ***if there were no other humans alive except Adam, Eve and their son Cain, after he killed his brother Abel, then there would not have been a need for 'the mark' that Cain received from God to protect him from being murdered by other people.*** For, the scriptures declared,

> **14 Behold. Thou hast driven me out this day from the face of the earth; and from thy face shall I be hid; and I**

shall be a fugitive and a vagabond in the earth; and it shall come to pass, that every one that findeth me shall slay me.

15 And the Lord said unto him, Therefore whosoever slayeth Cain, vengeance shall be taken on him sevenfold. And the Lord set a mark upon Cain, lest any finding him should kill him.

Ge 4:14-15.

In this Genesis 4:14-15 passage we learn that the Lord God drove Cain away from his home that was in Eden near his mother and father, because he had murdered his brother Abel *(Ge 4:8-11).* But, before he drove him away Cain begged for some form of protection to prevent other people (every one) from slaying (killing) him. So, the Lord God set a **'mark'** upon Cain, so that when other people saw the mark they would not kill Cain. Because, Adam's original sin had already caused all humans to become sinners, subject to death. *(Ro 5:12)* And, as a sinner, Cain knew and understood that anyone, including his sisters *(Ge 5:4)*, could become his slayer as he had become his brother's murderer *(Ge 4:8),* and as did Cain's offspring, La'-mech, became later. *(Ge 4:17-18, 23)*

We learn latter that the other people that Cain was concerned about were located east of Eden, in the land of Nod. For, the writer wrote,

...Cain went out from the presence of the Lord, and dwelt in the land of Nod, on the east of Eden.

Ge 4:16.

After arriving in the land of Nod, Cain met the other people that he had been concerned about killing him, but the mark protected him. In order for the mark to protect him it had to be an outwardly, visible sign that could be easily seen and not covered up by his clothing. And while there, although he was a marked man, Cain found himself a woman to marry. The question that now presents itself is,

Who were the other people from which came Cain's wife?

The answer is twofold. They were the descendants of the first man *(Ge 2:7)* and the first woman *(Ge 2:20-23)*, created by God. And, or, in addition to being Adam and Eve's descendants they were also descendants of the daughters that married the fallen angels *(Ge 6:1-4)* who had taken on terrestrial bodies—having left their first estate and their own habitation *(Jude 6)* during the war in Heaven that they and Satan lost. *(Rev 12:7-9)*

The ***tenth proof*** concerns the fact that ***after Cain began living in the land of Nod, he found a woman.*** For the scriptures declare,

> **And Cain knew his wife; and she conceived, and bare E`-noch...**

Ge 4:17a.

The point of this proof is that, if no children had been born in the garden of Eden, then where did Cain find a wife to marry. For, we know that Cain was the first, named child born outside of the garden of Eden. *(Ge 4:1)* Abel was the second, named child. *(Ge 4:2)* And, the third named child, Seth, *(Ge 4:25)* was not born until: **(1)** after Cain killed Abel *(Ge 4:8-12);* **(2)** after Cain moved to the land of Nod *(Ge 4:16);* **(3)** after Cain married a woman *(Ge 4:17)* that was fully grown and of child bearing years, for, "*...Cain knew his wife; and she conceived, and bare E`-noch...*" *(Ge 4:17a);* and, **(4)** after Cain built a city. *(Ge 4:17)* All of the named children born at this time were male children.

Therefore, the woman that Cain married must have been born before Cain, while Adam and Eve were living in the garden of Eden *'multiplying'* as they had been commanded to do by the Lord God *(Ge 1:28);* or, the woman was a descendant of Adam's daughter that married a fallen angel.

The ***eleventh proof*** concerns the fact that ***Cain built a city*** called Enoch, in the land of Nod, as the writer wrote,

> **And Cain knew his wife; and she conceived, and bare E`noch: and he builded a city, and called the name of the city, after the name of his son, E'noch.**

Ge 4:17.

The point of this proof is that, a city is not needed for three people, if there were only Cain, his wife and his son, E'noch. For, a city is a division of labor. There had to have been a lot of people already born from the *'multiplying'* acts of Adam and Eve to supply the labor needs to operate and run a city. A husband, wife and a son would only require a place to stay and several out buildings, not a city.

For, the word **city** *(sit-ē),* here, is translated from **`ayar** *(aw-yar'),* meaning a place guarded by waking or a watch; a city. And looking further into the word **city** we learn that it is an inhabited place of greater size, population or importance than a town or village.

The ***twelveth proof*** concerns the order in which ***Eve began bearing children based on gender,*** either sons or daughters. For, scripture declares that,

> **And it came to pass, when men began to multiply on the face of the earth, and daughters were born unto them,**

Ge 6:1.

Thus, we learn from this verse that when mankind, Adam and Eve, began to obey the seventh commandment to multiply on the face of the earth, daughters and not sons were born unto them. One might ask,

"Why were just daughters born and not sons,
while they were in the garden of Eden?"

The answer is found in the fact that the Lord God gave the commandment to the male (man) of the species called human. The woman was not yet brought forth into creation when the man Adam began keeping the garden of Eden *(Ge 2:15)* and working for God. *(Ge 2:19-23)*

However, the tree of the knowledge of good and evil had already been created *(Ge 2:8-9)* after the garden of Eden was planted *(Ge 2:8-9)* and before the woman was created. Therefore, with the tree of the knowledge of good and evil in existence, Adam had to be commanded *(Ge 2:16-17)* and taught about its dangers. For, it was only through the fellowship and eating of this tree could death enter the world and the garden of Eden, by sin. *(Ro 5:12-14)* And that sin had to be committed by the man and not the woman. For, we see that when Eve sinned *(Ge 3:6)* nothing happened to Adam or to the world. No sin was imputed to anyone else but to herself when she sinned. She was a woman and the commandment had not been given to her, but she was taught it by her husband. Satan began his reign as the ruler of this world with the birth of Cain. For, the scriptures declare that the first man child, Cain, born to Adam and Eve

> **...was of that wicked one, and slew his brother. And wherefore slew he him? Because his own works were evil, and his brother's righteous.**

1Jo 3:10-12.

So, Satan's reign and rule of the world involves the destruction of righteousness within the lives of mankind even if to do so means to murder and kill those who live righteous lives. For, the writer wrote,

> **6 And the Lord said unto Cain, Why art thou wroth? and why is thy countenance fallen?**
>
> **7 If thou doest well, shalt thou not be accepted? and if thou doest not well, sin lieth at the door...**

8 And Cain talked with Abel his brother: and it came to pass, when they were in the field, that Cain rose up against Abel his brother, and slew him.
Ge 4:6-8.

Thus Cain, a male child, began the long line of Satan, the serpent's, seed. *(Ge 3:15)* Abel and then Seth began the long line of the woman's seed. Cain and his offspring, being the enmity (enemy) *(Ge 3:15; 1Jo 3:11-12)* of the righteous seed, set out to persecute Abel *(Ge 4:8a)* who was righteous *(Heb 11:4)* and murdered him. *(Ge 4:8)* But God appointed the woman another man child seed, named Seth, to replace Abel, as the writer wrote,

And Adam knew his wife again; and she bare a son, and called his name Seth: For God, said she, hath appointed me another seed instead of Abel, whom Cain slew.
Ge 4:25.

This lineage went all the way to the cross of Calvary and the crucifixion of the righteous seed—Jesus Christ.

For, from Seth we get Enos, then Cainan, then Maleleel, then Jared, then Enoch then Mathusala. From Mathusala came Lamech, then Noah, then Sem, then Arphaxad, then Cainan, then Sala, then Heber, then Phalec, then Ragau, then Saruch. From Saruch came Nachor, then Thara, then Abraham, then Issac, then Jacob, then Juda, then Phares, then Esrom, then Aram, then Aminadab, then Naasson, then Salmon, then Booz, then Obed, then Jesse, then David. From David came Nathan, then Mattatha, then Menan, then Melea, then Eliakim, then Jonan, then Joseph, then Juda, then Simeon, then Levi, then Matthat, then Jorim, then Eliezer, then Jose, then Er, then Elmodam. From Elmodam came Cosam, then Addi, then Melchi, then Neri, then Salathiel, then Zorobabel, then Rhesa, then Joanna, then Juda, then Joseph, then Semei, then Mattathias, then Maath, then Nagge, then Esli, then Naum, then Amos, then Mattathias, then Joseph, then Janna, then Melchi, then Levi, then Matthat, then Heli, then Joseph then Jesus, as was supposed the son of Joseph *(Read Lu 3:23-38; Lu 23:26-47),* but who was fathered by the Holy Ghost. *(Mt 1:20)*

For the Lord God, himself, prophesied of the enmity between those who would follow the false doctrine of Satan, the serpent *(Re 12:9)* and the righteousness of Eve's seed. For, it is written,

> **14 And the Lord God said unto the serpent, Because thou hast done this, thou art cursed above all cattle, and above every beast of the field; upon thy belly shalt thou go, and dust shalt thou eat all the days of thy life:**
>
> **15 And I will put enmity between thee and the woman, and between thy seed and her seed; it shall bruise thy head, and thou shalt bruise his heel.**

Ge 3:14-15.

In addition to the enmity between the serpent's seed and the woman's seed, Genesis 3:15 also prophesied the manner by which Satan would lose some of his power, at the hands of the woman's seed. For, Judas Iscariot, Satan's seed, was the son of perdition. *(Joh 17:12)* It was he who betrayed the righteous seed of the woman which resulted in his, Jesus', crucifixion. And as a result, the Lord Jesus went down into hell, the heart of the earth, and took from Satan, the power of death *(Heb 2:14; 2Ti 1:10; Eph 4:7-10),* thereby bruising Satan's head by taking away some of the power possessed by Satan. At the same time Satan had bruised Jesus' heels—by crucifying him. This crucifixion prevented Christ from walking on the earth upon his heels for three days which was a three day heel bruise. *(Mt 12:40; Mt 16:21; Mt 17:22-23; Mt 20:18-19; Mt 26:61; Mt 27:40, 63; Mk 8:31; Mk 10:33-34; Lu 9:22; 13:32-33; Heb 5:7-9; Lu 24:6-7; 17-21; Lu 24:46; Ac 10:38-41; 1Co 15:3-4)* And later, in another place and time the Apostle John said,

> **10 In this the children of God are manifest, and the children of the devil: whosoever doeth not righteousness is not of God, neither he that loveth not his brother.**
>
> **11 For this is the message that ye heard from the beginning, that we should love one another.**

12 Not as Cain, who was of that wicked one, and slew his brother. And wherefore slew he him? Because his own works were evil, and his brother's righteous. 1Jo 3:10-12.

So, Cain was the seed of Satan and Abel was the seed of Eve. And Cain was a murderer *(Ge 4:8),* because he hated his brother *(1Jo 3:15),* for his works were evil *(1Jo 3:12)* and rejected by God. *(Ge 4:5-7)* But his brother Abel's works were righteous *(1Jo 3:12)* and accepted by God. *(Ge 4:4)*

Therefore, if only girls were born in the garden of Eden, then, even if the serpent beguiled them and persuaded them to eat of the tree of the knowledge of good and evil—he still could not steal God's glory—the man. But, if you introduce sons, then the serpent could steal God's glory from an unlearned son without having to go through Adam. And by having this son to serve him the son would father more sinners, and the serpent, Lucifer, would have more servants.

So, to prevent this, only daughters were born. This way God gets more praise and more work done, because the woman was created as a help meet, to help the man perform God's work. *(Ge 2:18-24)*

After Adam sinned it was necessary to bridge the gap between life and death, God and man and to reconcile man back to God. And God, being omniscient and omnipresent, saw that this development would take place and prepared a plan of salvation before he created the foundation of the world. *(1Pe 1:18-20; Re 13:7-8; Heb 1:10; Eph 1:4; Mt 25:34; Re 17:8)* Then, God hid the wisdom of this plan within himself, and called it the hidden wisdom *(1Co 2:7),* thereby preventing the tree of the knowledge of good and evil from knowing it, finding it, or becoming aware of its existence. *(1Co 2:7-8; Lu 23:33-34)*

And so, after man was driven out of the garden of Eden, God set out to find a man that would stand in the gap for his most prized creation—man. *(Heb 2:6-8)* This search resulted in God, himself, coming in the likeness of sinful flesh *(1Ti 3:16; Ro 8:3)* to go man's bond and to be the ransom for the souls of all mankind *(Mt 20:28;*

Mk 10:45; 1Ti 2:5-6; Tit 2:14; Ho 13:14; Joh 3:14-17) that believe in the name of his son, Jesus Christ. *(Joh 3:18)*

IV. *The Womb Of The Bride Of Christ*

There is the spiritual ***Womb Of The Bride Of Christ***, the church—where the repentant sinner is reconciled and reborn as a son of God. For, the bridegroom's wife, the church, must possess a womb if she is to bear children in the likeness of the bridegroom. As John the Baptist commented, Jesus is the bridegroom and he has the bride. *(Read Joh 3:22-29)* But, before John commented about Jesus and his bride, Nicodemus, a ruler of the Jews *(Joh 3:1)*, asked Jesus the question,

> **...How can a man be born when he is old? can he enter the second time into his mother's womb, and be born?**

Joh 3:4.

At first glance this question may seem foolish coming from a ruler, and from a man of knowledge, but the question was in response to Jesus' statement where he

> **...said unto him, Verily, verily, I say unto thee, Except a man be born again, he cannot see the kingdom of God.**

Joh 3:3.

From Jesus' statement, Nicodemus understood the fact that for a man to be born naturally would require a womb of the flesh. But, he did not have knowledge of nor did Nicodemus possess the understanding that a man can have a spiritual rebirth from a spiritual womb, and that spiritual womb is the womb of the bride of Christ. *(Joh 3:9-10)* Jesus, knowing beforehand Nicodemus' ignorance, began to teach him knowledge of the womb of the bride of Christ, saying

> **5 ...Verily, verily, I say unto thee, Except a man be born of water and of the Spirit, he cannot enter into the kingdom of God.**
>
> **6 That which is born of the flesh is flesh; and that which is born of the Spirit is spirit.**
>
> **7 Marvel not that I said unto thee, Ye must be born again.**
>
> **8 The wind bloweth where it listeth, and thou hearest the sound thereof, but canst not tell whence it cometh, and whither it goeth: so is every one that is born of the Spirit.**

Joh 3:5-8.

Here, in the womb of the bride of Christ the potter molds, recreates, regenerates, forms, transforms and fashions the clay by using the gifts of the apostle, prophet, evangelist, pastor and teacher in conjunction with the experiences, tribulations and troubles of this life to make and bring the members of his bride unto perfection. *(Eph 4:11-12)*

> **13 Till we all come in the unity of the faith, and of the knowledge of the Son of God, unto a perfect man, unto the measure of the stature of the fullness of Christ:**
>
> **14 That we henceforth be no more children, tossed to and fro, and carried about with every wind of doctrine, by the sleight of men, and cunning craftiness, whereby they lie in wait to deceive.**

Eph 4:13-14.

For, the members who possess and exercise the five-fold ministry gifts are part of the branches and can bear no fruit except they stay connected to the vine. *(Read Joh 15:1-8)*

In another place, even the Apostle Paul, while admonishing the Galatian Church, compared the strengthening and perfecting of the saints to the process of natural child birth, saying,

> **My little children, of whom I travail in birth again until Christ be formed in you.**

Ga 4:19.

Planting the Seed:

Here, in the spiritual womb of the bride of Christ, the church, the ministry travails in pain while working to form Christ in the individual believers. As in the womb of the flesh, the womb of the bride of Christ conceives after the husbandman *(Joh 15:1)*, through the preaching evangelist, has planted the Gospel 'seed of life' within the earth of the new believer. For, the scripture declares, that

> **...it pleased God by the foolishness of preaching to save them that believe.**

1Co 1:21.

> **13 For whosoever shall call upon the name of the Lord shall be saved.**
>
> **14 How then shall they call on him in whom they have not believed? and how shall they believe in him of whom they have not heard? and how shall they hear without a preacher?**
>
> **15 And how shall they preach, except they be sent? ...**

Ro 10:13-15.

The act of preaching the Gospel by the preacher, to unrepentant sinners, is the process of *'planting the seed'* by the husbandman into the earth of the hearer. But, for the planted seed to produce fruit, the hearer must subdue that earth—the will of his flesh—by repenting. This is the same earth that Adam and Eve were commanded to **subdue** *(seb-`dū)* in Genesis 1:28. There, **subdue** is translated from the Hebrew **kabash** *(kaw-bash')*, which means to tread down, to conquer, subjugate, bring into bondage, force, keep under and bring into subjection. In agreement, many years later, another preacher commented saying,

> **But I keep under my body, and bring it into subjection: lest that by any means, when I have preached to others, I myself should be a castaway.**

1Co 9:27.

The first word of the Gospel requiring an active, freewill response to the preacher's message, by the unrepentant sinner, is Repent, as was the seeds planted by Apostle Peter, on the Day of Penteost *(Read Ac 2:1-41),* when he said

> **Repent, and be baptized every one of you in the name of Jesus Christ for the remission of sins, and ye shall receive the gift of the Holy Ghost.**

Ac 2:38.

This process of *'planting the seed'* is what Apostle Paul meant when he admonished the Corinthian Church saying,

> **I have planted…**

1Co 3:6.

> **…for in Christ Jesus I have begotten you through the gospel.**

1Co 4:15.

The Courting Process: God Seeking You

After the husbandman has been introduced to the unrepentant sinner by the word of the sent preacher, the unrepentant sinner then has to make a choice to reject the man Jesus or believe in the man Jesus; to become the wife of the bridegroom or to remain single, solitary and alone. For the man of God declared that the people must *"...choose you this day whom ye will serve..." (Jos 24:15)* And, years later in another place the writer wrote

> **4 For he spake in a certain place of the seventh day on this wise, And God did rest the seventh day from all his works.**
>
> **5 And in this place again, If they shall enter into my rest.**
>
> **6 Seeing therefore it remaineth that some must enter therein, and they to whom it was first preached entered not in because of unbelief.**
>
> **7 Again, he limiteth a certain day, saying in David, Today, after so long a time; as it is said, Today if ye will hear his voice, harden not your hearts.**
>
> **...**
>
> **10 For he that is entered into his rest, he also hath ceased from his own works, as God did from his.**

Heb 4:4-7, 10.

The LORD God loves the unrepentant sinner so much until

> **...he gave his only begotten Son, that whosoever believeth in him should not perish, but have everlasting life.**

Joh 3:16.

And to insure that the unrepentant sinner knows that He is interested in being reconciled back to him, forgiving him and loving him, working through the spoken, anointed words of the preacher He

> **...stand[s] at the door, and knock[s]: if any man hear my voice, and open the door, I will come in to him, and will sup with him, and he with me.**

Re 3:20 *(Letters in brackets added).*

While the Lord Jesus is standing at his door knocking, desiring to come in to give him life and that more abundantly *(Joh 10:10),* the unrepentant sinner must make a conscious choice to believe in the man Jesus, to become his bride and desire to live a life pleasing in his sight. For, the Lord Jesus came seeking and looking for the sinner—the lost, that he may become their personal saviour, as he stated,

> **For the Son of man is come to seek and to save that which was lost.**

Lu 19:10.

The unrepentant sinner cannot come to God of his own will and will not seek him out or think to do good without Christ first coming to him, for he sayeth

> **No man can come to me, except the Father which hath sent me draw him...**

Joh 6:44.

And,

> **All that the Father giveth me shall come to me; and him that cometh to me will I in no wise cast out.**

Joh 6:37.

Because,

9 ...we have before proved both Jews and Gentiles, that they are all under sin;

10 As it is written, THERE IS NONE RIGHTEOUS, NO, NOT ONE:

11 THERE IS NONE THAT UNDERSTANDETH, THERE IS NONE THAT SEEKETH AFTER GOD.

12 THEY ARE ALL GONE OUT OF THE WAY, THEY ARE together become unprofitable; there is none that doeth good, no not one.

Ro 3:9-12.

Therefore, since the unrepentant sinner cannot initiate the courtship of seeking Christ, the Lord must initiate the courtship by first seeking him. As he declared to his disciples,

Ye have not chosen me, but I have chosen you...

Joh 15:16.

The seeking by the Lord is accomplished by drawing the unrepentant sinner to him by the Word of God preached by the sent preacher. The Lord causes the sinner to understand the Word of God that is preached. As He declared,

And I, if I be lifted up from the earth, will draw all men unto me.

Joh 12:32.

For, the Lord said in another place,

So shall my word be that goeth forth out of my mouth: it shall not return unto me void, but it shall accomplish that which I please, and it shall prosper in the thing whereto I sent it.

Isa 55:11.

When the unrepentant sinner chooses Christ he repents of his ways by ceasing from his own works and from his own ways. For, with some understanding, acquired through his decision to repent, he begins to seek after Christ as Jesus said

> **7 Ask, and it shall be given you; seek, and ye shall find; knock, and it shall be opened unto you:**
>
> **8 For every one that asketh receiveth; and he that seeketh findeth; and to him that knocketh it shall be opened.**

Mt 7:7-8.

And, while seeking after Christ, he begins to realize that he must

> **6 Seek …the Lord while he may be found, call … upon him while he is near:**
>
> **7 Let the wicked forsake his way, and the unrighteous man his thoughts: and let him return unto the Lord, and he will have mercy upon him; and to our God, for he will abundantly pardon.**
>
> **8 For my thoughts are not your thoughts, neither are your ways my ways, saith the Lord.**
>
> **9 For as the heavens are higher than the earth, so are my ways higher than your ways, and my thoughts than your thoughts.**

Isa 55:6-9.

The Choice: Betrothal vs. Solitary Living

When the unrepentant sinner makes the decision to become a member of the bride of Christ's bride chamber *(See Mk 2:18-20)* the husbandman continues to work with the repentant bride chamber member through the gift of the pastor as Apostle Paul declared to the Corinthian brides

For I am jealous over you with godly jealousy: for I have espoused you to one husband, that I may present you as a chaste virgin to Christ.

2Co 11:2.

To be **espoused** *(i-spouz'd)* means to be betrothed, having been translated from the Greek **harmozo** *(har-mŏd'-zō)*. **Betrothed** *(bi-trōthd')* means to be engaged to be married; to have promised to marry another person; usually a promise by a father that his daughter will become the bride and marry a certain man. The Apostle Paul was the planter of the gospel seed for the Corinthian church that produced brides for Christ. *(1Co 3:6)* He was also the pastor and their spiritual father. *(1Co 4:15)* And as their spiritual father it was his obligation to choose a husband for the spiritual brides in the Corinthian church. As he stated,

...for in Christ Jesus I have begotten you through the gospel.

1Co 4:15.

At the moment the unrepentant sinner makes the choice to become a member of the bride chamber, by repenting, conception has occurred. However, not every sinner that hears the gospel message chooses to become a bride.

Why Some Seeds Do Not Lead To Conception

Rejection of Jesus Christ—God's Word: Some sinners reject the gospel and therefore they reject the Lord Jesus. And concerning His being rejected, Jesus said,

He that rejecteth me, and receiveth not my words, hath one that judgeth him: the word that I have spoken, the same shall judge him in the last day.

Joh 12:48.

When the unrepentant sinner reject the gospel seed conception cannot occur. And by rejecting the Word they choose to remain alone, to be solitary. And, because

God setteth the solitary in families...

Ps 68:6.

...the choice to remain alone and solitary, and not become a part of the bride chamber, the church, the bride of Christ or the family of God—is against the will of God and is therefore against God.

Preachers Who Went But Not Sent: Another reason why the gospel seeds do not fertilize and cause conception to occur is because the preacher was not sent. A basic requirement of the Lord for the people to hear and acquire an understanding, so that they may believe, is that the preacher be sent by the husbandman and not by the will of man. For the scripture instructs

14 How then shall they call on him in whom they have not believed? and how shall they believe in him of whom they have not heard? and how shall they hear without a preacher?

15 And how shall they preach, except they be sent?

...

Ro 10:14-15.

They who preach without being sent, by the man whom they claim to represent, are representatives of themselves without authority. For the Lord Jesus was clear when he said

...without me ye can do nothing.

Joh 15:5.

If He does not send the preacher, then, when the preacher goes the Lord will not be with him in what he does. Because, to go without

Christ is to go by the will of man and not by the will of the Father. Even Jesus, while speaking of himself, said

> **I can of mine own self do nothing: as I hear, I judge: and my judgment is just; because I seek not mine own will, but the will of the Father which hath sent me.**

Joh 5:30.

> **My doctrine is not mine, but his that sent me.**

Joh 7:16.

The preacher that *went*, and was not *sent* is the Matthew 7:21-23 Believer. *(Read Mt 7:21-23)* As the Prophet Samuel stated,

> **...Behold to obey is better than sacrifice, and to hearken than the fat of rams.**

1Sa 15:22.

The word of the Father commands us,

> **In all thy ways acknowledge him, and he shall direct thy paths.**

Pr 3:6.

Therefore, when a preacher *went* and was not *sent*, he rejects the requirement to acknowledge God in all his ways, so that God may direct the how, when and where that he should go. *(Pr 3:5-6)*

> **For God is not the author of confusion, but of peace, as in all churches of the saints.**

1Co 14:33.

When he sends a preacher out from the flock, to do a work for the ministry, he informs the leadership of the church in addition to the person that he is sending. For he declared,

Surely the LORD God will do nothing, but he revealeth his secret unto his servants the prophets.

Am 3:7.

A good example of this is found in the first century Church concerning the sending out of Saul (Paul) and Barnabas. For, before they were sent out, the scripture recorded,

1 Now there were in the church that was at Antioch certain prophets and teachers; as Barnabas,...and Saul.

2 As they ministered to the Lord, and fasted, *the Holy Ghost said, Separate me Barnabas and Saul* **for the work whereunto I have called them.**

3 And when they had fasted and prayed, and laid their hands on them, *they sent them away.*

4 So *they, being sent forth by the Holy Ghost*, **departed unto Seleucia; and from thence they sailed to Cyprus.**

5 And when they were at Salamis, they preached the word of God...

...

8 But Elymas the sorcerer ...withstood them, seeking to turn away the deputy from the faith.

9 Then *Saul, (who also is called Paul,) filled with the Holy Ghost*, **set his eyes on him,**

10 And said...

11 And now, behold, the hand of the Lord is upon thee, and thou shalt be blind, not seeing the sun for a season. And immediately there fell on him a mist and a darkness; and he went about seeking some to lead him by the hand.

12 Then the deputy, when he saw what was done, believed, being astonished at the doctrine of the Lord.

Ac 13:1-5, 8-12 *(Emphasis added).*

In this Acts 13:1-5, 8-12 passage we see that the Holy Ghost spoke to the leadership of the church. He let them know that He wanted the church leadership to separate Saul and Barnabas from the other members and work of the local, Antioch church. Their separation was so that they could be *'sent'* to do the work for which the Holy Ghost had called them to do. And they had indeed answered the call, because they were found fasting and ministering to the Lord at the local church. *(Ac 13:2)* The first call that they answered was the same call that the Matthew 7:21-23 Believers had failed to answer. That call was unto repentance,

> **And the times of this ignorance God winked at; but now commandeth all men every where to repent:**

Ac 17:30.

…resulting in the indwelling Spirit of the Lord—the Holy Ghost—living within them, directing their paths. *(Pr 3:6)* For this is the Original Will of God for Man. *(Read Ge 1:26-27; Ge 2:7; 2Co 3:18; Joh 4:24; Ro 8:9-11; Read also Ac 9:3-18; Ac 4:36-37)* However, it was not until the Holy Ghost spoke to the church leadership that Paul and Barnabas were actually chosen to be separated and sent out to do the work in the ministry, in the lives of others, which they themselves had already been called to do in their own lives. For the Lord Jesus admonishes men everywhere saying

> **3 …why beholdest thou the mote that is in thy brother's eye, but considerest not the beam that is in thine own eye?**
>
> **4 Or how wilt thou say to thy brother, Let me pull out the mote out of thine eye; and, behold, a beam is in thine own eye?**
>
> **5 Thou hypocrite, first cast out the beam out of thine own eye; and then shalt thou see clearly to cast out the mote out of thy brother's eye.**

Mt 7:3-5.

Moreover, the Lord himself said, in another place

> **...for many be called, but few chosen.**

Mt 20:16.

Furthermore, they who shall be with the Lord are not only called, but

> **...they that are with him are called, and chosen, and faithful.**

Re 17:14.

Saul and Barnabas did not awake one morning and decide that they were going to do a work for the ministry and then went. But, they waited on the Lord to tell the church leadership when it was time to be sent. They remained obedient to leadership. Once the church leadership received the word of the Lord, they then prayed and fasted, to be sure that it was the Lord and to be sure that they sent them out properly and in the right spirit. Later, they *'laid hands'* on them and *'they sent them away'*. Because the Holy Ghost had instructed the church leadership in what to do, when they did what they had been instructed to do, by *'sending them way'*, it actually was the Holy Ghost sending them through and by the leadership. For the record reflects

> **3 And when they had fasted and prayed, and laid their hands on them,** *they sent them away.*
>
> **4 So** *they, being sent forth by the Holy Ghost*, **departed unto Seleucia;...**

Ac 13:3-4 *(Emphasis added).*

Since they were sent forth by, that is, sent forth because of the Holy Ghost, the Acts 13:1-5, 8-12 passage records the success and the victory enjoyed by Paul and Barnabas, after they were 'sent' to labor in their calling. For, Saul was also called

> **Paul, a servant of Jesus Christ, called to be an apostle, separated unto the gospel of God,**

Ro 1:1 *(Read Ro 1:2-5).*

Therefore, when the Matthew 7:21-23 Believers run with zeal, but not according to knowledge, they do the church and the body of Christ a great disservice. For, they are church folk much like the church folk of Israel in Paul's day. The record of their works show us that

> **1 … they have a zeal of God, but not according to knowledge.**
> **2 For they being ignorant of God's righteousness, and going about to establish their own righteousness, have not submitted themselves unto the righteousness of God.**

Ro 10:2-3.

And because they have not submitted themselves unto the righteousness of God and therefore have rejected the word of God, God rejects them. *(1Sa 15:23)* For, He declared

> **My people are destroyed for lack of knowledge: because thou hast rejected knowledge, I will also reject thee, that thou shalt be no priest to me: seeing thou hast forgotten the law of thy God, I will also forget thy children.**

Ho 4:6.

This is why, when the zealous work outside of and without the knowledge of the righteousness and the Will of God, their works are judged as works of iniquity. *(Mt 7:23)* And, in agreement the Lord Jesus commented saying,

He that rejecteth me, and receiveth not my words, hath one that judgeth him: the word that I have spoken, the same shall judge him in the last day.
Joh 12:48.

Furthermore, rejection of the word of God is actually stubbornness and rebellion against God. The word of God admonishes us that,

...rebellion is as the sin of witchcraft, and stubbornness is as iniquity and idolatry.
1Sa 15:23.

And the scripture sayeth further,

Thou shalt not suffer a witch to live.
Ex 22:18.

Conception is Repentance:

When the unrepentant sinner hears and then reacts to the Gospel message by confessing his sins to Christ and repenting of and truly forsaking those sins, this is the *'process of conception'* that we call REPENTANCE. During conception a life has been conceived in the womb of the bride of Christ, in the same manner as in the womb of the flesh. And, as conception does not mean out of the womb birth, with the womb of the flesh, it does not mean out of the womb birth with the womb of the bride of Christ. Therefore, although a life is conceived, that life has not been born of the Spirit. *(Joh 3:5)* Without our sins being forgiven and remitted *(Read Acts 2:38),* we remain dead men walking in trespasses and sins in the vanity of our minds *(Eph 4:18; Read also Col 1:21),* alienated from the life that is only in God through Christ *(Eph 4:18),* by our sinful, selfish and ignorant ways and the blindness of our hearts. *(Eph 4:18)* And, without the shedding of blood there is no remission of sins. *(Heb 9:22)* This is why Christ shed his blood for us on Calvary's cross *(Joh 19:32-34; Col 1:14; 1Jo 5:6),* that we may have a right to the tree of life, and eternal life. *(Re 22:14)* For, the Lord Jesus informed us saying,

> **Verily, verily, I say unto you, Except ye eat the flesh of the Son of man, and drink his blood, ye have no life in you.**

Joh 6:53.

Now, the question arises,

"How do you know when conception has occurred in the person's life?"

Or, how do we know that the unrepentant sinner has repented? Is there a pregnancy test that we can use that will accurately tell us that a life has been conceived in the womb of the bride of Christ? Yes! There is a sure and safe way of determining whether the person has repented and is therefore pregnant with life. The surest way of knowing that the womb of the flesh has conceived and is pregnant with a life is by sight, and the same goes for the womb of the bride of Christ. When we can see with our eyes the changes that takes place in a woman that is pregnant—we know that she is pregnant. When the womb possesses a new life: **(1)** the woman's walk changes; **(2)** her appetite changes; **(3)** her mood, **(4)** emotional state and **(5)** spirit changes; **(6)** her conversation changes; **(7)** the things that she is most concerned with change; **(8)** her physical body changes; **(9)** her desires change; **(10)** her manner of living changes; **(11)** her manner of sitting, **(12)** rising and **(13)** sleeping change; **(14)** the places that she visits change; **(15)** the company that she keeps change; **(16)** her plans for life change; **(17)** her outlook on life changes; **(18)** her thought process changes; **(19)** the object of her daily meditations change; **(20)** even the clothes that she wears change. These same 20 life changing events occur in the life of the repentant sinner. For when the sinner truly repents he will have works meet for, or representative of true repentance, as John the Baptist admonished the spiritual leaders of his day, wherein the writer recorded,

> **5 Then went out to him Jerusalem, and all Judea, and all the region round about Jordan,**
>
> **6 And were baptized of him in Jordan, confessing their sins.**
>
> **7 But when he saw many of the Pharisees and Sadducees come to his baptism, he said unto them, O generation of vipers, who hath warned you to flee from the wrath to come?**
>
> **8 Bring forth therefore fruits meet for repentance:**

Mt 3:5-8.

We know that a person has repented by the fruit that we see him produce. For, the fruit that he bears will tell us whether it is fruit borne of repentance or whether the fruit is the result of a continued life of sin. Although we are not to judge with unrighteous judgment, and never to judge the person *(Mt 7:1-2),* we are required to be fruit inspectors. As fruit inspectors we are to

> **Prove all things; hold fast that which is good.**

1Th 5:21.

> **And we beseech you brethren, to know them which labor among you…**

1Th 5:12.

And,

> **1 Beloved, believe not every spirit, but try the spirits whether they are of God: because many false prophets are gone out into the world.**

2 Hereby know ye the Spirit of God: Every spirit that confesseth that Jesus Christ is come in the flesh is of God: 3 And every spirit that confesseth not that Jesus Christ is come in the flesh is not of God: and this is that spirit of antichrist, whereof ye have heard that it should come; and even now already is it in the world.

…

6 We are of God: he that knoweth God heareth us; he that is not of God heareth not us. Hereby know we the spirit of truth, and the spirit of error.

1Jo 4:1-3, 6.

They who have not been born of the spirit are not called to be fruit inspectors. Because, a person cannot know God in-order to confess Christ except he be born of the Spirit by the indwelling Holy Ghost. For, the scripture declares

…that no man can say that Jesus is the Lord, but by the Holy Ghost.

1Co 12:3.

Because, until a person is born of the Spirit of Christ by receiving the indwelling Holy Ghost, although he has life in him, yet his birth remains only in the natural womb of the flesh and not within the womb of the bride of Christ. And,

14 …the natural man receiveth not the things of the Spirit of God: for they are foolishness unto him: neither can he know them, because they are spiritually discerned.

15 But he that is spiritual judgeth all things, yet he himself is judged of no man.

16 For who hath known the mind of the Lord, that he may instruct him? But we have the mind of Christ.

1Co 2:14-16.

When we are spiritual and of full age our judgment is not of man or of our own, but is of Christ. For, now possessing the mind of Christ *(1Co 2:16b),* we seek not our will, but the will of Him that called, chose and sent us. As we do understand, that

> **I can of mine own self do nothing: as I hear, I judge: and my judgment is just; because I seek not mine own will, but the will of the Father which hath sent me.**

Joh 5:30.

And with the mind of Christ we do and say as he does and as he declared, when he said

> **49 For I have not spoken of myself; but the Father which sent me, he gave me a commandment, what I should say, and what I should speak.**
>
> **50 And I know that his commandment is life everlasting: whatsoever I speak therefore, even as the Father said unto me, so I speak.**

Joh 12:49-50.

True Repentance Brings Us Into Life From Death

When we are inspecting fruit, the fruit, which is the person's actions and lifestyle will speak louder than his confessing of sins and his confession of faith. For, the Lord Jesus gave us the test that we should use, saying,

> **43 For a good tree bringeth not forth corrupt fruit; neither doth a corrupt tree bring forth good fruit.**
>
> **44 For every tree is known by his own fruit. For of thorns men do not gather figs, nor of a bramble bush gather they grapes.**

45 A good man out of the good treasure of his heart bringeth forth that which is good; and an evil man out of the evil treasure of his heart bringeth forth that which is evil: for of the abundance of the heart his mouth speaketh.
Lu 6:43-45.

Wherefore by their fruits ye shall know them.
Mt 7:20.

We know the good from the corrupt, and the good from the evil, by the presence of life or the absence of life, which is determined by fruit representative of life or fruit representative of death. The Lord Jesus declared

...I am the way, the truth, and the life...
Joh 14:6.

For,

In him was life; and the life was the light of men.
Joh 1:4.

As he said,

...Except ye eat the flesh of the Son of man, and drink his blood, ye have no life in you.
Joh 6:53.

Without the shedding of blood, there is no remission of sins. *(Heb 9:22)* When a person repents with his whole heart, the enemy of the bride of Christ, Satan, will then tempt him to try and turn him back from a life of righteousness to the death of sin that he has come out of. For, Jesus said

Verily, verily, I say unto you, He that heareth my word, and believeth on him that sent me, hath everlasting

life, and shall not come into condemnation, but is passed from death unto life.

Joh 5:24.

So, the repentant sinner must remember that

There hath no temptation taken you but such as is common to man: but God is faithful, who will not suffer you to be tempted above that ye are able; but will with the temptation also make a way to escape, that ye may be able to bear it.

1Co 10:13.

When this temptation comes, the repentant sinner's faith is placed on trial to prove whether he will stay connected to the Lord in the bride's womb, through obedience to his commandments or leave the Lord and the bride's womb and return to being a servant of Satan. For we know that

...to whom...[w]e yield...[o]urselves servants to obey, his servants...[w]e are to whom...[w]e obey; whether of sin unto death, or of obedience unto righteousness...

Ro 6:16 *(Letters in brackets added).*

Life can be found only in the righteousness of Christ. For, after we have repented then we must be

4 ...buried with him by baptism into death: that like as Christ was raised up from the dead by the glory of the Father, even so we also should walk in newness of life.

5 For if we have been planted together in the likeness of his death, we shall be also in the likeness of his resurrection:

Ro 6:4-5.

Within our new life, born of repentance, the trying of our faith through temptation raises the question:

"When you are tempted, how do you continue in the newness of life that was born by repentance?"

For, we must be tempted in the same like manner as was Eve and the Lord Jesus. Although Eve failed her test and lost the trial *(Ge 3:2-7),* the Lord Jesus answered the question, after he was

> **1 ...led up of the Spirit into the wilderness to be tempted of the devil.**
> **2 And when he had fasted forty days and forty nights, he was afterward an hungered.**
> **3 And when the tempter came to him, he said, If thou be the Son of God, command that these stones be made bread.**
> **4 But he answered and said, It is written, MAN SHALL NOT LIVE BY BREAD ALONE, BUT BY EVERY WORD THAT PROCEEDETH OUT OF THE MOUTH OF GOD.**

Mt 4:1-4 *(Read also Lu 4:1-4).*

Here, in the similitude of the weakened flesh of man, we find the Lord Jesus, after having been weakened by forty days and nights of fasting. Then came the tempter, the bride's enemy, tempting Jesus, the groom, by playing on a need and desire that Jesus had in his weakened flesh. For, he was in fact hungry and in need of food to feed his natural body. But his answer was plain and simple, *'When you are tempted, to continue in the newness of life that was born by repentance the believer must live by every word that proceeedeth out of the mouth of God.' (Lu 4:4)*

He must continue daily eating the flesh of Christ and drinking his blood. For, without doing so he shall have no life in him. *(Joh*

6:53) To create a daily diet of eating and drinking Christ's flesh and blood the believer must

> **Study to shew thyself approved unto God, a workman that needeth not to be ashamed, rightly dividing the word of truth.**

2Ti 2:15.

For,

> **16 All scripture is given by inspiration of God, and is profitable for doctrine, for reproof, for correction, for instruction in righteousness:**
> **17 That the man of God may be perfect, thoroughly furnished unto all good works.**

2Ti 3:16-17.

For, it is by searching the scriptures and studying them that we learn of Christ and his ways. Because the scriptures, which is the Word of God, which also is Christ's flesh *(Joh 1:1-2, 14),* testifies of Jesus Christ. *(Joh 5:39)* So, through studying, the believer learns and understands what the Word of God says and how to do and perform the work of that Word. Otherwise, if he fails to study the believer will find himself unable to obey Christ's commandment that says,

> **...he that eateth me, even he shall live by me.**

Joh 6:57b.

And, being unable to obey the commandment, because of ignorance, the believer becomes the dreaded carnal Christian and forgetful hearer admonished by the Apostles Paul *(1Co 3:1-3; Ro 8:5-8)* and James unable to

> **...lay apart all filthiness and superfluity of naughtiness, and receive with meekness the engrafted word, which is able to save your souls.**

Jas 1:21.

For, his inability to *'lay apart all filthiness and superfluity of naughtiness and receive with meekness the engrafted word'* is due to his carnality resulting from his failure to maintain a proper diet of eating and drinking the flesh and blood of Jesus, he having become *'a hearer of the word, and not a doer...' (Jas 1:23)* As a consequence

> **23 ...he is like unto a man beholding his natural face in a glass:**
>
> **24 For he beholdeth himself, and goeth his way, and straightway forgetteth what manner of man he was.**

Jas 1:23-24.

And now,

> **11 ...seeing ye are dull of hearing.**
>
> **12 For when for the time ye ought to be teachers, ye have need that one teach you again which be the first principles of the oracles of God; and are become such as have need of milk, and not of strong meat.**
>
> **13 For every one that useth milk is unskillful in the word of righteousness: for he is a babe.**

Heb 5:11b-13.

The Birthing Process:

The husbandman is the Father, the Spirit of the Lord. *(Joh 15:1)* After conception has occurred the Holy Ghost enters the womb of the bride of Christ, as He did with the virgin Mary *(Mt 1:18-21; Lu 1:31, 35),* and causes the new believer to be born of the Spirit. *(John 3:5)* We know that the bride has birthed a live, newborn babe into the Church when we hear the baby crying, that is, speaking in tongues. For, when we come out of the womb of the Lord's bride we cry out in the same manner as the bride's first 120 babies *(Ac 1:15)* did on the day of Pentecost, and thereafter. For,

> **...they were all filled with the Holy Ghost, and began to speak with other tongues, as the Spirit gave them utterance.**

Ac 2:4.

> **44 While Peter yet spake these words, the Holy Ghost fell on all them which heard the word.**
>
> **45 And they of the circumcision which believed were astonished, as many as came with Peter, because that on the Gentiles also was poured out the gift of the Holy Ghost.**
>
> **46 For they heard them speak with tongues, and magnify God...**

Ac 10:44-46.

> **And when Paul had laid his hands upon them, the Holy Ghost came on them; and they spake with tongues, and prophesied.**

Ac 19:6.

As shown in the above passages, in the fullness of time, out of the womb of the Lord's bride, the church, came forth the sons of God. For,

> **12 ...as many as received him, to them gave he power to become the sons of God, even to them that believe on his name:**
>
> **13 Which were born, not of blood, nor of the will of the flesh, nor of the will of man, but of God.**

Joh 1:12-13.

When believers are first born of the Spirit, they are first willing *(Ps 110:3)* and obedient sons led by the Spirit of God. *(Ro 8:14)*

Of his own will begat he us with the word of truth, that we should be a kind of firstfruits of his creatures. Jas 1:18.

Is there a set time to be born of the Spirit?

In the womb of the flesh the normal and natural time period for a life to grow from conception to full term birth is nine months. That is, in the fullness of the time—nine months—the life within the womb will spring forth to be born. Although the full term for the birthing process, in the womb of the Bride of Christ, is not set in length of time, as in months, it is set to occur in the fullness of time. The length of time for a repentant sinner to go from conception to being born of the Spirit depends upon the person's sincerity and level of repentance. That is, if the person is slow about departing from evil, from their thoughts and from their ways, then the birthing process will be a long, slow and full of travail birthing process. For, the bride of Christ did not birth her first 120 babies until the time for all of them to be born were the same. That is, the fullness of time came about for all 120 people at the same time and on the same day. For the scriptures recorded their new birth on this wise,

1 And when the day of Pentecost was fully come, they were all with one accord in one place.

2 And suddenly there came a sound from heaven as of a rushing mighty wind, and it filled all the house where they were sitting.

3 And there appeared unto them cloven tongues like as of fire, and it sat upon each of them.

4 And they were all filled with the Holy Ghost, and began to speak with other tongues, as the Spirit gave them utterance.

Ac 2:1-4.

The day of the new birth of the first 120 souls was the Day of Pentecost. But, their birth was not 12:01 at night, nor was it during the night. But the scripture reflect that their birthing occurred *'when the day of Pentecost was fully come'*. That is, the daylight had arrived and it was the third hour of the daylight. *(Ac 2:15)* However, the significance of the day itself is less important to what they, as a group had accomplished. For, they were all—120 souls—in one place with one accord. The phrase **'with one accord'** is translated from the Greek **hŏmŏthumadŏn** *(hom-oth-oo-mad-on')*. **Hŏmŏthumadŏn** means unani-mously, with one accord, with one mind. The 120 souls did not go into the one place where they found themselves on the day of Pentecost of their own, independent or individual accord, mind or will. But, they were all in the one place out of obedience to the word of the bridegroom whom they desired to marry. For the bridegroom, Jesus the Christ,

4 ...being assembled together with them, commanded them that they should not depart from Jerusalem, but wait for the promise of the Father, which saith, ye have heard of me.

5 For John truly baptized with water; but ye shall be baptized with the Holy Ghost not many days hence.

Ac 1:4-5.

After receiving instruction and direction from the bridegroom the believing souls

12 ...returned they unto Jerusalem from the mount called Olivet, which is from Jerusalem a Sabbath day's journey.

13 And when they were come in, they went up into an upper room…

14 These all continued with one accord in prayer and supplication…

15 …(the number of names together were about a hundred and twenty)

Ac 1:12-15.

In The Fullness Of Time: The Fullness of Time for each soul is different. As discussed earlier, the time for a person to be born will depend upon that person's sincerity and level of repentance. For, the Preacher declared

1 To every thing there is a season, and a time to every purpose under the heaven.

2 A time to be born, and a time to die; a time to plant, and a time to pluck up that which is planted;

Ec 3:1-2.

Therefore, as it was with the first 120 souls that were born of the Spirit when the day of Pentecost had fully come, **the repentant sinner will be born of the Spirit when he finds himself with one accord in one place with the Word of the Lord.** For, he must be in complete agreement with what he has been taught to understand about receiving Christ—about receiving the Holy Ghost indwelling. The Lord Jesus will come and indwell us, as the Holy Ghost, only after he justifies us by grace.

24 Being justified freely by his grace through the redemption that is in Christ Jesus:

25 Whom God hath set forth to be a propitiation through faith in his blood, to declare his righteousness for the remission of sins that are past, through the forbearance of God;

26 To declare, I say, at this time his righteousness: that he might be just, and the justifier of him which believeth in Jesus.

Ro 3:24-26.

The repentant sinner's will and mind must become one with the Word of the Lord Jesus with regards to salvation. That is, when the repentant sinner comes into agreement with the Lord by word and deed—then his walk will match and be in agreement with his talk. At this point the Lord justifies the repentant sinner by his grace and gives him the Holy Ghost after he has counted the repentant sinner as righteous. For, at this time the repentant sinner having entered the Lord's rest has ceased from his own works.

For he that is entered into his rest, he also hath ceased from his own works, as God did from his.

Heb 4:10.

Things That Prevent Or Hinder the Birthing Process:

There are many things that can hinder and—or prevent the birthing process. Before a person has been born of the Spirit, and after he has been born of the Spirit what hinders his birth and his growth are unrighteous things, unrighteous persons and—or unrighteous spirits. *(Read Ga 3:1; Ga 5:7)*

1. Confidence and Trust in Money and Wealth

An example showing how confidence and trust in money and wealth hinders and prevents the birth process is the rich young ruler, wherein the writer recorded,

17 And when he was gone forth into the way, there came one running, and kneeled to him, and asked him,

Good Master, what shall I do that I may inherit eternal life?

18 And Jesus said unto him, Why callest thou me good? There is none good but one, that is, God.

19 Thou knowest the commandments, Do not commit adultery, Do not kill, Do not steal, Do not bear false witness, Defraud not, Honor thy father and mother.

20 And he answered and said unto him, Master, all these have I observed from my youth.

21 Then Jesus beholding him loved him, and said unto him, One thing thou lackest: go thy way, sell whatsoever thou hast, and give to the poor, and thou shalt have treasure in heaven: and come, take up the cross, and follow me.

22 And he was sad at that saying, and went away grieved: for he had great possessions.

Mk 10:17-22 *(Read also Mt 19:16-22; Lu 18:18-23).*

In the above example of the rich man, we see that he was obedient to the Word of God up to a point. That point came when he was confronted with the thought of having to separate himself, for a season, from his worldly things—his great wealth and riches. For, the separation was only temporary, until he had followed Jesus into the regeneration to overcome the love of money, because the Lord Jesus has promised, saying

He that overcometh shall inherit all things; and I will be his God, and he shall be my son.

Re 21:7.

And when the disciples questioned Jesus about leaving all and following him, the record states,

> **28 Then Peter began to say unto him, Lo, we have left all, and have followed thee.**
>
> **29 And Jesus answered and said, Verily I say unto you, There is no man that hath left house, or brethren, or sisters, or father, or mother, or wife, or children, or lands, for my sake, and the gospel's,**
>
> **30 But he shall receive a hundredfold now in this time, houses, and brethren, and sisters, and mothers, and children, and lands, with persecutions; and in the world to come eternal life.**

Mk 10:28-30.

And Saint Luke wrote,

> **28 Then Peter said, Lo, we have left all, and followed thee.**
>
> **29 And he said unto them, Verily I say unto you, There is no man that hath left house, or parents, or brethren, or wife, or children, for the kingdom of God' sake,**
>
> **30 Who shall not receive manifold more in this present time, and in the world to come life everlasting.**

Lu 18:28-30.

In the Mark 10:17-22 passage above, the rich man's spiritual birth and entrance into the kingdom of God was prevented because his faith and his trust were in his riches and not in God. For the Lord declared,

> **24 ...how hard is it for them that trust in riches to enter into the kingdom of God!**
>
> **25 It is easier for a camel to go through the eye of a needle, than for a rich man to enter into the kingdom of God.**

Mk 10:24-25.

And again, He said

> **No man can serve two masters: for either he will hate the one, and love the other; or else he will hold to the one, and despise the other. Ye cannot serve God and mammon.**

Mt 6:24.

The rich ruler had obeyed some, but not all, of the Word of God up from his youth. And, by believing in Jesus, he thought he was ready to continue on as Jesus' disciple to inherit eternal life. But, when he was told to *"...come, take up the cross, and follow me" (Mk 10:21),* he found that he had more faith in his possessions than he had in the Lord. For, the scripture declared

> **31 Then said Jesus to those Jews which believed on him, If ye continue in my word, then are ye my disciples;**
> **32 And ye shall know the truth, and the truth shall make you free.**

Joh 8:31-32.

The rich ruler refused to continue in, that is, obey the word of the Lord. For, he discovered that he loved his possessions more than he loved God, and more than he desired to inherit eternal life. And, unknown to himself, he was in violation of the first commandment,

> **Thou shalt have no other gods before me.**

Ex 20:3.

The rich ruler had placed his possessions as his god before God, for *"...he was sad ... and went away grieved: for he had great possessions." (Mk 10:22)* Because the rich ruler refused to remain in the womb of the bride of Christ, as a repentant sinner, so that he could be born of the Spirit—he was not made free. For, had he obeyed the Lord and continued to fulfill the commandments in his own life, he would have known the truth about riches and the love of money. He would have been free to serve God and to use unrighteous mammon in a manner and a way that was pleasing in the sight of God.

2. Envy, Strife and Confusion within the Body of Christ

Envy, strife and confusion within the body of Christ will hinder and prevent a person from receiving the Holy Ghost, because it prevents the repentant sinner's mind from being with one accord with the Word of God and with the body and bride of Christ. For, we are admonished that

> **14 ...if ye have bitter envying and strife in your hearts, glory not, and lie not against the truth.**
>
> **15 This wisdom descendeth not from above, but is earthly, sensual, devilish.**
>
> **16 For where envying and strife is, there is confusion and every evil work.**

Jas 3:14-16.

And the evil works are also called the works of the flesh, and

> **19 Now the works of the flesh are manifest, which are these; Adultery, fornication, uncleanness, lasciviousness,**
>
> **20 Idolatry, witchcraft, hatred, variance, emulations, wrath, strife, seditions, heresies,**
>
> **21 Envyings, murders, drunkenness, revellings, and such like: of the which I tell you before, as I have also told you in time past, that they which do such things shall not inherit the kingdom of God.**

Ga 5:19-21.

So, if a new Believer is trying to receive the Holy Ghost in an environment that consists of the works of the flesh, he will be confused as to what is right and what is wrong. Because, those that he is supposed to follow are presenting themselves as hypocrites and are not walking the walk that they are talking, teaching and preaching.

3. The Talebearer

The talebearer within the body of Christ will hinder and prevent a person from receiving the Holy Ghost, by preventing the repentant sinner from believing the Word taught to him by the preacher. This in turn hinders and prevents his mind from being with one accord with the Word of God and with the body and bride of Christ, because now he is against the preacher, whom he needs. Jesus gave an example of this in the parable of the sower where he taught, that,

> **5 A sower went out to sow his seed: and as he sowed, some fell by the way side; and it was trodden down, and the fowls of the air devoured it.**
>
> ...
>
> **12 Those by the way side are they that hear; then cometh the devil, and taketh away the word out of their hearts, lest they should believe and be saved.**

Lu 8:5, 12.

Thus, as a thief, the devil can steal and take away the hearer's joy of the Word when he kills the preacher's influence by slandering his name, reputation and character. In doing so, Satan thereby destroys the hearer's chance, at that time, to receive salvation and deliverance from the bondage of sin. Because, Satan knows that the hearer cannot be saved without the preacher. As it is written,

> **13 For whosoever shall call upon the name of the Lord shall be saved.**
>
> **14 How then shall they call on him in whom they have not believed? and how shall they believe in him**

of whom they have not heard? and how shall they hear without a preacher?

Ro 10:13-14.

For...it pleased God by the foolishness of preaching to save them that believe.

1Co 1:21b.

Satan, the enemy, knows that if he makes the preacher irrelevant in the lives, hearts and minds of men then they cannot be saved. Therefore, Satan seeks out partners to become the devil, diabolos the traducer, to partner with him in using their vocal chords and their tongues to become busybodies, talebearers and whisperers, knowing that God has com-manded us saying,

Thou shalt not go up and down as a talebearer among thy people...

Le 19:16a.

And that,

He that goeth about as a talebearer revealeth secrets: therefore meddle not with him that flattereth with his lips.

Pr 20:19.

A talebearer revealeth secrets: but he that is of a faithful spirit concealeth the matter.

Pr 11:13.

Thus, Satan will partner with men outside and inside of the body of Christ to assist him in maintaining the captivity of the sinner. For, the word **talebearer** *(tāl-ber′-ər)* in Leviticus 19:16a, Proverbs 20:19 and Proverbs 11:13 is translated from **rakiyl** *(raw-keel′),* which means a scandal-monger (as traveling about); slander, carry tales, talebearer. Thus, the Lord admonishes us to not become a traveling talebearer carrying and repeating slanders, tales and scandals about our neighbors. But, rather we should be found of a faithful spirit by concealing the matter *(Pr 11:13; Pr 19:11; Pr 29:11)*, that we might win a soul. For, we are to love our neighbor as we love ourselves. *(Mt 19:19)* And we would not spread scandals or slanderous tales about ourselves to others.

When we use our tongue to utter a slander to diminish and defame another person's character, name or reputation we partner with Satan and have become a diabolos, traducer, and a fool that hates his own soul. For,

> **Whoso is partner with a thief hateth his own soul: he heareth cursing, and bewrayeth it not.**

Pr 29:24.

And,

> **He that hideth hatred with lying lips, and he that uttereth a slander, is a fool.**

Pr 10:18.

Here, to **partner** *(pärt′-nər)* with Satan, the thief, in Proverbs 29:24 is to **chalaq** *(khaw-lak')* in the Hebrew, meaning to be smooth; to apportion or separate; deal, distribute, divide, flatter, give, have part, have partner; take away a portion, receive, separate self, be smooth (er). Thus, the person who becomes a traducing devil with Satan actually thinks he is a smooth dealer and flatterer, because he refuses to reveal or bewray the truth that he has traduced and slandered his fellow man in the hearing of another. For, to **bewray**, taken from **nagad** *(naw-gad),* means to front, to stand boldly out opposite; to manifest; to announce (always by word of mouth to one present); to expose, predict, explain, praise; bewray, certify, declare, denounce, expound, messenger, profess, rehearse, report, shew (forth), speak, tell, utter. Thus, the partnering talebearer, traducer and slanderer does not reveal to the hearer the truth concerning the thief's intent which is to kill, steal and destroy the preacher's influence when he slanders and traduces the preacher.

Furthermore, a talebearer brings and maintains strife in the body of Christ thereby hindering the process and work of saving and delivering souls out of the kingdom of Satan. As it is written,

> **Where no wood is, there the fire goeth out: so where there is no talebearer, the strife ceaseth.**

Pr 26:20.

Because,

> **The words of a talebearer are as wounds, and they go down into the innermost parts of the belly.**

Pr 18:8 *(Read also Pr 26:22-28).*

And here, in the Proverbs 18:8 and the Proverbs 26:20 passages, the word **talebearer** is derived from **nirgan** *(neer-gawn)* meaning to roll to pieces, a slanderer; a talebearer, whisperer. Whispering, so that others with truth cannot hear, is a very effective method of name, reputation and character assassination used by the strife bringing talebearer. For, King David said,

> **All that hate me whisper together against me: against me do they devise my hurt.**

Ps 41:7.

And his son, King Solomon, wrote

> **...a whisperer separateth chief friends.**

Pr 16:28b.

And,

> **He that covereth a transgression seeketh love; but he that repeateth a matter separateth very friends.**

Pr 17:9.

And finally, as it was with the Hebrews, so it is with the church wherein the apostles, on occasion, had to admonish the wrongdoing talebearers, busybodies and tattlers within the congregations, saying,

> **But let none of you suffer as a murderer, or as a thief, or as an evildoer, or as a busybody in other men's matters.**

1Pe 4:15.

> **For we hear that there are some which walk among you disorderly, working not at all, but are busybodies.**

2Th 3:11.

> **And withal they learn to be idle, wandering about from house to house; and not only idle, but tattlers also and busybodies, speaking things which they ought not.**

1Ti 5:13.

Thus, in 2Thessalonians some members in the congregation had become hard working **busybodies** as a Greek **periergazomai** *(per-ee-er-gad'-zom-ahee)* working all around; bustling and hurrying about meddling and doing the work of a busybody. In 1Timothy 5:13 some had become Greek **periergos** *(per-ee'-er-gos)* **busybodies** working all around, even engaging in curious arts and magic, and being officiously meddlesome and overbearingly so offering unwanted advice and services to others; all the while being a Greek **phluaros** *(floo'-ar-os)* which is a **tattler** *(tat'-lər),* a prater, a garrulous person that talk much and a lot especially about unimportant things. And, in 1Peter 4:15 some saints had become a **busybody** *(biz'-ē-bad'-ē),* a Greek **allotriepiskopos** *(allot-ree-ep-is'-kop-os)* overseeing other's affairs; a meddler; a busybody in other men's matters. This ought not to be in the church.

4. Divisions within the Body of Christ

Divisions within the body of Christ will hinder and prevent a person from receiving the Holy Ghost, by causing the repentant sinner to believe what one preacher says and not what another preacher says simply because they are not from the same congregation or under the same bishop or overseer. This in turn hinders and prevents his mind from being with one accord with the Word of God and with the body and bride of Christ, because now he is against a portion of the body of Christ whom he needs. *(Read 1Co 12:4-27)* Because, the various gifts given to men *(Eph 4:7-12)* by the Lord Jesus Christ are necessary,

> **13 Till we all come in the unity of the faith, and of the knowledge of the Son of God, unto a perfect man, unto the measure of the stature of the fulness of Christ:**
>
> **14 That we henceforth be no more children, tossed to and fro, and carried about with every wind of doctrine, by the sleight of men, and cunning craftiness, whereby they lie in wait to deceive;**
>
> **15 But speaking the truth in love, may grow up into him in all things, which is the head, even Christ:**
>
> **16 From whom the whole body fitly joined together and compacted by that which every joint supplieth, according to the effectual working in the measure of every part, maketh increase of the body unto the edifying of itself in love.**

Eph 4:13-16.

So, if a repentant sinner has set his heart against a portion of the body of Christ, by taking sides in an evil division, he cannot receive the Holy Ghost because he has become carnal. And,

> **6 ...to be carnally minded is death; but to be spiritually minded is life and peace.**
>
> **7 Because the carnal mind is enmity against God: for it is not subject to the law of God, neither indeed can be.**

Ro 8:6-7.

There are two types of evil **divisions** in the body of Christ. The first is **sedition** and the second is a **schism**. An example of the **sedition** type of **division** was in the Corinthian Church where Apostle Paul admonished them saying,

> **For ye are yet carnal: for whereas there is among you envying, and strife, and divisions, are ye not carnal, and walk as men?**

1Co 3:3.

When a repentant sinner goes carnal he is unable to receive the Holy Ghost because his carnality causes him to walk by the flesh and not by the Spirit.

> **So then they that are in the flesh cannot please God.**

Ro 8:8.

The word **divisions** *(də-vizh'ən)* here, in the 1Corinthians 3:3 passage, is translated from the Greek **dichostasia** *(dee-khos-tas-ee'-ah)* meaning disunion, dissension, division, sedition. **Sedition** *(si-dish'en),* which means a stirring up of rebellion against the governing leadership, is an evil work of the flesh as listed by the Apostle Paul in Galations 5:20. This form of division is rebellion against God by rebelling against his messengers and leaders, thereby causing discord among the brethren which is an abomination unto the Lord. *(Pr 6:16, 19)* By sowing discord sedition causes offences contrary to the apostolic doctrine. And rather than fostering unity within the body of Christ it causes disunion, and weakness contrary to the work of the five fold ministry gifts of the apostle, prophet, evangelist, pastor and teacher as discussed in Ephesians 4:11-14. For, the brethren are to be found

> **Endeavouring to keep the unity of the Spirit in the bond of peace.**

Eph 4:3.

And not destroying the unity, for

> **1 Behold, how good and how pleasant it is for brethren to dwell together in unity!**
> **2 It is like the precious ointment upon the head, that ran down upon the beard, even Aaron's beard: that went down to the skirts of his garments;**
> **3 As the dew of Hermon, and as the dew that descended upon the mountains of Zion: for there the Lord commanded the blessing, even life for evermore.**

Ps 133:1-3.

And, because of this, we are admonished

> **17 Now I beseech you, brethren, mark them which cause divisions and offences contrary to the doctrine which ye have learned; and avoid them.**
> **18 For they that are such serve not our Lord Jesus Christ, but their own belly; and by good words and fair speeches deceive the hearts of the simple.**
> **19 For your obedience is come abroad unto all men. I am glad therefore on your behalf: but yet I would have you wise unto that which is good, and simple concerning evil.**

Ro 16:17-19.

The second form of **division** found in the body of Christ is a **schism**, and to prevent a schism from developing and expanding in the church Apostle Paul admonished the Corinthian Church, saying

> **Now I beseech you, brethren, by the name of our Lord Jesus Christ, that ye all speak the same things, and that there be no divisions among you; but that ye be perfectly joined together in the same mind and in the same judgment.**

1Co 1:10.

Here, **divisions** *(də-vizh'ən)* is translated from **schisma** *(skhis'-mah)* which means a split or gap; division, rent, schism. And **schism** *(skiz'em)* means a split, as in a church because of a difference of opinion or doctrine. When the brethren are not speaking, preaching and teaching the same thing it causes a split or division within the apostolic doctrine. And, thereby we create a split within the church congregation and the body of Christ. This schism will prevent and hinder a repentant sinner to receive the Holy Ghost because he is confused as to what side of the division is truth and what is error. Therefore, his mind and his heart cannot be with one accord with the Word of God or the body of Christ.

Thus, the brethren are commanded to speak the same things. When we do this we avoid doctrinal schisms, factions and splits within the congregation. And we are able to wear and possess the same mind and the same judgment as we walk and work to build the kingdom of God—one soul at a time. For, when there is a question, doctrine or judgement that causes different mind sets we are to obey the scriptures wherein we are told to

> **Come now, and let us reason together, saith the Lord…**

Isa 1:18.

For, if we do not sit and reason together, about our differences, then we cannot work together in building the kingdom of God because we will not be *"...perfectly joined together in the same mind and in the same judgment. (1Co 1:10)* As Prophet Amos asked

> **Can two walk together, except they be agreed?**

Amos 3:3.

For, it is by coming and reasoning together to work out our differences that we *"[e]ndeavour... to keep the unity of the Spirit in the bond of peace... (Eph 4:3)* amongst the brethren. As this is the same remedy used by the Apostles when the dispute and great dissension arose in the church concerning a new doctrine taught by some leaders, to non-Jewish converts, saying, *"Except ye be circumsied after the manner of Moses, ye cannot be saved." (Ac 15:1)* The issue and dispute was settled by sending the Apostles and elders to Jerusalem where many of them discussed the issue and came to an agreement. Thereby, they were all with one accord and avoided a **schism** from developing in the church, the body of Christ. To announce their one judgment and singleness of mind they wrote and sent letters saying,

> **23 ...The apostles and elders and brethren send greeting unto the brethren which are of the Gentiles in Antioch and Syria and Cilicia:**
>
> **24 Forasmuch as we have heard, that certain which went out from us have troubled you with words, subverting your souls, saying, Ye must be circumcised, and keep the law: to whom we gave no such commandment:**
>
> **25 It seemed good unto us, being assembled with one accord, to send chosen men unto you with our beloved Barnabas and Paul,**
>
> **26 Men that have hazarded their lives for the name of our Lord Jesus Christ.**
>
> **27 We have sent therefore Judas and Silas, who shall also tell you the same things by mouth.**
>
> **28 For it seemed good to the Holy Ghost, and to us, to lay upon you no greater burden than these necessary things;**
>
> **29 That ye abstain from meats offered to idols, and from blood, and from things strangled, and from fornication: from which if ye keep yourselves, ye shall do well. Fare ye well.**

Ac 15:23-29.

5. Zealous works not according to Knowledge

Another great offence within the body of Christ that prevents and hinders repentant sinners from receiving the Holy Ghost is due to men engaged in zealous works for God but not according to knowledge. As the Apostle Paul commented,

> **2 For I bear them record that they have a zeal of God, but not according to knowledge.**
>
> **3 For they being ignorant of God's righteousness, and going about to establish their own righteousness, have not submitted themselves unto the righteousness of God.**

Ro 10:2-3.

When preachers and leaders fail to study and acquire an understanding of God's righteousness they instruct new converts in the error of their ways. This error prevents and hinders the new Believer's minds from being with one accord with the Word of God and with the body and bride of Christ, because now, although they are sincere, yet they are believing and trusting in a lie. If a new Believer would receive the Holy Ghost based upon a lie, then after he receives the Holy Ghost he will not want to change to obey the truth. So, he remains in a partial repentant state until someone with the truth can instruct him in a more perfect way. For,

> **1 Now the Spirit speaketh expressly, that in the latter times some shall depart from the faith, giving heed to seducing spirits, and doctrines of devils;**
>
> **2 Speaking lies in hypocrisy; having their conscience seared with a hot iron;**
>
> **3 Forbidding to marry, and commanding to abstain from meats…**

1Ti 4:1-3a.

We are now living in those latter times. Amen.

The Feeding and Growth Process:

After we are born of the Spirit, it is necessary for the bride of Christ to begin the feeding process so that we may grow up in the Lord. To accomplish the initial feeding of the newborn babe, the Father, who is the husbandman teaches and feeds by the spiritual gift called the pastor. For, the husbandman declared,

> **And I will give you pastors according to mine heart, which shall feed you with knowledge and understanding.**

Jer 3:15.

Newborn babes are fed the milk of the word, and not strong meat.

> **13 For every one that useth milk is unskillful in the word of righteousness: for he is a babe.**
> **14 But strong meat belongeth to them that are of full age, even those who by reason of use have their senses exercised to discern both good and evil.**

Heb 5:13-14.

The milk that the pastor feeds the babes in Christ comes out of the bosom of the Father.

> **...the only begotten Son, which is in the bosom of the Father...**

Joh 1:18.

The bosom is the breasts. Christ is in the breasts of the Father. And, when we are in Christ, then we are in the Father and he in us, because Christ and the Father are one. *(Joh 10:30)* When we are lying on the breasts then we can receive and are fed milk which is the principles of the doctrine of Christ. *(Heb 6:1)* The doctrine of Christ is the first things, the first principles of the oracles of God that brings us and leads us to Christ. Therefore, the doctrine of Christ is the sincere milk of the Word. For, Christ fills the bosom of the Father, He, being the word made flesh *(Joh 1:14)* and the express image of God *(Heb 1:2-3)* with the fullness of the godhead bodily dwelling in him. *(Col 2:8-9)* For, all that are born of the Spirit into the bride of Christ—the church—are admonished

> **2 As newborn babes, desire the sincere milk of the word, that ye may grow thereby.**
> **3 If so be ye have tasted that the Lord is gracious.**

1Pe 2:2-3.

For, the Psalmist declared,

> **O taste and see that the Lord is good…**

Ps 34:8.

> **How sweet are thy words unto my taste! Yea sweeter than honey to my mouth.**

Ps 119:103.

After we have begun to grow, by drinking the sincere milk of the word, then we are to learn to eat the butter and the honey that we may know to refuse the evil, and choose the good. *(Isa 7:15)* And, then we are to proceed on to perfection *(Mt 5:48),* to manhood, eating the strong meat *(Read Heb 5:11-14)* after we leave the first principles of the oracles of God, that is, the milk of the word, the principles of the doctrine of Christ, namely:

> **1 …the foundation of repentance from dead works, and of faith toward God,**
> **2 Of the doctrine of baptisms, and of laying on of hands, and of resurrection of the dead, and of eternal judgment.**

Heb 6:1-2.

To leave the principles of the doctrine of Christ, means to be weaned from the milk and drawn from the breasts, from the first, basic doctrines, preaching and teachings that brought us and led us to Christ. But, now that we are in him, it is necessary for us as believers to go on unto manhood, prepared to be taught knowledge and made to understand doctrine by our Father, the husbandman. *(Isa 28:9)* For, as did the Lord Jesus, we must grow up in Him, increasing in wisdom, in stature and in favor with God and with man. *(Lu 2:52)* For the ministry of the apostles, prophets, evangelists, pastors and teachers are intended to work together in bringing us

> **...unto the measure of the stature of the fullness of Christ.**

Eph 4:13 *(Read also Eph 4:11-13).*

That measure and that stature is the same measure and stature that Jesus achieved during his life and ministry here on earth. For, we are to

> **5 Let this mind be in you, which was also in Christ Jesus.**
> **6 Who, being in the form of God, thought it not robbery to be equal with God:**
> **7 But made himself of no reputation, and took upon him the form of a servant, and was made in the likeness of men:**
> **8 And being found in fashion as a man, he humbled himself, and became obedient unto death, even the death of the cross.**

Php 2:5-8.

Babies Born Premature:

The premature birth babe in Christ is not actually born of the Spirit, but the person believes that he has all that is necessary to live for, work for and live with God in the Spirit. The word **premature** *(pre'me-tyoor')* means happening, done, arriving, or existing before the proper time; unexpectedly early; too early. Since the premature birth baby came out of the womb too early he is not fully developed, and requires additional outside help to live and survive. Premature babies are the rocky, no root, no depth, no moisture believers discussed by Jesus in his Parable of the Sower. *(Read Mt 13:3-6, 20-21; Mk 4:2-6, 14, 16-17; Lu 8:4-6, 11, 13)* They are believers who have acquired some under-standing through repentance and have been called and given gifts of the Kingdom of God *(Read Mk 16:17-18),* but not chosen or sent by God to exercise and utilize those gifts.

> **For the gifts and calling of God are without repentance.**

Ro 11:29.

These premature babies are the immature, Matthew 7:21-23 believers who, by their zeal of God are more concerned with operating the gifts of the kingdom than with strengthening their relationship with God, the giver of the gifts. They are like the souls of Apostle Paul's day when he described them saying,

> **2 For I bear them record that they have a zeal of God, but not according to knowledge.**
>
> **3 For they being ignorant of God's righteousness, and going about to establish their own righteousness, have not submitted themselves unto the righteousness of God.**

Ro 10:2-3.

The potter appoints man and gives him gifts while he is yet in the potter's house—within the womb of the flesh of our natural mother. *(Read Jer 1:5)* Pursuant to the Mystery of Election and Calling of God *(Ro 9:11; Ro 11:25),* some are appointed as vessels of honor, while others, born from the same, fleshly womb, are appointed as vessels of dishonor. All of this electing and calling by God is done without man's input for the purposes of God, the potter. For, although the unborn child has done no evil or performed no good, God places him in this life as he sees fit, in the same manner that he placed the twins of Rebecca. For, the Apostle Paul commenting, stated,

> **10 ...when Rebecca also had conceived by one, even by our father Isaac;**
>
> **11 (For the children being not yet born, neither having done any good or evil, that the purpose of God according to election might stand, not of works, but of him that calleth;)**
>
> **12 It was said unto her, The Elder shall serve the younger.**
>
> **13 As it is written, Jacob have I loved, but Esau have I hated.**

Ro 9:10-13.

Because they possess the gifts of the kingdom and not the gift giver, again, the premature birth babies are as the Matthew 7:21-23 Believers—they have not done the will of the Father in their own lives. That is, they have not allowed themselves to be made and recreated into the image and likeness of God, their creator Father, which is the Original Will and Plan of God for man. For, we

> **...are changed into the same image from glory to glory, even as by the Spirit of the Lord.**

2Co 3:18.

Commenting, the Lord Jesus said,

21 Not every one that saith unto me, Lord, Lord, shall enter into the kingdom of heaven; but he that doeth the will of my Father which is in heaven.

22 Many will say to me in that day, Lord, Lord, have we not prophesied in thy name? And in thy name have cast out devils? And in thy name done many wonderful works?

23 And then will I profess unto them, I never knew you: depart from me, ye that work iniquity.

Mt 7:21-23.

An unborn child is not given a place in the family until after his birth, although he is carried in his mother's womb. The same goes for the unborn child in the womb of the Lord's bride. The repentant sinner, although he possesses gifts belonging to the kingdom, he is not a member of the kingdom, the bride or the church until after he has been born of the Spirit of the Lord. For, until he is born of the Spirit, although he has repented, he is still in the flesh, having not the power of the Holy Ghost indwelling to enable him to walk in the Spirit of Christ.

9 But ye are not in the flesh, but in the Spirit, if so be that the Spirit of God dwell in you. Now if any man have not the Spirit of Christ, he is none of his.

10 And if Christ be in you, the body is dead because of sin; but the Spirit is life because of righteousness.

Ro 8:9-10.

When the child, the believer, has not been born of the Spirit he does not possess the Spirit of Christ and he therefore does not belong to Christ. And, Christ does not know him as a saviour, because he has not entered him as an indwelling saviour. This is why Christ declared to the Matthew 7:21-23 Believers that he never knew them. He did not know them, not as a person knows and possesses knowledge of facts, figures and information, but rather Christ did not know them as a man knows his wife. He had never entered them, to give them his power, and therefore the authority to represent him as his representatives. When Christ enters the womb of his bride, to give birth to the repentant sinner, he does so by the will of the Father and not by the will of man. For,

> **12 …as many as received him, to them gave he power to become the sons of God, even to them that believe on his name:**
>
> **13 Which were born, not of blood, nor of the will of the flesh, nor of the will of man, but of God.**

Joh 1:12-13.

The word **image** in Genesis 1:26-27 is translated from the Hebrew **tselem** *(tseh'-lem).* **Tselem** means a representation, profile, to shade, a phantom, an illusion, image, vain shew, a likeness or resemblance. We become his image and therefore his representative in power and authority by being changed into his image by the Spirit of the Lord. *(2Co 3:18)* We acquire the authority and the power to represent Christ only after receiving him indwelling as the Comforter, the Holy Ghost. For the Lord Jesus said,

> **5 For John truly baptized with water; but ye shall be baptized with the Holy Ghost not many days hence.**
>
> **…**
>
> **8 But ye shall receive power, after that the Holy Ghost is come upon you: and ye shall be witnesses unto me both in Jerusalem, and in all Judea, and in Samaria, and unto the uttermost part of the earth.**

Ac 1:5, 8.

The Matthew 7:21-23 believers were not born by the will of the Father, but by the will of man. They decided within themselves that they were ready to go and represent the Lord. Someone told them that they were saved and ready to go. But, if the Lord had sent them to represent him, surely he would have known them first. The Matthew 7:21-23 believers became workers for the kingdom, without the authority and power of the Holy Ghost indwelling. Rather than being sent by Christ, they went by the authority, power and word of man. Therefore, their spiritual birth was not by the will of the father, but by the will of man. Because man's judgment convinced them to go out prematurely, without the power and authority of the Holy Ghost, the Matthew 7:21-23 believers cut the umbilical cord of life and were born prematurely. They became unauthorized witnesses for Christ even to the point of assisting in destroying the kingdom of Satan, by casting out demons. *(Mt 7:22)* Yet, because they had not been authorized by the giver of the gift, He, the Lord, professed that all of their works were works of iniquity. *(Mt 7:23)*

Chapter 18

No. 8: The Commandment to Replenish

> ***And God blessed them, and God said unto them, … replenish the earth…***
> ***Ge 1:28.***

The LORD God commanded the one flesh, Adam and his wife Eve, to replenish the earth. Here, **replenish** *(ri-`ple-nish)* is translated from the Hebrew word **male** *(maw-lay')* which means to fill, be full of, accomplish, confirm, to consecrate, satisfy, furnish, to replenish. Here, the Lord's commandment is concerned with mankind consecrating the earth by multiplying and filling it, satisfying it and furnishing it with people. For, the earth is a very large place, and it would take more than two people to accomplish all that God had commanded them to do. By filling the earth with people consecrated to do God's work, God would get more praise.

More light is placed upon the subject when we consider Genesis Chapter 9, verses 1, 7 and 19. There the writer wrote,

> **1 And God blessed Noah and his sons, and said unto them, Be fruitful, and multiply, and replenish the earth.**
>
> **…**

7 And you, be ye fruitful, and multiply; bring forth abundantly in the earth, and multiply therein.

...

19 These are the three sons of Noah: and of them was the whole earth overspread.

Ge 9:1, 7, 19.

In the above passages of scripture we see that, even after the Lord had destroyed the earth by flood waters, the word replenished was not used with a mere reference of rebuilding an earth that had just been destroyed. But replenish, here, signifies the act of multiplying and fruitfully filling and overspreading the earth with people, in the image of God. For, they were instructed to bring forth abundantly and multiply in the earth.

Put another way, the word replenish is used to inform Adam and Eve, Noah and his sons, by what degree or extent did the Lord require them to be fruitful and to multiply, and in what manner were they to be taught and instructed.

How much is enough, and by whose standard?

The answers are, until the earth is full, satisfied, consecrated and furnished with workers dedicated to accomplishing the work of God. And, they were to

Train up [the children] in the way [they] should go: and when [they are] old, [they] will not depart from it.

Pr 22:6 *(Words in brackets added or modified for clarity).*

For, the word **train** *(trān)* translated from the Hebrew word **chanak** *(khaw-nak')* means to narrow, to initiate, discipline, dedicate. As the writer declared,

3 Great is the Lord, and greatly to be praised; and his greatness is unsearchable.

4 <u>One generation shall praise thy works to another, and shall declare thy mighty acts</u>

Ps 145:3-4 *(Emphasis added).*

The Training Process

Because of Adam's sin, in the garden of Eden, every person born unto a woman is born a sinner *(Read Ro 5:12-14, 19)*, except for John the Baptist who was born with the indwelling Holy Ghost *(Read Lu 1:11-15)*, and Jesus Christ who is the Holy Ghost. *(Joh 14:16-18, 26)* For, sin is imputed to all men because of Adam's initial sin of violating the fourth commandment—not to eat from the tree of the knowledge of good and evil. *(Ge 2:16-17; Ge 3:6-7, 9-12)* Therefore, all men are made to be sinners even if they have not committed any sin like unto Adam. *(Ro 5:12-14)* As a consequence, in these last days, the world is full of wickedness, evil and violence committed by adults, young adults and children *(Read 2Ti 3:1-5)* that are sinners.

The Default Position

Therefore, after man fell into sin through Adam's disobedience to the commandment of God, his Father, the **default position** of mankind became one of sin, committing sin and seeking to satisfy and fulfill the lust of the flesh, the lust of the eyes and the pride of life none of which is of God. But all is of the world. *(1Jo 2:16)*

By **default** *(de-folt')* we mean a failure to do or appear as required. Adam failed to obey the fourth commandment by failing to abstain and not eat the forbidden fruit from the tree of the knowledge of good and evil. Thus, he defaulted on his agreement with his Father God, by not doing and living his life in the manner required. For, his creation was so that he would exist in the image and likeness of God. *(Ge 1:26-27; Ge 2:7)* In addition, by **position** *(pe-zish'en)* we mean the way in which a person or thing is placed or arranged; one's attitude or opinion; the place where one is; the usual or proper place, a post of employment. Adams proper place and initial post of employment was as a watchman for God, dressing and keeping the garden of Eden *(Ge 2:15),* including the job of naming every living creature. *(Ge 2:19)* When Adam defaulted on his promise and responsibility to abstain and not eat from the forbidden tree he changed jobs and his employer. By his acts of rebellion and disobedience, Adam switched his employment to Lucifer, the serpent, because his mind had become carnal. With a carnal mind his attitude towards Lucifer, the serpent, and those things pertaining to the serpent were positive, while his attitude towards God and the things of God became his enemy.

Now, with a carnal mind Adam became the enemy of God—the servant of Satan, a servant of Lucifer. For, when he ate from the forbidden fruit from the tree Adam caused his physical body to be used as an instrument of unrighteousness to perform an act that the Lord God had forbidden. *(Ge 2:16-17)* As a result, he became Lucifer's servant of sin unto death. *(Ro 6:16)* For, if a person lives his life in the manner that he thinks is right for him or in the way the world and his culture thinks is right for him, then he will always be a servant of the ruler and prince of this world, Lucifer. This is so, because the ways of God are not the ways of man or the world and the thoughts of God are not the thoughts of man or the world. *(Isa 55:8)* For, God's ways and thoughts are higher than man's ways and thoughts, as the heavens are higher than the earth. *(Isa 55:9)* Lucifer became the prince and ruler of this world when Adam gave Lucifer his power and dominion, over the whole earth *(Read Ge 1:28),* by worshipping Lucifer when he ate *(Ge 3:6-7*) from the forbidden tree of the knowledge of good and evil. *(Ge 2:16-17; Lu 4:5-7)* So, with a new ruler of the world, the world took on and spiritually adopted the rebellious, wicked and ungodly ways of its new ruler Lucifer. As Jesus said,

> **Ye are of your father the devil, and the lusts of your father ye will do. He was a murderer from the beginning,**

and abode not in the truth, because there is no truth in him. When he speaketh a lie, he speaketh of his own: for he is a liar, and the father of it.

Joh 8:44.

Man's thoughts are naturally vain, he, having been created from the dirt which is worthless. Vanity is not of God, but God made and created man *"... subject to vanity, not willingly, but by reason of him who hath subjected the same in hope." (Ro 8:20)* Here, in this Romans 8:20 passage the word **vanity** *(`va-ne-tē)* is translated from the Greek word **mataiotes** *(mat-ah-yot'-ace)* meaning moral depravity, transientness, inutility. **Mataiotes** is derived from **mataios** *(mat'-ah-yos)*, which means that which is empty, profitless, vain, and vanity. Dirt is profitless. But, God breathed into the man the **neshamah** (breath) of life, which is the Spirit of Christ—the Holy Ghost that changed Adam from a mere brute beast created and formed from the profitlessness of dirt to being also a living spirit. Thus, Adam was both human and divine, in the image and likeness of God *(Read Ge 1:26-27; Ge 2:7)* in "*...the figure of him (Jesus Christ) that was to come." (Ro 5:14b)*

Now that man was made subject to vanity, with the Spirit of God (the neshamah of life) dwelling on the inside, man acquired the ability to choose to continue in life, in God or to follow the ways and thoughts of his flesh. This ability is called **freewill**. Everyone, including children, have **freewill**—the ability to choose good over evil or evil over good. But, a child has to be taught and trained up to know and understand what is good and what is evil. If a child is not given the holiness standard of life from God so that he may be able to determine what is good and what is evil, then, his moral standard will be of the world, of Lucifer its ruler, and not of God. A child cannot train himself, because the flesh desires nothing of God. Moreover, because sin dwells in his *flesh (Ro 7:17, 20, 23),* in his flesh no good thing dwells. *(Ro 7:18)* For, "*...there is none righteous." (Ro 3:10)* No. There is none that seek after God or the things of God on his own accord. *(Ro 3:11-12)*

So, when parents fail or refuse to train by example, by teaching and through discipline when their children display acts of foolishness, which is bound up in their hearts *(Pr 22:15),* those same children, if they survive, will grow up to become undisciplined young adults and undisciplined older adults. If the foolishness is not corrected when they are young, then, when they are older the foolishness of the world will be their way and manner of life. Moreover, because they were trained up in the ways of the world to be worldly, when they are old they will have no desire to depart from the ways of the world.

For, a child must be weaned from the milk and from his mother's breast if he is to be taught the doctrine, knowledge and understanding necessary to become a responsible adult of full age. *(Isa 28:9)* Before a child can be taught to choose the good and refuse the evil, by eating butter and honey *(Isa 7:15)* he first must be fed, required and allowed to drink the sincere milk of the Word of God. *(1Pe 2:2)* And, as he grows into manhood, in order for him to be able to discern both good and evil *(Read Heb 5:12-14),* he must first have been fed and allowed to eat the butter and the honey. *(Isa 7:15)*

For, in human growth and understanding there are three stages of development. The first stage is the newborn baby stage. The second stage is the youthful stage. And, the third stage is the full age stage—perfection—which is accepting the personal responsibility of overcoming one's own faults and short comings. A person's training up and discipline within the ways of God in all three stages of carnal, human growth and development will greatly affect his ways and manner of life as he grows and matures within each developmental stage. For, an infant becomes a product of his environment and his surroundings. Therefore, even a child is known by his ways and the things that he does. *(Pr 20:11)* If he, as an infant, is fed the sincere milk of the Word of God *(1Pe 2:2),* who is Christ Jesus manifested in the flesh *(Read Joh 1:1-3, 14),* then, some of his ways will reflect the moral and spiritual values and ideas taught and found within the sincere milk of the Word that he was required and commanded to drink.

On the other hand, a child left to himself to do as he sees fit for himself and to himself is not a disciplined child, and he will bring his mother to shame. *(Pr 29:15)*

Training: Corporal Punishment—The Rod of Correction

The rod of correction is a useful and sometimes necessary tool for the proper training of children and the youth. The rod of correction is known to drive out the foolishness bound up in the heart of a child. *(Pr 22:15)* This **rod** *(räd)* in the Hebrew is **shebet** *(shay'-bet)* meaning to branch off; a stick (for punishing, writing, fighting, ruling, walking), correction, dart, rod, staff, scepter. So, in correcting a child sometimes it requires the use of the rod, but many refuse to use the rod of correction out of fear of hurting the child or because of the child's crying. *(Pr 19:18)* But, as parents we should not fail to correct our children with the rod, if it is required, to turn him from a wayward path and deliver his soul from hell. *(Read Pr 23:13-14)* And, when it is required, our failure to use the rod of correction to discipline our children means that we do not really love them, or their souls. *(Pr 13:24)* Even the Lord God chastens his sons whom he loves and delights in. *(Pr 3:11-12)* So, when a parent says that they will not use corporal punishment, when it is necessary, to chastise and correct their children because they love them, then they actually hate their children. If they loved their child they would do by him as God does by those that he loves. Therefore, the love of a parent who refuses to use the appropriate punishment to correct their children is the love of the world. Moreover, since they love the world and the things in it, including the worldly doctrines of child rearing, they make themselves the enemy of God because the love of God is not in them. *(1Jo 2:15)* For, it is impossible for a believer to conform his life and child rearing practices to that of the world and still be transformed by the renewing of his mind that he *"...may prove what is that good, and acceptable, and perfect, will of God." (Ro 12:2)*

In addition, an undisciplined child will bring his mother and his father to shame *(Pr 29:15), because* without the Word of God to lead and guide him he will possess no light for his feet to walk in safety and no lamp for his path of life *(Pr 6:23)* towards eternal salvation. As the law was for the Israelites, the sincere milk of the Word of God is like a schoolmaster *(Read Ga 3:19-26)* for an infant to lead him towards the safety, security and prosperity of being full age which is found only in Christ Jesus. [1] When the infant learns to exercise faith he is no longer under a schoolmaster. *(Ga 3:25)* For, by faith, he learns to be obedient to the commands and statutes of God.

The Soft Answer

Another means of training up a child is to teach him by using words. Words are a very powerful tool to instruct and correct a person. The Word of God is all words. So, by using words from the Word of God a parent or teacher is better able to train a child in the way that he should go. For, in addition to the rod, reproof through words will give wisdom to those who receives it. *(Pr 29:15a)* As the Apostle Paul informed brother Timothy,

> **All scripture is given by inspiration of God, and is profitable for doctrine, for reproof, for correction, for instruction in righteousness…**

2Ti 3:16.

Many ideas can be transferred, conveyed and understood by communi-cating through words.

[1] Additional scripture passages to read and consider are: Pr 29:1; Pr 21:2; Pr 23:13-14; Pr 23:22a; Pr 23:23; Pr 26:12; Pr 29:17; Pr 30:33; Pr 30:11-12; Pr 21:16; Pr 10:13; Pr 11:5; Pr 11:6; Pr 11:19; Pr 12:15; Pr 13:13; Pr 13:20; Pr 13:24; Pr 14:7; Pr 15:9; Pr 15:10; Pr 15:26; Pr 15:28; Pr 15:32; Pr 16:2; Pr 16:7; Pr 16:9; Pr 16:23; Pr 17:21; Pr 17:25; Pr 18:6; Pr 19:3; Pr 19:13; Pr 19:18; Pr 19:20; Pr 19:21; Pr 19:26; Pr 19:29; Pr 20:11; Pr 20:20; Pr 20:24; Pr 1:24-31; Pr 3:1-7; Pr 3:11-12; Pr 3:31; Pr 4:14-27; Pr 6:23; Pr 9:4-6; Pr 9:10-11; Ps 89:30-32.

THE CHARACTER OF WORDS

Words also have character. For, words spoken with the tongue possess the power of life and death. *(Pr 18:21)* By it we bless God and curse men. *(Jas 3:9)* Also, a person can be encouraged to learn or discouraged to learn based upon the character of the words used towards him or in his presence. For, as wrath is turned away by giving a soft answer, anger is stirred up by grievous words. *(Pr 15:1)* Words used should be appropriate for the work they are sent to accomplish. As God's words always accomplishes what he sends them to do and never return void. *(Isa 55:11)* Furthermore, a believer's words, as a teacher and trainer, and the thoughts and meditation of his heart towards his students should always be acceptable in the sight of the Lord Jesus. *(Ps 19:14)* For, the wise teacher uses his tongue to disperse knowledge right *(Pr 15:2, 7),* because his wholesome tongue is a tree of life—tending to life and not death. *(Pr 15:4)*

Training By Living the Example

A third manner of training up a child in the way that he should go is by becoming and being an example of the person, thing, idea or standard being taught. This is a teaching method used by the Apostles. For, the Apostle Paul instructed the Philippian congregation saying

Brethren, be followers together of me, and mark them which walk so as ye have us for an ensample. Php 3:17.

When a child, whether naturally or spiritually, witnesses the standard, doctrine or idea being taught in a believer's life, he then sees how the standard is applied in life and he understands that the standard is attainable and doable. This is why Jesus said

7 Nevertheless I tell you the truth; It is expedient for you that I go away: for if I go not away, the Comforter will not come unto you; but if I depart, I will send him unto you.

8 And when he is come, he will reprove the world of sin, and of righteousness, and of judgment:

9 Of sin, because they believe not on me;

10 Of righteousness, because I go to my Father, and ye see me no more;

Joh 16:7-10.

When a believer becomes a living example of the righteous standard of God, in Jesus Christ, those who refuse to repent of their sins are judged by the lives of the believers. For, the believer's lives and moral living standards prove and testify to the justness of the standard. For, being an example for others to follow and learn by requires active participation and demonstration on a daily and continual basis.[2] It is not an act or a part in a play or drama. An example is a way of life, a way of thinking and responding to the challenges and troubles of living in this world.

[2] Additional scriptures to read are: 1Pe 2:21-24; 1Jo 2:6; 1Co 4:14-17; 1Co 11:1-2; Php 3:17-19; 1Th 1:5-10; 1Th 2:1-12, 14; 3Jo 11; 2Th 3:7, 9.

Chapter 19

No. 9: The Commandment to Subdue

> ***And God blessed them, and God said unto them, ... subdue it...***
>
> ***Ge 1:28.***

The LORD God commanded Adam and Eve to subdue the earth. The word **subdue** *(seb-`dū)* is translated from the Hebrew **kabash** *(kaw-bash')*, which means to tread down, to conquer, subjugate, bring into bondage, force, keep under and bring into subjection. In agreement with this commandment to subdue the earth we learn that God put the whole of creation in such an order so as to enable man to accomplish God's will of bringing into subjection, the newly created, unconquered earth. For, David wrote,

> **6 Thou madest him to have dominion over the works of thy hands; thou hast put all things under his feet:**
>
> **7 All sheep and oxen, yea, and the beasts of the field;**
>
> **8 The fowl of the air, and the fish of the sea, and whatsoever passeth through the paths of the seas.**
>
> **Ps 8:6-8.**

Man had already been called by God to work for God and to consecrate the earth by filling it with mankind, in God's image and for God's purpose. With his calling in plain view it was then necessary to enable man to make the earth subject to man. For, through the earth's consecration and subjection to man, God is praised and glorified. Because, the holy and righteous man, who keeps the law of God, is the praise, honor and glory of God.

Also, when we view the commandment to subdue the earth from a spiritual point we see the greater concern. In Revelation 2:7, we see the Lord Jesus relating back to the world and the tree of life. For he said,

> **He that hath an ear, let him hear what the Spirit saith unto the churches; To him that overcometh will I give to eat of the tree of life, which is in the midst of the paradise of God.**

Re 2:7.

The word **overcometh** *(ō'ver-kŭm'ef)* in the above passage is translated from the Greek word **nikao** *(nik-ah'-o)*. **Nikao** means to subdue, conquer, overcome, prevail, get the victory. Thus, while Adam and Eve were busy subduing the world in the natural, the commandment also required them to not be in love with the world or to be a friend of the world, but to overcome it. For, Apostle James said,

> **...know ye not that the friendship of the world is enmity with God? whosoever therefore will be a friend of the world is the enemy of God.**

Jas 4:4.

And, Apostle John stated, in another place,

15 Love not the world, neither the things that are in the world. If any man love the world, the love of the Father is not in him.

16 For all that is in the world, the lust of the flesh, and the lust of the eyes, and the pride of life, is not of the Father, but is of the world.

1Jo 2:15-16.

Adam and Eve were to get the victory over the cares of this world. The part of this earth and this world that they had to subdue and overcome was within themselves. For, they were created from the dirt of this world. And, the dirt itself, being carnal, is the enemy of God having no desire for heavenly things. The dirt, having been created to remain on the earth, is earthy. And so,

The first man is of the earth, earthy:...

1Co 15:47.

But, God used the same dirt to create mankind and then God breathed life, part of heaven, into him. This creative process created a war within man, wherein the flesh of man wars against the law of his mind, the seat of his soul. *(Read Ro 7:23)* For the flesh, made from earthly dirt, desires nothing of God. And the life, the soul of man, desires nothing of the earth. So, man's greatest battle and duty was to subdue, overcome the earth that was a part of him. Man was commanded to subdue the earth, to *"...abstain from fleshly lusts, which war against the soul;" (1Pe 2:11b)* As long as Adam and Eve abstained from fleshly lusts there would be no need for a marriage counselor. There would be no wars and fightings amongst them. For, the writer wrote,

From whence come wars and fightings among you? come they not hence, even of your lusts that war in your members?

Jas 4:1 *(Read also Jas 4:2-8).*

Adam and Eve were created to be soldiers in the army of God, to do and work for him. And they had been commanded to replenish, to fill the earth with consecrated soldiers ready for the service of God. For, after God had created Adam and his wife, Eve, the writer wrote,

> **Thus the heavens and the earth were finished, and all the host of them.**

Ge 2:1.

The word **host** *(hōst)*, here, is translated from the Hebrew word **tsaba** *(tsaw-baw').* **Tsaba** means a mass of persons, soldiers, a campaign, an army organized for war, service, host. As the earth's host, mankind were to be good soldiers for the Lord, by subduing the worldly lust that were within themselves. Adam and Eve, having been made overseers over God's creation and commanded to train others in the service of the Lord were required to,

> **[Keep] under [their] ...body, and bring it into subjection: lest that by any means, when [they] ...had preached to [and trained] others, [they themselves] ...should be a castaway.**

1Co 9:27 *(Words in brackets added).*

For,

> **No man that warreth entangleth himself with the affairs of this life; that he may please him who hath chosen him to be a soldier.**

2Ti 2:4.

Mankind was commanded to subdue, to completely overcome the lusts that is of this world, and that was in them. They were to force and bring the lusts of this world into subjection unto the law of God. Then, they would have acquired the right to and made able to eat of the tree of life that stood in the midst of the garden of Eden. As the Lord Jesus declared,

> **He that hath an ear, let him hear what the Spirit saith unto the churches; To him that overcometh will I give to eat of the tree of life, which is in the midst of the paradise of God.**

Re 2:7.

And, as the residents of the garden of Eden continued to strive for perfection through obedience to the commandments of God, they continued to be a blessed people, who were allowed to remain in the garden of God. *(Read Re 22:14)* For, the tree of life that stands in the midst of the paradise of God is the same tree of life that stood in the midst of the garden of Eden. The word **paradise** *(păr'a-dīs')*, as used in Revelation 2:7, is translated from the Greek word **paradeisos** *(par-ad'-I-sos)*. **Paradeisos** means a park, an Eden, a place of future happiness, paradise. The word **Eden** *(ēd'n)* is translated from the Hebrew word **`Eden** *(ay'-den)*. **`Eden** means pleasure, delight, delicate, to live voluptuously, delight self. **Voluptuous** *(va-lŭp'choo-as)* means to be full of, producing or characterized by sensual pleasures; fond of luxury, the pleasures of the senses. The word **garden** *(gärd'n)* is translated from the Hebrew word **gan** *(gan)*, which means a fenced garden. **Gan** is derived from the root word **ganan** *(gaw-nan')*, which means to hedge about, protect, defend.

We find that the garden of Eden was: full of joy, gladness, thanksgiving and the voice of melody *(Isa 51:3)*; and, it was well watered by one river *(Ge 2:10; Ge 13:10)*.

Chapter 20

No. 10: The Commandment To Have and Exercise Dominion

> ***And God blessed them, and God said unto them, ... have dominion over the fish of the sea, and over the fowl of the air, and over every living thing that moveth upon the earth.***
>
> ***Ge 1:28.***

God commanded ***them*** to exercise dominion, control over the sea life, the birds of the sky and over every living thing that moves upon the earth. *(Ge 1:28)*

Good Stewardship of the Earth's Resources

Therefore, the Lord God made Adam and Eve stewards over his creation. And in agreement the writer declared,

> **3 When I consider thy heavens, the work of thy fingers, the moon and the stars, which thou hast ordained;**
>
> **4 What is man, that thou art mindful of him? and the son of man, that thou visitest him?**

5 For thou hast made him a little lower than the angels, and hast crowned him with glory and honour.

6 Thou madest him to have dominion over the works of thy hands; thou hast put all things under his feet:

7 All sheep and oxen, yea, and the beasts of the field;

8 The fowl of the air, and the fish of the sea, and what- soever passeth through the paths of the seas.

Ps 8:3-8.

So, as stewards over the earth and its resources, God intended for man to govern, control and manage the earth and its resources for the benefit of all living creatures. As,

...it is required in stewards that a man be found faithful.

1Co 4:2.

And, just like man, all of the other forms of life on earth are in need of the earth's resources for growth and a sustainable life. However, because of the love of money, many have been and will be found unfaithful as stewards of God's house and of his creation. For, the word **steward** *(stū'ĕrd)* in 1Corinthians 4:2 is translated from **oikonomos** *(oy-kon-om'-os)*. **Oikonomos** means a house distributor, a manager, an overseer; a fiscal agent, a treasurer; a preacher of the Gospel; chamberlain, governor, steward. In an attempt to acquire and amass more money and wealth man continues to engage in the destruction and waste of the earth and it's life sustaining resources. And, man has caused some parts of the earth to become uninhabitable and non-life sustaining. As a result of his waste and destruction, in the end, when the Lord returns he will recompense those who have destroyed the earth and have been unjust and unfaithful stewards. For the writer declared,

And the nations were angry, and thy wrath is come, and the time of the dead, that they should be judged, and that thou shouldest give reward unto thy servants the prophets, and to the saints, and them that fear thy name, small and great; and shouldest destroy them which destroy the earth.

Re 11:18.

For, the earth belongs to God. *(Ps 50:12)* He created the earth *(Ge 1:1)* with his hands *(Ps 8:3; Ps 19:1; Ps 95:5; Ps 102:25)* and everything in the earth *(Ac 14:15; Ac 17:24; Re 14:7; Ps 119:73),* for the benefit of the whole of mankind *(Heb 2:6-8; Ps 8:4-8),* and not just for the rich and the powerful to pollute and to destroy for the love of money. As the writers declared,

The heavens are thine, the earth also is thine: as for the world and the fullness thereof, thou hast founded them.

Ps 89:11.

To be a good steward of the earth's resources one must guard against waste. For a steward can be an overseer, a house distributor, a fiscal agent, a treasurer, a manager, a governor or a preacher. Therefore, he is given charge and the responsibility to insure that the assets, wealth and resources belonging to the household, the kingdom and God's total creation called the earth are not wasted, ruined, polluted or destroyed for the sole purpose of acquiring more wealth. Thus, the scriptures declare,

He also that is slothful in his work is brother to him that is a great waster.

Pr 18:9.

This is so because when a person is slothful he is a waster of the earth's resource called time. And when he misuses or fails to use material wealth, in a responsible manner, he is a waster of the earth's natural resources which requires time to earn and accumulate.

And so, when we reconsider the Proverbs 18:9 passage above we realize that it paints the same negative picture of the slothful worker who must use time to accomplish his work and the great waster who consumes the material wealth accumulated through the use of time. Furthermore, when we review the concepts of being slothful and a great waster we also learn that these two types of people are not examples of being good stewards of the earth's resources.

The Great Waster

First, the word **waster** *(wāst'ĕr)* in the Proverbs 18:9 passage is translated from the Hebrew word **shachath** *(shaw-khath').* **Shachath** means to decay, ruin, batter, cast off, corrupt, destroy, lose, mar, perish, spill, spoiler, waste, waster. Therefore, when a person is a waster he assists in spoiling the earth, corrupting the earth and causing decay and ruin to occur in the earth. And as such, as a waster, he does not exercise the dominion and control of the earth's resources in a responsible manner that is beneficial to all plant, animal and human life as is required of stewards by the Lord God. For, as it was stated earlier,

> **...it is required in stewards that a man be found faithful.**

1Co 4:2.

For, if he fails to use the earth's resources responsibly his stewardship will be taken away and he shall come to want. This is demonstrated in Jesus' parable of the Unjust Steward, wherein he taught,

> **1 ...There was a certain rich man, which had a steward; and the same was accused unto him that he had wasted his goods.**

2 And he called him and said unto him, How is it that I hear this of thee? give an account of thy stewardship: for thou mayest be no longer steward.

3 Then the steward said within himself, What shall I do? For my lord taketh away from me the stewardship: I cannot dig; to beg I am ashamed.

4 I am resolved what to do, that, when I am put out of the stewardship, they may receive me into their houses.

5 So he called everyone of his lord's debtors unto him, and said unto the first, How much owest thou unto my lord?

6 And he said, An hundred measures of oil. And he said unto him, Take thy bill, and sit down quickly, and write fifty.

7 Then said he to another, And how much owest thou? And he said, An hundred measures of wheat. And he said unto him, Take thy bill, and write fourscore.

8 And the lord commended the unjust steward, Because he had done wisely: for the children of this world are in their generation wiser than the children of light.

9 And I say unto you, Make to yourselves friends of the mammon of unrighteousness; that, when ye fail, they may receive you into everlasting habitations.

10 He that is faithful in that which is least is faithful also in much: and he that is unjust in the least is unjust also in much.

11 If therefore ye have not been faithful in the unrighteous mammon, who will commit to your trust the true riches?

12 And if ye have not been faithful in that which is another man's, who shall give you that which is your own?

13 No servant can serve two masters: for either he will hate the one, and love the other; or else he will hold to the one, and despise the other. Ye cannot serve God and mammon.

Lu 16:1-13.

In this parable we learn that the rich man placed another person as a steward and overseer over his goods, his wealth. And, someone else that knew the rich man and the steward, and had been observing the steward, accused the steward of wasting, spoiling, destroying and ruining his lord's, the rich man's, goods, his wealth. In this parable the accusation of waste was so great until the rich man required his steward to give an accounting of his stewardship, of what he had been doing with his lord's goods. And if the accusations were proven true, the rich man informed the steward of his intent to take away the stewardship from the steward. The steward's actions, after being accused, were commendable because his actions fostered good will towards the rich man's business, and made friends for the steward, of the rich man's debtors, through the act of forgiving the debtor's debts.

Additional lessons learned from this Luke 16:1-13 parable of the unjust steward are: **(1)** the differences between serving unrighteous mammon and serving the Lord God; **(2)** the mystery behind success in business and ministry; **(3)** the Lord's manner of determining a person's likelihood of success in his own program, business or ministry and the tests he uses; and, **(4)** the comparison or correlation between mammon and the true riches of heaven.

Serving Unrighteous Mammon—Trust and Confidence in Wealth

Serving the accumulation of wealth, which is unrighteous mammon, will lead to a desire to be rich, and a snare in the believer's soul *(1Ti 6:9; Ec 9:12; Ps 91:3; Pr 22:5; Jos 28:12-13),* resulting in the love of money which is the love of wealth. For,

> **...they that will be rich fall into temptation and a snare, and into many foolish and hurtful lusts, which drown men in destruction and perdition.**

1Ti 6:9.

When a person falls in love with money and wealth he then possesses within himself the root of all evil. And, with the root of everything evil now planted, growing and established within his soul the root will then began to produce the harvest of sin, evil and the seventeen (17) works of the flesh within his life

> **19 ... which are these; Adultery, fornication, uncleanness, lasciviousness,**
> **20 Idolatry, witchcraft, hatred, variance, emulations, wrath, strife, seditions, heresies,**
> **21 Envyings, murders, drunkenness, revellings, and such like...**

Ga 5:19a-21b.

In agreement another writer commented, saying

> **...the love of money is the root of all evil: which while some coveted after, they have erred from the faith, and pierced themselves through with many sorrows.**

1Ti 6:10.

Here, in this 1Timothy 6:10 passage, the Apostle Paul teaches us that coveting after money will eventually lead to a love of money causing us to possess the root of all evil. For, **coveted** *(kuv'it-d)* is translated from **oregomai** *(or-eg'-om-ahee).* **Oregomai** means to stretch oneself, to reach out after, to long for, covet after, desire. Thus, we are admonished that when a believer stretches himself out, by using most of his time, talents and abilities to accumulate and acquire money and wealth he will develop and acquire a love for that money and wealth. And that which he love he will serve.

To serve unrighteous mammon is to put one's confidence and trust in the acquisition, possession and accumulation of wealth rather than in the provisions of God that are accessed through faith in and obedience to his Word. And, when we consider the desire and practice of serving unrighteous mammon we should be mindful of the great fall of the anointed, cherubim *(Eze 28:14)* angel named Lucifer. *(Read Isa 14:12-15; Re 12:7-12)* For, he was in heaven with the Lord God and in the garden of Eden *(Eze 28:13)* perfect in his ways from the day of his creation. *(Eze 28:15)* But, the love of material riches and wealth caused him to fall. *(Eze 28:4)* The pursuit of material riches and wealth took his mind off of serving God and placed his attention upon acquiring material wealth, the things of this earth that belonged to man. *(Eze 28:5)* As the Lord Jesus said of him in another place,

> **...Get thee behind me, Satan: thou art an offence unto me: for thou savourest not the things that be of God, but those that be of men.**

Mt 16:23 *(Read also Mk 8:33).*

For, Adam and Eve, mankind had been given total control and dominion of the earth. *(Ge 1:28)* And therefore the things found upon the earth were for their benefit, and were theirs to give away if they chose to do so. We understand this more perfectly when we consider Satan's comments to Jesus during Jesus' forty-day, wilderness fast. *(Read Mt 4:1-11, and Lu 4:1-13)* For, there it is recorded that,

> **5 ...the devil, taking him up into an high mountain, shewed unto him all the kingdoms of the world in a moment of time.**
>
> **6 And the devil said unto him, All this power will I give thee, and the glory of them: for that is delivered unto me; and to whomsoever I will I give it.**
>
> **7 If thou therefore wilt worship me, all shall be thine.**

Lu 4:5-7.

From this Luke 4:5-7 passage Satan, the devil, reminds Jesus that all of the kingdoms of the world had been delivered unto him. That is, Satan acquired these kingdoms from the man, Adam, during the

Genesis Affair *(Read Ge 3:1-24)* when he beguiled and tricked the woman *(Ge 3:1-6, 13)* to worship, taste and eat from his worldview doctrine found in him, the tree of the knowledge of good and evil. Once the woman became his servant, as the scripture admonishes us saying,

> **Know ye not, that to whom ye yield yourselves servants to obey, his servants ye are to whom ye obey; whether of sin unto death, or of obedience unto righteous-ness.**

Ro 6:16.

The woman served Satan by enticing her husband, Adam, who was with her, to begin worshiping, tasting and eating from Lucifer's worldly doctrine. And because Adam had now become Lucifer's servant *(Read Ro 6:16)*, all of the earthly power, dominion and material possessions that the Lord God had given mankind in Genesis 1:28 was delivered to and transferred to their new master, boss, Satan. For, by this creation groaning and travailing deception *(Ro 8:22)* Lucifer, the anointed cherubim angel of the Lord God, became Satan, the devil and the prince of this world. *(Joh 12:31; 2Co 4:4; Joh 14:30; Joh 16:11; Eph 6:12; Eph 2:2)* And now that the power and dominion of the world had been acquired by him, through the deceit of the lie *(Ge 3:1-4, 13; Joh 8:44)*, Satan could give it to whomever he desired pursuant to his own will. *(Lu 4:6)* Just like he gave it to the Israelite enslaving Pharaoh of Egypt *(Ex 1:8-14)* and King Nebuchadnezzar *(Da 5:18-19; Da 2:37-38),* who were both world rulers *(Ge 41:56-57; Da 2:37-38),* he now offered this worldly power and glory to Jesus the Christ. But Jesus, although he was being tempted in the same like manner and points as the first Adam and Eve had been tempted *(Heb 4:15; Heb 2:18)*, said unto Satan,

> **...Get thee behind me, Satan: for it is written, Thou shalt worship the Lord thy God, and him only shalt thou serve.**

Lu 4:7b.

The love of material wealth and the things of man corrupted Lucifer's wisdom and he thereby fell into spiritual darkness from the light of the righteousness of God. For, as we know,

> **...the love of money is the root of all evil: which while some coveted after, they have erred from the faith, and pierced themselves through with many sorrows.**

1Ti 6:10.

And, in agreement, even the Lord Jesus spoke concerning Lucifer's spirit that had begun leading Peter in his thinking. For, the writer recorded,

> **21 From that time forth began Jesus to shew unto his disciples, how that he must go unto Jerusalem, and suffer many things of the elders and chief priests and scribes, and be killed, and be raised again the third day.**
>
> **22 Then Peter took him, and began to rebuke him, saying, Be it far from thee, Lord: this shall not be unto thee.**
>
> **23 But he turned, and said unto Peter, Get thee behind me, Satan: thou art an offence unto me; for thou savourest not the things that be of God, but those that be of men.**

Mt 16:21-23.

By studying Lucifer's fall we learn that no one, not even an anointed angel of God in heaven, can serve both the accumulation of wealth (unrighteous mammon) and the Lord God. As the Lord Jesus declared,

> **… for either he will hate the one, and love the other; or else he will hold to the one, and despise the other. Ye cannot serve God and mammon.**

Lu 16:13.

Mammon (mam'en), here, is translated from **mammonas** *(mam-mo-nas').* **Mammonas** means confidence in wealth; wealth personified; avarice (deified). **Mammon** is riches regarded as an object of worship and greedy pursuit. So, once Lucifer placed the pursuit of riches as his object of worship and his trust and confidence therein he could no longer serve God. Because the first commandment is *'Thou shalt have no other gods before me'. (Ex 20:3)* For, Ezekiel wrote of him saying,

> **2 Son of man, say unto the prince of Tyrus, Thus saith the Lord God; Because thine heart is lifted up and thou hast said, I am a God, I sit in the seat of God, in the midst of the seas; yet thou art a man, and not God, though thou set thine heart as the heart of God:**
>
> **3 Behold, thou art wiser than Daniel; there is no secret that they can hide from thee:**
>
> **4 With thy wisdom and with thine understanding thou hast gotten thee riches, and hast gotten gold and silver into thy treasures:**
>
> **5 By thy great wisdom and thy traffic hast thou increased thy riches, and thine heart is lifted up because of thy riches:**
>
> **…**
>
> **12 Son of man, take up a lamentation upon the king of Tyrus, and say unto him, Thus saith the Lord God; Thou sealest up the sum, full of wisdom, and perfect in beauty.**
>
> **13 Thou hast been in Eden the garden of God; every precious stone was thy covering, the sardius, topaz, and the diamond, the beryl, the onyx, and the jasper, the sapphire, the emerald, and the carbuncle, and gold: the workmanship of thy tabrets and of thy pipes was prepared in thee in the day that thou wast created.**
>
> **14 Thou art the anointed cherub that covereth; and I have set thee so…**

15 Thou wast perfect in thy ways from the day that thou wast created, till iniquity was found in thee.

16 By the multitude of thy merchandise they have filled the midst of thee with violence, and thou hast sinned...

17 Thine heart was lifted up because of thy beauty, thou hast corrupted thy wisdom by reason of thy brightness...

Eze 28:2-5, 12-17.

Here, in this passage, we learn that Lucifer is an anoninted, cherub angel *(Eze 28:14)* that was perfect in beauty *(Eze 28:12)*, full of wisdom *(Eze 28:12)*, wiser than Daniel *(Eze 28:3)*, was a musician *(Eze 28:13)*, had the power to know everyone's secret *(Eze 28:3)* but God's *(1Co 2:7-8)*, and was perfect in all his ways when he was created. *(Eze 28:15)* But, rather than serving and seeking God, his creator, with his wisdom and understanding he began serving and pursuing mammon (riches) by using his wisdom and understanding for the pursuit of wealth and riches. *(Eze 28:4-5)* Until finally, by doing so, the multitude and greatness of his riches and wealth caused his heart to be lifted up in pride, corrupting his wisdom *(Eze 28:16-17)* and causing him to believe that he was as great as the Lord God, and sat in God's place. *(Eze 28:2)*

Furthermore, in the above Matthew 16:23 passage, we learn also that Lucifer, as Satan, had a mind and mental state that was disposed to seek out and taste the things of men—worldly riches and wealth—rather than the things of God. But, to savour the things of man rather than the things of God, one would have to be of a carnal mind. And Lucifer, since his fall that made him Satan *(Re 12:3-4, 7-12; Isa 14:12-15),* always possesses a carnal mind, because the word **savourest** is translated from the Greek **phroneo** *(fron-eh'-o).* **Phroneo** means to exercise the mind, to entertain or have a sentiment or opinion; to be mentally disposed more or less in a certain direction; to interest oneself in with concern or obedience; to set one's affection on; be of the same mind; regard, savour, think. To **savour** *(sā'vẽr)* means to get gratification from or taste for something; to taste or smell with pleasure; to delight in; to relish; to suit; to have a taste or smell, as of a certain kind or quality; to be agreeable to one's taste; power to arouse interest or zest.

Thus, we learn that Lucifer, sometime during his service unto the Lord God, with his clothing and attire being covered in all of the precious stones found in Eden *(Eze 28:13)*, acquired a mind and mental state that desired nothing but the riches and wealth of the world, rather than the riches and glory of heaven. *(Mt 16:23)* The things belonging to the world are carnal and earthly, and the things belonging to God are spiritual. Therefore, the anointed angel of God became a carnal minded, anointed angel. And, we know that,

> **6 ...to be carnally minded is death; but to be spiritually minded is life and peace.**
>
> **7 Because the carnal mind is enmity against God: for it is not subject to the law of God, neither indeed can be.**

Ro 8:6-7.

Thus, Lucifer's mind, after becoming carnal, became the enmity of God and as such he acquired the name of Satan. For,

> **6 ...there was a day when the sons of God came to present themselves before the Lord, and Satan came also among them.**
>
> **7 And the Lord said unto Satan, Whence comest thou? Then Satan answered the Lord, and said, From going to and fro in the earth, and from walking up and down in it.**

Job 1: 6-7.

The word **Satan** *(sāt''n)* in this passage is taken from the Hebrew word **Satan** *(saw-tan')* which means an opponent, the arch-enemy of good, adversary, to withstand, Satan. Thus, with the Lord God being the only one that is good *(Nah 1:7; Lu 18:18-19),* Lucifer acquired the name Satan to announce that he had become the Lord God's number one opponent, enemy, adversary and withstanding spirit. And so, being against God, in his spiritual essence, Satan—the Devil, always possesses a carnal mind. For, Lucifer showed up as Satan during his campaign to steal God's glory that was resident in the lives of Adam and Eve. *(Ge 3:1-7)* By acquiring Adam and Eve's obedience, in disobeying God in the garden of Eden *(Ge 3:1-7),* Lucifer was able to acquire the power of death *(Heb 2:14)* and the dominion and kingdom of the world from man, from Adam. *(Lu 4:5-7)* For, after he had acquired the taste and smell for the things of man rather than God, as Satan the Devil, he created the lie *(Joh 8:44)* and with it acquired all of the wealth of the earth. The writer declared further,

> **5 For they that are after the flesh do mind the things of the flesh; but they that are after the Spirit the things of the Spirit.**
>
> …
>
> **8 So then they that are in the flesh cannot please God.**
>
> **9 But ye are not in the flesh, but in the Spirit, if so be that the Spirit of God dwell in you. Now if any man have not the Spirit of Christ, he is none of his.**

Ro 8:5, 8-9.

The prophet Ezekiel declared that Lucifer, the anointed, cherubim angel of God, was created on a specific day. *(Eze 28:13, 15)* And we know that 'a day' is a measurement of time and that time did not begin to exist until the Lord God began creating heaven and earth. *(Read Ge 1:1-2)* After God created heaven and earth he created 'light' on the earth. *(Ge 1:3)* And then he separated the light from the darkness of the earth.

> **And God called the light Day, and the darkness he called Night. And the evening and the morning were the first day.**

Ge 1:5.

So, from the first chapter of Genesis we learn that the first day came about while God was creating heaven and earth. And, according to Ezekiel 28:13 and 15, we know that Lucifer, the anointed, cherubim angel was created on 'a day', but it was not the first day. Later on in Genesis chapter one we learn that on the sixth day of creation God created the man and the woman, male and female, in his own image and likeness. *(Read Ge 1:26-31)* Then Genesis chapter 2 explains how and in what time sequence the Lord God brought forth the man, the tree of life, the tree of the knowledge of good and evil and the woman. Genesis chapter 2 verses 7 through 23 informs us that the man was first, and the woman was last, the tree of the knowledge of good and evil was after the man and before the woman. And all of this occurred on the sixth day of creation. Three physical bodies and souls were created on this day—one man, one angel who possessed a physical body, and one woman. And the writer stated,

> **Here is wisdom. Let him that hath understanding count the number of the beast: for it is the number of a man; and his number is six hundred threescore and six.**

Re 13:18.

So, the number is **666**. Adam was created on the sixth day. Lucifer, the tree of the knowledge of good and evil, was created on the sixth day. And the woman was created on the sixth day—**666**. The combined works of these three brought about the fall of man, his separation from God and the transfer of the power of death and of the dominion and control over the earth from Adam to the angel with the cunning, subtle, serpent spirit, Lucifer. After the passing of many generations and the founding of the salvational church through the coming of Jesus the Christ, Lucifer, the serpent, the beast, the dragon shall begin his direct rule of the earth, by declaring and making war with the church, the remnants of the righteous seed of the woman *(Re 12:17; Re 13:4-7)* and by physical control of all of the inhabitants of the earth. For the writer said of him,

> **16 And he causeth all, both small and great, rich and poor, free and bond, to receive a mark in their right hand, or in their foreheads:**
>
> **17 And that no man might buy or sell, save he that had the mark, or the name of the beast, or the number of his name.**

Re 13:16-17.

Therefore, the tree of the knowledge of good and evil was created on the sixth day because the man and the woman were created on the sixth day and the tree of the knowledge of good and evil was created before the woman, but after the man.

And, Moses wrote in the book of Genesis that the tree of the knowledge of good and evil was made from the ground *(Ge 2:9)* just like the man Adam. *(Ga 2:7)* For, he recorded

> **8 And the Lord God planted a garden eastward in Eden; and there he put the man whom he had formed.**
>
> **9 And out of the ground made the Lord God to grow every tree that is pleasant to the sight, and good for food; the tree of life also in the midst of the garden, and the tree of knowledge of good and evil.**
>
> **10 And a river went out of Eden to water the garden; and from thence it was parted, and became into four heads.**
>
> **11 The name of the first is Pison: that is it which compasseth the whole land of Havilah, where there is gold;**
>
> **12 And the gold of that land is good: there is bdellium and the onyx stone.**

Ge 2:8-12.

As the anointed, cherub angel of God, Lucifer was created full of wisdom and perfect in beauty. *(Eze 28:12)* The prophet Ezekiel describes his precious stone, jeweled, covered clothing while he was in the garden of Eden saying,

> **Thou hast been in Eden the garden of God; every precious stone was thy covering, the sardius, topaz, and the diamond, the beryl, the onyx, and the jasper, the sapphire, the emerald, and the carbuncle, and gold: the workmanship of thy tabrets and of thy pipes was prepared in thee in the day that thou was created.**

Eze 28:13.

Now when we compare Ezekiel's descriptive covering of the anointed angel of God in verse 13 with Moses' description of the land of Eden in Genesis chapter 2 verses 11 and 12 we see that Moses describes the precious stones of Eden, gold, as being good. He also mentions the bdellium and the onyx stone as being part of the land. Therefore, when we consider the writings of Moses and Ezekiel, we realize that the anointed angel of God wore upon his physical person, the precious, jeweled stones of Eden that came out of the same ground that his physical body was made from. It is true that Lucifer is an angel. It is also true that angels can adorn physical bodies that can be seen with the human eye. For, even the Apostles admonishes us about the entertaining of angels, saying,

> **Be not forgetful to entertain strangers: for thereby some have entertained angels unawares.**

Heb 13:2.

Apostle Paul went on to say, that,

> **There are also celestial bodies, and bodies terrestrial: but the glory of the celestial is one, and the glory of the terrestrial is another.**

1Co 15:40.

The word **celestial** *(sə-les'chəl)* is translated from the Greek **epouranios** *(ep-oo-ran'ee-os)* which means above the sky, celestial, in heaven, heavenly, high. And the word **terrestrial** *(te-res'tri-el),* taken from **epigeios** *(ep-ig'-i-os)* means worldly (physically or morally); earthly, in earth. So, the angels who reside in heaven were created with heavenly (celestial) bodies capable of living in heaven. For, they were created a little higher than man. And man, who was created a little lower than the angels *(Ps 8:4-5; Heb 2:6-7),* was created to live in terrestrial bodies capable of living only on the earth.

Furthermore, the scriptures contain many examples of angels adorning physical, celestrial bodies, such as: **(1)** the angels that appeared to Abraham *(Ge 18:1-3);* **(2)** the angel that appeared to Haggai *(Ge 16:6-13);* **(3)** the angel that appeared in the fiery furnace with the three Hebrew boys *(Dan 3:23-28);* **(4)** the angel that appeared unto Mary *(Lu 1:26-38),* and Zacharias *(Lu 1:11-20);* **(5)** the angels that appeared to the shepherds out in the fields *(Lu 2:8-14);* **(6)** the angel that appeared unto Jacob and physically wrestled with Jacob *(Ge 32:24-28);* **(7)** the angels that appeared unto Lot, unto Lot's family and unto the citizens of Sodom and Gomorrah *(Ge 19:1-16);* **(8)** the angel that appeared unto Balaam *(Nu 22:22-34);* and, **(9)** the angel that appeared unto Samson's mother *(Jg 13:2-20).*

Also, serving the accumulation of wealth will lead to the wasting of the earth's resources for the sake of more wealth. An example of this is the Parable of the Rich Fool, wherein Jesus taught

> **16 ...The ground of a certain rich man brought forth plentifully:**
>
> **17 And he thought within himself, saying, What shall I do, because I have no room where to bestow my fruits?**
>
> **18 And he said, This will I do: I will pull down my barns, and build greater; and there will I bestow all my fruits and my goods.**

19 And I will say to my soul, Soul, thou hast much goods laid up for many years; take thine ease, eat, drink, and be merry.

20 But God said unto him, Thou fool, this night thy soul shall be required of thee: then whose shall those things be, which thou hast provided?

21 So is he that layeth up treasure for himself, and is not rich toward God.

Lu 12:16-21.

In this parable the man was already rich and his barns were already filled when the blessed increase came to him. With the increase there was no room in his barns to receive and store the increase. He could have chosen to be rich toward God by giving the over abundance to the poor and recognizing that the increase was a blessing that enabled him to give to others less fortunate. As Apostle Paul stated

I have shewed you all things, how that so labouring ye ought to support the weak, and to remember the words of the Lord Jesus, how he said, It is more blessed to give than to receive.

Ac 20:35.

But, rather than sharing with the weak and less fortunate to avoid destroying and wasting his barns to build larger barns the rich man chose to tear down his barns and build larger ones so that he could keep all of the blessing for himself. And by doing so he placed his trust and confidence, for his future wellbeing, in his riches, in unrighteous mammon. For, had he placed his trust in God and not in his riches he would have been able to testify of his richness towards God, as did the Apostle Paul. *(Ac 20:35-37)* Instead, God considered him a fool and he lost his soul the same night and all of his goods became the property of someone else.

Another good example of the waster is found in a parable used by the Lord Jesus wherein he taught the people saying,

11 ...A certain man had two sons:

12 And the younger of them said to his father, Father, give me the portion of goods that falleth to me. And he divided unto them his living.

13 And not many days after the younger son gathered all together, and took his journey into a far country, and there wasted his substance with riotous living.

14 And when he had spent all, there arose a mighty famine in that land; and he began to be in want.

15 And he went and joined himself to a citizen of that country; and he sent him into his fields to feed swine.

16 And he would fain have filled his belly with the husks that the swine did eat: and no man gave unto him.

17 And when he came to himself, he said, How many hired servants of my father's have bread enough and to spare, and I perish with hunger!

...

20 And he arose, and came to his father, But when he was yet a great way off, his father saw him, and had compassion, and ran, and fell on his neck, and kissed him.

21 And the son said unto him, Father, I have sinned against heaven, and in thy sight, and am no more worthy to be called thy son.

22 But the father said to his servants, Bring forth the best robe, and put it on him: and put a ring on his hand, and shoes on his feet:

23 And bring hither the fatted calf, and kill it; and let us eat, and be merry:

24 For this my son was dead, and is alive again; he was lost, and is found, And they began to be merry.

Lu 15:11-17, 20-24.

Here, in this parable, the young son had worked for his father and had earned a portion of the family's undivided wealth held by his father. For, the word **falleth** *(fôl'if)* in verse 12 is translated from the Greek word **epiballo** *(ep-ee-bal'-lo).* **Epiballo** means to belong to. Therefore, in verse 12 the younger son requested that portion of the family's wealth that belonged to him, because he had worked and earned it. For, had he refused to work then no portion of the family's wealth would have belonged to him, as the scriptures admonish us saying,

> **10 For even when we were with you, this we commanded you, that if any would not work, neither should he eat.**
>
> **11 For we hear that there are some which walk among you disorderly, working not at all, but are busybodies.**
>
> **12 Now them that are such we command and exhort by our Lord Jesus Christ, that with quietness they work, and eat their own bread.**

2Th 3:10-12 *(Read also 1Th 4:11).*

And in another place the scriptures admonish us saying,

> **Let him that stole steal no more: but rather let him labour, working with his hands the thing which is good, that he may have to give to him that needeth.**

Eph 4:28.

Also, in the beginning, the Lord God commanded the man to work when

> **...the Lord God took the man, and put him into the garden of Eden to dress it and to keep it.**

Ge 2:15.

And, the second time the Lord God commanded the man to work was after he had sinned, saying

> **19 In the sweat of thy face shalt thou eat bread, till thou return unto the ground...**
>
> **...**
>
> **23 Therefore the Lord God sent him forth from the garden of Eden, to till the ground from whence he was taken.**

Ge 3:19a, 23.

Thus, the father's youngest son in Jesus' Luke chapter 15 parable, above, had to have been working to assist in building the family's wealth in order for him to rightfully request the portion of the wealth that 'belonged to him', be given to him. And because, by working, he had earned the right to take his portion the father did not hesitate to give the younger son the wealth that he had earned. In the same manner, when we work and labor for the Father's kingdom, we are encouraged to keep on working by knowing that,

> **...God is not unrighteous to forget your work and labour of love, which ye have shewed toward his name, in that ye have ministered to the saints, and do minister.**

Heb 6:10.

So, in the parable, the problem was not that the younger son had requested his portion of the wealth and received it. The problem was what the younger son did with the wealth after he received it. He did not invest his wealth or use it in a manner to acquire more wealth, to sustain the wealth that he possessed or to make his life's situation or the lives of the needy better. *(Eph 4:28)* Instead he wasted all of his wealth on riotous living. **Riotous** *(ri'ət-əs)* in Luke 15:13 above is translated from **asotos** *(as-o'-toce)*. **Asotos** means dissolutely, unsavedness, profligacy, excess, riot, riotous. And, **riotous** means having the nature of a riot, engaging in a riot; loud and disorderly; boisterous;

hilarious. **Riot** *(ri'ət)* means wild or violent disorder, confusion, tumult; a violent disturbance of the peace by a number of persons assembled together; debauchery; unrestrained revelry. **Profligacy** *(prof'lə-gə-si)* means to be in a profligate state; to be abandoned to vice; dissolute; recklessly wasteful. **Dissolutely** *(dis'ə-lōōt'li)* means dissipated and immoral; debauched. And **debauchery** *(di-bôch'ẽr-i)* means extreme indulgence of one's appetites; dissipation; orgies; a leading astray morally.

The younger son left home with his wealth and moved to a far country away from his father and his father's teachings and ways so that he could live the type of life that he would choose for himself. And the lifestyle that he chose was one of waste filled with immorality. The long distance into another country gave the young son privacy and no interference from his family, relatives and those that knew him. Although his moving away kept his father and his relatives from personally interfering with his lifestyle, the younger son was not able to escape the impact of his father's moral teachings upon his life. For, the scriptures foresaw the straying away of man during his youthful days and therefore admonished the parents to

Train up a child in the way he should go: and when he is old, he will not depart from it.
Pr 22:6.

When we review this Proverbs 22:6 passage we learn that there is a time when a person is a young child in need of teaching and training in the way that he should go in life. And then in this passage we learn that the child is now old, a mature adult. It is this time in his life that he returns to the teaching and instruction of his mother and father. And, now he keeps the teachings and follows them. But there is a time in this person's life when he is neither a child, nor is he old, but rather he is a young adult without much experience in life. And, just like the younger son, this is the time when young adults leave home and therefore the teachings of their parents. It is during this time in their lives that they become transgressors of the ways taught to them by their parents. And as a result, the scriptures foretells of their future plight, admonishing us that

...the way of transgressors is hard.

Pr 13:15b.

And to be sure, we learn from the parable that the younger son's way, his life's condition and situation became very hard. This is so partly because the younger son's moving away for the sole purpose and cause of living alone, on his own, was a direct violation of God's will and his word. For, the Lord Jesus declared,

6 But from the beginning of the creation God made them male and female.

7 For this cause shall a man leave his father and mother, and cleave to his wife;

8 And they twain shall be one flesh: so then they are no more twain, but one flesh.

Mk 10:6-8 *(Read also Ge 2:24; Mt 19:4-5).*

When we review the parable we learn that the younger son did not leave his father to marry a wife but to engage in orgies and other immoral behavior. His cause was one of selfishness, waste and extreme indulgence in acts of immorality. His cause was one of rebelling against the moral ways of his father. And, as a result the young son became a great waster squandering and scattering all of his wealth abroad in another country. *(Lu 15:13)* As the word **wasted** *(was'-təd)* in the Luke 15:13 passage of scripture is translated from the Greek word **diaskorpizo** *(dee-as-kar-pid'-zo),* we realize that he **diaskorpizoed** his wealth and substance. For, **diaskorpizo** means to dissipate, to rout or separate, to winnow, to squander, disperse, scatter abroad, strew, waste.

And so, we learn from this parable that when young adults leave home for the purpose of living their own lives, alone, outside of Jesus Christ, they are living outside of the will and plan of God for their lives. And they are not being good stewards towards the earth's resources. For, it is the will and therefore the plan of God that everyone should live within the family structure, as evidenced by the scriptures, wherein we are informed that,

God setteth the solitary in families...

Psa 68:6.

And that the Lord God announced that a man living alone without the companionship of other humans was not part of his plan for the life of mankind. For, the writer recorded,

And the Lord God said, It is not good that the man should be alone...

Ge 2:18a.

The Slothful Worker and the Resource of Time

The earth possesses many, natural resources including things such as water, air, oxygen, vegetation, dirt and time. But, the resource of time is extremely important to all of the other resources found on the earth. Although time has not always existed it began with the beginning of creation, by the Lord God, of heaven and earth. *(Ge 1:1, 5, 8, 13-14, 19, 23, 31; Ge 2:1-2)* And the natural resources found on the earth were created after the earth's creation, in time. *(Read Ge 1:1-31)* So, when we consider a thing coming after an event or before an event we are talking about time. For, the word **after** *(af'ter),* here, means behind, later, next, later than, as a result of. Time affects the duration of the other natural resources, because, at the end of days, sometime after the angel of the Lord declares time to be no more—the Lord God will destroy the earth and create a new heaven and a new earth. For, the writer declared,

5 And the angel which I saw stand upon the sea and upon the earth lifted up his hand to heaven,

6 And sware by him that liveth for ever and ever, who created heaven, and the things that therein are, and the earth, and the things that therein are, and the sea, and the things which are therein, *THAT THERE SHOULD BE TIME NO LONGER***:**

Re 10:5-6 *(Emphasis added)***.**

And since time affects everything in this life, everything and everyone is awarded a set amount of time to exist, to grow, change, produce or transform. Even a person's wisdom and understanding is affected by time. For,

With the ancient is wisdom; and in length of days understanding.

Job 12:12.

The phrase 'length of days' is a measurement of time. Also, Solomon, the wise king of Israel, wrote about time saying,

1 To every thing there is a season, and a time to every purpose under the heaven.

2 A time to be born, and a time to die; a time to plant, and a time to pluck up that which is planted;

3 A time to kill, and a time to heal; a time to break down, and a time to build up;

4 A time to weep, and a time to laugh; a time to mourn, and a time to dance;

5 A time to cast away stones, and a time to gather stones together; a time to embrace, and a time to refrain from embracing;

6 A time to get, and a time to lose; a time to keep, and a time to cast away;

7 A time to rend, and a time to sew; a time to keep silence, and a time to speak;

8 A time to love, and a time to hate; a time of war, and a time of peace.

Ec 3:1-8.

By far, time is the most abundant of all of the earth's resources. For, it is renewed every day. And it is the one resource that everyone who lives has an equal share of each day that they live. In time, the poor and the rich are equal.

For man also knoweth not his time: as the fishes that are taken in an evil net, and as the birds that are caught in the snare; so are the sons of men snared in an evil time, when it falleth suddenly upon them.

Ec 9:12.

The rich man can buy many things, but time he cannot purchase. Because, when it is his time to die his money, his wealth, his pedigree and his fame shall all fail him. He will not be able to add any time to his life, just like the poor man cannot. As King Solomon stated,

I returned, and saw under the sun, that the race is not to the swift, nor the battle to the strong, neither yet bread to the wise, nor yet riches to men of understanding, nor yet favour to men of skill; but time and chance happeneth to them all.

Ec 9:11.

It is our freewill that allows us to use our time in the manner that we choose within the conditions and circumstances that we find our lives in.

Time and Spiritual Wealth

If we waste our time, then we become poorer, both naturally and spiritually. For example, the scriptures admonish us to,

> **Study to shew thyself approved unto God, a workman that needeth not to be ashamed, rightly dividing the word of truth.**

2Ti 2:15.

By reviewing this scripture we learn that if we fail to use a portion of our time to study, then we prevent ourselves from showing ourselves approved unto God. And being unapproved, when we attempt to perform God's work and the work of the kingdom of God, we will find ourselves being put to shame as a workman because we are unable to rightly divide the word of truth. That is, God does not approve of our ignorant attempts to proclaim his word and perform his work when we do not possess the knowledge, understanding and wisdom of his requirements of time, place and manner. Because he said in his word,

> **To every thing there is a season, and a time to every purpose under the heaven.**

Ec 3:1.

And, concerning spiritual things,

> **I would not have you to be ignorant…**

1Th 4:13a *(Read Ro 1:13a; Ro 11:25a; 1Co 10:1a; 1Co 12:1a; 2Co 1:8; 2Co 2:11; 2Pe 3:5-8).*

Because,

> **…he that winneth souls is wise.**

Pr 11:30b.

For, the purpose of the church, the kingdom of God and the birth, life death and resurrection of Jesus Christ is to save those that are lost. *(Mt 18:11; Lu 19:10)* And to be successful and fruitful in the winning of souls for salvation one must possess the wisdom, knowledge and understanding that comes only from becoming and continuing steadfastly as a disciple of Christ and of the Word of God. As the Lord said unto Joshua

> **This book of the law shall not depart out of thy mouth; but thou shalt meditate therein day and night, that thou mayest observe to do according to all that is written therein: for then thou shalt make thy way prosperous, and then thou shalt have good success.**

Jos 1:8.

Therefore, when the wise men, the leaders, the teachers and the pastors refuse knowledge, by not taking out the time to study, the people of God become and remain ignorant of the remedies and rescue options available to them, from God, through faith in the promises found within the Word of God. For, God's plan for the people, to be fed knowledge and understanding, is through the pastors and teachers *(Read Eph 4:11-14; Jer 3:15),* wherein he declared,

> **And I will give you pastors according to mine heart, which shall feed you with knowledge and understanding.**

Jer 3:15.

Therefore, a pastor or leader within the kingdom of God that will not spend time studying the word of God cannot righteously lead a flock of God's sheep to green pastures. And now, not being able to righteously lead them to green pastures he is rendered unable to feed them the knowledge and understanding that comes only from the Lord God. This is so, because, by not studying the Word of God he rejects the knowledge of God. And without the knowledge of God he cannot righteously lead God's people for God. As the writer declared,

...the priests lips should keep knowledge, and they should seek the law at his mouth: for he is the messenger of the Lord of hosts.

Mal 2:7.

And now, since the pastor, priest and leader is ignorant of the knowledge of God's word, hereby is the manner by which the people, the flock of God is kept ignorant of the will of God concerning their condition and their situation. So, out of ignorance they err and commit sin by engaging in worldly, self-help, feel good activities that fail them and lead them into spiritual captivity that in the end leads them to a real Hell. For, Jesus said,

Ye do err, not knowing the scriptures, nor the power of God.

Mt. 22:29.

And, in agreement the Prophet wrote,

13 Therefore my people are gone into captivity, because they have no knowledge: and their honourable men are famished, and their multitude dried up with thirst.

14 Therefore hell hath enlarged herself, and opened her mouth without measure: and their glory, and their multitude, and their pomp, and he that rejoiceth, shall descend into it.

Isa 5:13-14.

Furthermore, as for the willful and intentionally ignorant pastor, priest or leader of the flock, God rejects them and their work. For, he said,

6 My people are destroyed for lack of knowledge: because thou hast rejected knowledge, I will also reject

thee, that thou shalt be no priest to me: seeing thou hast forgotten the law of thy God, I will also forget thy children.

7 As they were increased, so they sinned against me: therefore will I change their glory into shame.

8 They eat up the sin of my people, and they set their heart on their iniquity.

9 And there shall be, like people, like priest: and I will punish them for their ways, and reward them for their doings.

Hos 4:6-9.

The Prophet Hosea went on to admonish the people saying,

1 Hear the word of the Lord, ye children of Israel: for the Lord hath a controversy with the inhabitants of the land, because there is no truth, nor mercy, nor knowledge of God in the land.

2 By swearing, and lying, and killing, and stealing, and committing adultery, they break out, and blood toucheth blood.

3 Therefore shall the land mourn, and every one that dwelleth therein shall languish, with the beasts of the field, and with the fowls of heaven; yea, the fishes of the sea also shall be taken away.

4 Yet let no man strive, nor reprove another: for thy people are as they that strive with the priest.

5 Therefore shalt thou fall in the day, and the prophet also shall fall with thee in the night, and I will destroy thy mother.

...

10 For they shall eat, and not have enough: they shall commit whoredom, and shall not increase: because they have left off to take heed to the Lord.

11 Whoredom and wine and new wine take away the heart.

12 My people ask counsel at their stocks, and their staff declareth unto them: for the spirit of whoredoms hath caused them to err, and they have gone a whoring from under their God.
Hos 4:1-5, 10-12.

Time and Natural Wealth

Time also affects our natural wealth. For the scriptures declare that

By much slothfulness the building decayeth; and through idleness of the hands the house droppeth through.
Ec 10:18.

Thus, when we are slothful or our hands are idle and not working, during the harvest, we waste and misuse the valuable resource of time. And, by wasting time we also waste our wealth, riches and money as a result of the high cost of repairing and rebuilding the portions of the house that dropped through or the portions of the building that decayed. Had we not been slothful we would have been richer and wealthier by saving the time and the money spent on repairs. Therefore, believers must be careful to not become like as the fool that,

...foldeth his hands together, and eateth his own flesh.
Ec 4:5.

Or, the slothful man that

...hideth his hand in his bosom, and will not so much as bring it to his mouth.
Pr 19:24.

Or, the sluggard who

...will not plow by reason of the cold; therefore shall he beg in harvest, and have nothing.
Pr 20:4.

For, if the believer becomes as the fool, the slothful or the sluggard, then while in his poverty he will be more easily tempted and enticed by the tempter to violate and offend God's Word out of need, want and survival, knowing that the Lord will not answer his prayer in the midst of his disobeying the command to work. *(Ge 2:15; Ge 3:19; 2Th 3:10-12)* Therefore, the man that is poverty stricken because of his slothfulness, sluggardness, laziness or foolishness will find himself living within the condition of poverty that was rejected by the Prophet Agur, when he said

8 ...[G]ive me neither poverty nor riches; feed me with food convenient for me:

9 Lest I be full, and deny thee, and say, Who is the Lord? or lest I be poor, and steal; and take the name of my God in vain.
Pr 30:8-9.

For, when the fool eateth his own flesh, in the Hebrew, it is said that he **'akal** *(aw-kal'),* that is, consumes, burn up, devour, dines and feeds on his own **basar** *(baw-sawr')*—his **flesh**, his body fat, his lean meat, his skin. And, unwilling to work, he should not look for those who do work to feed him. Agreeing, the Apostle stated

10 For even when we were with you, this we commanded you, that if any would not work, neither should he eat.

11 For we hear that there are some which walk among you disorderly, working not at all, but are busybodies.

> **12 Now them that are such we command and exhort by our Lord Jesus Christ, that with quietness they work, and eat their own bread.**

2Th 3:10-12.

The poverty conditions of the sluggard, the slothful and the foolish will cause them to steal *(Pr 30:8-9),* but after we become believers we should

> **Let him that stole steal no more: but rather let him labour, working with his hands the thing which is good, that he may have to give to him that needeth.**

Eph 4:28.

For,

> **In the sweat of thy face shalt thou eat bread, till thou return unto the ground...**

Ge 3:19a.

Furthermore, the believer should not become known as a sluggard, loving sleep, when there is work to be done. As King Solomon asked,

> **9 How long wilt thou sleep, O sluggard? When wilt thou arise out of thy sleep?**
> **10 Yet a little sleep, a little slumber, a little folding of the hands to sleep:**
> **11 So shall thy poverty come as one that travelleth, and thy want as an armed man.**

Pr 6:9-11 *(Read also Pr 24:33-34).*

As a consequence of loving sleep, relaxation and entertainment many believers are poverty stricken and will remain so, because they actively love and seek out sleep, relaxation and entertainment during harvest time refusing to exercise even the wisdom of the ant. For, if he would just,

6 Go to the ant, thou sluggard; consider her ways, and be wise:

7 Which having no guide, overseer, or ruler,

8 Provideth her meat in the summer, and gathereth her food in the harvest...

Pr 6:6-8.

...the sluggard would be able to avoid structural and generational poverty within their lives. But, as we are told,

25 The desire of the slothful killeth him; for his hands refuse to labour.

26 He coveteth greedily all the day long: but the righteous giveth and spareth not.

Pr 21:25-26.

The slothful man roasteth not that which he took in hunting: but the substance of a diligent man is precious.

Pr 12:27.

Slothfulness casteth into a deep sleep; and an idle soul shall suffer hunger.

Pr 19:15.

13 The slothful man saith, There is a lion in the way; a lion is in the streets.

14 As the door turneth upon his hinges, so doth the slothful upon his bed.

15 The slothful hideth his hand in his bosom; it grieveth him to bring it again to his mouth.

16 The sluggard is wiser in his own conceit than seven men that can render a reason.

Pr 26:13-16 *(Read also Pr 22:13).*

As vinegar to the teeth, and as smoke to the eyes, so is the sluggard to them that send him.
Pr 10:26.

And,

The soul of the sluggard desireth, and hath nothing: but the soul of the diligent shall be made fat.
Pr 13:4.

Also, this is why

The hand of the diligent shall bear rule: but the slothful shall be under tribute.
Pr 12:24.

After considering the word choice used by the writers we learn that there are degrees and levels of slothfulness, foolishness and sluggardness. For, the words **slothful** *(sloth-fəl)* and **sluggard** are at times translated from the same word such as in the Proverbs 19:24, Proverbs 21:25 and the Proverbs 26:13-15 passages above. There, the word **`atsel** *(aw-tsale')* is translated meaning indolent, slothful and sluggard.

On the other hand in Proverbs 12:24 and 27 **slothful** is taken from **remiyah** *(rem-ee-yaw')*. **Remiyah** means false, guile, idle remissness, treachery, deceit (ful, fully), slack, slothful. But then, in the Proverbs 18:9 passage **slothful** is taken from **raphah** *(raw-faw')* which means to slacken, abate, cease, consume, fall, (be) faint, be (wax) feeble, forsake, idle, leave, let alone (go, down), (be) slack, stay, be still, be slothful, (be) weak (-en).

So, there is the slothful person that is just lazy as in Proverbs 19:15, Ecclesiastes 10:18 and Proverbs 24:30-34. Then you have the slothful that is idle with his time, slack, feeble and faints or quits in the midst of the work during harvest time as in Proverbs 18:9. Then there is the slothful that is not only idle, false and slack with his time but he uses deceit, treachery, guile, remissness and lies to cover up his slothfulness. On the other hand the **slothful** is, in the Greek, **nothros** *(no-thros'),* that is, sluggish, dull, lazy and stupid as in Hebrews 6:12. And in Romans 12:11 and St. Matthew 25:26 he is **okneros** *(ok-nay-ros)*—tardy, indolent, irksome, and grievous.

It does great harm and causes great detriment, to the kingdom of God and the cause of Christ, when a believer lives his life as a foolish person, a sluggard or a slothful person. To highlight the danger of falling into an indolent and slothful lifestyle the Lord Jesus taught against this condition when he admonished the people saying,

> **14 For the kingdom of heaven is as a man travelling into a far country, who called his own servants** *(Ro 8:28-30; 1Co 7:20-24; 1Co 1:23-24; 1Th 2:12; 2Th 2:14-15; 1Pe 1:15; 1Pe 2:9-10, 21; 1Pe 3:9; 2Pe 1:3),* **and delivered unto them his goods.** *(Eph 4:8-12)*
>
> **15 And unto one he gave five talents, to another two, and to another one; to every man according to his several ability; and straightway took his journey.**
>
> **16 Then he that had received the five talents went and traded with the same, and made them other five talents.**
>
> **17 And likewise he that had received two, he also gained other two.**
>
> **18 But he that had received one went and digged in the earth, and hid his lord's money.**
>
> **19 After a long time the lord of those servants cometh, and reckoneth with them.**
>
> **20 And so he that had received five talents came and brought other five talents, saying, Lord, thou deliveredst unto me five talents: behold, I have gained beside them five talents more.**
>
> **21 His Lord said unto him, Well done, thou good and faithful servant: thou hast been faithful over a few things, I will make thee ruler over many things: enter thou into the joy of thy lord.**

22 He also that had received two talents came and said, Lord, thou deliveredst unto me two talents: behold, I have gained two other talents beside them.

23 His lord said unto him, Well done, good and faithful servant; thou hast been faithful over a few things, I will make thee ruler over many things: enter thou into the joy of thy lord.

24 Then he which had received the one talent came and said, Lord, I knew thee that thou art an hard man, reaping where thou hast not sown, and gathering where thou hast not strawed:

25 And I was afraid, and went and hid thy talent in the earth: lo, there thou hast that is thine.

26 His lord answered and said unto him, Thou wicked and slothful servant, thou knewest that I reap where I sowed not, and gather where I have not strawed:

27 Thou oughtest therefore to have put my money to the exchangers, and then at my coming I should have received mine own with usury.

28 Take therefore the talent from him, and give it unto him which hath ten talents.

29 For unto every one that hath shall be given, and he shall have abundance: but from him that hath not shall be taken away even that which he hath.

30 And cast ye the unprofitable servant into outer darkness: there shall be weeping and gnashing of teeth.

Mt 25:14-30 *(Citations in **italics** added).*

In this parable, of the slothful servant, we learn that the slothful servant caused the lord's kingdom to not grow due to his unwillingness to go out and work for the kingdom. Here, the **slothful** servant was so lazy until he was in the Greek **okneros** *(ok-nay-ros)*—tardy, indolent, irksome, and grievous to his lord.

Instead of working, the slothful servant hid his talent and thereby refused to make an attempt to use it. Then he wasted time by sitting down and waiting on his lord to return from his journey. And this is why King Solomon said

He also that is slothful in his work is brother to him that is a great waster.

Pr 18:9.

The fear and possibility of failure gave the slothful servant his rational reason for not going out and using his talent to work, in the same manner that the thought of possibly being eaten by a lion caused the man who refused to go to work to say,

...There is a lion without, I shall be slain in the streets.

Pr 22:13.

Believers must guard against slothfulness least they fall from their own steadfastness and receive the punishment prepared and waiting for the slothful and lazy servant—which is losing their talent to another brother and being cast into outer darkness along with those who shall be weeping and gnashing their teeth. For, we are commanded to be

Not slothful in business; fervent in spirit; serving the Lord...

Ro 12:11.

Because, it is desired

11 ...that every one of you do shew the same diligence to the full assurance of hope unto the end:

12 That ye be not slothful, but followers of them who through faith and patience inherit the promises.

Heb 6:11-12.

Success or Failure in this Life

Many of the brethren wonder why their ministry or business in the kingdom of God and in this life are failures or does not have long term success although they engage in the same activities as other brethren who are successful.

Failure: Lack of Faith

First of all the believer must walk by faith, for,

...without faith it is impossible to please him:...
Heb 11:6a.

And, if he is walking by faith, living holy and obeying the commandments of God there are several additional reasons why they experience failure in their ministry or business.

Failure: Not Called To Do that Type Ministry

For *one,* they may be engaged in ministry or a business that is not within their calling. If the Lord did not give him or anoint him for the ministry in which he is engaged he and the ministry shall surely fail. For, Jesus said,

> **4 Abide in me, and I in you. As the branch cannot bear fruit of itself, except it abide in the vine; no more can ye, except ye abide in me.**
> **5 I am the vine, ye are the branches: He that abideth in me, and I in him, the same bringeth forth much fruit: for without me ye can do nothing.**

Joh 15:4-5.

So, if the Lord did not call, choose and anoint the believer for the particular ministry in which he is engaged, then, to engage in the ministry without the anointing and blessings of Christ is abiding in the ministry and not abiding in Christ Jesus. And, to engage in ministry without Christ is sure failure, because without Christ the believer can do nothing to be successful in ministry or in business.

Failure: Went but Not Sent

Another reason for failure may be that the believer went too soon to start the ministry, although he had been called to do so. However, being called to minister, and being chosen and sent to perform and engage in that ministry calling are two separate events. For, the scripture commands all believers saying

> **...let us wait on our ministering...**

Ro 12:7.

For,

> **In your patience possess ye your souls.**

Lu 21:19.

And, we are taught that

> **...In the mouth of two or three witnesses shall every word be established.**

2Co 13:1b.

An example of this doctrine of waiting patiently until the witnesses of God's will are revealed, to the waiting minister, is found in Acts 13:1-3, wherein,

1 Now there were in the church that was at Antioch certain prophets and teachers; as Barnanas, and Simeon that was called Niger, and Lucius of Cyrene, and Manaen, which had been brought up with Herod the tetrarch, and Saul.

2 As they ministered to the Lord, and fasted, the Holy Ghost said, Separate me Barnabas and Saul for the work whereunto I have called them.

3 And when they had fasted and prayed, and laid their hands on them, they sent them away.

4 So they, being sent forth by the Holy Ghost, departed...

Ac 13:1-4.

Therefore, if the believer did not wait on his ministry by waiting on God's witnesses to be revealed, as Barnabas and Saul (Paul) did, and went and began his ministry anyway, then, he went without Christ, began his ministry without Christ and therefore was not sent by Christ. As a result, the believer's ministry is not in Christ and Christ is not with him in his ministry. Thus, failure is the only outcome, because without Christ Jesus he can do nothing. *(Joh 15:5b)*

God Rewards Faithfulness

The Lord God loves, commands and rewards faithfulness. For he commanded

...be thou faithful unto death, and I will give thee a crown of life.

Re 2:10b.

Failure: Unfaithful in the least, in the small things

Yet, a further reason for failure in the believer's life, ministry or business may be because he has been unfaithful in the small things, the things that are least, the small foxes.

> **Take us the foxes, the little foxes, that spoil the vines…**

Ca 2:15a.

For, if within his assignment to accomplish something of small (of least) importance he is not dedicated, steadfast and responsible, then, as he takes on larger and much more important things he will yet remain unfaithful and therefore a failure. As the Lord Jesus taught, saying,

> **He that is faithful in that which is least is faithful also in much: and he that is unjust in the least is unjust also in much.**

Lu 16:10.

Failure: Unfaithfulness by Misapplication, Misuse and Waste of Money and Wealth

Furthermore, the Lord Jesus compares unrighteous mammon to the true riches of heaven. In this comparison unrighteous mammon is the least and the true riches are the much. Failure results when a believer is unfaithful or unjust in paying tithes, freewill offerings and when he waste, misuses or misapplies unrighteous mammon. For, the prophet asked,

8 Will a man rob God? Yet ye have robbed me. But ye say, Wherein have we robbed thee? In tithes and offerings.

9 Ye are cursed with a curse: for ye have robbed me, even this whole nation.

10 Bring ye all the tithes into the storehouse, that there may be meat in mine house, and prove me now herewith, saith the Lord of hosts, if I will open you the windows of heaven, and pour you out a blessing, that there shall not be room enough to receive it.

11 And I will rebuke the devourer for your sakes, and he shall not destroy the fruits of your ground; neither shall your vine cast her fruit before the time in the field, saith the Lord of hosts.

12 And all nations shall call you blessed: for ye shall be a delightsome land, saith the Lord of hosts.

Mal 3:8-12.

Here, in this Malachi 3:8-12 passage we learn that failure comes from robbing God of tithes and offerings. For, with our failure to pay our obligations to the Lord comes a curse upon our lives, our money, our labor and our hopes. Also, in another place the prophet warned,

2 Thus speaketh the Lord of hosts, saying, This people say, The time is not come, the time that the Lord's house should be built.

3 Then came the word of the Lord by Haggai the prophet, saying,

4 Is it time for you, O ye, to dwell in your ceiled houses, and this house lie waste?

5 Now therefore thus saith the Lord of hosts; Consider your ways.

6 Ye have sown much, and bring in little; ye eat, but ye have not enough; ye drink, but ye are not filled with drink; ye clothe you, but there is none warm; and

he that earneth wages earneth wages to put it into a bag with holes.

7 Thus saith the Lord of hosts; Consider your ways.

8 Go up to the mountain, and bring wood, and build the house; and I will take pleasure in it, and I will be glorified, saith the Lord.

9 Ye looked for much, and, lo, it came to little; and when ye brought it home, I did blow upon it. Why? saith the Lord of hosts, Because of mine house that is waste, and ye run every man unto his own house.

10 Therefore the heaven over you is stayed from dew, and the earth is stayed from her fruit.

11 And I called for a drought upon the land, and upon the mountains, and upon the corn, and upon the new wine, and upon the oil, and upon that which the ground bringeth forth, and upon men, and upon cattle, and upon all the labour of the hands.

Hag 1:2-11.

In this Haggai 1:2-11 passage the Lord promises a drought upon his people who fail to take action by using their personal money, wealth, gifts and talents to assist in building, rebuilding and maintaining the physical house and temple of the Lord. He promises that they who earn money shall lose it as if they were placing the earned wages into a bag with holes in it. And finally, he promises failure by his hand, because he shall call ruin and desolation upon the man, his goods, his business, his crops, his efforts to labor to earn wealth and the land. For, the word **drought** *(drout),* here, is translated from the Hebrew word **choreb** *(kho'-reb)* which means desolation, drought, dry heat that causes utterly waste. **Drought** means a prolonged shortage, prolonged dry weather. And, **desolation** *(des'ə lit-shən)* means misery, loneliness, a desolate condition or place that is uninhabited, laid waste, solitary, ruined. This type of failure results because the person has not been fair and faithful in the paying of tithes and offerings and in giving general assistance to the kingdom of God with his gifts and talents. For, again, we are admonished that,

> **10 He that is faithful in that which is least is faithful also in much: and he that is unjust in the least is unjust also in much.**
>
> **11 If therefore ye have not been faithful in the unrighteous mammon, who will commit to your trust the true riches?**

Lu 16:10-11.

Failure: Unfaithfulness In Serving Under Leadership

If there is failure and not success and none of the above causes of failure exist, in the believer's life, then the question should be asked,

"Was he faithful to the church leadership and the congregation under which he was born into the body of Christ?"

For success, it is necessary that a believer be found faithful in the ministry into which he was spiritually born or experienced spiritual growth—before he seeks to begin and engage in his own ministry. For, we are admonished

> **Therefore, my beloved brethren, be ye stedfast, unmoveable, always abounding in the work of the Lord, forasmuch as ye know that your labour is not in vain in the Lord.**

1Co 15:58.

The believer that desires to have his own work must first be found faithful in another man's work. For, if he is faithful in the work of another man's, then he will learn how and what is required to be faithful and successful in his own work. In agreement, the Lord Jesus commented, saying

And if ye have not been faithful in that which is another man's, who shall give you that which is your own? Lu 16:12.

Jesus is the author of our salvation *(Heb 5:9),* the finisher of our faith *(Heb 12:2)* our good Shepherd *(Joh 10:14),* our provider and the giver of our gifts within the kingdom of God. *(Eph 4:7-8)* And, as such he knows what ministry and business is necessary, required and needed to grow, expand and to build his church here on earth. He also knows who he has equipped with certain attributes, gifts, talents and abilities to carry out specific works and ministries for the benefit of His Church.

So, when a believer engages in ministry without Christ leading him, in the work, he is wasting the time, talent, ability and resources of the Church and the Kingdom of God.

Amen.

Recycling

Protecting and Keeping the Earth by Reusing its Resources

Another means of proving our good stewardship of the earth's resources on behalf of the Lord God is to reuse the waste products generated from our use of the earth's resources. This process of reusing waste products on the earth is called **recycling**. It is more convenient to use throwaway, one use items. However, single use items are more expensive for the user and consume more of the earth's resources. When we **recycle** *(rē-sī-kəl)* we reclaim waste materials by using the materials in the manufacture of new products. When we **renew** *(ri-nū')* a thing we make new or as if new again; make fresh or strong again; we reestablish, we begin again and we resume.

When we take waste and used materials, to save it, and to make a new thing from it we act in the same manner as the Lord God acted regarding man's fall into sin. For, God first made man upright *(Ec 7:29),* because he

> **...created man in his own image, in the image of God created he him; male and female created he them.**

Ge 1:27.

However, after man had lived in the garden of Eden for a while they began to seek *"...out many inventions..." (Ec 7:29)* and forsook the image and likeness of God for which they had been created. For,

> **...when the woman saw that the tree was good for food, and that it was pleasant to the eyes, and a tree to be desired to make one wise, she took of the fruit thereof, and did eat, and gave also unto her husband with her; and he did eat.**

Ge 3:6.

So, by transgressing the commandment of God, to not eat of the tree of the knowledge of good and evil *(Ge 2:15-17; Ge 3:8-12),* Adam and his wife, Eve, made themselves transgressors and servants of Lucifer, Satan, the Devil, the serpent. As the Apostle stated,

> **Know ye not, that to whom ye yield yourselves servants to obey, his servants ye are to whom ye obey; whether of sin unto death, or of obedience unto righteousness?**

Ro 6:16.

And now, having become a servant of Lucifer, Adam brought sin to all of mankind and with sin came death pursuant to the commandment *(Read Ge 2:15-17; Ge 3:8-12; Ro 7:8-11), "...[f]or as by one man's disobedience many were made sinners..." (Ro 5:19a)*

> **12 Wherefore, as by one man sin entered into the world, and death by sin; and so death passed upon all men, for that all have sinned.**
>
> **...**
>
> **14 Nevertheless death reigned from Adam to Moses, even over them that had not sinned after the similitude of Adam's transgression...**

Ro 5:12, 14.

Therefore, with mankind existing in a fallen, used, sinful state rather than as an upright soul in the image of God, who is upright *(Ps 25:8; Ps 92:15),* man stepped out of life to exist in the death of sinful flesh. As a consequence God, his creator, knowing beforehand that man would fall into sin *(1Pe 1:19-20; Eph 1:4; Re 13:8; Mt 13:35)* prepared and developed a rescue and recycling plan to save man from sin and hell by transforming and renewing his soul and mind making him a new creature. For,

> **16 God so loved the world, that he gave his only begotten Son, that whosoever believeth in him should not perish, but have everlasting life.**
>
> **17 For God sent not his Son into the world to condemn the world; but that the world through him might be saved.**

Joh 3:16-17.

And all that will believe and obey are commanded to

> **...be not conformed to this world: but be ye transformed by the renewing of your mind, that ye may prove what is that good, and acceptable, and perfect, will of God.**

Ro 12:2.

Because,

> **...if any man be in Christ, he is a new creature: old things are passed away; behold, all things are become new.**

2Co 5:17.

Thus, the entire plan of salvation is a plan of spiritual and natural recycling. For, the Lord God is as the potter that takes vessels that are ruined because of sin and reuses and remakes them into good vessels of honor. As the Lord said to Jeremiah,

> **2 Arise, and go down to the potter's house...**
>
> **3 Then I went down to the potter's house, and behold, he wrought a work on the wheels.**
>
> **4 And the vessel that he made of clay was marred in the hand of the potter: so he made it again another vessel, as seemed good to the potter to make it.**
>
> **5 Then the word of the Lord came to me, saying,**
>
> **6 O house of Israel, cannot I do with you as this potter?**
>
> **saith the Lord. Behold, as the clay is in the potter's hand, so are ye in mine hand, O house of Israel.**

Jer 18:2a-6.

In this, Jeremiah 18:2-6 passage, we see the Lord comparing himself to the potter who made a vessel that was ruined. In the same manner the Lord forms us and places within us a living soul that dies and is ruined upon entering and living inside of sinful flesh, because of Adam's sin. In the above passage the potter took the ruined clay vessel and remade the vessel again into a new and good vessel. Likewise, when we believe in his name Jesus and obey the commandment as

> **...Peter said unto them, Repent, and be baptized every one of you in the name of Jesus Christ for the remission of sins, and ye shall receive the gift of the Holy Ghost.**

Ac 2:38.

The Lord God, as does the potter, makes us and molds us into vessels of honor even after we have been created, initially, as vessels of dishonor—thereby recycling our wasted, used and ruined souls rather than casting us away. Therefore, as believers, we are commanded to

5 Let this mind be in you, which was also in Christ Jesus:

6 Who being in the form of God, thought it not robbery to be equal with God...

Php 2:5-6.

God is a recycler, renewing our inward man day by day. *(2Co 4:16)* And so, to be like him, we must be recycled and become recyclers. For, we are to

23 ...be renewed in the spirit of your mind;

24 And that ye put on the new man, which after God is created in righteousness and true holiness.

Eph 4:23-24.

For, we

...have put on the new man, which is renewed in knowledge after the image of him that created him.

Col 3:10.

Therefore, as believers we should not waste by being of the same mind as those who

...shall build the old wastes, they shall raise up the former desolations, and they shall repair the waste cities, the desolations of many generations.

Isa 61:4.

Amen.

This discussion on The Mystery of the Will of God is continued in Book 4, Believing Warriors in Combat.

Key Word Index

Symbol

A

B

C

D

E

G

H

Q

T

Scriptural Index

Printed in the United States
By Bookmasters